The Poetics of Authorship in the Later Middle Ages

Studies in the Humanities
Literature—Politics—Society

Guy Mermier
General Editor

Vol. 21

PETER LANG
New York • Washington, D.C./Baltimore
Bern • Frankfurt am Main • Berlin • Vienna • Paris

Burt Kimmelman

The Poetics of Authorship in the Later Middle Ages

The Emergence of the Modern Literary Persona

PETER LANG
New York • Washington, D.C./Baltimore
Bern • Frankfurt am Main • Berlin • Vienna • Paris

Library of Congress Cataloging-in-Publication Data

Kimmelman, Burt.
 The poetics of authorship in the later middle ages: the emergence of
 the modern literary persona / Burt Kimmelman.
   p.   cm. — (Studies in humanities; vol. 21)
 Includes bibliographical references and index.
 1. Poetry, Medieval—History and criticism. 2. Poetics. 3. Authorship.
 4. Oral tradition—History and criticism. I. Title. II. Series: Studies in
         humanities (New York, N.Y.); vol. 21.
       PN688.K56   809.1'02—dc20   95-32874
         ISBN 0-8204-2856-6 (hardcover)
         ISBN 0-8204-4567-3 (paperback)
             ISSN 0742-6712

Die Deutsche Bibliothek-CIP-Einheitsaufnahme

Kimmelman, Burt:
The poetics of authorship in the later middle ages: the emergence of the
modern literary persona / Burt Kimmelman. – New York; Washington,
D.C./Baltimore; Bern; Frankfurt am Main; Berlin; Vienna; Paris: Lang.
    (Studies in the humanities; Vol. 21)
     ISBN 0-8204-2856-6 (hardcover)
     ISBN 0-8204-4567-3 (paperback)
              NE: GT

Cover design by James F. Brisson.

Cover illustration is credited to Bibliotheca Bodmeriana (Cologny-Geneva).

© 1996, 1999 Peter Lang Publishing, Inc., New York

All rights reserved.
Reprint or reproduction, even partially, in all forms such as microfilm,
xerography, microfiche, microcard, and offset strictly prohibited.

Printed in the United States of America.

In memory of my father
David B. Kimmelman

and my teacher
Robert O. Payne

♦

For Diane and Jane
tot iorn meillur et esmeri

ACKNOWLEDGMENTS

Mind and memory inherently fallible, I am nonetheless sure of one thing: I will forget someone, now, who deserves naming. There are many—for whose criticism, emotional and moral support, often great warmth and enthusiasm, at least equally often great intelligence and knowledge, I am deeply grateful. Let me begin with those who have read and commented on my book when it was in manuscript: George Economou, Frederick Goldin, Robert O. Payne, Eugene Vance and Henry Weinfield. Special thanks to Allen Mandelbaum, who was my doctoral adviser, is now my friend and advocate; to David Greetham, for what is already way back when; and to Jeff Cassvan, who read the manuscript in its final draft, whose acuity and creativity were indispensable.

I am also greatly beholden to my teaching colleagues who have assisted me in innumerable ways: Dennis Donahue, Robert Lynch, John Opie, Nikki Stiller—and particularly Norbert Elliot. I am lucky to be able to work with people who share in my intellectual and pedagogical pursuits and who go out of their way to see them realized. As well, I am quite indebted to Dr. Gary Thomas, Provost, Dr. Robert Pfeffer, Vice President for Research, and his staff including Lauren Rethwisch and Adrienne Walker, at New Jersey Institute of Technology, who have been instrumental in supporting my scholarly activities through arranging for summer research and equipment grants and publication subvention.

I save the best for last: my partner in life, my wife Diane Simmons, and our daughter Jane Zvi Kimmelman—whose love and devotion have made me a better human being, whose presences in my life make it and all worldly things vibrant and essential. I must also not forget to thank, for their encouragement and at times scintillating conversation, my brother Michael Kimmelman, and his wife Maria Simson who discovered the illuminated letter that appears on the front cover of this book.

Acknowledgment is also gratefully made to these copyright holders for permission to reprint copyrighted material: John D. Bernard, Ed., *Vergil at 2000*. AMS Press, 1989. John M. Bowers, *The Crisis of Will in* Piers Plowman. Catholic University Press, 1986. Lucie Brind-Amour and Eugene Vance, Eds., *Archéologie du signe*. Institut Pontifical d'Études Médiévales, 1982. Janet Coleman, *Piers Plowman and the Moderni*. Edizioni di storia e letteratura (Cod. Az. 3002-3 CAB 05022-9 c/c n. 650106/31 BANCA DI ROMA—Piazza San Pantaleo, 1—00186 ROMA—Ag. 211), 1981. Jesse M. Gellrich, *The Idea of the Book in the Middles Ages*. Cornell University Press, 1985. Frederick Goldin, *German and Italian Lyrics of the Middle Ages*, and *Lyrics of the Troubadours and Trouvères*. Anchor Press, 1973. Linda M. Paterson, *Troubadours and Eloquence*. Oxford University Press, 1975. Eugene Vance, *From Topic to Tale*. University of Minnesota Press, 1987.

CONTENTS

Introduction 1
   Alterity and History

Chapter One 37
   Text and Word, History and Fiction

Chapter Two 89
   The Poetics of the "I"

Chapter Three 121
   The Poet as Text, the Text as Name

Chapter Four 159
   Poetic Voice, Poetic Text, Thematics and the Individual

Afterword 229
   The Middle Ages and the Modern Persona

Appendix A 237
Appendix B 238
Appendix C 241
Works Cited 243
Index 269

"Translationem voco cum vel similitudine unum nomen fit multis rebus...."

"I call it transference when by similarity one name is used of many things...."

    – St. Augustine, *De Dialectica*

"We may creaunce whil we have a name...."

    – Geoffrey Chaucer, *The Shipman's Tale*

Introduction

Alterity and History

> *However the topic is considered, the* problem of language *has never been simply one problem among others.*
> – Jacques Derrida, *Of Grammatology*

Beginning in the eleventh century, poets and other intellectuals began to view language in a dramatically new way: as distinct from the language user. Later medieval language theory eventually split itself off from the discipline of theology to become a branch of philosophy. From today's perspective, this interest in language anticipates, albeit distantly, modern linguistics and post-structuralism. The emergence of medieval philosophy of language was gradual but inexorable—and it was mirrored by developments in poetry. Even so, several hundred years after Anselm and Abelard, after Guillem IX and Marcabru, the line between theology and other bodies of knowledge was drawn so faintly as to be, at times, indiscernible. Today we find ourselves in a similar position—which prompts us to reevaluate what is still, basically, our scholarly belief in two worlds, theirs and ours, the medieval past and the "postmodern" present. This absolute division has become useless except where it has been qualified by recognizing what people of the two worlds have shared. Post-structuralism teaches, among other things, how fragile our own categories of knowledge can be. On the other hand, our present separations of philosophy and theology, and philosophy and poetry, are widely accepted with a degree of clarity unknown in that "other" world. The modern reader can readily tell a philosophical tract from a poem, will never confuse the rigorous logical formulations of a Willard Quine with the exquisite verbal flights of a John Ashbery. In comparison, works like Bernard Silvestris' *Cosmographia*, Dante's *Commedia*, and Langland's *Piers Plowman*, attest the human search for truth throughout various imaginative realms—mythology, theology, philosophy, esthetics—each of the four a strand within the same fabric. To be sure, the work of a philosopher like Derrida, and that of a poet like William Bronk, will each resist easy classification, the one poetically philosophical, the other philosophically poetic; but our thinking of them as at least vaguely similar is grounded in a different sense of writerly intention, and readerly expectation, than that which underlies the medieval experience of a work like *Piers Plowman*. For that matter, a medieval reader could regard Langland's poem as embodying manifold intentions—particularly because later medieval categories, in their shifting and perhaps duplicating of each other, could be acknowledged even as they were changing. Edmund Reiss reports (in "Chaucer's Fiction and Linguistic Self-Consciousness in the Late Middle Ages" 111) that at least one fifteenth-century commentary, Jean Gerson's *De Modis Significandi*, expresses anxiety over "the different disciplines of knowledge [which were] losing their traditional distinctiveness and sense of purpose" as a result of investigations, on the part of "logicians and grammarians, as well as poets and storytellers," into "the transformations of language." The problem, Reiss observes, was that "the particular modes of signification proper to one discipline [were] being used to solve problems pertinent to other disciplines"—which led to confusion.

> According to Gerson, the masters of grammar, whose object should be "the congruity of discourse," have been attempting to solve their problems by using methods proper to logic, whose object should be "the truth or falsity of propositions." At the same time, by employing these same methods, the masters of logic have been trying to solve the problems of metaphysics. Moreover, grammarians, logicians, and metaphysicians alike would seem to believe that by using these methods all at once they can solve the problems of theology.
> (Reiss 111)[1]

My book argues that there were two groups of language users, poets and philosophers, who were writing out of a fecund relationship with one another, during a period of great intellectual tumult lasting for over four hundred years. For us, grasping this relationship will mean holding a key to later medieval cosmology and philosophy of language, and to textual autocitation, which is the focus of the book. The art of fictional self-inclusion was practiced by poets ever more widely and with ever greater acumen and imagination as the later Middle Ages got underway. I believe this art was the forerunner of what we now call the modern literary persona. Autocitation took many forms. It occurred less significantly as word puzzles and anagrams that were used to spell out an author's name within a poem, as other forms of "signature," and as explicit self-naming within a literary work. By calling these writerly ploys "less significant," however, I do not mean to diminish their importance either to us or to medieval readers.[2] On the contrary, I will demonstrate here and in the following chapters that "signing" one's literary work happened in direct relation to a medieval author's approach to the idea of literature. The use of an anagram, for example, as Laurence de Looze puts it (in "Signing Off in the Middle Ages" 170), "reaffirm[ed] the materiality and the limits of the text and [drew] attention to the fact that the text [was] nothing but a web of signification." Hence, the signature

---

[1] *De Modis Significandi*, I.12-32. Cf. Etienne Gilson, *History of Christian Philosophy in the Middle Ages*, 529.
[2] There have been many studies of medieval literary signatures. Recent and admirable studies include: David F. Hult, *Self-Fulfilling Prophecies: Readership and Authority in the First* Roman de la Rose; Erik S. Kooper, "Art and Signature and the Art of the Signature"; Anne Middleton, "William Langland's 'Kynde Name'"; and Laurence de Looze, "Signing Off in the Middle Ages: Medieval Textuality and Strategies of Authorial Self-Naming."

bespeaks a poet's sensitivity to and understanding of, not simply one or another poem, but textuality itself. In fact, individual texts were thought of within a larger world of signs—in a fashion not too different from that of our contemporary critical theory. This world was comprehended through the Western and most of all Christian metaphor of *the* text, the biblical Word of God, which was metamorphosed in the poetic imagining of Augustine's *Confessions* into an unfurled scroll. Thus these kinds of textual self-inclusion were the surface features of what I choose to call "the poetics of authorship"—for in their very materiality they resonated a vast authorial tradition, yet this was a tradition that was articulated in the terms of *text*.

Autocitation takes other forms as well, forms that more incisively disclose the connections between medieval poetry and medieval philosophy, and between medieval and modern narratology. Chapters Two and Three of this book examine the songs of Marcabru in which we find, for the first time in European literature, the unequivocal mark of a truly new literary attribute. I will show how Marcabru establishes all the ground rules for the later proliferation of "character-narrators." These narrators bear their authors' names and vocations as poets. However, even the creation of a character-narrator—a poet within a poem written by a namesake—is not the most profound manifestation of the authorship trope. Finally, the most revealing display of autocitation—that is, what constitutes true autocitation—is one that goes well beyond simple convention; it transpires, rather, as a discussion, carried on by this narrator, about poetry—about poetry's nature. This discussion leads to the contemplation of the poet's existential role in the world. The ultimate purpose of this discussion is to reflect upon the purpose and efficacy of writing and ultimately of language per se.

That poetic narrators would come to be known by the names of their authors was inevitable. In his famous essay, "What is an Author" (123), Michel Foucault maintains that when a text is linked to an author's name it is characterized in a particular manner:

> Discourse that possesses an author's name is not to be immediately consumed and forgotten; neither is it accorded the momentary attention given to ordinary, fleeting words. Rather, its status and its manner of reception are regulated by the culture in which it circulates.

In fact today, often enough, window shoppers are drawn to books because of their authors' names prominently displayed across their covers; many books now exist within a culture of celebrity. Yet Foucault's thesis is exactly wrong when applied to the medieval book:

there was a time when those texts which we now call "literary" (stories, folk tales, epics, and tragedies) were accepted, circulated, and valorized without any question about the identity of their author. [And texts] that we now call "scientific" (dealing with cosmology and the heavens, medicine or illness, the natural sciences or geography) were only considered truthful during the Middle Ages if the name of the author was indicated.
(125-26).

This monolithic distinction has recently been qualified by Roger Chartier (in *The Order of Books* 58),[3] and I too may usefully exploit it. First of all, let us observe that not all authoritative "scientific" texts were signed by individuals in the Middle Ages, although enough of them were, especially those of the philosophical variety. But, as I suggested before, in many instances there was no clear resolution as to what constituted "literary" and what "scientific." Neither, say, the *Cosmographia* nor the *Commedia* can be glibly categorized, in terms of intention, doctrine—even genre.

In trying to make his point about who, or should we say what, an author is, Foucault is peculiarly wrong concerning the medieval text—when his discussion turns to a consideration of grammar. He writes, "an author's name is not simply an element of speech (as a subject, a complement, or an element that could be replaced by a pronoun or other parts of speech)" (123). In other words, the author resides beyond the language of the text. In the later Middle Ages, however, especially *literary* authors (I concede how problematic this term is—and how rich) assert their names precisely because they view the proper noun, philosophically, as momentous. Foucault principally distinguishes between the "proper name" and the "name of the author"; the former "moves from the interior of a discourse to the real person outside who produced it," while the latter "remains at the countours of

---

[3] Chartier writes:
> Foucault was right to recognize a presence of the author in the Middle Ages, when texts circulated in manuscript, but his hypothesis that authorship as a function for the classification of discourses was attached to medieval "scientific" texts while "literary" works fell under the rule of anonymity seems somewhat more fragile. In reality, a basic distinction must be made between the ancient texts—whatever their genre—that founded their authority on the work's attribution to a name (not only Pliny or Hippocrates, whom Foucault mentions, but also Aristotle and Cicero, St. Jerome and St. Augustine, Albert the Great and Vincent of Beauvais) and works in the vulgar tongue for which the author-function was constituted around a few great "literary" figures—in Italy, Dante, Petrarch, and Boccaccio. In this sense the trajectory of the author can be thought of as a gradual change in the way texts in the vernacular were regarded, attributing to them a principle of designation and election that had long been characteristic only of works that were referred to an ancient *auctoritas* and that had become part of a corpus of works continually cited and tirelessly commented upon.

Cf. Chartier's "Figures of the Author," 21. I find, however, that Chartier is also falling into some of the same traps he has come to recognize in Foucault, as I hope will be evident shortly.

texts—separating one from the other, defining their form, and characterizing their mode of existence" (123). The differentiation here is both subtle and slippery.

Foucault is referring to the condition of the modern text; a few sentences later he declares that "[t]he author's name is not a function of a man's civil status, nor is it fictional [. . .]." To be sure, the theory behind this assertion is both ingenious and provocative, and to my mind it holds fast to my own reading of modern literature. Conversely, it falls short (as perhaps any theory will, in the end) of being comprehensive. It does not take into account the later medieval phenomenon of self-naming: Chaucer's use of a persona named "Geffrey," or Langland's use of a figure called "Will," or Dante's use of a narrator referred to by Beatrice, also a character in the *Commedia*, as "Dante" (Purg. XXX.55), and this is to say nothing of the fact that an author like Chrétien de Troyes, in all probability, employed a pseudonym.[4] Self-naming called attention to an author whose "literary" and social status became elevated through association with the

---

[4] I do assume that "Chrétien de Troyes" is a nom de plume; this assumption, while it may come to seem contradictory of my argument, does, rather, assist it. What is primarily important in Chrétien's act of autocitation is that he claims authorship for himself and in doing so associates himself with the text he is claiming to have composed and within which this claim is being made. Just because a Dante or a Chaucer was *in fact* an author is no reason to overlook the significance of other authors who take certain names, which become to some extent historicized. Not only *Chrétien* but *William Langland* as well may have been a pseudonym (as John Bowers has suggested in a letter to me of 3 June 1992). On the other hand, we need to avoid falling into the old trap of "autobiographical assumption." As Sarah Kay writes (in *Subjectivity in Troubadour Poetry* 2, 3), regarding the Provençal songs (but what she says provides a starting point for addressing the work of poets who lived in later periods too), extant *vidas* and *razos* encourage the notion "that the 'I' of an individual text refers in some way or other to its supposed author and that the ideas and feelings expressed there are in some sense his or hers." To make this leap in one's reading is to embrace "an over-literal understanding of 'autobiography' as anecdotal truth." I hope to demonstrate that over time an autonomous "I"—one whose subjectivity, in the words of David R. Olson (in *The World on Paper* 234), "is tied to consciousness [. . .] of mind and the vulnerability of one's beliefs"—evolves from a starting point of a textual subject position determined, fundamentally, by grammar. I also must add that self-naming is not a phenomenon exclusive to the later Middle Ages, yet it is more prevalent then than in earlier times. In Ursula Schaefer's essay "Hearing from Books," for example, she writes that "Cynewulf obviously did not care much about the 'poetic I', but he tried all the harder to make the 'auctorial' person known to his audience" (134). Cynewulf's self-naming supports my argument that there was gradually a trend of the sort I have been describing, which gained momentum and focus—a trend deeply conditioned by the spread of literacy. Schaefer concludes her essay:

> Fictionality is imminent whenever writing is involved. Cynewulf may well have been aware of that. And this could have been his ultimate reason for tying his poetry forever to the name of its author: to keep it from lapsing forever into the never-land of fictitious discourse. He himself, however, had no choice but to open the way in that very direction.

(134)

text he or she had composed—here Foucault is right on target. Still, the text made the author, not the other way around—here Foucault does not quite see how the uniquely medieval text, more fundamentally how medieval language, and even more primally how medieval grammar, were responsible for this dynamic.

How, then, can I have implied earlier that the medieval and modern worlds are not all that different? In ways, they are not. Yet no period is like another, and one particular aspect of medieval culture seems to me, after all, to be definitive. The role of authority in the lives of medieval people can hardly be overstated— although, shortly, I should like to whittle away at what I believe is our reductivist image of it. The cliché (like all clichés, it contains a measure of truth) is that in the Middle Ages *auctoritas* reigned supreme as it defined the individual's sense of *communitas*. True enough, this book will describe how poets of the later Middle Ages asserted themselves in their works, not so much for the sake of self-promotion in the modern sense, but rather in response to past as well as current intellectual and spiritual issues. Speculative grammar, realism and nominalism, often provided the poetic material for poets to be discussed at length: Guillem IX, Marcabru, Dante, Chaucer and Langland. The process in which their poems were created must have been inflected, perhaps directly and certainly indirectly, by the achievements of medieval philosophers whose diction and ideas are so very often present in the poets' verses, and whose insights into the nature of language these poets absorbed. Such transference took place within a literate community to which all writers, all composers of texts, belonged. Thus the philosophers, again either directly or indirectly, must also have benefited from the work of the poets.

As literacy and Aristotelian logic became widespread, these poets contributed to a distinction being made between history and fiction; they employed contemporary ideas about language and its relationship to experience as both metaphor and theme. Furthermore, they elaborated a Western sensibility that had been articulated at least as early as Plato, Paul, and Augustine who, as has been indicated, essentially viewed the world as a text. This basic metaphor ultimately formed the later medieval outlook; *text*, and *language* and/or *discourse*, maintained fluid interrelationships. Anselm, moreover, set aside Augustine's criterion of intentionality as the most important factor when determining falsehoods. In doing so, he was recognizing the separateness of language; he proposed that statements could have a "natural" cogency despite their lack of objective reference. This autonomy of language formed the ground for individual poetic identity. We shall look into these developments in Chapter One. In the face of a hierarchical authority inherited from the past, poets insisted upon their presence as individuals by aligning themselves with their texts. They could hold their poetry, and the very idea of poetry, at a distance from themselves, and so they could contemplate them because of the advantage of their new perspective, as never before.

From our present vantage point, the medieval poet's perspective is quite familiar. In other words, as I have been arguing, the two worlds, medieval and (post)modern, are not that far apart, and maybe are not separated by any sure gulf. Medieval scholarship today, for all its forays into deconstruction, new historical and gender criticism, is still haunted, in the words of Wallace Stevens, by "that absolute foyer beyond Romance." We have yet to outlive our philological parents. I think that we still must revise to our satisfaction two canonical assumptions, one of which was built on the other. The bedrock premise is, according to Jacob Burckhardt in *The Civilization of the Renaissance in Italy* (1860), that medieval "man was conscious of himself only as a member of a race, people, party, family or corporation—only through some general category" (81).[5] The second, put forth by Julius Schwietering in *Die Demutsformel mittelhochdeutscher Dichter* (1921), is that the medieval writer was self-effacing in following the precepts of Salvian, Sulpicius Severus (c. fifth century) and others who caution authors not to commit the sin of *vanitas terrestris*. Surely the earlier Middle Ages has a greater purchase on this assessment. But when speaking of literature after the millennium, and especially after the eleventh-century, some adjustment is in order. Anonymity, earlier, was in fact prescribed; as Ernst Robert Curtius tells us (in *European Literature and the Latin Middle Ages* 515), if an author ever finally chose to give his name, he did so "to gain forgiveness of his sins through the intercession of his hearers and readers." Even St. Bonaventure (1221-74), taking the Song of Songs as his model of anonymity, thought that the name of an author would get in the way of a song's meaning, as A. J. Minnis has noted (in *The Medieval Theory of Authorship* 132).

Bonaventure's comment notwithstanding, Schwietering's view, in particular, prevents us from focusing on the literary *maker*. By the later Middle Ages we find authors creating opportunities for self-advancement, for recognition as individuals, through the very craft of authorship. The sign of what I have chosen to call the "poetics of authorship" was the text's narrator, or persona, which advertised itself *as* a sign, since it bore its creator's *name*. Even more crucial is the fact that the persona was characterized in its poem *as a poet*. The persona became the poet's essential *verbal* gesture. Thus, rather than the typical *Adamo me fecit*, the medieval manuscript's perennial coda—whose inscription acts as what Derrida might call a "supplement" faintly asserting a scribe's latent individuality—the poet of the later Middle Ages found numerous and increasingly ingenious ways of insinuating, of weaving into the very fabric of poetry the modern claim, *ego auctor*. The name of the first man Adam was generalized in a formula for anonymity. *Adam* becomes *Marcabru, Chrétien, Dante*.

This persona did not evolve without critical notice. For instance, Dante develops a rationale for self-referentiality in the *Convivio* (I.2). The *Confessions*, as John Freccero notes (in *Dante: The Poetics of Conversion* 2-3), which was the first text that could be judged to be autobiography proper, is cited by Dante as an instance of an author's speaking of himself altruistically. Augustine wanted to set an example for all humanity; and his description in the *Convivio* seems "almost to herald Dante's own 'testament'," the *Commedia*. One reason to speak of oneself, Dante writes, is to offer the

---

[5] Cf. Lee Patterson, *Chaucer and the Subject of History*, 7.

greatest advantage [. . .] for others by way of instruction; and this reason moved Augustine to speak of himself in his confessions, so that in the progress of his life, which was from bad to good, and from good to better, and from better to best, he furnished example and teaching which could not have been obtained from any other equally truthful testimony.[6]

Freccero's understanding of the *Commedia*'s structure is illuminating in that it provides the basis for an ultimate merging of the pilgrim-figure with the author of the poem. Moreover, given the critical heritage that was defined by scholars like Schwietering, it is easy to see what motivates this more recent commentator to strike a balance between total self-effacement and total self-assertion: "By naming himself at the moment of his confession [Purg. XXXII.1003]," Freccero writes, "[Dante] gives to the abstract *exemplum* the full weight of *vero testimonio*, exactly as had St. Augustine before him" (3).[7]

The narrator Dante created in the *Commedia*, seen with the aid of our hindsight, is the pivotal moment in the evolution of the medieval authorship trope. Here the name of the author, and his vocation as poet, come together with a full blown discussion of poetry's uses and travails. Thus poetry, which is profoundly an act of naming in the sense of describing experience, such as first practiced by Adam, is shown to be the very same as the one who creates it, the author, who has named himself within it. Furthermore, as it merges with a discussion of language's efficacy, the named Dante-figure divulges the origins of authorship poetics and thereby delineates its developmental trajectory.

Dante is no modern. Even so, like other poets of his time, he can be utterly self-promoting in his references to himself. In their identifications with the very language and poetics they employ, medieval poets manage to single themselves out *from their surrounding literary tradition*—a tradition that could be seen as all-engulfing. Be that as it may, this is a tradition that not only nourishes them but also proffers a language whose very structure invites self-reference. It is a tradition that exists within the larger world of the text. And Dante is an intellectual who, as a poet, is responding to the ideas of his time.

Freccero points out that as the *Commedia* begins there is a great distance between persona and author; this separation gradually dissolves because of "the dialectic of the poetic process until the pilgrim and poet coincide at the ending of the poem" (25). This poetic process will involve meditations on the nature of both language and interpretation, through which the full depth of the Dante-figure will be realized. The poem is structured according to "the spiral paths the pilgrim

---

[6] Trans. Freccero

[7] Cf. Leo Spitzer, "Note on the Poetic and Empirical 'I' in Medieval Authors," 416-18.

[takes]"; these paths, in turn, are "spatial analogues of the temporal paradox of *terza rima* forward motion which recapitulates the beginning in the end." Such a structure reflects the merging of author and figure, and mimics the pattern of discourse that comprises the kind of autobiography to be found in the *Confessions*. Indeed, the movement of the Dante poem serves to represent

> the paradoxical logic of all such narratives [in which] the beginning and end must logically coincide, in order for the author and his *persona* to be the same. This exigency, analogous to what Kenneth Burke in another context refers to as "the Divine tautology," takes the form, "I am I, but I was not always so."
> (264)

Michel Beaujour (in "Speculum, Method and Self-Portrayal" 189) writes that "self-portrayal is inherently involved in epistemological speculation because it questions the validity of the procedures that program its own dialectical intervention, as it attempts to map out a new field of inquiry: the individual, thinking object, and the very process of thinking." What also becomes evident, in the spiritual autobiography, is that historical time and the eternity of divine grace are conflated, but within the conflation they are distinguishable in relation to one another, so that the Dante-figure can be viewed as a religious pilgrim. More so, significantly, this pilgrim is also a poet. And, as a poet, Dante will always locate himself in time, yet the manifestation of this temporality will be word and number—the poetic process itself. Virgil the poet, moreover, is his guide, and if wisdom is to be attained, it will have to come through the pilgrim-poet's ability to ascend beyond his guide's provenance. This the pilgrim does, with the aid of Grace; in the poem, so does the author, through poetic ingenuity that forms the poet's overall signature in which he will surpass the ability of his poetic master Virgil.

We will take up Dante's poetics shortly and again in Chapter Three. But first I need to fortify that discussion by returning to the issue of naming in order to amplify it. Let me begin by claiming that, simply, the act of naming lies at the heart of Dante's poetic strategies, and, further, that when we can comprehend the act of naming within the context of his time, we will be in a position to appreciate, in an accurate and detailed manner, the fundamental tension in the later Middle Ages between authority and individuality. The very conception of naming became, increasingly throughout the later Middle Ages, the fundamental preoccupation of language theorists from Anselm to Ockham. Anselm's semantics introduced the idea that statements in and of themselves possessed integrity; also noteworthy is his belief that within these statements the functions of adjectives and nouns differed, a difference designated as "signification," and "naming" or "*appellatio*," respectively (*De Grammatico* 4.30 ff.). By the time of Ockham, the noun or *nomen* had become a mere word, ontologically empty. In both of these thinkers' views, however, as well as in the views of many others since Anselm, language is set off as discrete from the language user. Language comes to exist as over and against the speaker or, gradually with the spread of literacy, the writer.

Furthermore, language came to exist within a unique dynamic exploited by those language users par excellence, the later medieval poets. The first troubadour, Guillem IX, was intent on creating dialectical structures in songs that reveal his interest in *how* language could be used to its full effect. His various discussions of language-as-object form a metapoetry out of which the persona as such emerges. Often enough, in fact, the troubadour or trobaritz song makes clear that this persona—in terms of grammar and in terms of poetry per se—besides marking its author as individualized, is the very sign of its metatextual nature. The persona, then, was a hypersign.

This literary persona, at various stages of its growth, both reflected and was the outcome of concomitant beliefs about language, more specifically about the noun, and even about the proper noun. In its capacity to signify a text's author directly, the proper noun served a historical function while, at the same time, it contributed to the author's fictional characterization or what Wayne C. Booth has called (in *The Rhetoric of Fiction* 67 ff.) a "second self."[8] Or, as David F. Hult comments (in *Self-Fulfilling Prophecies* 63), the "authorial name [. . .] alludes to an exteriority without ever relinquishing its fundamental textual determination." To this end, my book especially focuses on the work of Marcabru, Dante and Langland. Each, in his act of self-naming and contentions about poetry and language, provides a critical way station in an investigation of how a modern form of literature eventually came into being—that which, over a half millennium later, is meant when speaking of *fiction* (the newly recognized genre of *creative nonfiction* notwithstanding), a fiction divorced from the supernatural and therefore unlike prior literatures such as mythology. But in order that each way station can be understood for what it is, some attention must also be paid to Guillem IX and Chaucer. Their works represent, respectively, the beginning and end of this earliest stage in the development of modern fiction. Guillem's arguments about what makes for good poetry point to where the authorship trope is going. Chaucer's similar arguments not only tell us where the trope has been but also how it has established a ground in which literary realism can flourish—and by now they are being made by a fully realized "fictional" character named Geffrey, a narrator-poet who somewhat resembles his author and who "incarnates himself," in the words of Charles Owen (in "The Tales of Canterbury: Fictions within a Fiction" 179). Both poets employ narrative voices that speak about the problems of being a poet. By the time of the *Canterbury Tales*, the voices in those narratives reveal an understanding of, as John M. Hill asserts (in *Chaucerian Belief* 19), what their characters "do, for better and worse, because their posturings, responses, and feelings—their self-revealing, narrating voices—are crucially involved" (19). Chaucer, then, anticipates the modern sensibility. Yet to understand the how and why of this persona, Geffrey, that poetic function driving Chaucer's protomodernity, its predecessors must be taken into account.

---

[8] In Foucault, 129.

Another, synchronous figure, also demands our scrutiny. The final stage in the early development of the literary persona occurs when William Langland names the dreamer-narrator of *Piers Plowman* Will. From the medieval point of view, arguably, Will is the greatest achievement of all. Langland's persona is meant to represent human *voluntas* or *will*, as John Bowers has shown (in *The Crisis of Will* 176 ff.); at one level of signification, Langland's poem is about the struggle to exercise one's individual will in the striving for salvation.[9] Like Geffrey, more importantly like Dante, Will is named after his author—and, again, like the real life author, Will is a poet deeply concerned with the problems of writing poetry and more broadly of using language to get at the truth of experience. Yet as a figure Will also represents the theme of Langland's poem. Lastly, in representing the theme, Will is meant to comment on the specific form of the poem—allegory, which was the Middle Ages' primary expressive mode. That this figure, Will, evolved as it did should perhaps not be surprising. An argument can be made for such an occurrence as the natural outcome of the literary impulse. David Lawton (in *Chaucer's Narrators* xiii) speculates that the first person narrator might have been understood by a medieval reader as a personification. The effect of this point of view is that history, such as it then might have been conceived of, and fiction, which was also a rather loosely construed abstraction, were modulated:

> The narratorial "I," sometimes *persona*, always voice, is a personification of the text or, since all these tropes are related to allegory, it is an allegory of the author's presence in the text. Both presence and author are thereby allegorised, signified by unstable, because shifting, abstractions.

This "I," a "rhetorical trope," which is "mobile in the field between deixis and evaluation," is rooted in the earliest textual impulses, such that among the ancient Greeks it "might have been listed under *ethopoeia* [. . .] or *prosopopoeia*" (xii-xiii). The increasing emphasis on grammar generally and on the noun particularly, after the millennium, served to encourage the trope's evolution. The trope manifests itself in Chaucer's early dream poems, Robert R. Edwards comments (in *The Dream of Chaucer* 44), as "representational dimensions [existing] in a dynamic relation to the rhetorical dimensions [. . .]. The narrator stands, albeit uncomfortably and perhaps uncertainly, at the point where mimesis and rhetoric converge."

Sarah Kay contends (in *Subjectivity in Troubadour Poetry* 52) that the first-person subject of the troubadour lyric was an outgrowth of allegory "whose original purpose was the assertion of community"; further, this lyric "I" becomes the means of elaborating difference. Amelia Van Vleck writes in a similar vein (in *Memory and Re-Creation in Troubadour Lyric* 9) that the content of troubadour

---

[9] Bowers includes a comprehensive review of scholarship on this topic; cf. pp. 41 ff.

lyric, which was so often about its own "self-conscious artifice" and literary ideas, was freely exchanged among poets and their audiences in an atmosphere of "competition and controversy." The competition encouraged the emergence of literary individuality, since one point of view would often be asserted within a group holding another. The milieu of this poetry, more fully defined by Lee Patterson (in *Chaucer and the Subject of History* 8), was structured in terms of a

> dialectic between an inward subjectivity and an external world that alienates it from both itself and its divine source [and which] provides the fundamental economy of the medieval idea of selfhood. Medieval anthropology defined the subject as desire: as the Augustinian will, with its opposed movements of *caritas* and *cupiditas*; as the Boethian *intentio naturalis* that tends ineluctably toward the *summum bonum*; as the scholastic powers of appetition, in which the intellectual appetite seeks to govern its concupiscible and irascible partners; or as *amor*, an inward sense of insufficiency that drives the Christian self forward on its journey through the historical world. Among the impediments placed in the way of the Christian is the social identity—the stoic *persona* or *karaktera*—derived from the historical communities of the medieval world. The medieval conception of selfhood is typically understood as a dialectic between the Christian subject and this objectified historical identity.

The idea that the literary persona might have been comprehended as allegorical comes about as a logical conclusion especially when we take the *word*, that basic linguistic metaphor of Christianity, into account. Consider, for instance, Ovid's story of Narcissus, in which the self becomes, according to John Brenkman (in "Narcissus in the Text"), a denominal replacement founded on resemblance, or according to Paul de Man (in *Allegories of Reading* 188) a "parable of denomination."[10] By the fourteenth century Chaucer and Langland are, each in his own way, forcing a distinction between two selves, a distinction best appreciated in the context of de Man's claim (in "Autobiography as De-Facement" 70) that trying to separate autobiography and fiction is an ultimately fruitless task. In contrast to De Man, Derrida (in "From Psyche" 332) has (somewhat fancifully) proposed the notion of a "fabulous invention," a poeticizing that

> becomes the invention of truth, of its truth as fable, of the fable of truth, the truth of truth *as fable*. And of that which in the fable depends on language (*fari*, fable). It is the impossible mourning of truth: in and out through the word. For you have seen it well, if the mourning is not announced by the breaking of the mirror [i.e., the ostensibly fictionalized text that reflects actuality], but consists in the mirror, if it comes with specularization, well then, the mirror comes to be itself solely through the intercession of the word. It is an invention and an intervention of the word [. . .].

---

[10] Both are in Jonathan Culler, *On Deconstruction*, 257.

In Derrida's terms, the persona becomes the author's imperfect mirror image of himself. And this figure does in fact speculate about truth—or rather, a persona such as Chaucer's Geffrey often blindly stumbles over it in attempting to find the true words he desires to describe his experiences; these experiences are invariably characterized by a contemplation of both the power and futility of language. Chaucer's question, which had been Augustine's, is how can words comprehend truth? What question could be of greater interest to a poet? Chaucer's mode of inquiry can be excruciatingly funny, but we need to note how seriously busy Geffrey is, as he is made to reflect the dramatic, intellectual changes of his time.

Frederick Goldin has said (in *The Mirror of Narcissus* 22) that medieval poets "saw in the tale of Narcissus"—which they altered to suit their varying individual beliefs—"a representation of an indispensable human experience, the birth of self-consciousness through love." In the *Confessions* Augustine had written that the Word of God appears in the clouds as an enigma because of Heaven's mirror ("quod nunc in aenigmate nubium et per speculum caeli") although the mortal condition will mean that human beings cannot see the truth, the word, as it truly is (XIII.15.18). Thus the *"speculum Scripturae,"* Goldin comments, "reflects the image of what we long for, and gazing upon it we struggle to understand what is not clear" (11). The association of mirror and language, or alternatively mirror and text, is one that medieval poets greatly exploited. Among the troubadour and minnesäng lyrics particularly, as a poetic image and as a paradigm for poetics, the mirror

> takes on many meanings, although their common source is in the mirror of Narcissus: the mirror enables a man to see himself in another. But a new necessity requires the use of a mirror. The courtly man and the class to which he claims adherence are defined by an ideal that is often difficult to delineate and always impossible to fulfill. In the mirror, however, that ineffable courtly ideal is made visible down to the last detail, and is united with the knight's own image reflected there. His quality as a courtly man is thus confirmed.
> (70)

Hence, all these poetic attributes—the naming of the persona and the ascribing to it of the vocation of poet, the discussion on the persona's part of poetics and of language overall, the aligning of the persona's name with the poem's theme—all these components of the poetics of authorship are finally synthesized in *Piers Plowman*'s Will, as they indicate a turn in European literature that is transforming itself into its modern form. There are other attributes too, which must be noted but which I believe are less central to the emergence of the persona. "Medieval literature," writes Scott D. Troyan (in *Textual Decorum: A Rhetoric of Attitudes in Medieval Literature* 259), "marks a watershed, a major turning point in the development of rhetoric, a time during which rhetoric becomes re-oriented toward vernacular languages and a time during which narrative evolves toward romance and begins its movement toward the novel." The romances of authors such as Chrétien will surely tend in the direction of the novel; so, in its own way, will the

Canterbury Tales. Yet I would like to argue that the voicing in the *Tales*, in the last analysis, comes from Chaucer's deeply intuited relationship with his material, with tradition, with the very notion of text—all of which are bound up in the creation of Geffrey in his earlier work. This sense of "character" can be seen to lie at the heart of the various voices in the tales whose tellers are, in all of medieval literature, unique and yet utterly familiar from the modern standpoint—Chrétien's figures cannot be described in this manner. The modern "novel is of course marked by its tendency to develop interiority, to explicate internal character motivations, to make evident character attitudes" (259). In comparison with the *Tales*, *Piers Plowman*—not unlike, say, *Erec et Enide*—is alien to the modern expectation. In Will, however, we can see the convergence of rhetoric and various themes. This consolidation is identifiable as an individual person—at least in the sense that we can speak of Will as occupying the subject position within the code of Langland's text, within the code of its narrative. Even more, the consolidation is identifiable as an author. Most of all, *Piers Plowman* is quite conscious of itself as a text. And it is this factor, more than any other, which I believe has led to the creation of Will.

As a unique creature, though, it is Geffrey who will be viewed as anticipating the modern realm of the psychological, that which we treat as the supreme construct of truth. Psychology as such is a way of understanding what was virtually unknown and in any event would have been irrelevant to the medieval poet. Quite otherwise, the difference between Will and Geffrey reflects their authors' different aesthetically and epistemologically based reactions to allegory. Both Langland and Chaucer discerned this form's limitations and strengths and capitalized on them. It is only after Chaucer, in Thomas Hoccleve's work, that we catch the tiniest glimmers of what Troyan has called "interiority" in the poet's fascination with his own mental state. David Greetham notes (in "Self-Referential Artifacts" 245) that "[s]elf-referentiality (not merely of the work to the artist but of the work to itself) has become such a decidedly modern conceit—part of the legacy of Formalist defamiliarisation of the fictiveness of art—that its presence in the fifteenth century may come as a surprise." In his poem *Complaint* (ll. 162-75) Hoccleve suffers from what, by the time of Burton, will be called a "melancholy." Furthermore, while "looking at a mirror to adjust his appearance (an 'image' which obviously acquires particular sensitivity for the Lacanian psychological critic), Hoccleve realizes that because of his emotional state, he may not be able to see 'reality' as observed by friends, but only the 'illusion' caused by his own illness" (Greetham 247). What is important to see here is that Hoccleve's fears are couched in a rhetoric he not only inherits from Chaucer but openly credits to him. Hoccleve's narrator, Thomas, extends "the reach and competence of his inherited" poetics of authorship (244).[11]

Greetham's analysis suggests that extensive explorations of the works of other poets should be included in this book—such as those of Chrétien, or of Francesco

---

[11] Cf. Albrecht Classen, "The Autobiographical Voice of Thomas Hoccleve," "Hoccleve's Independence from Chaucer," and "Autobiography as a Late Medieval Phenomenon."

Petrarch. I have omitted them from the present study because, ultimately, their works are superfluous to understanding the literary persona's basic stages of development. Both Chrétien and Petrarch deserve incorporation into a broader study of the authorship trope. Chrétien does mention himself by name in his own work—an important constituent in any writer's poetics of authorship. All the same, he is cited, not as a literary character, but as the author proper; consequently he exists, for the reader or hearer, beyond the linguistic code of the story. To borrow a phrase from Lawton, we can say that the speaker claiming authorship in Chrétien's romance subsists as "an extratextual sign"; here we can differentiate between the persona and what Bakhtin called voice (Lawton x, xi, xii), a speaking personality driven by a will or desire. Even more intriguing, perhaps, is the fact that Chrétien seeks to elevate his authorial status—another ploy that is key to authorship poetics—by grandly proclaiming that his work will last throughout all of Christian time ("tant que durera chrétiente"—from the prologue to *Erec et Enide*);[12] and, simply by taking the name that he does, which brings together in him all of history and literature, pagan and Christian,[13] he can also be viewed as indulging himself in a kind of self-aggrandizement. But he is not the first author to include himself, in any manner, in his own poetry. Furthermore, he does not engage in an explicitly linguistic inquiry of a magnitude such as is carried out by Marcabru, Dante or Langland. The other writer, Petrarch, ushers humanism into literature. He is a Christian who looks back to the classics and ahead as well. Both his poetry and philosophy, in the words of Charles Trinkaus (in *The Poet as Philosopher* 125), embrace an "ideal of psychically autonomous individuality [which] has remained basic to Western Culture." Yet, as in the case of Chrétien, analyzing Petrarch's poems is not necessary to a fundamental comprehension of the authorship trope.[14] Petrarch also names himself in his work, but the form of autocitation he practices will tell us nothing beyond what we can learn from the poets we will be studying here.[15] Nonetheless, evoking Petrarch's verse prompts

---

[12] Paul Zumthor discusses this in "Autobiography in the Middle Ages," 31 ff.

[13] Cf. Roger Dragonetti, *La vie de la lettre au moyen âge*, 13-14; and Gregory B. Stone, *The Death of the Troubadour*, 208 n. 1.

[14] There is also the question of prose, its role versus poetry, which is beyond my scope. After about 1200, Paul Zumthor writes (in *Toward a Medieval Poetics*, p. 69),
> prose explicitly [adopts the function of] setting itself in opposition to verse and accentuating the role of language as a witness to facts. Prose eliminated a certain depersonalizing, refractive effect between author and listener, and lifted the veil of fictitiousness.

[15] But note J. A. Burrow's comment (in *Langland's Fictions* 87):
> Petrarch's use of his baptismal name, rather than his more distinctive surname, has a slight generalising effect; but his "Franciscus" is, much more clearly and continuously than Langland's Will, the author himself, the historical Francis Petrarch imaginatively submitting himself to the scrutiny of that master of moral and spiritual self-examination, the Augustine of the *Confessions*.

I do not reject Burrow's assertion. However, my concern has to do with the later medieval literary trajectory toward fiction, not history, even though that vector passes through the

me to make some pertinent comments about humanism, historicism, subjectivity and individuality, all of which are normally taken to be the hallmarks of modernism as originating in the Renaissance.

---

language of autobiography. The key to understanding this difference is indeed language. Langland's persona is essentially a creation of language and is in a sense only coincidentally autobiographical—as will be become clear. Indeed, Burrow also writes (citing Lawton's article "The Subject of *Piers Plowman*" 11) that

> [i]n speaking of Langland's self "or selves" I had in mind the variety of roles adopted and behaviours exhibited by his persona Long Will in the course of the poem. Here I agree with David Lawton, who has argued that it is just not possible to understand Will as a single consistent "character." As Lawton says, Will displays "a bewildering number of attributes," and "there are simply too many of these, some contradictory and not all in play simultaneously, for the notion of characterization to cope with."

(Burrow 90)

In Chapter Four I hope to show a consistency of a kind. Of course, Bowers' suggestion (above), that there was no actual author by the name of William Langland, may support my thesis. A like implication is to be found in Middleton's essay, "William Langland's 'Kynde Name'." Burrow is emphasizing one aspect of a phenomenon; I am emphasizing another. Burrow speaks of "a "'writer self'" and concludes that "[t]he 'persona', in other words, is in no way an exclusively literary phenomenon." And he cites Stephen Greenblatt in support of his claim, who writes (in *Renaissance Self-Fashioning* 3), "self-fashioning derives its interest precisely from the fact that it functions without regard for the sharp distinction between literature and social life" (89 and n. 16). Middleton's article also takes this tack; while laying the groundwork for asserting the non-existence of a person going by the name of William Langland (e.g., "Langland" can mean "land of longing" and therefore this signature gestures toward a theme in the poem rather than to a person), she demonstrates convincingly how Langland's ever more elaborate, subtle, deeply embedded and profuse authorial signatures, as *Piers Plowman* is revised finally in the C text, are determined by the social and political events of his time. Perhaps, then, what I am hoping to show (indirectly) is that these events, as they may have involved the person of the author, were to a significant degree contingent upon the author's language, at least in terms of the author's possible interpretations of events, and more so in terms of instigating, shaping and otherwise guiding the author's actions in making poetry and in other activities as well. In any case, what is crucial to my argument is the understanding of how language provides a kind of resonance in which self-knowledge arises, without which full-fledged fiction cannot come into being. The poets I will be analyzing reveal the struggle toward the attainment of fiction, which means toward a full self-realization that comes about through criticism, within their writing, of what they are writing and of the act and effect of writing overall. They also criticize language in and of itself, but increasingly that criticism is inflected by the spread of literacy as it changes them personally and within their societies. Middleton's essay, "*Piers Plowman*," contains some discussion of the authorship question in Langland's poem and a full bibliography to date. There are also George Kane's earlier studies, *Evidence for Authorship* and *The Autobiographical Fallacy in Chaucer and Langland Studies*.

It must be acknowledged that for quite some time this view of the Renaissance, a great turning point, in contrast to the twelfth century "renaissance," has been undergoing scrutiny. As has been suggested, the act of mythologizing a majusculized Renaissance arises out of a natural desire for a narrative, for a cogency. Unavoidably, the "recording" and or "interpreting" that are part and parcel of historiography will involve categorization in the attempt to comprehend discrete events of a past time. But this tendency has been shown to undo its own best efforts to arrive at truth.[16] The anti-historicist argument proceeds as follows. In ideal terms, it can be said that truth is unique, univocal—an idea, it must be observed, which implies that history does not really repeat itself—contrary to the adage that in effect stipulates basic historicist procedure. Modern historicism was first challenged by archetypalism and structuralism; the making of history inevitably came to be viewed as the shaping of the past according to the desires and assumptions of the present. That is, the past was believed to be beyond the ability of the historian to reach. By this reasoning, employing the tools of the *literatus* to describe his or her subject, the historian may not, in any absolute way, manage the past's rescue by endowing it with the writer's subjective presence. Such a debunking of the historical project has become more pronounced with the arrival of post-structuralism that specifically demonstrates how our view of ourselves, of our "modern" world, need not depend on what is still widely held to be a fundamental and monumental change in the way people of the Western world lived and thought—a change that ostensibly occurred first in Italy between 1300 and 1600.[17]

Yet in some sense history *can* repeat itself. We can somehow learn from the events of our past through their flawed contemplation—as if in an imperfect mirror. Historiography remains a rigorous procedure when its tenets are reassessed periodically in keeping with the changes in the way we interpret all experience, the present and the past. The work of Patterson bears out this point. As he has eloquently stated (in "On the Margin" 92), the conception of the modern Western world has depended on a "*grand récit* that organizes Western cultural history, the gigantic master narrative by which modernity identifies itself with the Renaissance"; moreover, this *récit* or formula "rejects the Middle Ages as by

---

[16] For a comprehensive summary of this problem, and its proposed viable solution, see Gabrielle M. Spiegel, "History, Historicism, and the Social Logic of the Text in the Middle Ages."

[17] Philosophers of history such as Hayden White (in *Metahistory*, *Tropics of Discourse* and *The Content of the Form*) and Valentine Cunningham (in *In the Reading Gaol*) have come to see the project of historiography as an "embarrassment." Cunningham also quotes Greenblatt (in "Shakespeare and the Exorcists" 102) to the effect that historicizing "has lost its 'epistemological innocence' as a consequence of post-Saussurean theory. 'History cannot be divorced from textuality'" (96).

definition premodern." From the time of the Renaissance, "medieval premodernity has with few exceptions been experienced by modernity as 'Gothic'—obscure, difficult, strange, alien." Closer to the present, after Hegel, history was based on a dialectic. Gregory B. Stone argues (in *The Death of the Troubadour* 2) that Burckhardt saw the Middle Ages as "a primitive or infantile stage of human history during which the subject, being essentially objective, does not know the difference between subject and object." And Michel Zink observes (in *La subjectivité littéraire* 11) that Hegel could not help but have viewed medieval art in the contemporary terms of Romanticism.

The problem with the Romantic, and later the modern, critical approach becomes obvious when studying, say, the literature of moral exhortation so popular in the Middle Ages. As Edwards has put it (in *Ratio and Invention* xii),

> However much we recover and come to grasp the techniques of didacticism and allegorical elaboration, the literary values that authorize didactic and allegorical works and elevate them to a level of cultural prestige remain largely alien to the modern age. We can learn to appreciate the rhetorical tactics of Chaucer's Tale of Melibee, for example, but it is hard to imagine preferring the moral tale the poet assigns to himself over the stories he assigns to the other Canterbury pilgrims. As a practical measure, when we find these areas of intractable difference, we reinscribe them in history. They are read back as part of the difference of the Middle Ages, even if the difference is to be explained by the historical fiction of an audience's "horizon of expectations," which differs fundamentally, though perhaps indefinably, from our own.[18]

Différance, deferral and difference, on the other hand, has made for new historiographical approaches that take the recognition of alterity as their starting point in attempting descriptions of the chimerical past, but question the need for the overarching, definitive "master narrative" into which, by definition, the historian strives to fit all that there "is" within the "historical" purview. Patterson strongly questions Burckhardt's thesis (cf. above).[19] Within the *grand récit* determined by the exigencies of the present, which comprise a self-vision to which we hold fast, pre-structuralist history-making allowed us the choice to ascribe to the Renaissance and deny to the Middle Ages "both a historical consciousness and a sense of individual selfhood"—as if such a sense, and with it the capacity for original thinking, were by definition the very gift of the Renaissance to the future (Patterson 93).

Yet certainly, since the millennium, the medieval world knew of the individual and maintained its own sense of history, as is well documented in theological and

---

[18] Edwards quotes from Stephen G. Nichols, Jr., "A Poetics of Historicism? Recent Trends in Medieval Literary Study."

[19] In *Chaucer and the Subject of History* (7-8) he reviews Burckhardt's acceptance and development in numerous ways by Terry Eagleton, Greenblatt, Jonathan Dollimore, Joel Fineman, and Francis Barker.

literary documents of the time. Colin Morris explains (in *The Discovery of the Individual 1050-1200* 10-11) that by the twelfth century

> [s]elf-awareness and a serious concern with inner character [was] encouraged by the conviction that the believer must lay himself open to God, and to be remade by the Holy Spirit. From the beginning, Christianity showed itself to be an "interior" religion. It also contain[ed] a strong element of respect for humanity. Its central belief, that God became man for man's salvation, is itself an affirmation of human dignity which could hardly be surpassed, and its principle ethical precept is that a man must love others as he loves himself.[20]

What Morris suggests is that the very notion of self, such as we usually conceive of it when speaking about the Renaissance self, was latently present in medieval social structures, religion and philosophy; the medieval self was determined by a subjectivity, autonomy, and an individuality within but also separate from community. The term *individual* was in all likelihood construed as *individuum*, *individualis*, or *singularis*—philosophical conceptualizations having to do with logic and possible relationships between the singular, and the category or species; *individual*, as a word, did not signify the realm of human affairs.[21] Anselm, who was a philosophical realist, saw the individual human being as subsumed within the species *human*, whereas Abelard, in discussing salvation, saw that people differed from each other in terms of form and matter. As for the *self*, the "age had," Morris writes, "other words to express its interest in personality. We hear a great deal of 'the self', not expressed in that abstract way, indeed, but in such terms as 'knowing oneself', 'descending into oneself', or 'considering oneself'." Another related term was *anima* to indicate *soul* or *mind*. Selfhood was indicated in other

---

[20] Cautioning against Morris and others of his persuasion (her article contains a comprehensive review of scholarship in favor of this position) is Carolyn Bynum (in "Did the Twelfth Century Discover the Individual?"), who writes (citing John Benton's article, "Individualism and Conformity in Medieval Western Europe") that people of this time viewed themselves as members of a corporate body. Moreover,

> When we speak of "the development" of "the individual" we mean something open-ended. In contrast, as Benton has noted, the twelfth-century regarded the discovery of *homo interior*, of *seipsum*, as the discovery within oneself of human nature made in the image of God—an *imago Dei* which is the same for all human beings. [. . . .] Thus, if the twelfth-century did not "discover the individual" in the modern meaning of expression of unique personality and isolation of the person from the firm group membership, it did in some sense discover [. . .] the self, the inner mystery, the inner man, the inner landscape.
> (Bynum 4, 15)

Cf. below. I draw the following remarks, except where stated otherwise, from Morris' book, 10-11 and 64 ff..

[21] Bynum points out, à la Benton, that the "word *individuum* (*individualis*, *singularis*) was a technical term in the study of dialectic; what [the twelfth-century people] thought they were discovering when they turned within was what they called 'the soul' (*anima*), or 'self' (*seipsum*), or the 'inner man' (*homo interior*)" (4).

ways too. Guibert of Nogent wrote about an "inner mystery," Otloh of Saint Emmeram about "the inner man." William of Saint Thierry, Bernard of Clairvaux and Peter Damiani all spoke of "knowing oneself." The sermons of the day, furthermore, revealed a desire for self-expression. And one particular school of preachers, of which Guibert was a member, emphasized the value of one's own experience in exegesis.

Clearly, the focus of theological attention was shifting to the human side of the equation. Since about the seventh century the word *humanitas* had been used pejoratively to stress frailty. But by the twelfth century the term "recovered its formal dignity" so that it indicated "philanthropy and kindness" (Morris 10). Augustine's *Confessions*, coupled with a new interest in individuality, moreover, led to the writing of many quasi-autobiographies. Suger of Saint-Denis, for example, wrote about his political activities, and, while Otloh did not formally compose a history of his life, he was given to reminiscing in a number of his books, which culminated in a work called *On his Temptations and Writings*.

There was no linguistic invention on the order of what in the Renaissance was meant by the term *poetry*, and for the medieval historian there could never be "a sense of the otherness and lostness of the past" (Patterson 93) that to a great extent accounts for the Renaissance and modern historical as well as literary sensibility. Yet the Middle Ages produced unique poetry that concerned itself with the individual poet's travail, with his or her attempt to provide a fitting description of experience, and overall with the art of making literature. Witness Dante and his Virgil. Dante chooses to employ a literary language and usually a subject matter inherited from the past. He seeks to be a part of a tradition. Indeed Dante— among other medieval poets—locates himself within this tradition by partaking of the "matter" of his literary heritage, and by refashioning this literary matter according to the demands of his own temperament and sense of what constitutes eloquence. In the later Middle Ages we see this intent manifested variously, for instance in the large number of Troy stories composed since the twelfth century. Some of them were considered to have been "literary," others "historical." These stories range widely from the twelfth century's *Erec et Enide* and the *Roman de Troie* by Benoit de St. Maure, to the *Historia Destructionis Troiae* (a quasi translation of Benoit) by Guido delle Collone, to *Troilus and Criseyde* by Chaucer. Considering the profound differences among these literary works, it might be argued that each of them is so distinct as to have to be considered original, in the sense that we take the notion of *originality* to mean that authorial intention and linguistic construct which have instigated and ordered works written by the time of Romanticism and perhaps as early as the Renaissance (i.e., certainly in the sense that Stephen Greenblatt intends in his book *Renaissance Self-Fashioning*).[22]

These medieval poets, just the opposite, were not interested in originality. Rather, the poets of the later Middle Ages were concerned with reworking the language—the matter and, ultimately, the textual nature—of an inherited tradition. And in fact this was a tradition that might be thought of by them to have been first

---

[22] Cf. my note above.

and foremost textual. These poets were not interested in going outside that tradition. They were part of a self-involving system in which their enunciatory activity could give rise to nothing that might exist beyond the system's comprehension. The nature of the system was doctrinally Christian, and, inasmuch as Jesus Christ was the Word incarnate, it followed that the cast of the entire Christian "system" was substantially textual (perhaps, the better term to describe the "system" is *literal*, yet the Christian *word* was not at all limited to a fixed or written form and could imply both explicit discourse and implicit, silent thought). As I shall explore at length, in the later Middle Ages all that existed could be seen and understood in textual terms. Textuality was the field on which medieval poets endeavored both to fit into the world in its Christian sense and to transcend what was fundamentally a Christian hierarchy of value and authority. James Hans describes (in *The Play of the World* 90) how the very activity of a poet allows the employment of "the furrows of [a] predictable range [of experience] to get outside of those furrows of predictability and, in going outside of them, [to enlarge] the field of some of the furrows." Thus the Christian system, which inevitably came to embrace purely literary esthetics, paradoxically made possible the promotion of individual *literati* who could turn the hierarchical impulse of (now, a literary) authority and value back on itself, and in so doing elevate themselves as the new authorities or at least the new spokespersons of the prevailing truth. These poets did indeed desire to assert themselves as poets—that is, as *auctores*—yet their enterprise took the form of an evolved sense of eloquence that in part derived from, and could be tested by, a reader's or listener's commitment to a literary past.

These poets wished to express the thing understood as the literary tradition better than it had ever been done before and better than it ever would be after them. To say it best—or to sing it best, as in the case of the troubadours, who were the primary formulators of this poetic—was to say it truthfully. In this light, we can understand the troubadours' preoccupation with judging both peers and forebears, with their praise or scorn; a variety of characterizations in poems allowed authors to set themselves up, dramatically, in either implied or outright contention with their *others*. In doing so, the troubadours invoked the past and placed their present beside it. Indeed, in verse and other endeavors, the medieval world provided a scheme by which it could explain itself vis-à-vis the past, for this period "saw temporality as an unbroken continuity from past to present, which is why it consistently presented the elements of antique culture anachronistically" (Patterson 93).

Ironically, perhaps, it has taken the urgency and vocabulary of a post-structuralist critique to reveal the very seeds of its epistemological approach in the philosophy of the Middle Ages. Early developments in epistemology, in turn, have now made the vitality and indeed the contemporaneity of the latter period clearly evident. This is a symbiosis that is most apparent in literary studies. Since the 1960's, the influence of post-structuralist theories has caused a radical reevaluation of medieval literature. In textual studies the principle of alterity, for example, has taught that variants of a text can be valid in their own right, as

Eugene Vance writes (in *From Topic to Tale* xxvii): the "necessity for medievalists to define relationships between variants of a given text extends to that of defining relationships between a single text and the network of *other* texts that constitutes its cultural horizon." Or consider Julia Kristeva (in *Desire in Language* 66): "Any text is constructed as a mosaic of quotations [and is] the absorption and transformation of another. The notion of intertextuality replaces that of intersubjectivity" (66). At the climax of the Middle Ages, poems begin overtly to presentا consciousness of themselves; in this they look ahead to a Modernist "art for art's sake" credo. Judson Allen's comparison (in *The Ethical Poetic of the Later Middle Ages* 32) of medieval and modern esthetics is instructive:

> The moral centre of most modern art is the value of the particular as such, taken either in the personalist sense exemplified by Wordsworth's *Prelude*, or in the verbal and lapidary sense most perfectly illustrated by "Twas brillig, and the slithy toves . . ." The two come together in *Finnegans Wake*, as the world of literature achieves perfect verbal solipsism. All these works, of course, make truth claims of various sorts, but they all have in common the axiomatic divisions of post-Renaissance times: life from art, mind from matter, science from religion, fact from value, word from thing. Whether these are accepted or opposed makes no difference; they are there. The medieval claim [for poetry, however,] presumes an axiomatic that these divisions do not exist—before Descartes, obviously, there was a profound sense in which they had not yet been thought of.

As we shall see, what Allen has called a "verbal solipsism," which he rightly claims is a sign if not a product of the twentieth century world, may very well, distantly, owe its existence to Anselm's recognition that statements in and of themselves enjoy an integrity or rather an internal logic of their own, quite apart from any objective reality. Perhaps it is not going too far to suggest that the way for Joyce's "solipsism" is prepared by Dante, who especially looks ahead to Kant's *Einbildungskraft* in the Paradiso's "ephemeral balance [*l'equilibrio fuggente*] between idea and symbol," as Allen Mandelbaum has said (in *Visione e Visibilia* 35).[23] There is a similarity although not a sameness between the Middle Ages and our own time, particularly the fourteenth and twentieth centuries. Both are eras of great change and uncertainty.[24] The one still had no precise, authentic notion of literary fiction, and the other has now arrived at an equivalence of fiction and fact in the crisis of genre that conflates poetry and prose and demystifies the fictive moment. For better or worse, Deconstruction may make no distinction between the fictional text and a news article or a philosophical argument. Indeed, what was perceived by Augustine as a linguistic breach is mirrored by a modern belief only in language's inability to supply stable meanings, and it is here that we can locate the primary symptom of complementary upheavals. For instance, Dante has Adam say

---

[23] My trans.
[24] See Jacques Le Goff, *The Medieval Imagination*, 20-23, for the medieval side of this story.

> Or, figliuol mio, non il gustar del legno
> fu per sé la cagion di tanto essilio,
> ma solamente *il trapassar del segno*
> (Par. XXVI 115-17, my italics)
> [My son,] the cause of my long exile did not lie
> within the act of tasting of the tree,
> but solely in my trespass of the boundary [i.e., of the sign][25]

in order to invoke an ancient epistemological meditation that for him has its origin in, after Paul, the "semiological consciousness" of Augustine (as Vance phrases it in *Mervelous Signals* 34): "What the Apostle says pertains to this problem: 'For the letter killeth, but the spirit quickeneth'" (*De Doctrina Christiana* II.6.8; in Vance 29). The *Summa Theologiae*, philosophically at the heart of the *Commedia*, augments Augustine in phenomenological terms; the *Summa* is echoed in Purgatorio XVII's paen to imaginative power:

> O imaginativa che ne rube
> tavolta sì di fuor [. . .]
> chi move te, se 'l senso non ti porge?
> (13-16)
>
> O fantasy, you that at times would snatch
> us so from outward things [. . .]
> who moves you when the senses do not spur you?

Then Thomas is specifically paraphrased in what essentially derives from the Pauline and Augustinian meditation (*ST* I.60.5) on natural knowledge and its necessary adjunct, mental knowledge, by which the sign of an object is apprehended (the sign, according to Augustine, being what he calls the *verbum mentis*):

> Lo naturale è sempre sanza errore,
> ma l'altro puote errar per malo obietto
> o per troppo o per poco di vigore.
> (94-96)
>
> The natural is always without error,
> but mental love may choose an evil object
> or err through too much or too little vigor.

Post-structuralist systems take up like issues. As Erich Auerbach observed (in *Dante* 18-19), there is an inherent discrepancy in the Christian idea of a singular word or sign that might represent a paradoxically plural Holy Trinity; similarly,

---

[25] This and all further translation of the *Commedia* are by Allen Mandelbaum in *The Divine Comedy of Dante Alighieri*. The text of the poem has been taken from Mandelbaum, who based his text on that in The *Enciclopedia Dantesca*, Ed. Umberto Bosco et al.

nineteenth century positivism is undermined by relativity, quantum theory, and the principle of uncertainty, and more recently the theories of chaos and complexity. Hence, we cannot entertain a faith in mimetic language, just as medieval people could not apprehend signs heuristically but rather instrumentally—since, Marcia Colish points out (in *The Mirror of Language* 222 ff.), knowledge came only with God's assistance.

The issue of a shifting semantic ground speaks directly to the question of self-citation that is an *Ur* form of the modern autobiographical impulse. Take, for example, the common misconstrual of Augustine's *Confessions*. For Augustine confession, as Vance writes, was a profession of faith in which,

> far more than the admission of sins committed [. . .] it meant also the speech act of *praising*, as when Christ says to God, "I confess to you [*Confiteor tibi*], Father, Lord of heaven and earth, since you have hidden these things from the wise." (*Marvelous Signals* 5)

Self-knowledge, in Augustine's view, was an unworthy enterprise. Augustine also tended to reject the notion of esthetic pleasure that the art of rendering such knowledge might otherwise afford. Such an outlook could not have persisted after Descartes. This perspective explains how narratology, by definition, cannot comprehend the last four books of the *Confessions*, which deal not with the events of Augustine's life but with the epistemology of memory in the human soul, the first chapters of Genesis, and so forth. His "autobiography" praises, and professes faith and sacrifice, so to bear out one or another sense of the word *confession* (5). The *Confessions* does not present an objectified, historical "I," but in fact declares its intention (in Book X) to reveal "what I now am and what I still am" (in Vance 2). Here we are confronted, as Jacques Le Goff contends (in *The Medieval Imagination* 80), with a "dialectic between the time of history and that of Salvation," a dialectic that became acutely operative with the emergence in the twelfth century of the *exemplum* as a literary form. While Augustine's conception of *communitas* is determined by divine love, by the time of Aquinas—particularly Dante's version of him—the events of one's life had become truly integral to the sense of the Christian community. This ethical sense served as the metaphor for poetics in Dante's *polis*; and it is this same sense of the personal life within a community, a self-conception driven by the realization of alterity, which drives poets like Guillem IX, Marcabru, Chaucer and Langland.

Recent critical theory allows us to see, moreover, that to a degree all historiographical perception, not just the medieval variety, must ultimately be anachronistic. Even so, "[o]ur anachronisms are not falsehoods," write Bill Readings and Bennet Schaber (in *Postmodernism across the Ages* 15), "but the thinking of the unaccountable and yet necessary phrase-events upon which every act of historical recounting and epistemological accounting is based." What the medieval poet's struggle for selfhood, for authorship, makes vividly clear is that a linguistic act inhabits a uniquely perceptual, linguistic space, and more so writing, which can be used to formulate laws or rather formulas that are by nature resistant to such truth claims. Speech and the literary impulse—because they employ ambiguous wording—at once comprehend a world beyond their direct statements and reject that world as unlike what they are. Hence the recounting of events in hindsight is inherently problematic. What becomes important, then, is to understand how one or another culture sees its past, and perhaps to resist the urge to embrace either oversimplified or overarching contrivances.

> History is not a panoply of past events, written about in an unhistorical present. We think that writing and reading cannot be understood as merely contingent or secondary in their effects upon the history to which they happen. On the contrary, we think that they structure history in ways that upset the understanding of it as a procession of moments independent of acts of inscription. Nor, however, do we think that history is a purely present act of inscription (nothing other than "what is said about it now"). On the contrary, we think that the "it" of historical difference uncannily haunts the "now" of the historian's discourse. We inhabit neither the distant past nor the distance of the present.
> (15)

Yet it is out of the historical perspective that the notion of the self becomes substantial and gains resonance. To be sure, what occurs is the dissolution of any clear definition of *self*—and this phenomenon has been the dilemma in medieval studies. Since the advent of post-structuralism, Paul Zumthor has, like Burckhardt, undermined the idea of medieval individualism.[26] In 1972, Zumthor spoke of the medieval poet (in *Toward a Medieval Poetics*) as one who is subsumed into a textual tradition, thus in effect as nothing more than the language of the poem. This recognition is a necessary one in order to arrive at, considering the enormous importance of authority in the Middle Ages, a balanced definition of pre-Renaissance individuality. Thus Zumthor is forced by the implications of his own theory to claim that the medieval text had to have been composed by a

> *someone*, to whom it still belongs, even if that someone's outline has faded. A shift has thus occurred, which must be taken account of without our being taken in by it. The author has disappeared; what remains is the subject of the enunciation, a communicating psyche, integrated in the text and indissoluble from the way it functions: a talking id.
> (44)

---

[26] Yet his idea of "Poet as Text"—the title of a chapter from his book—is crucial to my own argument.

Almost two decades later, H. Marshall Leicester, writing about the fourteenth century (in *The Disenchanted Self* 9), essentially repeats Zumthor's assertions about the provenance of the text but also establishes the ground for believing in a flesh and blood individual. Both critics draw upon the work of Emile Benveniste's *Problems in General Linguistics* and the idea of linguistic codes.[27] The *Canterbury Tales* is described by Leicester as "a collection of individually voiced texts [. . .]." The very fact of their textuality

> insist[s] that there is nobody there, that there is only the text. But if a written text implies and enforces the absence of the self, the real living person outside the text who may or may not have expressed himself or herself in producing it, the same absence is emphatically not true of the voice *in* the text, which I might also call the voice (or subject) *of* the text.[28]

Benveniste, Saussure, Barthes, Derrida, structuralism and post-structuralism have led to the dissolution of what was once thought of as an autonomous and integral selfhood. As Stone asserts,

> [w]hat is questioned by postmodern poetics is the very notion of the "self" that began to be constructed and to emerge, in *narrative*, precisely when courtly lyric was at is zenith, during the twelfth century. That is, the "renaissance" of the twelfth century is marked by the conjunction of two diametrically opposed literary models of subjectivity. The name of Chrétien de Troyes, who was both lyric poet and courtly novelist, is emblematic of this conjunction. On the one hand, there is the disembodied lyric "I," nothing other than a word, a generalized subjectivity, no one in particular, a fragmented, anonymous voice that can speak another's language, an inherited, conventional, or "found" language. On the other hand, there is the unique narrative self, the novelistic self of romance, an extraordinary, self-determining subject whose language is decidedly different. Narrative champions a hero who masters his destiny, who proves his special worth, whose quest is a frontal attack against discursive anonymity precisely insofar as it is a struggle to make a name for oneself or, more precisely, for one self. The self of story is historically, geographically, and genealogically localized. [The] subject of story is not determined by an inherited and conventional language but rather determines a new language.
> (58)[29]

[27] The idea has a special force when speaking of what is Chaucer's literate culture—that is, a less residually oral culture, as Walter Ong would say—in comparison with that of the troubadours. See Ong's groundbreaking book, *Orality and Literacy* (especially 31-77).

[28] Compare Michel Zink in *La Subjectivité littéraire au moyen âge* (1985), where he argues that subjectivity arises out of a poet's relationships with antecedent texts (171 ff.).

[29] Stone also writes, however, that the "Middle Ages consciously insists that I am *they*: that the individual subject is never singular, is always in some essential sense general, collective, objective" (4). I cannot help but express sympathy with him, since what he, and others, as well as myself, are striving for is the definition of *medieval individualism*, a term that can be regarded as an oxymoron, but this is because the language of a serviceable definition is still in the process of being forged.

Stone's remarks overlook the importance of self-naming in the lyric, prior to Chrétien, even as they trade on the notion of naming as critical to romance machinery. What lies at the heart of both romance and lyric is the court, where one exists both within and apart from its society, and where one may derive a sense of nobility, of being made better, through eloquence. The name as subject underwrites both courtly genres as well as the theme of "life and art as one"—as Chaucer recollects, centuries later, at the start of the *Parliament of Fowls*, echoing Horace's "ars longa, vita brevis":[30]

> The lyf so short, the craft so long to lerne,
> Th'assay so hard, so sharp the conquerynge,
> The dredful joye alwey that slit so yerne:
> Al this mene I by Love [. . .].
> (1-4)[31]

Both genres, romance and lyric, broadly speaking, are examples of the poetics of authorship. What happens in the lyric, however, describes this poetics more precisely and deeply (as we shall see). Yet in Chaucer's day the two converge and lead to the *Canterbury Tales* whose characters seem to have "interiors."

On the one hand, if the idea of the individual is determined by a psychological critique, and on the other by a textual one, then we need to resolve exactly how the particularized literary persona emerges and what its meaning is for its medieval readers, inasmuch as readers of later ages may all too easily make the mistake of ascribing attributes to medieval works that were simply not there. Furthermore, in contrast, later readers will often fall into the trap of alterity in which they view the medievals as other, as unlike themselves as can be. My study, I confess, wants it both ways. The argument of this book is that the medieval persona came into being in response to philosophies of its time. The medieval poets we read were deep thinkers; they were intellectuals, and, as poets, they could not resist exploring and otherwise playing with contemporary beliefs about language, epistemology and ontology. As the persona took shape, various poets and readers came to realize the implications of this poetics, and thus extrapolated new meanings. Slowly, a new sense of the human experience takes shape.

I am not alone in this contention. Writing about *Piers Plowman* (in "William Langland's 'Kynde Name'"), Anne Middleton describes the essential dynamic of the authorship poetics, specifically of "the pervasive practice of complex literary signature [which] is not an illustration of [a] cultural phenomenon, but an

---

[30] Cf. Lawton, *Chaucer's Narrators*, 45-47. On the Horace paraphrase, cf. Dorothy Everett, "Some Reflections on Chaucer's 'Art Poetical'," 1 ff.
[31] All quotations of Chaucer are taken from *The Riverside Chaucer*. 3rd Ed. Ed. Larry D. Benson.

important grammatical operator in bringing about a broader cultural transformation [in] a rearguard action" (25). As correct as I believe Middleton to be here, I must also take cognizance of Kay's assertion that, as early as the troubadours, the "subject" could be "read not just as a grammatical position, but as articulating a self" (213). The context of this remark is amply laid out by Stone who, just the same (and I think in the last analysis incorrectly), maintains that the lyric is not really individualized. While he reveals a deep understanding of the lyric moment's timelessness, so to speak, he does not fully appreciate the tension and thereby the power of the lyric when a self is being asserted however neoterically:

> The language of troubadour love poetry does not permit the identification of its speaker as a certain historical and singular individual: the time and place of the *I* is no particular place. Grammar or the language of song transcends the concrete historical situation; in Heideggerian terms, it is an ontological rather than an ontic language; it expresses Being in general rather than a certain particular being. (5)

Surely any history of ideas will take philosophical and theological writings as the signs of an evolving human self-consciousness. Poetry has more than ever to be taken in this fashion. I hasten to emphasize here, though, that what I am arguing for should not be understood as negating the medieval poet's reverence for and dependence upon *auctoritas*. Rather, the textual tradition provided a role for the poet in the present, as R. A. Shoaf explains (in "Medieval Studies after Derrida after Heidegger" 12): "All medieval writing posits relations among this or that discrete individual entity, person, or thing, and other entities, within structures of ever-increasing articulation and hierarchical interconnectedness." Grammar is the map that traces and at times gives rise to self-enunciation. I will show in Chapter Four how Langland employs grammar both conceptually and metaphorically to elaborate a metapoetry involving allegory and the exercise of the will, which is central to Langland's sense of authorship and to his act of self-assertion within his poem.

Langland is building on a poetic tradition that was perhaps most eloquently and subtly elaborated by Dante. In the *Commedia* Dante reveals himself to be, arguably, both a lyric and narrative poet (albeit this is not the narrative of romance). As a poet, Dante will always locate himself in time. For him the ultimate manifestation of this temporality is word and number—the poetic process itself. Virgil the poet is his guide, and if wisdom is to be attained from him, it will have to come through the pilgrim-poet's ability to ascend beyond his guide's provenance; this the pilgrim does, with the aid of Grace. In the poem, so does the author, through poetic ingenuity that forms the poet's overall signature by which he will surpass the ability of his poetic master, Virgil. We see this virtuosity in Dante's use of the trope "io sol uno":

> [. . .] e io sol uno
> m'apparecchiava a sostener la guerra

sì del cammino e sì de la pietate,
che ritrarrà la mente che non erra.
(Inf. II.3-6)

[. . .] and I myself
alone prepared to undergo the battle
both of the journeying and of the pity,
   which memory, mistaking not, shall show.

This poetic maneuver is the emblem of Dante's poetic performance in large. In its triple insistence on the acolyte's powers and future journey to Paradise, where Virgil cannot go, it places the pilgrim within and associates him with the very matrix of his thought, actions, aspirations, beliefs and fears—for it is in the number three that we find the links Dante has forged among himself, his poetry of *terza rima* and of three canticles, and the Holy Trinity. Here we see a direct attempt, in writing, at self-reflection, which was in some sense meant to be taken as fiction—however loosely, in our minds, the Middle Ages in general construed fiction and history. Yet a work like the *Commedia* is not to be easily defined. At one level of signification it is an allegory, yet real people and events are included in the fictional telling, which can suggest that the *Commedia* is the story of Dante's real spiritual journey. But the true, the actual, the quantifiable and most fascinating signs of Dantean autobiography lie elsewhere, in the poem's very language. When Dante singles himself out in Inferno II (above), he is, as a poet, intent on establishing himself as an individual who is both a part of and distinct from an immensely influential literary and philosophical tradition.

The relationship of Virgil and Dante in the *Commedia* of course constitutes the supreme instance of this dynamic. Virgil is both lauded and subtly undermined in favor of the Dante persona in whom the tradition is not only alive but flourishing as never before, through the role of the witness. The witness "merely" reports a depth and grandeur that even Virgil, we are finally left to ponder, could not achieve. In fact it is through the praise of Virgil that we first come to appreciate both the enormity and grace of the Dantean project, which is most profoundly spoken in its inter- and especially intratextual undertones. Virgil is Dante's "author," first identified as such in Inferno I (85) by the approbations *maestro* and *autore*: "Tu se' lo mio maestro e 'l mio autore."[32] The bounteous acknowledgment on the part of the Dante-figure is still to be augmented; it is not long before Virgil, twice praised, will be referred to as Dante's *guide, governor,*

---

[32] Cf. Giuseppe Mazzotta, *Dante, Poet of the Desert*, 154: "The language of this appeal is strongly reminiscent of Vergil's neoplatonic commentators. The reference to him as 'maestro e autore' recalls the Chartrian debate over *authentica* and *magistralia*: the conventional opposition between incontrovertible *auctoritates* and the learned, but not binding, opinions of the *magistri* seems to collapse in Dante's line as the two terms are applied to Vergil but, in effect, they are symptomatic of the ambiguous reading that Dante will have of Vergil." M.-D. Chenù discusses the background of the Chartrian debate in *La Théologie au douzième siècle*, 351-65.

master—"Or va, ch'un sol volere è d'ambedue: / tu duca, tu segnore e tu maestro" (Inf. II.139-40). Here, notably, the machinery for praise and acknowledgment is to be found in the very fabric of the praiser's language, in his recurring cadence that in its reprise serves to increase the depth and volume of that praise, and therefore the language further ennobles its subject as well as itself.

The key to this ploy lies in what are otherwise the least significant parts of Dante's speech—the pronouns containing in themselves, by definition, no semantic power. Yet used here in the larger discourse of praise, they serve to convey the primal meaning of that praise in the rhythm of their speaker. In fact, they form Dante's voice in these cantos. In their repetitions they suggest the measured, utterly sober realization on the part of their speaker that the source of his very meaning lies in his "father poet," Virgil—who is his *other*. Analogically, Dante is the pronoun to the noun Virgil—first in the twice proclaiming pronoun *mio*, and then a canto later in the thrice uttered *tu* (cf. above). Language theory of Dante's time focused on such semantic, and by extension ontological, distinctions. For instance the fifth century grammarian, Priscian, whose views still held sway in the late thirteenth and early fourteenth centuries, wrote that pronouns were without being,[33] that they were hollow and empty as they definitely stood for nothing.[34] While Priscian's teaching is challenged in later centuries, once the greater portion of the Aristotelian corpus has been rediscovered, the difference between noun and pronoun is only more sharply drawn based on a distinction between substance and accident, where only the noun could signify its referent both substantially and accidentally.[35] The Speculative Grammar movement, which emerged in Dante's years, "took the form of an attempt to provide an Aristotelian ontology of language, finding analogues in the various parts of speech for matter, form, substance, process, and so on," writes Norman Kretzman (in "History of Semantics" 374). The nominalist-realist debate also flourished, which served to underscore this difference, as did, in various ways, the schools of thought known as Terminism and Modism. We shall see in the following chapters the extraordinary attention other poets also paid to this difference.

Dante's acute sensitivity to textual features is evinced in the subtlest kind of augmentation. Specifically, his use of pronouns serves to point up the effusive quality inherent in any act of praise, which is quite possibly what drives the perception of praise when it is considered to be beautiful. And it is in this manner that he establishes his debt to the one being praised. Dante's tactics are not so far removed from, for instance, what we find in the French *margerite* genre, or the later Chaucer's overly abundant lauding of Alceste in the Prologue to the *Legend*

---

[33] "[P]ronomina esse non possunt [. . . .]"; *Institutio de Nomine et Pronomine et Verbo* II.37, in *Grammatici Caesariensis*.
[34] "Pronomina . . . cassa sunt et vana . . . , nihil certum et determinatum supponerent." In Stone 7; Stone cites Giorgio Agamben, *Il linguaggio e la morte: un seminario sul lungo della negatività*; and for Priscian's text, C. Thurot, "Extraits de divers manuscrits latins pour servir à l'histoire des doctrines grammaticales au moyen âge."
[35] Cf. Colish, *The Mirror of Language*, 72.

of Good Women. She is the goddess of love, who is the "flour of al floures." Chaucer's epithet is but one manifestation of what Peter Dronke has identified (in *Medieval Latin and the Rise of the European Love-Lyric* 181-82) as the *flos florum* trope that was common when both Dante and Chaucer were alive. Dante, however, had another purpose in his progressively grand enunciations of his debt to his "other" and great poet.

The problem for Dante is how to name himself as *the* poet and still acknowledge the literary past that has made his own poetry a possibility. Hence he must valorize Virgil while carefully laying the groundwork for the demonstration of his own poetic provenance. He initiates this strategy by praising Virgil twice (Inf. I.85). Then a triadic configuration recalls the thematic structure of that praise (Inf. II.140), to say nothing of its meter and cadence. As mentioned, of all numbers the number three orders the *Commedia*, structurally and doctrinally: the three line stanzas of thirty-three syllables, thirty-three cantos in each canticle (Canto I of the Inferno serving as an introduction to the poem as a whole), the thirty-three years of Jesus Christ's life on earth, and so forth.[36] In effect, the *viator*'s early praise of Virgil helps to create a resonance that will continue throughout the *Commedia* as an important subtext serving a number of poetic functions; one of these is to create the context for Dante's self-naming that, through the virtuosity of his poetic demonstration, will prove the truth of his claim for poetic mastery.

Again, it is what Dante sets between the two tropes of acknowledgment that fully marks him as the greater poet. As Mandelbaum makes clear (in "Taken from Brindisi" 233), Dante's unique maneuver originates in the finely wrought tour de force of Inferno II's "io sol uno" (3) that encapsulates the singularity of the pilgrim's circumstance and his destined envisioning of a celestial truth residing beyond the grasp of language:

> Lo giorno se n'andava, e l'aere bruno
> toglieva li animai che sono in terra
> da le fatiche loro; e io sol uno
>   m'apparecchiava a sostener la guerra
> sì del cammino e sì de la pietate, [. . . .]
> (1-6)

> The day was now departing; the dark air
> released the living beings of the earth
> from work and weariness; and I myself
>   alone prepared to undergo the battle
> both of the journeying and of the pity [. . .].

At least one of Dante's sources here is Arnaut Daniel's song "En cest sonet coind'e leri" where the troubadour writes, "Ieu sui Arnautz q'amas l'aura" (43). It is quite possible that Arnaut means to elevate romance by pointing to its origins

---

[36] Cf. Freccero, 258-71.

in pagan verse; his line recalls the *Aeneid*'s "Polydorus ego" (3.45). But it is with Dante that the trope fully blossoms. It should come as no surprise that Dante employs the trope to praise Arnaut.

> Dante is a most adroit user, especially in the *Purgatorio*, of the styleme of "I am" followed by the proper name. Its chief incarnation is the Provençal *ieu sui Arnaut*, citation-steal from Arnaut Daniel (Purg. 26.142), and its first incarnations are the negative of Inf. 2.32, *io non Enea, io non Paolo sono*, and then the affirmative, *I' son Beatrice* (Inf. 27.70 [sic]).
> (Mandelbaum 232)

In this regard, Mandelbaum goes on to make a crucial observation, one that goes to the heart of Dante's poetic:

> The proper name is one part of natural language that mimes—and engenders— poetic language. It is the emblem of poetry as nominalization [. . .] for the proper name collapses class and membership in the class into one. Even the reading aloud of a catalogue list, with that most elementary of structures, the alphabet, to be found in a telephone book, or an unalphabetic random sampling of registered voters, gives us some poetic lift. (And the pairing of the un-pairable proper name with the common noun in a rhyme pair yields even more poetic surplus.) But in *io son*, it is the coupling of that already-poetic proper name with the pronominal, indefinite, hovering shifter of "I am" that condenses the chiaroscuro of shadowed presence emerging into the light of particularity [. . .].

More than this skillful tactic, however, Dante evokes Virgilian mystery by precisely *not* naming; this profound yet understated "namelessness" is attested

> in the long wait between Dante's *io sol uno* and Beatrice's utterance of his name, "Dante," and, more hauntingly, in Matilda's nameless appearance in the Earthly Paradise, where the *donna soletta*, the "solitary woman" (*Purg.* 28.40) waits for some six cantos to be named.
> (232-33)

This strategy for self-naming is set against the background of the naming of the other (poet) at the beginning of the poem when Virgil is introduced into the story as the pilgrim's guide; here the namer's self-assertion occurs through delicately managed, subversive maneuvers such as has been noted in the use of the pronouns *mio* and *tu*. If Dante had wanted a literate reader to contemplate the philosophical implications of such language, moreover, specifically the play of its constituent parts, he could have done no better than to have placed the unique citation "io sol uno" midway between his first and second measured approbations of Virgil who, in effect, becomes the source of Dante's poetry, of his linguistic play. Thus, by implication, Virgil becomes the origin of this pilgrim-poet's *ego* ("io"). Within the framework of what Auerbach called the *sermo humilis*, Dante manages to elevate himself through a triad of self-reference while, ironically, he remains anonymous precisely by foregoing the use of a proper noun. The power of his trope comes from, again, understatement—that is, through "humble" (*humilis*) pronouns, through terms of number, which serve to raise the poet above all others. This configuration exists within a tradition but it is unprecedented in its virtuosity; in its agility and plenitude of self-signification it establishes its poet's preeminence. As Mandelbaum cleverly remarks,

> Dante the maker knew when to dismiss Vergil, but Vergil of all poets is the poet who knows when to disappear, and that knowledge is shared by Dante's Vergil and the author of the *Aeneid*. Yet as moving as Vergil's final disappearance in the *Purgatorio* is [cf. XXX.49-54], the most Vergilian moment of his absence is to be found in the opening of canto 2 of the *Inferno*. There, with the three Vergilian night scenes behind him, Dante forgets the presence of Vergil and concentrates on Dante's own shadowed aloneness—in that aloneness remembering Vergil most[...]. (234)

Here is a *presence* that can be profoundly invoked through its opposite, *absence*. This understanding of complementaries pervades Dante's language, even to the use he makes of parts of speech such as the pronoun, in order to point up both the paradoxicality of presence within absence and to show what such a dynamic can suggest about all language in its attempt to comprehend experience.

For Dante, it is finally the very music of his poem which establishes the proof of his superiority, particularly as he defines music in *De Vulgari* (II.4) as the ordering of rhetoric. He arrays the evidence of his rhetorical mastery before his audience, from which it can judge his claim. The claim is never baldly asserted; to do so would be to deny the very tradition that makes such a claim possible in the first place. Virgil is the great one, but in establishing the conditions for this greatness, Dante reveals the greater magnitude of his own poetry.

It should also be noted that Dante has included within his stratagem not only Virgil, his literary antecedent, but strictly historical antecedents in Aeneas and Paul ("io non Enea, io non Paolo sono," above). In itself this inclusion is a mark of the deep, ultimately inseparable connections among literature, theology and philosophy, and history, all of which are understood in Dante's time under the aegis of what we can call *textuality*. In a general sense we can say that the poet of the later Middle Ages, in this case Dante, was busy establishing himself or herself through the articulation of a relationship with a predecessor poet, or alternately with a received text, a text inherited from the older poet yet one whose conditions were determined by forces beyond the narrow field of the purely literary.

It is in such terms that an attempt should be made to understand the later medieval poets as authors writing both within and against the literary *auctoritas* whose hierarchy and very subject matter were beholden to a past understood through the supporting structure of Christianity. The poets strove to stake out an area of purely literary authority. This authority, however, would never be won at the expense of the tradition. All the same, the poets distinguished themselves from the received, "authorized" *text*, in a fundamentally subliminal manner, which necessarily included and in fact was determined by an author's understanding of what *text* meant. Contained within their poetry, their basic question was: "How can there be a meaningful statement about the nature of truth when my text departs from *the* text that is as close to the truth as any language will allow?" This question embraces a poet's self-conception in which he or she is in some sense to be self-described as a "textual being" or perhaps as a being who inhabits the language understood to be "textuality" per se.

The elucidation of such a rich and complex idea requires an examination of textuality as a force in the medieval Christian community. It cannot be otherwise, for, as will become evident, the origins of the concepts of *text* and *author* are one and the same; they are both aspects of a particular cultural discourse, and what Christianity first nurtures and then undermines can be seen in terms of language philosophy, which describes in part the integral relationship between what is said and the person or persons who say it. Christian history very much parallels that of the concept of textuality in its time. How could it not, since the text was first and foremost a Christian text, and furthermore a text founded upon all of the assumptions of a world that was derived from the *Word made flesh*?

As rationalism slowly emerges, the emphasis on grammar, as a force by which to order perception, wanes. In the eleventh century, the text and its author grow both distinct and distant from each other. Yet holding each to the other, despite the phenomenon of a new and ever increasing distance, is Christian and, eventually, literary *auctoritas*. Each author delineates and explores connections to a text that is the ground of that author's own definition and that makes possible, ironically perhaps, a growing distinction from the very text of which the author is a part. In his examination of the origins of the sonnet form (in *The Birth of the Modern Mind* 182-83), Paul Oppenheimer has argued convincingly that the sonnet derives from a tradition other than that of the troubadours. The earliest sonnets, such as those written by Giacomo da Lentino, are immediately striking due to

> the absence of two elements essential to successful performed poetry and ubiquitous in troubadour poetry: the absence of any even implied address to a listening audience, and the absence of multiple or dual personae [such as] the persona who actually suffers the pains of unrequited love, and the "poet-persona," who makes the song.

Indeed, especially in a poem like "Molti amadori la lor malatia"—whose brevity of form and meditative tone, it is suggested, alter poetry's rhetoric—the poetic discourse is addressed instead to the "poet himself" and may in fact address "the very form in which it is written" (183). The sonnet's brief and asymmetrical octave-sestet structure, which derives from a developing literate rather than the older oral tradition, goes far in engendering the form's meditative quality. We can discover a metapoetical stance, however, in the work of someone like Marcabru. All the same, the sonnet can be set apart "from those treatments of love to be found in the songs of the troubadours" because of "its dialectical structure" (183). Here again, though, we find a similarity with the troubadours whose very posture toward either implied or explicit interlocutors depends on an understanding of dialectic that had been broadened and deepened with the spread of a revived Aristotelianism. While it may be true that, as a form, the sonnet does not stem directly from the troubadours, we can say that it nevertheless fits into any fundamental attempt at understanding the Western, Christian world of the twelfth and thirteenth centuries.

In the *Confessions*, Augustine elaborates a basic textual metaphor that describes the crux of language and the reality that language seeks to portray—language and perception. In fact, the whole issue of *auctoritas* implicates the fundamental dynamic of language's relationship to experience, a relationship that is explored and intensified in Augustine's thought, and, moreover, one that is compounded with an overt meditation on textuality as the means of articulating this relationship. Within the framework of Augustine's thinking, the notion of textuality is arranged in relation to the individual of the society, as a part of a hierarchical, neoplatonic and unified structure. In the later Middle Ages, as the balance between orality and literacy became altered by technological and other forces—and because of the wider dissemination of Aristotle's writings, in part as the result of those forces—the unity of the Augustinian world was vitiated. "Technology is a way of revealing," Martin Heidegger has written (in "The Question Concerning Technology" 12). What persisted, despite the shift from singing and speaking to writing, was the Augustinian textual metaphor. In Augustine's works, this metaphor described the split between language and reality, the *verbum mentis*. With a renewed, more vigorous Aristotelianism, the metaphor came to describe the widening gap between the author and his or her language, and, too, between the author and experience or reality. More importantly, a self-referentiality had inhered in the Augustinian epistemological system; this was later applied to a metapoetics in which poets increasingly tended to refer to and to carry on discussions about themselves as poets and about the possibility of making poetry that might reflect the true state of things in the world. Three related perceptions were the result of this transformation, of what Etienne Gilson called "the demise of Christianity": 1) The poem took the form of the author. 2) The poem was a text and the intertextuality of its discourse increased, especially through the treatment of its own and other authors. 3) As a consequence, the author fully became his or her text. We see this final development in William Langland's *Piers Plowman*, whose persona is named Will. He is a poet, whose preoccupation is centrally concerned with the individual capacity for *voluntas*. In the testing of his will to be able to write the truth of what he sees and believes, we witness the dramatization of his effort to become his very poem, and so he becomes the mark of his larger textual tradition.

Chapter One

Text and Word, History and Fiction

A congruence of religious, social, political, technological, philosophical, esthetic, and even natural events created what we now recognize was a renaissance in the twelfth century. These events provided the backdrop for the unfolding of a drama that, when scrutinized, discloses elements common in all of them. That drama was the gradual appearance of a poetics of authorship. This poetics evolves as the medieval poet strives to establish a ground for his or her own singular identity—even though to do so, to assert one's individuality, will mean having to set aside the authority of the collective, Christian community. The authorship trope reflects the tension between the group and the unique poet who was a part of the group. The group was, in turn, in its present, determined profoundly by the past. Christian *auctoritas* was an ethical force manifest in all aspects of the medieval citizen's life, underwriting moral codes and their intellectual principles that satisfied, explained and justified them. Thus the doctrines of the Christian community as well as the pursuits of individual poets became increasingly concerned with language, with grammar most of all, and in relation to this focus with the concept of textuality—not least of all as it related to language but also, simply, in and of itself. For the idea of a *text*, as it was handed down from the past to theologians after the millennium, was modified by them as they undertook diverse explorations into the nature of language. Furthermore, their intellectual gains provided a foundation upon which poets and other writers could create and elaborate a distinction between fiction and history.

The emergence of the individual was a slow, an incremental and inevitable process that can be traced through the history of various medieval disciplines of thought. In this chapter, we will be especially concerned with two "disciplines"—philosophy and poetry; in order to appreciate what they shared with one another, let us think of them each as being, simply, a "mode of expression," or perhaps it would be better to think of each as a form of epistemological inquiry. To consider a poem as such may seem awkward and, worse, obtuse, since it implies that poets created verse in their search for intellectual truths rather than, say, because of the sheer pleasure a poem could render—although, no doubt, an aspect of this pleasure had to do with the ways in which ideas and music could come together. Yet it is important to see that both philosophy and poetry had much in common. Both fields of endeavor were conceived in terms of the authority of the past. Both, as well, were deeply changed by the spread of literacy and by the resuscitation of once lost classical texts.

What is particularly remarkable is the fact that the authorship trope emerged because of a constant intercourse among various fields of knowledge, or, more to the point, among various epistemological systems. And the sign of this overall change was a shared approach to language as an idea. Both philosophy and poetry deeply involve themselves in questions about parts of speech, and then, most of all, about names. The poetics of authorship evolves as an intercommunication among disciplines—to apply modern labels to medieval categories, for convenience—like music, poetry, philosophy, and theology. As it evolves, this poetics increasingly articulates the image of individuality, an image that becomes an idea. The story of this emergence, then, will reveal a struggle characterized by starts, stops and regressions, within many fields of thought; underlying these changes will be the two intertwining conceptualizations of language and text, as they continually developed, often moving closer to one another in their respective meanings, and at times growing individually more distinct.

As has been said, the act of naming, as that broadest, basic impulse to describe experience, centrally defines the sensibility of later medieval poets. For them the significance of naming, in its intent to comprehend the world, becomes immediately apparent when we consider them as a component in a large picture of intellectual change—especially involving a deepening division between theology and philosophy. Long before the millennium, the relationship of word to thing had become a critical issue within the Western tradition—such as we find in the Creation story of Genesis and in a number of classical texts, for example Plato's *Cratylus*. To name a thing, in some fundamental manner, is to attempt to bring order to perception. Or perhaps it can be said that naming is the very substance of perception; and naming may even be—to push this notion to its logical extreme—perception per se. Through naming, articulation becomes possible; moreover, it can be argued that it is only through articulation that being itself, as it were, can *be*. Nomination, in other words, is critical to any discursive and perhaps to any cognitive impulse.

The name, the medieval *nomen*, will define the thing named in the sense that the name can act in relation to the thing as a classifier: a name sets a thing named off from other things as being distinct; or, at least, the name must implicitly make such a claim. Distinction can vary widely within the range of the name. We can distinguish if an entity performs an action (e.g., grammatically, the entity as it exists in its nominative case), or if it is acted upon either directly or obliquely by another agent (e.g., genitive, accusative, dative, ablative cases). Such distinctions, furthermore, may include the recognition that the entity is not an agency of an action, as is embodied in language's verbal mode.

In the thirteenth century, Thomas Aquinas exploits a basic ontological premise that formed the basis for conceptions of noun and verb. He wishes to establish a ground for recognizing the difference between the *essence* of a thing and that thing's actual *existence*. William of Ockham, in the fourteenth century, undermines this difference by dint of what Aquinas would have viewed to have been an overly determined logic—or rather a logic whose purview comprehended areas formerly reserved to metaphysics. Aquinas could justify his analysis of reality by positing existence as a verbal mode (*esse*); thus he could claim that existence was, as F. C. Copleston has paraphrased it,

> an act, the created act of a created essence, the two [i.e., existence and essence] being distinguishable but not separable. At the same time in the phrase "essence and existence" *esse* functions as a verbal noun, and the two words tend to suggest two entities. That is to say, there is a temptation to regard "essence" and "existence" as names which stand for distinct entities.
> (*Medieval Philosophy* 335-36)[1]

Ockham the nominalist will reject Aquinas' metaphysics. In our attempt to understand the view of language generally held by poets throughout these centuries, it is important that we recognize a certain significance in Ockham's thinking. That he discards Aquinas' assertion is not as nearly as interesting to us, within the confines of our discussion, as the fact that he does so by adhering to his predecessor's epistemological procedure. Ockham sees no distinction between *essence* and *existence* since to him they signified the same thing, the one as a noun (*nominaliter*) and the other as a verb (*verbaliter*). Yet in maintaining this linguistic analogy, Ockham has to admit that, because the two words function differently in speech, they cannot be perceived as being interchangeable. The principle underlying this recognition is what Ockham (in *Summa Logicae* III.2.27) calls *propriety* (*convenienter*). His struggle to place language within the larger perspective of his theology is notable for his dependence on terminology. In fact, overall, medieval logic had increasingly come to rely on such tools as

> terms and propositions and the relations between them. That is to say, it became clear to the medieval logicians that they were dealing not with extramental substances, nor even with concepts as psychical realities, but with terms and propositions.
> (Copleston 268)

The rejection of Aquinas could only have occurred after the discoveries of ancient texts in both Greek and translation, especially Aristotle's *Categories*, which more than any other single factor caused a renaissance that, by the twelfth century, was fully underway. A renewed emphasis on Aristotle, who could now be read without recourse to Boethius' translations, profoundly altered the intellectual climate of the day. It is at this point in the progress of the Middle Ages that a pivotal feature of overall Christian cosmology is developed. As reflected in the *Categories*, a name may distinguish species from genus or one species from

---

[1] Cf. *De Ente et Essentia* 5; *De Potentia* 7.2. Reply 9; *Summa contra Gentiles* II.54; *Summa Theologiae* I.75.1.

another. Distinctive concepts of this order are the domain of the simple noun, of course, while the proper noun, by the very condition of its terms, the condition that brings it into being, seeks to make unique distinctions. One may wish to name the man Socrates as he who is neither Plato nor any other human being, which is to say that *proper* nomination dissolves the difference between category and membership within it.[2] This semantic, philosophical, and otherwise theological issue of class also involved questions of grammar.

Colish has carefully documented how, even before the twelfth century, a more vigorous Aristotelianism created exceptionally disturbing problems, some of which could be found in Boethius. In the eleventh century, grammarians could not avoid thinking about questions of "substance and accident, genera and species. The idea that a given thing might be looked at in a variety of ways called into question the classical definition of the part of speech used to denote a thing, the noun." In the Boethian translation of *De Interpretatione* nouns can signify in one way or another. Yet "[i]f they signify with respect to accidents they cannot properly signify with respect to substance, and vice versa" (*Mirror of Language* 69–70). This distinction was lost on these grammarians who continued to maintain, with a remarkable tenacity, the ideological boundaries of their received sense of the world. They held to the traditional views of Donatus, Priscian, Remigius of Auxerre and Alcuin, who determined that nouns defined things in terms of substance and accident, in all cases, both general and specific. These "traditional" grammarians had failed to recognize the two kinds of designation without furnishing any insight into possible changes nominal signification might undergo when moving from one to another act.

The tendency to cling to the past remains operative beyond Scholasticism. As for the eleventh century, although "the [contrary] testimony of Boethius" was embraced, simultaneously it was set beside the already-known; and so thinkers continued to accept the "massive authority of grammar" (Colish 70). Thus the influence of newly discovered classics, while eventually they would fundamentally transform Europe, was at first only tentative. The doctrines of the past, the past itself, for that matter, could be altered but only slowly, in small steps. Medieval philosophy of language undergoes great change, eventually, but at first the ideas of the new texts barely compete with, in Curtius' apt phrase, "the cloudy lees of the medieval curriculum of study and reading" (*European Literature and the Latin Middle Ages* 27).

The same can be said about poetry. The poets of the twelfth to fourteenth centuries also adhered to a received past. Their poetics typified a changing intellectual landscape; poetic practice reflected an increasing separation of theology and philosophy. Yet their poetic sensibility had its roots, too, in the splitting off from Latin of the vernacular languages, and, concomitantly, in a widening gap between oral and written textual traditions. While change could happen gradually, certain hallmarks of change start to appear in the twelfth century when poets first begin to practice autocitation, when they begin to speak of themselves in their

---

[2] As Mandelbaum noted in "Taken from Brindisi," 232 (cf. the Introduction).

poems. These "selves" were left to be interpreted ambiguously as being neither wholly the poets' real selves nor their apparently fictional versions that nevertheless were to be referred to by the names of the actual poets. Marcabru, for instance, scorns other rival poets who are to him merely *joglars* incapable of either true love or poetry containing truth; these *joglars* bear the *names* of actual personages. In the *Commedia*, Virgil acts as Dante's guide but he is also Dante's mentor, and his rival. By the fifteenth century, for the first time among medieval poets, Thomas Hoccleve writes verse that can qualify as being truly literary and *autobiographical* in the modern sense of this term as opposed to a form of self-naming that instead falls generally within the purview of simple rhetorical coloration. Hoccleve employs a poetics of self-referentiality. He represents a dynamic that had already been operative for several hundred years, one which developed and came to be used in increasingly subtle forms (as has already been discussed in the Introduction). Indeed, he relied on the past in order to establish his own poetic authority, as Greetham explains:

> The "discipleship" topos (with its inevitable acceptance of *humilitas* before the master) is very common, and is supported by such ancillary topoi as the "Golden Age" and the "dwarves on the shoulders of giants."[3] But the evidence of such perennial debates as the *moderni* versus *antiqui* demonstrates that the topos can in fact be used as an ironic stick with which to beat one's predecessors (Bloom's tessera perhaps). The pose is all, for it provides the poet's invention with a respectable heredity, gives scurrility, obscenity, libel, or esthetic deficiency a decent cover, and yet allows the work great freedom and independence through the apparent artlessness and objectivity of the narrator.
> (244)

What Greetham makes clear here is that the immense weight of the past, the result of Christian *auctoritas*, is at one and the same time a burden and virtue in the hands of someone like Hoccleve. The description of Hoccleve's "artlessness" brings Chaucer's narrator immediately to mind (who was clearly Hoccleve's model in *La Male Regle*, the *Regement of Princes* and other works). As we have said, moreover, contemporary with Chaucer's poignantly comical persona Geffrey is Langland's Will the dreamer, whose name includes a pun on the human capacity for volition—a concept that was intimately involved in the fourteenth century's heated controversy over the respective roles of human will and intellect, a dispute that inevitably drew to itself current ideas about language. And Langland's Will is not unlike the earlier Chrétien de Troyes' self-pun on the idea of what constitutes Christian truth. This kind of naming, which suggests that a poet is writing about either or both a real or fictional self, is a poetic act that plays a role in asserting individual poetic authority through names. More powerfully, however, later medieval poets iterate themselves through their manipulations of inherited notions of language as it relates to that reality of which naming is an integral part. It is

---

[3] For the discussion of "dwarves on the shoulders of giants" by Bernard of Chartres and its surrounding context see Curtius, 83-85, 252-55, 407-13; and cf. below.

within these very notions that we can discover the fundamental rhetorical gesture of these poets, who make nascent claims in their poetry for originality and individuality.

The manner in which these poets have appropriated the philosophies of their times entails some discussion at length, for theirs is a complex procedure. In this discussion, at the risk of stating the obvious, we must acknowledge nonetheless that a fundamental, Christian, underlying world view supported the manner in which medieval poets depicted both their personae and themselves, as well as their writing. Yet we should especially observe that Christian *auctoritas* contained a central paradox: In defining themselves as individuals, the poets of the later Middle Ages remained within the Christian community. Poetic *auctoritas*, an outgrowth of purely Christian, Church authority, had been a rigidly determinative force, one which commanded the poet's awe. Christian *auctoritas* defined poetry as well as other intellectual disciplines, yet out of its hierarchical system poets devised a new dynamic in their poems, one that illustrated poetry's unique value in relation to its inheritance. The context for the poetic assertion of individuality was the realization of an inherent play in language that the Christian establishment had long ago relegated to itself as being that which could most powerfully and authentically demonstrate Christian tenets. As will shortly become evident, this appropriation of language's potential was particularly articulated by Augustine whose metaphors for Christian truth, moreover, preeminently invoked issues of textuality. On the other hand, medieval poets' self-naming, as well as the naming of other poets who were at times either or both revered ancestors and competitors, was the symptom of a new poetics that had its sources in the currently transforming epistemology of scholars in both monasteries and universities. As well, poetic naming was one of the poets' several strategies that gestured toward a socialized definition of self within the courts of the aristocracy. However, as I have suggested already, the individual poet most profoundly underwent self-discovery by defining his or her poem in terms that often deliberately resonated contemporaneous theological and philosophical movements.

In Augustine's time, the intellectual emphasis was placed on rhetoric. As we shall see, beginning with Anselm in the eleventh century, that emphasis, which since Augustine had shifted to grammar, shifted once again, slowly and not without backward steps, to logic. This gradual movement is reflected in the contemporary poetry. Also, the transition paralleled a passage from a collective society to one that contained individuals at its center, which came about largely as a consequence of a changeover from orality to literacy. And, again, these fundamental changes in the lifeblood of European society could but only have effected a change in the society's literature—more precisely, in literary narrative structure.[4] Older forms of narrative, employed by an orally based culture, had primarily served a commemorative function and existed as a counterpart to a theology grounded in the Augustinian epistemology of memory, as Vance explains:

> Christianity, especially Augustinian neoplatonism, is founded on a theology of memory and on commemorative rituals of the purest sort. Its Eucharist is centered upon the gestures of a Son recalling men to his Father on the eve of his crucifixion by breaking his bread and exhorting his apostles thus: "This is my body, which is given for you; do this in remembrance of me" (*in meam commemorationem*; Luke 22:19). In the story of Christ's return to men after his resurrection, his disciples will be unable to *know* Christ until they *remember* him as he breaks bread and eats fishes among them (Luke 24).
> (*Mervelous Signals* 52)

In *De Magistro* (X, XIV) Augustine writes that true things cannot be taught, that pupils can only be reminded of what they know already. Augustine's *De Trinitate* (XV.22.42) holds that humans can know intelligible things (i.e., timeless spiritual things) in their minds through the agency of divine illumination, which occurs in their memory, in collaboration with the operations of intellect and will. All that occurs, therefore, will be colored by a sense of the past. Hence, as Wlad Godzich writes (in his introduction to *From Topic to Tale* xiv), it is not coincidental that the "performance or the telling of stories in oral societies is essentially commemorative," and that, concomitant with the spread of both Aristotelianism and Averroism in the early twelfth century, as well as with the emergence of new secular forms of literature, a new literary impulse is defined by the esthetics and cognitive demands of a now written textuality. This new impulse, furthermore, embraces the distinction between an emerging sense of literary fiction and that of historiography.

With the spread of literacy, however, and the springing up of what Brian Stock has fittingly called "textual communities," persons of the older commemorative communities came to be defined within their societies ontologically rather than discursively. In the orally based group of *memoria*, individuals could not, Godzich observes, "choose their roles but [had] them thrust upon them"; they experienced these roles as "fate." These persons were in fact "the loci in which discourses intersect[ed] and produce[d] subject positions," for "memoria" was the "treasure trove of discourses" that comprised the community's *hystoria* (xvi).

Gradually, Western society becomes dependent on written texts—the older culture having relied on the collective consciousness, the newer increasingly influenced by individuals, some of whom composed the texts. The newer culture was, as well, an intellectual community dependent on cognitive paradigms that ultimately came to be logical instead of grammatical. Yet, as has been noted briefly in connection with Aquinas and Ockham, descriptions and proofs of the real

---

[4] See Wlad Godzich's discussion of this change in his "Foreword" to Eugene Vance, *From Topic to Tale*, xiv; and cf. Godzich's book, *The Culture of Literacy*, 77-80.

as well as of the metaphysical increasingly turned to linguistic models both in order to derive a viable descriptive vocabulary and to establish a ground for measuring truth. Consider the case of Abbo of Fleury in the tenth century. He employed the received assumptions about language, and its relationship to reality, to formulate a rationale for an ostensibly perceived truth, by attempting to reconcile one of a number of what had become conundra surrounding the holy trinity. Abbo's problem arose from the acknowledgment that, even as he might choose to think of Christ as the begotten son of an unbegotten Father, he could not posit the Holy Spirit in either of these ways. He tried to solve his dilemma through a consideration of grammar and the question of negation, by observing that some forms of negation are relative. A grammatical principle supported Abbo's conclusion "that the Holy Spirit, although absolutely unbegotten, is also begotten in a *relative* sense, since He proceeds eternally from the Father and the Son" (Colish *Mirror of Language* 67; my emphasis). A more radical analogy with the structure of grammar—one that, notably, reveals the tyranny of Scriptural tradition in all areas of contemporary intellectual endeavor—occurs in the eleventh century. In the writings of Berengarius we see how reasoning by analogy had come to reside at the heart of Christian doctrine. Through analogy, they argued against the actuality of Christ's presence in the Eucharist. In his querying of the phrase "*Hoc est enim corpus meum*," Berengarius was led to construct a dichotomy of two truths, one spiritual and the other physical. Interestingly, in order to demonstrate his assertion and so to arrive at his "objective" position, he cites a crucial difference in the formula of noun and pronoun. Colish spells out his thinking:

> "hoc" [in the sentence *Hoc est enim corpus meum*] is a pronoun, and its grammatical function is to signify the Eucharistic bread on the altar. "Corpus," signifying Christ's body, is, to be sure, a noun. However, it functions as predicate nominative in the sentence, and, as such, is controlled by "hoc," the subject of the sentence, with which it must agree. Since the pronoun "hoc" has limited significative possibilities, good grammar dictates that these limitations must also extend to "corpus" in the context of the sentence. If [. . .] the substance of the bread were actually changed into Christ's body during the consecration, the subject of the sentence would be annulled and destroyed by its own predicative nominative, a manifest grammatical impossibility.
> (72–73)

Both Abbo and Berengarius elevated pronoun and noun to the status of arbiter of perception. Their intellectual procedures paved the way for the speculative grammarians—Peter of Elia, a University of Paris professor of grammar, Siger of Courtrai, and, prominent among them, Thomas of Erfurt—who, even more radically, assert the primacy of grammar as the measurement of truth. An article by Thomas Maloney discussing the background of Roger Bacon's thinking ("Roger Bacon" 187), makes the observation that more than any other ancient text Aristotle's *Sophistici Elenchi*, which was discovered in the early twelfth century, "forced logicians to draw help from the grammarians and develop semantic theories capable of the resolution of the linguistic problems rooted in the

[Aristotelian] fallacies [of division and composition in statements]." The speculative grammarians, in recognizing grammar's importance vis-à-vis logic, had applied its tools, as well as those of categorical thinking, to a widely held idea that Latin was different from all other languages. They concluded that there was a basic linguistic—that is, a grammatical—structure common to any and all languages. In fact, grammar was thought to be able to fit the Aristotelian concept of a science, and the speculative grammarians set out to prove that it was. As Copleston writes,

> The characteristic feature of speculative grammar was its attempt to deduce the parts of speech from the forms of thought, from basic concepts, that is to say, which were themselves expressions of the ontological studies of reality. For example, the noun was thought to express the concept of that which is stable, of substance, while the verb expressed the concept of becoming and, in the infinitive at least, the concept of "matter." A word becomes a definitive part of speech through its "mode of signifying" (*modus significandi*), these modes being concepts of the understanding which bind the word, as it were, to some mode of being. (*Medieval Philosophy* 269-70)

These grammarians, then, emphasized the machinery of signification, and thereby privileged grammar over metaphysics and logic.

It is not too difficult to appreciate what a poet as skilled as Dante could do within the context of such thinking. His use of the pronouns *mio* and *tu* in counterpoint with substantives, in a line like "Tu se' lo mio maestro e 'l mio autore" (Inf. I.85), and with the proper names of himself and others, indicates intellectual struggles of his contemporaries and forebears (as discussed in the Introduction). Likely enough, Dante helped to increase the importance of pronouns in the minds of thinkers who came after him—whether or not they actually knew of or had even read his work. After Dante, the nominalist-realist controversy reaches its height. We need to see how it begins, though, with the epistemological efforts of Abbo and Berengarius—and of others, Anselm not least among them, in his search for the proper name of the Deity (as in the *Monologion*). These thinkers were not clearly either practitioners of logic or grammar, since there were as yet no such explicitly defined disciplines. Under the influence of the *Categories*, with its concepts of substance and accident, genera and species, Anselm and others were able to grasp the idea of multiple perspective, and this led them to reassess the definition of a noun (as Colish has said, above). This recognition, in turn, instigates a great enterprise of redefinition and the postulating by Anselm in *De Grammatico*, notwithstanding his philosophical realism, of a "fittingness" that any true noun, or more specifically any true *name*, might enjoy in its act of signification, as he cautions against "logicians [who might] make assertions about words insofar as they signify, and yet, in speaking, given the appellative function of those words, use them in a fashion which is at variance with those assertions [...]."[5] In distinguishing between God and all other possibilities in the universe,

[5] IV.620. Trans. Desmond P. Henry, *The Grammatico of St. Anselm*. Consider this

furthermore, Anselm observes that the language used to denote anything else in the world will not suffice in the struggle to evoke the Supreme Being; normal attributes are not of the same kind as that which a divine attribute should be. Moreover, as Anselm says in *De Veritate* (esp. Books II, IV and V), the name for the thing, divine or otherwise, must be proper; it must possess rectitude (*rectitudo*), which means that its mechanics of signification must be cogent or rather what he calls *natural* ("*naturaliter*"), and, as well, that its signification must refer to an objectively true situation:

> Vera quidem non solet dici cum significat esse quod non est; veritatem tamen et rectitudinem habet, quia facit quod debet. Sed cum significat esse quod est, dupliciter facit quod debet; quoniam significat et quod accepit significare, et ad quod facta est. [. . . .] Alia igitur est rectitudo et veritas enuntiationis, quia significat ad quod significandum facta est; alia vero, quia significat quod accepit significare. Quippe ista immutabilis est ipsi orationi, illa vero mutabilis. Hanc namque semper habet, illam vero non semper. Istam enim naturaliter habet, illam vero accidentaliter et secundum usum.
> (Book II)

> [A term] is not ordinarily said to be true when it signifies that that which is not, is. But it has truth and rightness in that it does that which it should. But when it

---

passage (from the same, bilingual edition), which reveals the full flavor of Anselm's critique of the Categories:

> Nullatenus itaque credam sine aliqua alia ratione tractatores dialecticae tam saepe et tam studiose in suis libris scripsisse, quod idem ipsi colloquentes dicere erubescerent.
> (IV.210)

> So I just find it impossible to credit that authors of logical works can have no further grounds for so frequently and seriously committing themselves in their books to positions that they would be ashamed to exemplify in conversation.

Anselm's distinction, qualifying Aristotle, is brought out when he writes as follows (he analyzes the ambiguous term *grammaticus*, which could signify either "precisively" or "obliquely"—i.e., as noun or as adjective, roughly).

> Appellativum autem nomen cuiuslibet rei nunc dico, quo res ipsa usu loquendi appellatur. Nullo enim usu loquendi dicitur: grammatica est grammaticus, aut: grammaticus est grammatica; sed homo est grammaticus, et grammaticus homo.
> (IV.231)

> Here I want to lay it down that the name of a thing is *appellative* of that thing when it is the name by which that thing is itself called in the customary course of utterance. Thus assertions such as "Literacy is literate," or "Literate is literacy" run counter to such customary usage; we say, rather, "The man is literate," or "The literate is a man."

signifies that that which is, is, it does doubly what it should, since it signifies both what it has the power to signify and what has happened. [. . . .] Consequently, the one is rightness and truth of statement, in that it signifies that which it was made to signify; the other in that it signifies that which it undertook to signify. So the latter is the immutable possession of speech itself, but the former is mutable; for speech always has the latter, it does not always have the former; for it has the latter naturally, but it has the former accidentally and according to use.

All in all, for Anselm, "the beauty of the name lies in the fact that it is a self-evident definition; it virtually proves itself" (Colish 100-101). In other words, he observed that the proper name of a thing has its virtue in its self-evidence.

What we find here, then, are epistemological systems that are inevitably self-involved in the ways in which they have reverted to their own self-descriptions—their own languages—in order to arrive at self-validation. Likewise, the poetry of this period also directly addressed the issue of poetry. Moreover, beyond the question of the poem, which was being asked from *within* the poem, the poetry engaged in philosophical speculation about the nature of reality and the efficacy of comprehending that reality within a net of language. Not dissimilar to the philosophy, poetry began quite consciously to manipulate the language of the new ideas. Sensitivity to contemporary intellectual milieux produced the language that poets had at their disposal. To put it more broadly, the poems of this time derived from a society that was profoundly aware of its linguistic foundation. The concept of signs, signs that were held to be of divine origin, informed the consciousness of the later medieval intellectual. In fact, the Augustinian understanding of signs was compounded by a new, specifically *intellectual* apprehension of them, as a consequence of the societal shift away from orality and toward literacy. Laura Kendrick (in *The Game of Love* 21) notes, for example, that the newness of vernacular reading and writing, their "unregulated procedures," meant that

> men recognized the imperfections of writing as an instrument for conveying meaning. Thus early vernacular written charters do not claim to be more than aids to living memory. Medieval people placed the responsibility for the meaning of the inscribed vernacular text on its interpreter even more than on its original author. They recognized that condensation, omission, and various idiosyncracies in a scribe's use of signs to represent speech made the written text ambiguous.[6]

---

[6] One interesting consequence of this phenomenon was that the meanings of troubadour verses were changed through their reception. Kendrick writes that "[i]n effect, the transmission of troubadour lyrics in writing, instead of authenticating and stabilizing them as we might imagine, had the opposite effect of freeing interpreters to appropriate and make what they wanted of other men's signs; the ambiguous abbreviation of early vernacular writing freed interpreters to discover in the lyric whatever [. . .] they desired, to recreate the text in their own images, making their own new texts [...]" (42).

The spread of written communication distanced authors from both their texts and audiences, and implicitly demanded that a visual activity of *reading* would take place; reading in this sense meant mental reflection instigated by the visual engagement of a document, and, moreover, engagement by a some*one*. In the one to one relationship between text and reader that this act of reading provided, private meditation was being encouraged. Thus, an ever more widespread literacy gave rise to abstract thought processes, replacing the orally based listener's awareness of "true" internal signs, which had been founded in the epistemology of memory, with external signs of monumentality and new social and political orders.

Janet Coleman (in *Medieval Readers and Writers* 158) shrewdly parallels this transformation in Europe with what had occurred in sixth-century Greece, when literacy first became widespread. The change was profound. Once reading laws and history became generally possible, the Greek language underwent a transformation in order that it could express "for the first time metaphysical and political ideas, and abstract ideas [. . .]." So, too, in the high Middle Ages there occurred a

> shift from what is called the mythical to the logico-empirical mode of thought [.... For writing] appears to establish a different kind of relationship between the word and its referent which is a more general and abstract one, less closely connected with a particular person, place or time, than obtains in oral communication. This [happens because] certain mental potentials are activated by communication when it is frozen in the written text, and memory becomes akin to a vestigial organ.

Literacy, furthermore, meant seeing the past in terms of objectivity, and therefore meant separating myth out from history. And, as in ancient Greece,

> when a widespread alphabetic culture was becoming a reality, the very idea of logic as an unchanging and impersonal mode of discourse could and did develop. Such a new methodology for the learning and analysis of language led to fourteenth-century universities basing their curricula on logic as an abstract methodology that could investigate questions of how the mind perceived, learned and responded to the natural and the supernatural.
> (159)

Reading generally fostered a new critical attitude that had its impact on all walks of life and engendered in readers a psychological detachment from the larger community, which contributed to a nascent sense that a person could be a unique individual. This was a fatal point of view for feudal society, since literacy "encouraged the mobility of men and their ability to conceive of themselves as having a function apart from the land." In England, for instance, people "came to distinguish themselves either as 'lewed' or 'lered' far more frequently than as free or unfree" (160).

Perhaps more than at any other time, a semiotically based world view now affected all human endeavor, whether as narrowly linguistic provisions or within a more broadly conceived linguisis as can be found in the contemporary architecture, art, music—in short, in all walks of life. At the heart of all these semiotic "systems," however, lay the general system of grammar, one that Scholastics eventually argued for as being, vis-à-vis Aristotelian standards, a true science. Aristotle's thinking had instigated new struggles, owing to its skepticism regarding the possibilities for linguistic meaning. Originating with the mistaken belief, deriving from Boethius' translation of the *Perihermenias*, that Aristotle had defined names as the direct or indirect signs of the things they named, medieval semantics evolved by way of "a long and tortuous" path (Maloney 187 and n.1). Yet semantics really began in the early twelfth century with the discovery of the *logica nova*, particularly with, as has been noted, the *Sophistici Elenchi*. It was then that logicians felt compelled to turn to contemporary theories of grammar for a paradigm that would foster a resolution of the problem of language versus logic.

It is in England—ironically, where Latin had never been the native tongue— that grammar becomes the paradigm par excellence, the model of truth. All assertions of the real were being measured, analogically, against grammar's inherent wisdom. In the eighth century, Western textual repositories and centers of learning had to be shifted from the south of Europe to the north, in the face of Muslim threats. As Dronke observes (in *Poetic Individuality in the Middle Ages* 2), this shift contributes to vernacular literature's emergence in the ninth century. Copleston writes that many intellectuals of this time adopted an "ultra-realism which was the expression of the unwarranted assumption that there must be some real entity corresponding to every noun." Documents such as the *Letter on Nothing and Darkness*, written by Alcuin's pupil, Fredegisius of Tours (d. 834), perpetuated analogical thinking that took language as its starting point. Fredegisius "maintained, among other things, that there must be something corresponding to the word "nothing," and as every noun must refer to a corresponding reality, God must have created the world out of a pre-existing undifferentiated material or stuff" (*Medieval Philosophy* 69).

Although the Latin tradition had to be perpetuated, it became necessary to simplify Latin for the less sophisticated northern Europeans. This artificially emphasized grammar came to enjoy a privilege beyond its intrinsic merit, until by the time of Anselm it was being used to define both sensible and divine truths. This was a grammar, however, which was slowly being infused with Aristotelian reason. It was inevitable that grammar should have come to occupy such a central position in the perceptual framework of the mid to late Middle Ages. An expression of a cognito-linguistic inheritance from earliest times, it was most abundantly elaborated in the writings of Augustine. The *Confessions*, for example, presupposes an essential alignment between language and experience—indeed, a more intimate relationship between the two than is to be found in either the Presocratics or in Plato's conception of the *logos*. The *Confessions* (XIII.15) not only draws this relationship more acutely but also in more copious fashion than previously. Augustine's sense of the eternal is articulated as a heavenly text, echoing Apocalypse 6:14; the created world is "spread out like a canopy of skins," deriving from Psalms 103:2. Here Augustine exploits the biblical interassociations of skin, clothing, scroll, text and language:

> The authority of your divine Scriptures is all the more sublime because the mortal men through whom you gave them to us have now met death which is man's lot. You know, O Lord, how you clothed men with skins when by sin they became mortal. In the same way you have spread out the heavens like a canopy of skins, and these heavens are your Book, your words in which no note of discord jars, set over us through the ministry of mortal men. Those men are dead, and by their death this solid shield, the authority of your words delivered to us through them, is raised on high to shelter all that lies beneath it. While they lived on earth, it was not raised so high nor spread so wide. You had not yet spread out the heavens like a canopy of skins; you had not yet heralded to all the corners of the world the fame that came with their death.[7]

Vance writes (in "Augustine's *Confessions*" 8) that Augustine conceives of the mortal world as a "scroll of the firmament, a layer of 'skin'" (i.e., parchment as well as garment) on which "the primal dictation of creation is dispensed as a written text, as Scripture." Mortals must *read* the *word* of God, Augustine continues, unlike the angels, who as more refined beings read the eternal will without the aid of the syllables of time.[8]

Experience, whether the metaphysically Christian (or, for that matter, the formally Real of Plato) or that of the sensible, the material, must ultimately take the form of an expression that will have to be embodied in linguistic terms. All forms, whether Platonically Ideal or fallen in the Christian sense, obtain to metaphoric or catachretic expression that employs the terms of language per se. The very idea of the Christian Word incarnate must by definition adhere to such a parameter. Perhaps this observation merely states the obvious, that the dilemma of an ineluctable language is an eventuality, or, rather, that language is a given. The attempt had been made, of course, to separate oral from written language, and thereby to account for the "distancing effect" that the naming of the thing has on that thing's very comprehension. In the *Phaedrus*, according to Socrates, Theuth's invention of writing is repudiated by King Thamus because it can only resemble wisdom and therefore gets in the way of knowing and remembering; writing will cause a rupture in memory.[9] Augustine and later medieval thinkers go to great

---

[7] This and all further translations of the *Confessions*, unless otherwise indicated, are by R. S. Pine–Coffin.

[8] Cf. Jesse Gellrich, *The Idea of the Book in the Middle Ages*, 29 ff.

[9] Theuth calls writing "an elixir of memory and wisdom," yet Thamus fears that "this invention will produce forgetfulness in the minds of those who learn to use it, because they

lengths to distinguish between a word and the idea that may or may not be the cause of the word's inception. On the one hand, the alignment of word and idea includes discourse, and on the other, the alignment includes experience or rather reality. Colish observes that Augustine's view of the efficacy of language was a consequence

> of his conversion from pagan rhetoric to Christian eloquence [. . .]. On the level of rhetoric, the immediate application that Augustine perceives in the Word made flesh is the redemption of human speech. Since he is a rhetorician after his conversion as well as before it, he therefore interprets the theologian's role as a participation in the Incarnational task of expressing the Word to the world. (*Mirror of Language* 223)

For Augustine, discourse comprehends both the oral and the written, the sacred and the secular, the historical and the exegetical. Discourse ultimately transcends language, even though it is grounded in the linguistic expression of the truth as it is contained within any particular language. Such thinking about the possibilities of any finite expression is much in keeping with Jerome, whose ideas regarding translation stem from the understanding that there is a *sensum* or perhaps a "spirit" of any given thought, one that needs to be "extorted" (*exprimere*) from the actualized thought by a translator when making any linguistic transposition (*Epist.* 57 *Ad pamm.*).[10] Direct transference might not only be wrong but impossible. In the *Instituto Oratorio* (8.6.4), for instance, Quintilian equates Latin *translatio* with Greek *metaphor*.[11] Thus Reiss comments that "along with being a trope, or adornment of language, *translatio* represents the process of creating and altering meaning [. . .]" (103). Indeed, in *De Dialectica* (10.15), Augustine speaks of it as equivocation or rather as the creation of a "tangle of ambiguities" ("ambiguitatum perplexio"). *Translatio* was a necessity since language was viewed as inadequate. As Reiss notes, for

> medieval grammarians and logicians, *translatio* not only presented the possibility—as well as the possibilities—of transformation of which language was capable, but it went beyond language itself. That is, it was a principle of indicating relationships, not only between words, but between things, and between words and things. (103)

Jerome contributed to this conceptualization. Yet it is Augustine who, for the

---

will not practise their memory. Their trust in writing, produced by external characters, which are no part of themselves, will discourage the use of their own memory within them" (Trans. H. N. Fowler 563). Cf. relevant discussions by Curtius, 304; Gellrich, 33; and Derrida, *Of Grammatology*, 15.

[10] "[N]on verbum de verbo, sed sensum de sensu exprimere," *Patrologia Latina* XXII.571. This is a revision of Cicero's "non verbum pro verbo," *De Optimo Genere Oratorum* V.14–15; cf. Rita Copeland, *Rhetoric, Hermeneutics, and Translation in the Middle Ages*, 2.

[11] "Incipiamus igitur ab eo, qui cum frequentissimus est, tum longe pulcherrimus, *translatione* dico, quae μεταφορα Graece vocatur."

Middle Ages, establishes the authority under which notions of text and reality are to be ontologically, inextricably woven together, so that textuality and experience each come to define the other. As Vance declares, the written

> scroll of the firmament [. . .] is impelled and sustained by force of the creative—and recreative—oral performance. Enunciation, then, is the mode of moral and prophetic truth, of *auctoritas*; the "writing" of the Scriptures is only ulterior mediation, merely a supplement. The skin of the scroll once covered man, who was as a hieroglyph of authority. When Adam and Eve sinned, however, they covered the true text of their skin with the garments of an alien world. Martyrs, by contrast, are men who refuse to cover themselves with the skins of this world and with the fig-leaves of false eloquence, and who continue to articulate God's authority to sinners in the "infirmity" below.
> (8-9)[12]

Vance clearly evinces the debt Augustine owes to the language that is employed in the very elaboration of his cosmology. And in this enterprise Augustine establishes a long lived tradition, one the later Middle Ages struggles to supersede although the struggle must be lost. Jesse Gellrich writes (in *The Idea of the Book in the Middle Ages* 33) that

> [w]hile medieval instructors surely appreciated the distinction between "reality" and "semblance"—between Augustine's eternal text and temporal writing—they nonetheless tried rigorously to locate divine wisdom within the letters of the *sacra pagina*. Instead of a stumbling block to truth, the "semblance" was its "revelation" in the Bible, the "veil" (*integumentum*) or "mirror" (*speculum*) in which divine wisdom was present, if only readers had "eyes to see."
> (33)

Augustine's cosmology, in fact his etymology, still hold sway as late as the Renaissance, and in the twelfth century can be perceived, for instance, in the use made of a ceremonial Gospel book that was kept in the wardrobe of Edward I of England: "a book which [was] called *textus* upon which the magnates were accustomed to swear."[13] The twelfth century's association of *textus* with the Bible highlights the evolution of the English noun *text* from the Latin verb *texo* meaning "to weave, plait or interlace." In his essay "Medieval Literacy" (21) Stock initially establishes a relationship between, alternately, text or weaving, and discourse, by first pointing out the additional meaning of *texo*, "to compose," which implies composition, a form of composition that could include rhetoric:

> The notion of a *series verborum* survives as late as the *Oxford Dictionary*, which gives as the first meaning of text, "the wording of anything written or printed; the

---

[12] Cf. *Confessions* XIII.15, and *Enarratio in Psalmo* CIII.1.8.

[13] Chaplais, *Docs* 50, n. 2; in Thomas Clanchy, *From Memory to Written Record*, 205.

structure formed by the words in their order," a notion whose medieval roots were neatly summed up by the lexicographer Calepino when he wrote that *textus* equals *complicatio*, and that *textum* can be defined as *"quicquid contexitur aut componitur."*[14]

Gradually, *text* increasingly signified written instead of oral composition, and "[f]rom the eleventh century, *textus* began to refer more and more exclusively to the Bible" (21). In the later Middle Ages the Bible (Greek for *book*) could be seen as the *central* text of the world, that first and ultimate description of experience. The mystical idea of a text as being the world itself was never far from this revelation. As Derrida has said (in *Of Grammatology* 18), the idea of the book is not limited—indeed it exists as prior to writing that is essentially superfluous to it; the book is a text that indicates the world through its significative capacity to totalize, to portray meaning as ever present and homogenous:

> The idea of the book is the idea of a totality, finite or infinite, of the signifier; this totality of the signifier cannot be a totality, unless a totality constituted by the signified preexists it, supervises its inscriptions and its signs, and is independent of it in its ideality. [The idea of the book] is the encyclopedic protection of theology and of logocentrism against the disruption of writing, against its aphoristic energy, and [. . .] against difference in general.[15]

Such mysticism, the expansive impulse toward totalization, influences both metaphysics and an emerging physics. Language's relationship to reality, particularly language's tendency to rely on imagery of itself in order to describe the manner in which it might signify the real, is inclusive in nature. Yet language also insists on setting itself off as a distinct entity. Always on intimate terms with the world it purports to describe, language nevertheless has at times been viewed as insisting upon a separate existence from the world, that world it appears to gesture toward, while, at other times, language has been actually identified with its world— as in the status of the Bible during the Middle Ages.

The recognition of this dual proclivity on the part of language originates at least as early as Plato. The roots of this perception can be found in ancient stoicism. The Stoics, who indirectly but profoundly influenced many medieval thinkers (as Colish has shown in her essay "The Stoic Theory of Signification" 20), proposed a unified world:

> Plato's main concern in the *Cratylus* is not so much to forge a compromise between the natural and conventional theories of verbal signification as it is to delineate the limitations of language itself, as a transient, sensory form, in communicating a knowledge of abstract and transcendent objects of knowledge. The Stoics, [however,] while they were vigorous supporters of the theory of natural signification, rooted it in a decidedly non-Platonic metaphysics.

---

[14] *Dictionarii Octolinguis* (Lyon, 1663), 703.
[15] Cf. Gellrich, 31.

According to them, the speech of humans was "the verbal *logos*, the expressive side of the rational *logos* in man"—and this was true whether such speech was oral or literal; the "human *logos*," then, was "consubstantial with God, the *logos* of nature." The conclusion to be drawn here is that

> Stoic physics sees the world in monistic terms; God is identified with the natural world and with the human mind. Words, thus, are intrinsically real, in a physical sense. Speech is a natural phenomenon. Both the denotations of words, their etymological derivations, and the grammatical structure of language are hence natural.
> (19-20)

The Stoics' alignment of semansis, and particularly grammar, with what is held to be natural and thus intrinsic to the universe, presents a rough parallel to the elevation of grammar in the tenth century as an unsurpassed epistemological tool— even as the discipline of logic was coming into its own. In its increasing application to theological and/or epistemological problems, logic came to be conceived of as a distinct entity. For their part, the Stoics had

> extended their belief in the intrinsic correspondence between words and things from linguistics and the science of grammatical declination to a pedagogical emphasis on grammar as the basis of the liberal arts and to a didactic and rationalistic theory of poetics and rhetorical style.
> (21)

The emphasis on language leads to the more sophisticated notion of a *text* as that which is the metonymic, metaphoric, or in some manner consubstantial representation of a perceived world. To be sure, the idea of a text as being either or both a composition or a woven fabric occurs as early as the *Gorgias*. While set in a contrast to dialectic, the notion of weaving here is associated with rhetoric (i.e., rhetoric conceived of as spoken and as affecting a listener's judgments):

> Socrates: [. . .] since you [Gorgias] claim to be skilled in rhetorical art, and to be able to make anyone else a rhetorician, tell me with what particular thing rhetoric is concerned: as, for example, weaving is concerned with the manufacture of clothes, is it not?[16]

Out of the Latin term *texo* English, German and the Romance languages eventually derive their respective words for *text* that, as we have seen, came to be identified with Scripture. Yet *text* was too semantically rich to remain within the province of a narrowly defined, religious discourse. While the conception of a *text* had held out, to Augustine and others, the opportunity to realize religious truths fully, Stock observes that

---

[16] Trans. W. R. M. Lamb, 267.

> [. . .] the more sophisticated notion of tissue, texture, or style of composition, which may have originated with Quintilian, also survived throughout the Middle Ages, and, to add to the many layers in the idea of a text, never lost touch with its original, tangible associations. Cicero, for instance, in a phrase known to medieval authors, speaks of "tegumenta corporum vel texta vel suta" ("the coverings of bodies or weavings or sowings"), and a glossary of late Latin, preserving usages between the second and the sixth century, refers to *texta* as connections or chains.
> (Stock "Medieval Literacy" 21)[17]

By the time of the high Middle Ages, derivations from *texo* had more to do with cloth than parchment. All the same, Augustine's felicitous conceptualization of martyrdom in the *Confessions* (cf. above), to say nothing of his version of Adam and Eve both within and without the Garden of Eden, influences the eventual emphasis of Scripture as *the* text, while it bridges the related notions of skin, parchment and cloth, as integral within the religious sensibility that informed the idea of a decidedly *Christian* biblical text. Moreover, by the twelfth century, *integumentum* (like *textus* and *texo*, rooted in the Latin *tegere*) had come to signify, as Stock puts it (in *Myth and Science in the Twelfth Century* 52) "the 'allegorical covering' of a secular fable or myth."

Text and *reality* as concepts, then, are virtually inseparable in Augustine's thought. In the high Middle Ages they evolve into components of a central dialectical construct. Inherent in the idea of textuality is the presumption of interpretive strategies that must result in two meanings, inner and outer, the familiar husk and seed metaphor (outer skin and inner truth) and so forth, such as can be found in an allegory like Bernard Silvestris' *Cosmographia*. In this sense, allegory may be understood to have been an overly determined *text*, an assumption that might have been derived from any number of ancient writers. For example, Cicero associates the terms *integumentum* (*skin* or *covering*) and *involucrum* (*wrap* or *covering*). They are used interchangeably. In *De Oratore* (I.35.161) Cotta says, "modo in oratione Crassi divitias atque ornamenta eius ingenii perquaedam involucra et integumenta perspexi" ("I discerned the wealth and magnificence of his talent [i.e., Crassus' speech] as through some wrappings and coverings, but though I was longing to scrutinize them, I had hardly the chance of a peep").[18] Both terms mean *physical covering*. But Cicero's juxtaposition of them creates a platonic metaphor suggesting that Crassus' wrapping of his meaning in the sheer veils of rhetoric "[parallels] the concealment of formal reality from the senses of man by the phenomenal appearance of things" (Stock 49–50). This kind of figure anticipates a medieval understanding of the close relationships among myth, truth and allegory. In the later Middle Ages, as Coleman asserts, allegory finds its proper context in a world of readers, not listeners. Ever more "fixed modes of discourse and a fixed logic to analyse discourse," which are the conditions of literacy, instigated.

---

[17] *De Natura Deorum* II.150; Souter, *s.v. texta*.
[18] Trans. E. W. Sutton and H. Rackham.

> the development of the use of allegory and figural interpretation as an attempt to "read" and reinterpret aspects of the fixed, cultural tradition, not least the Bible. This had already been developed by the literate minority in monasteries and cathedral schools of the earlier Middle Ages. Allegorisation, in general, seems to develop only in literate ages, when the complex traditions of a society, which are previously expressed in myths and disseminated orally, are now fixed in a text for all to read. Any evolution of the myth previously effected by a minstrel or singer's oral adaptation to the needs of his audience, is replaced by allegorical interpretation of the traditional story, explaining away the inconsistencies that an oral tradition, not based on fixed texts, would have been able to subsume.
> (*Medieval Readers and Writers* 159)

Within this literate community, moreover, allegory came to function as a means of equating one body of knowledge with another. For Bernard Silvestris, allegorical poetry was the only adequate means of scientific description (Stock *Myth and Science* 230). In *Cosmographia* allegory allows him to synthesize an "empirically definable world" and the "inherited authority of ideal moral law" by setting the one standard, empiricism, beside Platonic–Christian *auctoritas* (Stock 280-81). In part, the inherent contradiction of the two world views is dissipated in their subsumption within the poem's encyclopedic "comprehensiveness" that allows each view its own ground within the larger structure of *Cosmographia*'s vision, and provides a co-equal justification of both views in the poem's "playful ambiguity" (128-30)—an ambiguity, it must be added, which primarily rested on double entendres of a complexity only possible for the literate reader who has the leisure to entertain simultaneous and multiple significations and associations within a single utterance. A typical example of Bernard's subtle poetic play occurs early in the poem when the universe is being described. The description allows Bernard to bring together myth, history and geography within "a delicate architectural model" that continues the first "image of a visual structure unfolding before the creator" (Stock 132). The poem equally arrays the Christian and the pagan. Christ and the Pope, for instance, are grouped among an assortment of classical heroes:

> Exemplar speciemque dei virguncula Christum
>   Parturit et verum secula numen habent;
> Munificens deitas Eugenium comodat orbi,
>   Donat et in solo munere cuncta semel.
> (I.3.53-56)

> A tender virgin gives birth to Christ, at once the idea and the embodiment of God, and earthly existence realizes true divinity. Divine munificence bestows Eugene upon the world, and grants all things at once in this sole gift.[19]

Here Bernard is punning on *virgo* ("virguncula," i.e., the virgin birth and the astrological sign anticipating it), and when describing Christ's historical role he uses the pagan term *numen*. It is the depth and richness of the ambiguity here that

---

[19] Tr. Winthrop Wetherbee, *The* Cosmographia *of Bernardus Silvestris*.

most suggest the literate quality of this text, which would not have been possible, in fact, in a world devoid of the new forces of both writing and rationalism.

Puns, symbols, and other like figures, will inevitably raise more questions than such language originally hoped to put to rest. Bernard's "individuality," in comparison with other twelfth-century Platonists, as Stock says, "is best understood within a framework for cosmogenesis utilized in particular by Thierry and William of Conches" (124). However, Bernard stands apart from these writers and all other contemporary Platonists. All embraced the belief that rhetoric and philosophy were to be united, and each of these thinkers may have "possessed a poetic vision of the cosmos"; yet only Bernard "imposes a new symbolic view of the cosmos." Indeed, unlike all the others, Bernard constructed "a new *myth* of creation" (274).

Dronke, therefore, includes *Cosmographia* in his claim for the individuality of the medieval poet, in the use made of such linguistic strategies that produce both rich perception and deep mystery. The poet's conscious intentions can result in the presentation of "something deliberately enigmatic." It is as if the rich, albeit equivocal, texture of the poet's text—the product of an "inner vision"—is to be the mark of his or her unique self-assertion. Ultimately, we must regard the inexplicable—such as *Titurel*'s Sigune, who sends her beloved Schionatulander on the quest for the hound's leash, or Piers the Plowman's tearing up of the Pardon— as an author's insistence upon an audience's embrace of what is "intrinsically" intransigent:

> The problems of inner vision, finally, can touch every kind of attempt at embodying in images some aspect of the intelligible, immaterial world. Thus in the twelfth century alone the inquiry could extend to visions of very different kinds: in Hildegard's own mystical prose writings, we should have to ask, how and why do the visions she relates nearly always suggest so much more than her own allegoresis of them can express? So, too, with the prophetic visions of Joachim of Flora: in what ways are his images—such as those in the *Liber Figurarum*—able to reach beyond abstract concepts? And with the allegorical visions of the twelfth-century Platonists: what can be expressed by allegory can also in principle be expressed conceptually, yet do these visions at moments reach the limits of allegorical statement? Where Bernard Silvestris, for instance, requires three goddesses, each with her own equipment, for the fabrication of man, or Alan of Lille conjures up four spheres, each showing the relation between matter and form in a different light, is this merely the allegorist's playfulness, multiplying entities beyond necessity, or are these, too, attempts at saying what could not be said any other way, at using allegorical constructs as if they were myths, to extend the range of conceptual statement?
> (Dronke *Poetic Individuality* 200-1)[20]

Allegory is but one instance, indeed, of medieval bifurcated conceptualization

---

[20] Dronke's references are to: *Cosmographia* II.11-12, and Alan's *Sermo de Sphaera Intelligibili*.

and expression; for the dyadic structure existed within social, political and philosophical systems as well. These were also systems of thought and expression that informed and nurtured one another. In the twelfth century Abelard's division of *langue* and *parole*, which was achieved through a more fully rationalized intellectual system—a system that was capable of articulating a relationship between language and experience—anticipates a subtle parodying of allegory in the fourteenth century, in Langland's *Piers Plowman*. In line with an emerging rationalism, Abelard was able to construct a more elaborate model of what can be conceived of as abstract mental processes, and in so doing he distanced himself from the logical procedures of his time, procedures which were predicated on the grammatical example established by Priscian (as described in the Introduction). Abelard saw no reason why, for instance, Plato and Socrates should share an identity merely because two sentences—"Socrates is a man" and "Plato is a man"— share an identical predicate. Yet there was for Abelard a belief in universals, if not a somewhat qualified belief. In the *Ingredientibus* he proposed the notion of an *intellectus universalium*. When considering the question of nouns, however, he eventually acknowledged that there were two kinds of designation: *circa ad inferiora* and *ad speciem*, the latter being a noun of species that referred to a *fictio* obtained by *abstractionem*. For Abelard, things would always be individuals, yet there was a universal that named them, one that actually existed.[21] Such naming was not a *flatus vocis*—that is, a sound made from letters and syllables—but a meaningful expression, a *vox significativa* or what Abelard also recognized as a *nomen* and what later, in a revised edition of his logic, he called a *sermo*; either signified a "common likeness" though *flatus vocis* did not require the ascription to it of universality. Abelard would conclude that universals are not things but that they do denominate things; moreover, such common conceptions reside in consciousness. All the same, a term like *man*, which was universal, was not a proper name such as *Socrates*, even as it did name the individual, because it was predicable of all men including Socrates. Common nouns named indeterminately.

Finally, Abelard is to be seen as struggling to be free of—and only somewhat succeeding in his endeavor—the linguistic paradigm that first provoked his grappling with the concept of universals and his striving to derive a purely logical model out of that struggle. He had to turn away from the idea of logic as dealing with entities, including mental entities, and toward the belief that logic treated terms and propositions, in what Jean Jolivet (in *Arts du langage et théologie chez Abélard* 352) describes as "une entreprise de déréification." If Abelard's position appears equivocal, it may nonetheless be fairly judged within the context of a larger tension between grammatically and logically based world views.

---

[21] This discussion of Abelard is indebted to Maria Fumagalli, *The Logic of Abelard*, 62; Copleston, *Medieval Philosophy*, 82–83; Jean Jolivet, *Arts du langage et théologie chez Abélard*, 352; and Thomas Gilby, "Peter Abelard," 6.

Abelard could distinguish between an inner linguistic model based on Latin's explicit grammar that was common, at least in theory, to many members of a group, and an outer speaking capacity associated with the vernaculars, one that demanded undivided performance and flexible social allegiances (Stock *Implications of Literacy* 528). His work reflects, and was the product of, the tensions and rebalancings of grammar and logic, but also of orality and literacy, of the feudal society of *memoria* and a new kind of society comprised of individuals who were no longer bound to a single place, the common circumstance under feudalism (cf. above). These tensions are the condition of later medieval life, and even centuries after him they provide the background for *Piers Plowman* in which Langland raises the question of an inherent dichotomy in human experience between speech and action. The conflict they pose is highlighted in the poem's banquet scene when the Doctor is challenged by Will to practice, as it were, what he has been preaching. As Middleton has smartly phrased it (in "Two Infinities" 170), their dispute is reconciled when, in speaking of Dowel, Dobet and Dobest, "Clergy offers more than a bizarre analogy to explain *what*" is meant by these *terms*:

> 'Now thow, Clergie,' quod Conscience, 'carpe us what is Dowel.'
> 'I have sevene sones,' he seide, serven in a castel
> Ther the lord of lif wonyeth, to leren hem what is Dowel.
> Til I se tho sevene and myself acorde
> I am unhardy,' quod he, 'to any wight to preven it.
> For oon Piers the Plowman hath impugned us alle,
> And set alle sciences at a sop save love one;
> And no text ne taketh to mayntene his cause
> But *Dilige Deum* and *Domine quis habitabit*;
> And seith that Dowel and Dobet arn two infinites,
> Whiche infinites with a feith fynden out Dobest,
> Which shal save mannes soule—thus seith Piers the Plowman.'
> (B XIII.118-29)[22]

The argument Clergy continues to advance is based on his knowledge of grammar. Here we may observe that the poem is departing from normal allegorical procedure. Langland is personifying what Middleton has correctly identified as "coined terms using several parts of speech"; the meanings of these terms will lie in their strictly formal properties (171)—indeed, as purely formal, they exist only within their poetic environment. Compare them, for instance, with the ideas they

---

[22] Unless otherwise specified, all quotations from the A, B and C texts of *Piers Plowman* come from, respectively, *Piers Plowman: The A Version*, Ed. George Kane; *The Vision of Piers Plowman: A Critical Editon of the B-Text*, Ed. A. V. C. Schmidt; and, *Piers Plowman: An Edition of the C-text*, Ed. Derek Pearsall.

signify as we find them in the *Convivio* (I.2) where Dante writes of Augustine's life that progressed "from bad to good, and from good to better, and from better to best."[23] In Langland's hands, allegory can function as a result of the "syntactic impossibility" of the terms indicating the Three Lives, as David Mills has expressed it (in "The Role of the Dreamer in *Piers Plowman*" 195).[24] Yet the poem is clearly allegorical. This approach to allegory, its assessment of its formal "possibilities," is reminiscent of the argument advanced by Abbo, Berengarius, and later the speculative grammarians, who held that reality is literally defined—

---

[23] Cf. the Introduction.

[24] Cf. Middleton, "Two Infinites," 170, and the Introduction. This issue is taken up at length in Chapter Four. While I am deeply indebted to Middleton's perceptions in "Two Infinites," I also must acknowledge her more recent work, particularly the long essay "William Langland's 'Kynde Name'." Yet in this book I am interested in pursuing the central line of inquiry of the earlier piece. In the later essay she writes, for example, of a "late fourteenth-century 'crisis of the proper' concerning representation itself, a crisis more fundamentally political than literary" (18-19)—a well chosen phrase here. Her explanation of Langland's signatures in each version of *Piers Plowman* tends in the direction I am going; on the other hand, she brilliantly links them to Langland's social context. She continues:

> It is within this broader, discursive field that Langland presents the status of his authorship as a matter of paradigmatic importance: the making of this poem, the nature of its representative claims, and the elusive social identity of its author, acquire—with more specificity in each of its revisions—the aspect of urgent contemporary political concerns.
> (19)

She focuses on the varied uses of Langland's name in the poem, and finds his
> progressively deeper understanding and more fully conscious acceptance—comparable to that of Augustine—of both the literary and social consequences of developing a philosophic and spiritual quest in the narrative form of an apparently specific life-story.
> (42)

I do not deny the truth of what she has written; yet I am presently interested, rather, in showing how the linguisis of the poem reveals its author's attitudes about allegory and poetics generally, which in turn embody the deepest of all his authorial signatures—as Middleton says, they "[regulate] properties that are in the first instance grammatical and ontological [. . .]" (27). Thus the later article also adds some important insights that I am happy to marshall in my behalf, to offer but one more illustrative example (which is an expansion of most of what I have already quoted in the Introduction):

> A good deal of recent discussion of medieval authorial self-representation has regarded [. . .] internal self-naming as but one aspect of the broader late medieval "discovery of the individual," and has considered literary manifestations of "poetic individuality" as among several kinds of evidence of new interest in the representative and signifying power of the self. But [. . .] the pervasive practice of complex literary signature [. . .] is not an illustration of this cultural phenomenon, but an important grammatical operator in bringing about a broader cultural transformation [. . .].
> (25)

perhaps it can be said to be invoked—by the language used to describe it. For Langland, the ultimate attempt at expressing the truth must come enigmatically, in a coded form, in language not merely imitating life but rather creating it. In the banquet scene his "grammatical argument"—whether we consider it the text of his narrative, his narrative text, the text of his intent, or the narrative's subtext—

> is crucial to the entire poem in showing *how* these terms have significance. Clergy shows that their meaning lies in the forms of the words themselves, and his account illustrates the way allegorical language works throughout the poem to order the search for perfection.
> (Middleton "Two Infinities" 170)

As will later be discussed at length, Langland purposely obscures his allegorical framework as a way of commenting on both the nature of allegory and what he believes is its sustaining structure—that of grammar. In this manner, furthermore, he has taken a step beyond the Augustinian allegorical expectation, where there is the surety of a one to one correspondence between outer and inner meaning (that is, if the reader can only apply the proper interpretive method). Langland, instead, "repeatedly calls attention to the heuristic shortcomings of [allegorical] personifications by exploding their narrative and dramatic consistency in mid-scene." Likewise, he questions "the very notion of linear narrative as adequate to the task of explanation" (185). The question to be asked at this juncture—one that was intensely pursued during Langland's day and for some time before it—is whether truly linear narrative, what for the historian might take the form of chronology, is a poet's viable alternative.

Piers Plowman is one of many examples of inter- and intratextual strategies that appeared in the later Middle Ages. Always residing at the center of the Christian imaginative experience, particularly after Jerome and Augustine, textuality continually instigates these kinds of strategy within the church, throughout the exegetical tradition; eventually, in the eleventh century, textuality provides the basis for a peculiar, new form of itself, in secular literature. And while interpretation was always a component of Augustinian cosmology, the later spread of literacy created a second order interpretive activity. The written text's temporal and spatial remove from its author meant that its readers could, at leisure, engage in a reflective negotiation of a text. Leisure and reflection "[promote] the ability to conceive more complicated structures" than is possible when there is only oral discourse (Coleman *Medieval Readers and Writers* 157). In turn, reflection allows for a reader's greater discernment of the issues a given text sets out. Increased abstract and critical thinking, moreover, help to form an individual consciousness, a self-consciousness distinct from that of the group. As Godzich has said (above), members of an oral community are defined "discursively" within that community, for these are persons who are individuals merely "in the etymological sense of the term, that is, [they are] material purports of roles which they do not write but accept, in the form of fate, from the power that resides in *memoria*." Within the community of readers, however, the individual will come to be defined as inherently and fundamentally human, in the sense that such an individual can play a role in forging his or her destiny; in other words, such an individual will come to be defined "ontologically" (xv–xvi). Walter Ong comments (in *Orality and Literacy* 105) that "writing makes possible increasingly articulate introspectivity, opening the psyche as never before not only to the external objective world quite distinct from itself but also to the interior self against whom the objective world is set."

One social outgrowth of this shift from oral to written discourse is that, in the latter case, the individual as a reader will come to be defined as separate from the overall societal discourse that would otherwise be all subsuming. Writing, and particularly reading, give rise to abstractive logic, which in turn engenders and sustains reflection on the part of the individual and defines a new kind of discourse that will ultimately change all social and political structures. It is logic, furthermore, unique among possible discourses, which comes to dominate all other epistemological systems. It is unique because

> it does not intersect with any other discourses and, as a result, it comprehends them all. It makes them all answerable to itself. The advantages are immediately obvious. Instead of a belief in the ultimate coherence of the universe of discourses, logic provides a verifiable methodology for the determination of such a coherence. Since it appeals to universals of reason, it is inherently more egalitarian as long as one is willing to consider all human beings as rational beings. (Godzich xvii)

Literacy and logic, therefore, establish a new importance for a society that could now be defined by its attachment to that aspect of the world which existed for the individual between his or her birth and death. Logic undermined the premise of Christian eternality that served as a cement to bind individuals to a common and dominant, broadly societal discourse. This was a community that gradually was perceived as being an entity apart from such an individual. Moreover, such a separation occurred in both secular and clerical worlds. A new rationalism, in short, pervaded all aspects of later medieval society in which persons played astonishingly new roles as both members and autonomous individuals; for logic "open[ed] the door to the emergence of the individual as someone endowed with rights" (xvii).

Likewise, the question of poetic *auctoritas* parallels exegetical activity that in the later Middle Ages began to be concerned with the *human* aspect of Scripture. As M.-D. Chenù first demonstrated (in *La Théologie au douzième siècle* 351–65), the word *auctor*, at one time, most often referred to the Church fathers.[25] The concept signified by the term *auctoritas*, derived from *auctor*, writes Hult, "was eventually emptied out of any ideas of human agency, coming to refer directly to the texts themselves [and,] at the same time, the word *auctor* came to be confused with another word of related meaning, *actor*, which recuperated the primitive meaning of human agency" (62).[26] Minnis observes that later medieval commentators were brought "considerably closer to their *auctores*" as the newly popular Aristotelian system of the four causes that "governed all activity and change in the universe" (efficient, material, formal, final) came to be "applied in literary analysis" (5). The revered *auctor*

> remained an authority, someone to be believed and imitated, but his human qualities began to receive more attention. This crucial development is writ large in the prologues to commentaries on the Bible. In twelfth-century exegesis, the primacy of allegorical interpretation had hindered the emergence of viable literary theory: God was believed to have inspired the human writers of Scripture in a way which defied literary description. Twelfth-century exegetes were interested in the *auctor* mainly as a source of authority. But in the thirteenth century, a new type of exegesis emerged, in which the focus had shifted from the divine *auctor* to the human *auctor* of Scripture. It became fashionable to emphasize the literal sense of the Bible, and the intention of the human *auctor* was believed to be expressed by the literal sense. As a result, the exegetes' interest in their texts became more literary.
> (5)

Minnis' particular focus on this one aspect of a changing intellectual climate discloses a change that reached into all walks of life. The individual, standing apart from the community, is a member of the larger Christian fold; however, within this Christian society there is an ever growing appreciation of each member's mortal, sensible life. The new emphasis on the individual, furthermore, altered society's literary sense and brought about the construction of definitions for fiction and history.

From our modern standpoint, we must view the distinction between fiction and history as remaining blurred in the twelfth century, yet it is from then that we can trace the separation into two unique fields of thought—when, simultaneously, there arose an increasing interest in literature that can conveniently be called *historically conscious*. For instance, Bernard of Chartres' analogy of twelfth-century thinkers, as dwarves who rest on the shoulders of the classical giants ("nos esse quasi nanos gigantium humeris insidentes"), was well known;[27] Jacqueline T. Miller surmises (in *Poetic License: Authority and Authorship* 9 ff.), from the fact of its citation in John of Salisbury's *Metalogicon* (III.4), that a spirited debate took place over the significance of what was deemed a renaissance and its debt to the rich, newly

---

[25] In Hult, 61-62.
[26] *Augere* and *agere*, respectively. Cf. Minnis' commentary below.
[27] Cf. Curtius, 119.

rediscovered antique past. It is important to note that Bernard's remark was double edged. In his own time, Bernard realized the debt his contemporaries owed to the classical past, seeing them as a continuation of it in faithful reproductions of antiquity's ideas, styles, and cultural paradigms; yet, too, he was ready to admit that in other respects the renaissance he was a witness of, and a part of, had perhaps surpassed even the ancients' reach.

Such doubleness of perception permitted the licensing of individual interpretation vis-à-vis a past that was revered as awe inspiring. The individual of the twelfth century saw himself as part of a flow from ancient times, yet he or she also represented a distinct turn in that literary–historical course of events. And in this he or she was, in fact, participating and continuing that flow of events by acting as an individual who could be viewed as being at one and the same time a part of it and a distinct entity regardless of any larger social structure or continuum. The twelfth-century individual's look backwards in time from a new vantage point, and with a decidedly altered attitude toward both the past and, secondarily, toward what constituted knowledge, inevitably had to raise questions about the nature of historiography itself. Such a development particularly obtained to the twelfth century's view of Virgil, who himself in the *Aeneid*—a crucial text in the medieval litero-historical imagination—had to synthesize past and present, myth and fact, according to the ethics, politics and esthetics of his own time. Virgil's amalgam of myth and history could and did readily serve as a model for medieval counterparts like Chrétien.

The extent to which Virgil exercised literary license was indeed to be theoretically justified in the twelfth century. Averroes, for example, allows that at times there occurs the need to depart from a literary standard. Of course, he feels himself to be sanctioned by the authority of Aristotle; his commentary on the *Poetics* asserts that "variation from proper and standard speech" is one aspect that defines poetry (ch. XXII).[28] Quintilian, Cicero and other *antigui*—the "shoulders" of their counterparts of the renaissance, the *moderni*—were also often invoked, by Donatus, Isidore and others. Eventually, John develops the notion of poetic license to such a degree that he can declare,

> License to use figures is reserved for authors and for those like them, namely the very learned. Such have understood why [and how] to use certain expressions and not use others. According to Cicero, "by their great and divine good writings they have merited this privilege," which they still enjoy. The authority of such persons is by no means slight, and if they have said or done something, this suffices to win praise for it, or [at least] to absolve it from stigma.
> (*Metalogicon* I.18)[29]

Here, importantly, John speaks of the use of less than transparent, figurative

---

[28] Trans. Hardison, 378, in Alex Preminger, Leon Golden, O. B. Hardison, Jr. and Kevin Kerrane, Eds., *Classicism and Medieval Literary Criticism: Translations and Interpretations*.
[29] Trans. Daniel D. McGarry. Cf. Miller, 27.

language, but what needs to be noticed is his great investiture in certain persons, "authors and for those like them," his contemporaries who might choose such language as an option in their own work.

Related to this idea was the question of *compilation*. As Neil Hathaway writes (in "Compilatio: From Plagiarism to Compiling" 19),

> Isidore's *Etymologies*, Gratian's *Decretum*, Peter the Lombard's *Sentences*, the *Glossa ordinaria*, Huguccio's dictionary, Vincent of Beauvais's *Speculum maius*, the innumerable florilegia are easily recognizable to us as compilations. They are the forerunners of our encyclopedias, catalogs, inventories. [. . . .] But they were not the only texts thought to be compiled: the vocabulary of compiling was expressed to describe the making of chronicles (arranged by date), saints' lives (arranged by the individual *res gestae* or *miracula*), cartularies.

In classical times the verb *compilo* had meant "to plunder" or "to pillage"—which yielded up the term "to plagiarize," to change meaning in written language. And then compilation was viewed negatively.[30] By the twelfth century, however, the notion of using the words of others had taken on a neutral connotation, and specifically *to compile* meant what it means today.[31] Thus a distinction was gradually being developed, between original authorship and what the modern world calls plagiarism. Yet what must be kept in mind is the fact that the medieval growth of awareness, whereby individual authorship could be acknowledged, was decidedly uneven, as is perhaps best exemplified by Isidore's definition of *compilator*, midway between the ancients and the intellectuals of John's time, as "someone who mixes the sayings of others with his own" (Hathaway 21). As for the exercising of literary license, it occurred in varying degrees and in various situations, with various consequences. For instance, Mazzotta notes that in the thirteenth century a version of poetic license was condemned by the bishop of

---

[30] Ong's commentary on plagiarism takes us beyond the scope of the present discussion, while it remains pertinent to the issue of poetic license. He writes that, overall, with the proliferation of literacy,

> resentment at plagiarism begins to develop. The ancient Latin poet Martial uses the word *plagiarius*, a torturer, plunderer, oppressor, for someone who appropriates another's writing. But there is no special Latin word with the exclusive meaning of plagiarist or plagiarism. The oral commonplace tradition was still strong. In the very early days of print, however, a royal decree or *privilegium* was often secured forbidding the reprinting of a printed book by others than the original publisher. [. . . .] Typography had made the written word into a commodity. The old communal oral world had split up into privately claimed freeholdings. The drift in human consciousness toward greater individualism had been served well by print.

(131)

[31] It must be noted in contrast, as Jay David Bolter points out in *Writing Space* (108), that "[t]he Latin word *lego* [. . .] literally means 'to gather, to collect', while one of its figurative meanings is 'to make one's way, to traverse'. By this etymology, reading is the process of gathering up signs [. . .]."

Paris, "under the rubric 'Errores in Theologia'," who strictly stated that poetic fictions are not the foundation for theology—"'quod sermones theologi fundati sunt fabulis'"—and that "in Christian dispensation there [can be no] fables and falsehoods" (*Dante's Vision* 10–11).

John of Salisbury's rather quixotic definition of poetic license amounts to a rationalization (the word is used here advisedly) of an otherwise rigidly determined hierarchy of specifically literary authority. He and others created sets of double standards, each standard held in tension by the other, which were instigated by the emergence of a more fully articulated logic and the consequent need to resolve the very dichotomies established by the dialectical discourse that logic engendered. The question of history, as posed by these dual standards—each related to the other of the set—presents a clear picture of the struggles intellectuals underwent in their various attempts to reconcile, within a wide array of circumstances, faith and empiricism. What is particularly remarkable in this regard is that the attempts at resolving dichotomies never fully succeeded, and that out of these "failures" an abundantly rich, unique culture was established.

There was to be nothing like the clarity of Erasmus' attack on St. Jerome: "Ciceronianus es, non es Christianus."[32] Erasmus felt that, because Jerome had appropriated pagan linguistic forms such as style and even syntax and lexis, the wisdom proffered by him was tainted; in fact, it could not be wisdom. Language and thought were simply not separable; to use the language of the pagan meant thinking and speaking as a pagan. In contrast, as Jeanette Beer writes (in *Medieval Translators and Their Craft* 4), the Middle Ages held the "'auctoritas' of Scripture [to be] absolute, its source obviously being beyond all reproach," while "the status of other literary works in the inherited corpus was variable and varying." Authors like Isidore of Seville and Boethius enjoyed nearly canonical status. An author such as Virgil was revered and copied, not only in an attempt to resuscitate his wisdom but to maintain a vital continuity with a tradition, so to invoke its authority. And, as has already been suggested, what the case of Virgil allows us to understand is the medieval sense of history, a sense intimately connected with a tension that arose between faith and empiricism (i.e., logic).

This tension, moreover, finds its clearest focus in the issue of medieval translation practices. As a rule, the medieval translator "abrogated" to himself "the right to act magisterially" with his *auctor*.

> Explicit intervention through commentary was one possible technique in the [medieval translation] process, but the translator's magisterial role often extended

---

[32] In K. Lloyd–Jones, "Humanist Debate and the 'Translative Dilemma' in Renaissance France," 351. See *The Collected Works of Erasmus*, Vol. 28, pp. 140–42.

far beyond such superficialities. If his responsibility was to his public, not to his source, the authority of that text *qua* text was correspondingly minimized. No period (*pace* Ezra Pound!) has been less servile to the literalities of a text, because the authority of that text was not recognized as absolute.
(Beer 4)

In part, what John of Salisbury and others were doing, in their theorization of and therefore their attempt to legitimize an individual author's poetic license, was to sanction the translator's, indeed the poet's, interpretive activity in relation to texts either poet or translator would regard as an inheritance from the past. For, considering the Christian textual tradition, especially after Augustine, the very idea of a text, as well as the actual texts that were the manifestations of that idea, were revered. Hence, it is possible to see these texts as possessing something approaching the power of a talisman, and there could have arisen the need to undo their absolute authority through various formulated theories of translation (such as Jerome's, perhaps) and poetic license (such as John's), which offered potent alternative forms or sources of authority. In great part, however, the impulse to sanction contemporaries came from the very sense of "pastness" in the texts that were to be altered.

Rather than Scripture or even the writings of the Church fathers, it was in Virgil's work that there occurred the greatest tension between what in later times could be clearly designated as historical factuality, and the myth(s) of the past that was also impressed into the service of esthetic and political concerns, in order to perpetuate the institutions of Virgil's day. Yet if in some broad sense Virgil's work was seen to be, in itself, a translation, such a definition of it, in the Middle Ages, could not help but establish its greater jurisdiction. It quite possibly could have been viewed as a conflation of the mythical and the empirical, and thus as a work of interpretation—considering the role of translation as the primary form of an interpretive act. The vexed reception of the *Aeneid*, Patterson remarks, also influenced "the nature of the central documents of the legendary historiography by which the Middle Ages imagined its origins." This conflict is central to medieval "historical consciousness *per se* [. . .]" (*Negotiating the Past* 160).

Virgil's poem, couched as it was in the language and cognitive structures of both myth and faith, prepared the way for an empirically grounded historicism.

> It was, after all, by means of the Virgilian model, transmitted through the topoi of Trojan foundation and *translatio imperii*, that the notion of a secular, purposive, linear historicity was made available to the Middle Ages. To be sure, Virgilianism was never able to achieve an unambiguous authority within medieval thought because it was subject to pressure from a variety of sources, including the Augustinian and Boethian dismissals of historicity *per se*, the tenacious dream of a prophetic *Geschichteestheologie*, and the dubious historiographical status of many of its crucial legitimizing texts (Geoffrey of Monmouth, the Arthurian romances, and the Trojan legendary). But it also contained, as an inheritance from Virgil himself, an inherent instability that rendered its project uncertain. Put simply, the tension that at once animates and inhibits the *Aeneid* is a struggle between, on the

> one hand, a linear purposiveness that sees the past as a moment of failure to be redeemed by a magnificent future and, on the other, a commemorative idealism that sees it as instead a heroic origin to be emulated, a period of gigantic achievement that a belated future can never hope to replicate.
> (160)

The potency of the past, pagan though it was, ultimately could not be denied; all the same, it was "endowed with a double, contradictory value." Particularly in the formative role it played in the medieval elaboration of a heroic vision, the past was "reinvoked and reenacted." Most notably in *Erec et Enide*, it emerges as the "site of both emulation and exorcism, of slavish imitation coupled with decisive rejection" (Patterson 160).

Not unrelated to this new historiography, furthermore, is the fact that societal structures throughout the vast stretch of time between Virgil and Chrétien had come to be based on discourses that were primarily oral. As we have seen, all social and political—indeed, often enough, religious—functions of European society, during this hiatus between literate antiquity and the literate Middle Ages, were fundamentally influenced by orality. The subsequent rebalancing of the oral and the literal in the later Middle Ages contributed to "the recuperation of historicity itself, a *prise de conscience* that, for all its qualifications, stands as a decisive moment in the development of the West" (157).[33] The *Chanson de Roland* presents a fine example of a balance between orality and literacy. Temporally, philosophically and esthetically, it is a pivotal poem in the literary history of this period. Its first half is indebted to the idiom of oral epic, while the second half is deeply affected by a new societal emphasis on writing and reading. The "tragedy" of *Roland*, Vance writes,

> is inseparable from the disclosure that not only words, but even things and events to which words refer, are equivocal. The *Roland* inaugurated in the most hallowed legends of vernacular culture a new but troubled consciousness of the radical difference between the knower and the known, between unquestioning memory and exercised judgment, between the claims of blind loyalty and of assumed responsibility, and between past or present actions and their future historical consequences. The *Roland* made its culture glimpse a terrifying centrifugality, not only in the institutions of political power, but also in the very discourse by whose conventional formulas that power had been celebrated. The tragedy was all the more brutal because of the poem's failure to invent and utter new, compensatory values upon which to base the hero's quest for unequivocal honor in this world—and for salvation in the next.
> (*From Topic to Tale* xxi)

There is a cause and effect relationship between the emergence of literacy as the dominant mode of the contemporary society's discourse and the transformation of that society's institutions of political power—a power, I might add, that began to

---

[33] Patterson is paraphrasing Chenù, "Theology and the New Awareness of History," 162.

see itself in new historical terms:

> If the *Roland* does indeed testify to a crisis in the discourse of power, surely this crisis stemmed in part from the impact of writing as it brought new constraints to vernacular language which disrupted the economy and latent *epistémè* of traditional discourse. Indeed, a shift from epic *mouvance* toward a culture of *grammatica* and monumentality is already indicated in the body of the *Roland* itself, for Charlemagne plans to perpetuate the memories of Roland and the twelve peers not by the invention of songs (*cantilènes*), but by the construction of white marble tombs that will presumably bear written inscriptions. To suggest that literacy was crucial to the disruption of the semantic processes of Old French epic is also to point to a broader relationship between writing and political power that was transforming the modalities of twelfth-century culture as a whole.
> (xxi–xxii)

Various mythical, quasi-historical and historically grounded discourses proliferated within the initiating framework of a more fundamental contest between orally and literally based societal mores. One possible esthetic response to this struggle was the construction of historiographically framed narrative that, in proclaiming its origin in the great past, could be seen as legitimate, and as sanctioning the institutions of power, as Patterson comments:

> *Verum quia vetus* is a medieval proverb that expresses a ubiquitous theology of origins in force across the whole range of medieval culture, and nowhere more visibly than in the political world. The disruptions of medieval political history were typically healed with the soothing continuities of a founding legend, and insecure rulers bolstered their regimes by invoking honorific if legendary precedents.
> (199)

Furthermore, the political exigencies affected literary production that "continued throughout its medieval life to concern itself with essentially historiographical issues, issues such as the relation of individual action to historical process, or the use and abuse of historical precedent itself" (199).

The emergence of the secularized individual, who stood apart from the community, was necessary to the development of secular governmental and other political institutions that could rival Feudal and Church authority. As individuality came into its own, writers of the period were capable of using the past "to delineate an instructive chronology of secular empire, more commonly to apprehend the plan of providential dispensation [. . .]" (199). Thus linear and empirically grounded history slowly takes its shape as the result of a new consciousness of the past, a historical tension whose two vectors were the lurch forward toward an "authentic apprehension of temporality and periodization" and the retreat, "under the pressure of various ideologies toward reification and idolization" (198). As especially to be found in the Romance epics, the literature contained a self-reflexivity, a lack of concern for the factual past; these were, therefore, fictions inasmuch as they contained a "[meditation] both upon the paradox of their own production—as historical fabrications designed to legitimize political power—and upon the problematic enterprise of reconstituting, *from within history*, a prehistorical origin" (199; my emphasis).

Romance was the result, then, of technological invention that produced widespread literacy and the concomitant renewed interest in Aristotle and in the pagans overall. Romance contended with Scripture for the twelfth-century reading audience; as such this literature was a function of the new world of the *literatus*, who, within textual communities, functioned as the *interpres*—that member of a community who could explicate its central texts (Stock "History, Literature" 12).[34] Literacy meant, in fact, the social reorganization around this interpreter. The new structure indicated the depth of transformation from the older orality. The orally based community could not afford an individuality that ran counter to the group need to sustain an ethical memory and hence a social cohesion. The shift to an emphasis on literacy entailed a restructuring that meant the creation of a new hierarchy, according to Godzich:

> The most curious, and ultimately the weakest, feature of the economy of *memoria* is the strange coexistence of the acknowledgment of a discursive multiplicity and even heterogeneity with the belief in their ultimate, and unverifiable, coherence. One could readily view this admixture of experiential fact and belief as an ideological strategy for the suspension of societal antagonisms in view of real differences between groups and individuals. These antagonisms can be held in check as long as no one identifies with a given subject position, that is as long as there prevails a realm of persons in which no one seeks to erase the difference between a subject position and the material purport that assumes it. For as soon as this difference, and the arbitrariness that presides over its assignment, are effaced, roles are taken to be entitlements and specific discourses are felt to be somehow natural to those who wield them, and they may not easily shed them in order to assume others. Furthermore, the entire universe of discourses is no longer conceivable as a general flux whose sense resides in its specific, yet unfathomable, economy, but must be hierarchized, that is, must be brought under the control of a discourse that can account for the operations, and especially the localization, of other discourses.
> (xvi–xvii)

The ruling discourse in the new, literate society, will be that of logic. Logic will, in turn, impart its peculiar form of order to an emerging historiography that seeks a ground in empiricism and thus rivals the older literature of *geste* and *memoria* in its privileging of the particular and the individual. The evolving logic, in other words, which offered a new framework for literature—even as that literature was driven by the cognitive demands that grammar continued to put upon it for quite some time—ultimately came to define modern consciousness.

---

[34] See also *Implications of Literacy*, 105 and 167.

Romance is an important signal of a dawning modern historical consciousness; in this regard, the most salient feature of this literary form is an historiographical self-reflexivity that resides within its narrative mode. Yet historicity is not the most profound materialization of a self-meditation. We have touched upon the practice, in secularized literary texts, of authorial self-acknowledgment and self-interpretation as a part of discussions about interpretation of the very text in which the discussion appeared; this literary criticism could focus on other texts as well. Langland's satire includes grammar as its subject; this very subject, the choice of it as subject, suggests the mechanism of his poem's self-meditation. Grammar still exercised a broad authority in Langland's time. Indeed *Piers Plowman*—perhaps more than any other single work of literature in the Middle Ages—exhibits the late medieval struggle between grammar and logic, with the Western mind as the prize. The poem is built out of a desire to resolve what was often an antithesis propounded by the two's respective epistemological ground rules; as such it reflected the post Ockham philosophical debate (which will be examined, especially in Chapter Four).

Traditionally, grammar included "not merely the knowledge of the Latin language but also the techniques of the gloss, the concordance, and the allegorical method"—all of which comprised "the necessary introduction to the science of Holy Scripture" (Colish *Mirror of Language* 65). In the sense that we may speak of a *text* as a woven pattern, one that by extension connotes the process by which discourse itself is generated (connoting, quite possibly, even the linguistic "space" in which discourse takes place), word and concept can thus be understood as linked to an *auctor*. If language can be said to be the matrix out of which ideas emerge, it follows that words sharing similar or common etymologies may in turn be the result of efforts to articulate a common experience or perception, a common idea. And therefore, just as discourse can be understood in various, similar aspects such as rhetoric or dialectic, interpretation can be considered to play an integral role in any ongoing discourse or dialogue.

By nature, any text will contain a measure of ambiguity, yet the duplicity of any posited, intended, meaning of a text is also a function of reading that in itself can perhaps be viewed as a paradoxical attempt to clarify what is held to have been ambiguous. As we have seen, reading lies at the heart of the decision in the *Roland* to construct monuments to the dead heroes who will be understood by individuals in various, albeit related, ways. Yet reading can be a process in which the reader assigns meaning to a text based on his or her desires. A reader may presuppose an author's or text's intention and genre. In the Middle Ages reading is, of course, first and foremost, a process understood in terms of Augustine's overall epistemology that foregrounds the interpretive act, as described, for example, in *De Doctrina Christiana* (I.36). Patterson points out that for Augustine the "Christian reader comes to the text (Scripture) already possessed of its message (the double law of charity), and his task is to understand not its meaning but its way of signifying that meaning." Of course, the Augustinian hermeneutic serves a decidedly utilitarian end: "to inoculate the reader against the sweetness of the letter by endowing him with the strength of moral interpretation—with, in effect, the spirit." However, *to read* in this manner is to raise the issue of textualization as a possible purpose unto itself, and a possibly dangerous undertaking—if the contemplation of textualization, or if the indulgence in the pleasure of reading for its own sake (to echo Roland Barthes), were to lead away from the doctrine of charity. Augustine found this to be a vastly rich problem. Even before him, reading necessarily included what might be called a reader's selective attitude, which established a connection between author's and reader's intentions. And with Augustine—especially in the worth he finds in figurative language—reading could begin to enjoy a greater vigor and variety of activity. By the time of the later Middle Ages, reading is allowed its greatest breadth. The intellectual revolution, beginning in the tenth century, led to a more abstractive comprehension of language, texts, reality, and their interrelationships, and indirectly, as Stock says, "to the polarization of attitudes towards textual methodologies in such writers as Abelard and Bernard" (*Implications of Literacy* 528).

By the later Middle Ages, reading represented a self-meditation that was being promoted by literary texts; as an act of interpretation, ultimately of itself as its own text, the ways in which reading was understood and practiced contributed to the newly developing historical impulse. It can be argued, furthermore, that this impulse evolved out of a textual consciousness of the time, a fascination with and a deep awareness of textuality per se. Textuality was rooted in the beginnings of Western culture and particularly in Augustine, but it took new forms in the later Middle Ages; as it became more and more distinct from a reality thought to lie beyond it, it profoundly altered the growing complex vision of text in relation to experience, as is evident in a new emphasis on reading that had far reaching implications.

> Everywhere, the presence of texts forced the elements of culture embedded in oral discourse to redefine their boundaries with respect to a different type of human exchange. This invariably resulted in contrasts between the "popular" and the "learned" which were themselves the by-products of literate sensibilities. Other opposites also became polarized: custom versus law, things versus linguistic ideas, synchrony versus diachrony, and sense versus interpreted experience.
> (Stock 529)

In his discussion of the Fourth Lateran Council of 1215, which mandated individual confession at least once a year, Le Goff observes that such a proclamation would mean the employment of a language and context unique to confessers who were acting as individuals in their acts of confession and who engaged other individuals, those who heard these confessions. In fact, individual confession was but one of many ancillary effects of the contemporary society's heightened sensitivity to texts of all kinds both spoken and written. Individual confession was a manifestation of a changing intellectual climate, one based on "introspective self-examination [within] a whole culture of the memory that developed in the thirteenth century."

In fact, priests were taught by manuals created for confessors, which specified how memory could be developed and shaped by inculcating a "spiritual and moral conscience, which was associated with a new idea of sin linked to the intentions of the sinner as well as with the new practice of auricular confession, based on introspective self-examination" (80). At first seemingly unrelated to these developments is the innovative use made of exempla, which represented a vital principle in the emerging, ever more codified *ars praedicandi*. A new species of literary exemplum, now to be used especially but not exclusively in preaching, owed its existence to the Greeks and Romans who saw it as an apt vehicle for "historical anecdote[s] employed in the rhetoric of persuasion" (78). Now this classical exemplum had been transformed so that the encouragement of individual introspection was coupled with an implied emphasis on textuality in the acutely literary nature of the new sermonizing. In its new incarnation in sermons, moreover, the exemplum served as an effective link between oral and written cultures. Thus it is a telling symbol of the radical shift from the one to the other, which brought together the palpability of written and transcendent truth.

In and of itself the exemplum also did much both to expand the possibilities of, and to atomize, conceptualized time. Implicit within the exemplum was the conception of time; Le Goff infers this

> from a study of sermons, in which three kinds of proof were used in argument: *auctoritates*, *rationes*, and *exempla*. The diachronic, narrative time of the exemplum, in a sense that of secular history, was combined with the retrospective and eschatological time of the auctoritates and with the atemporality of the rationes. Exemplum time must therefore be understood within the context of the sermon in which the exemplum occurs. The auctoritates, for the most part biblical citations, exhibit the temporal multiplicity of the Bible itself: the words are old but remain valid in the present and for the future, until the end of time and for eternal salvation. The homiletic commentary of the authorities is in the present, the timeless present of eternal truths. The rationes, on the other hand, are in the didactic present. Between the eschatological time of the Bible, brought up to date and oriented by commentary, and the eternal time of rational truths, the exemplum insinuated a segment of narrative time—historical, linear, and divisible. (78–79)

All tenses, all forms of time including linear time, and *auctoritas*, are conjoined under the aegis of Augustine's view of understanding as recollection. Yet in the new use made of exempla, ironically, Augustine's conception of time, which was a function of memory, yields to narrative's diachrony and hence to the time of historiography whose very principles of composition embrace rationalism and empiricism, and therefore undermine the Augustinian project of reading; for, as has been noted, Augustine held that, read "correctly," a text must yield its moral, its divine truth, no matter what its surface texture, its *littera* signified.

Later medieval "textual communities," Stock writes, were groups whose attitudes and behavior became determined by an "agreed meaning of gospel passages" or other revered texts, an agreement that in effect, in and of itself, became "the text, as opposed to the translation, transcription, or verbalization" of the prior text. Such communities founded their own, as it were informed, "meaningful pattern[s] involving an already established inner code through which outer behavior [could] be interpreted." Thus these communities duplicated the Augustinian exegetical procedure of divining the inner meanings of scripture, and they also duplicated the later allegorical tradition of correspondence through separate signification. Nevertheless, at the very moment that the members of a newly forming textual society were partaking of an "original textual experience" through their essentially Augustinian epistemology of reading, their "discourse acquired its historical dimension: for men and women not only presumed to understand" the actions of the *interpres*, who provided a conceptualized link between textuality and rationality, "but without consciously thinking about it [they] modeled their own behavior on his" ("History, Literature" 12, 15, 16). There is an attendant human individuality that emerges out of such communities, which requires the living out of a dual role. The individual is an "audience (a silent reader)" but also an "individual *auctor*; for in the older culture, intellectually dominated by Augustine, oral literature exists to keep alive the *memoria* of its people" (Godzich xv–xvi). Textuality, however, meant that

> the use and reuse of such familiar polarities as time and eternity, image and reality, and *figura* and *veritas*, whatever their particular sources, were justified by the belief that within the ontology of the written word lay an intimate reflection of reality [. . .].
> (Stock *Implications of Literacy* 530).

This reality could be revealed through "the study of grammar, syntax, and hermeneutics" (530). The literate, rational procedures of the *interpres*, then, whose interpretive strategies could be brought to bear upon newer literary forms such as sermons and especially the exempla they contained, adapted the singular temporality of the Augustinian cosmos, in which the eternal finally subsumed all other time frames, to the temporal span of the individual mortal's life and, as well, to the larger frame of narrative that too easily lent itself to historical time; in turn, historical time gradually undermined the intellectual notion of the eternal.

This transformation of conceptualized time is vividly demonstrated in the dynamic of two pivotal and, as I have suggested, related terms: *textus* and *auctoritas*. Etymologically, the two are primally associated. The oldest Indo-European root of *auctoritas* indicates *force, increase, supply, augmentation*, and so on; the Latin *augere*, besides these meanings, expresses the idea of *fertilization, the causing to thrive, strengthening, making more numerous*, and *making richer*.[35] We might also remind ourselves that the idea of *glossing* a text, which was of course a central tenet of the exegetical tradition, as Robert Hanning observes (in "I Shal Finde It in the Maner Glose" 28), has its roots in the Greek word for *tongue*.

---

[35] See J. Gonda, *Ancient Indian ojas, Latin *augos and the Indo-European nouns in -es-/-os*, 744–45.

Just as in a later evolutionary stage of the verb the classical Latin *texo* could mean *to connect* or *to link*—which might share to a degree the earlier Greek concept of rhetoric as a process of *weaving*, as defined in Plato's *Gorgias* (cf. above)—the medieval term *auctor* strikingly reveals an intimate association with the whole idea of discourse. It is no great surprise that, in the "literary context" of the later Middle Ages,

> the term *auctor* denoted someone who was at once a writer and an authority, someone not merely to be read but also to be respected and believed. According to medieval grammarians, the term derived its meaning from four main sources: *auctor* was supposed to be related to the Latin verbs *agere* "to act or perform," *augere* "to grow" and *auieo* "to tie," and to the Greek noun *autentim* "authority." An *auctor* "performed" the act of writing. He brought something into being, caused it to "grow." In the more specialised sense related to *auieo*, poets like Virgil and Lucan were *auctores* in that they had "tied" together their verses with feet and metres. To the ideas of achievement and growth was easily assimilated the idea of authenticity or "authoritativeness."
> (Minnis 10)

In the *Convivio* (IV.4) Dante elaborates on the verb "to link," spelled there as *auieo*, noting that the word is made up of the five vowels:

> And anyone who considers [the word] in its first voice will plainly see that it demonstrates itself, that it is made entirely of the links of words, that is of the five vowels alone which are the soul and connecting links of every word; and it is composed of them in a way that may be varied to represent the image of a link ("che solo di legame di parole è fatto, cioè di sole cinque vocali, che sono anima e legame d'ogni parole, e composto d'esse per modo volubile, a figurare imagine de legame"). Because beginning with A we then turn back into U and come directly by I into E, whence we turn again to the O; so that this figure of a link really represents the vowels aeiou. And how far "author" comes from this verb we learn only from the poets, who have linked their words together with musical art.[36]

To tie verses together with meters is perhaps in small to tie ideas together—as in *rhetoric*, *to weave* them, indeed to weave them into a tapestry (i.e., into a text or *textus*, into a textile or *textilis*). Kendrick notes that "the technical terms for composition" employed by the troubadours included "*tresar* ('to braid'), *entrebescar* ('to weave'), *lasar* ('to lace'). Whereas, in the textile arts, patterns of colored threads are woven together to evoke visual figures, the troubadours wove together patterns of letters representing patterns of sounds evocative of abstract senses" (205 n. 21). This overall system of interconnected significations forms the context in which we can rightly place a song like Guillem IX's "Ben vuelh que sapchon li pluzor" whose first stanza ends with the textual voice proclaiming that, once the verse will be finished or "laced up" ("lassatz"), it will be named "auctor":

---

[36] Trans. Katharine Hillard, in Mazzotta, *Dante, Poet of the Desert*, 258-59.

> Ben vuelh que sapchon li pluzor
> d'est vers si's de bona color,
> qu'ieu port d'ayselh mestier la flor,
> et es vertaz,
> e puesc en traire·l vers auctor
> quant er lassatz.
>
> I want everyone to tell
> whether there's good to this *vers* [literally: its colors]
> that I have brought out of my workshop:
> because I'm the one that gets the flower in this craft,
> and that is the truth,
> and I will call this *vers* to witness [literally: authority][37]
> when it is all laced up.[38]

Here the voice, singing from within its own song, considers the song as from a distance and by extension, therefore, considers itself. In other words, the poet's text, a linguistic fabric, is doubly woven through the use of a voice that refers to its own textual origin—even as the singing of the song, the unfolding of the text, is still in progress. But, in a more extended sense, either or both the *auctor* and *interpres* of a textual community, who speaks out or perhaps, intentionally or otherwise, "glosses" his or her *auctor*'s previously established text, "ties" together the members of the textual community. Again in Guillem IX, we should note, appropriately, the appeal of the textual voice to a community who will hear and judge the worth of the song and of the song's maker as well. In fact the act of tying is that of forming the group into a cohesive whole. In the song, the tying of the *vers* leads to the cohesion of the group. Furthermore, a secular author such as Guillem, like his or her religious counterpart, could act as the *interpres* of such a community or could even provide the text for interpretation. This notion is perhaps echoed in the following lines of the song:

> Ieu conosc ben sen e folhor,
> e conosc anta et honor,
> et ai ardimen e paor [. . .].
>
> I know what wisdom is, and foolishness,
> and I know what honor is, and shame,
> I can tell bravery and fear [. . . .].

In this and other ways the secular author played a role, in other words, in the institutionalization of literacy.

---

[37] Cf. Stephen G. Nichols, "Voice and Writing in Augustine and in the Troubadour Lyric," 154.
[38] The translation of this passage and all further translations of Provençal verse, unless otherwise specified, come from Goldin's anthology, *Lyrics of the Troubadours and Trouvères*.

Unquestionably, the role of the author and interpreter in the textual community of the later Middle Ages is a consequence of the new societal balance between oral and written discourse; yet the basis for this change in the medieval societal infrastructure can also be traced, and is perhaps most dramatically revealed, in various attacks on medieval language theory by contemporaneous logicians. New cognitive procedures, which comprised the intellectual matrix for the new roles of author and reader (or alternately author and interpreter) also arose, if indirectly, out of a renewed and intensified resultant bifurcation of the Word, which was accomplished by logicalist investigations of both grammar and the constituent that made up that grammar—the individual word.

What was the nature of that word? How might it have represented reality? The word is first of all seen to be *both* oral and written. It can also be viewed as being a reality in and of itself; or, as in the philosophy of someone like William of Ockham, it can be viewed as being merely a signifier. It can enjoy, as well, an intermediary status, as in Aquinas' thinking; Aquinas implies this status in his formulation of the concept of *essence* as well as in his distinction between the Aristotelian terms of intellection, *species impressa* and *species expressa*.[39] Questions surrounding the possibility of *universals*, and the specific issue of realism versus nominalism—which were basic to the theories of Anselm and Abelard—could find a focus in the ever more acute perception on the part of later theologian-philosophers that the *word* was a written, physical form on the page.

Under the influence of Boethianized Aristotelian logic, Anselm, for example, had to employ an "increasingly rationalized" grammar in order to continue to sustain the inherited Augustinian, what Colish calls the "ineluctably verbal," conception of knowledge. This "quasi-logical grammar," in fact,

> is Anselm's basic theological tool; its peculiar, and, as events were to prove, highly transitory methods and presuppositions dictate the operative conditions of his thought as a whole. Like Augustine [. . .] Anselm's major epistemological concern is the theological problem of speaking about God. But, where Augustine sees the task of theology as the eloquent expression of the Word, Anselm sees it as the conscientious and faithful definition of the Word.
> (*Mirror of Language* 58-59)

Thus in Anselm's view the Word has been set at a distance from the one who partakes of it, first of all by the very attempt at formulating its definition. In effect, the Word has been objectified, which is precisely what happens when words are set as spatial figures on a page and hence can be taken in, that is, can be read, can be processed by a reader rather than by a listener, over an extended period of time.

---

[39] For the concept of *essence*, see *De Ente et Essentia* II; and cf. above. For the concepts of *species impressa* and *species expressa*, see *Quaestiones Disputatae de Malo* 16, 8, *ad* 3; *In Librum Boethii de Trinitate*, 6, 2, *ad* 5; *Summa Theologiae* Ia, 16, 2; and cf. Copleston, *Aquinas*, 90-91, 177-78.

Such words, furthermore, usually have lost their proximity to their *auctor*—as Chaucer reminds us in his famous adieu, "goe litel boke." Not only has an integral connection between speaker and audience been severed, but so too have the speaker's—now the writer's—words been set apart from the knower, as independent of their author and as ontologically grounded in the conception of their own essential aspects qua words. This objectivity inevitably raises questions of definition, since the word may be contemplated at a leisure afforded by both the new temporal and spatial distances, and therefore it enlists the services of a burgeoning new discourse of logic. In querying the nature of the Word, Anselm had to seek a term with which to signify the divine adequately; yet he was only one of a series of theologian–philosophers, epistemologists—Augustine among them— who needed to describe reality, thought and language and the connections among them, less in terms of the *spoken* word and more often in the terms allowed by ever more abstractive procedures.

Anselm's view was only a step away from that of the ancient Stoics, a view he derived, however, through his reading of Augustine's *De Dialectica* and *De Doctrina Christiana*, where Augustine further elaborates and, in fully appropriating it, makes the Stoic theory of verbal signification uniquely his own as a theory that is now distinct and Christian. "Since the *Cratylus*," Colish observes,

> thinkers had used the terms "natural" and "conventional" to mean the ways in which words acquire their denotations. However, Augustine applies these terms to signs in the light of their intentional or unintentional character. His natural signs are unintentional. A fire signifies its presence unintentionally through the smoke it produces; a man signifies his feelings unintentionally through his facial expression. These signs do indeed signify physical and psychological realities, but they do so involuntarily. Augustine's conventional signs also correspond truly with the things they signify. But they are signs used deliberately by animate or intelligent beings to express their ideas, intentions, and feelings to other beings.
> ("Stoic Theory" 26–29)[40]

Augustine presents a middle stage, to be sure, between the notion of a universe of signs that are of equal stature, whether verbal or otherwise, and later medieval philosophers' positions specifically in relation to verbal signs, positions adopted under the influence of the growing spread of literacy when the word acts not only as a verbal sign per se but more often than not as a written representation of that verbal sign, and in fact a representation that is gradually gathering unto itself its own ontological authority. Augustine's "natural" sign, on the other hand, can be non-verbal. Even so, Augustine's distinctive interest is in the verbal, particularly in *De Doctrina Christiana* where he concerns himself with exegesis and preaching; words in these contexts are understood as being conventional and verbal (Colish 29).

The doctrine of intentionality, and the use made by the sign in this context, is an expansion of the Stoic theory of *lekta*. The Stoics believed in language as being

---

[40] See *De Doctrina Christiana* II.3.

inherently ambiguous. Chrysippus, for one, cited language's capacity to signify intentionality, even if an intended meaning was not identical with the language's objective referent. The Stoics viewed "intellectual intentions," Colish explains, as

> one member of a quartet of entities called incorporeals, along with space, time, and the void. The incorporeals are immaterial; thus, for the Stoics, they are not fully real. They do not exist but merely subsist. Time, space and the void have their assigned roles to play in physics. For their part, *lekta* are the foundation of logic. *Lekta* are the "stuff," if you will, out of which logical propositions are made. Logical propositions include predications, arguments, syllogisms, and fallacies. Such formulae have meaning; but, since they are not corporeal, they do not have full being. Unlike words, *lekta* and their logical by-products are not natural signs of natural objects. The relations between logical statements are governed by their own laws, which can and should be studied as a distinct and formal branch of philosophy. But logical statements and their relations, since they are composed of *lekta*, do not mirror the real, corporeal world. *Lekta* and logic have a purely intramental existence and validity. (23-24)[41]

On this basis, logic is elevated to the status of "an independent discipline," self-justifying according to "its own internal rules and criteria." Simultaneously, the Stoics would have avidly subscribed to "the later scholastic dictum, *a nosse ad esse non valet consequentia*" (24). In the first century a.d., Aulus Gellius writes *Attic Nights* in which he associates, after the Stoics, the question of intentionality with that of words existing as natural signs, and, furthermore, describes in one part of his work (XI.12.1) how one's inner intentions do not need to enjoy a connection to reality. *Attic Nights* was popular in the fourth century. It is Augustine who adopts Gellius' ideas and situates them within a broader context (Colish 24).

More than a millennium separates the Stoics and the grammarians of Anselm's time. Yet much of what is believed later has its roots in ancient and hellenistic Greece. We need only recall what was, oftentimes, a blind obedience to a language paradigm, in the attempt to describe reality, such as the tenth-century controversy surrounding the Eucharist initiated by Berengarius (cf. above), which, along with the writings of Abbo of Fleury, lays a foundation for the speculative grammar movement. In this historical light, moreover, we might better understand the nominalism of someone like Ockham as being a reaction to a deeply entrenched realism. And, in this context, we can locate the earlier Anselm's tireless search for the transcendental signifier that might represent the divine. All of these intellectual movements (whose tensions are elaborated in contemporary imaginative literature as early as the songs of Guillem IX and Marcabru, and as late as Langland's *Piers Plowman*) owe much to the Greeks and particularly to the Stoics' conception of language as being, first and foremost, naturally engendered. According to Stoic reasoning, words—"as natural signs," as "sounds" and hence as "material" and

---

[41] Cf. *Stoicorum Veterum Fragmenta* II.93-95, 132, 166, 170, 181, 183, 331, 335, 488, 501-2, 511, 514.

"corporeal"—enjoyed an "automatic correlation with the material and corporeal realities" for which they stood, which was in keeping with the Stoic belief in the substantiality of "all real beings." The Stoic sense of a body included "agents, such as God and the human soul." The criterion that defined language was "the articulate human voice" rather than the "inarticulate sounds made by animals."[42] And both spoken and written human speech could but only include the perception that the "human *logos* [was] consubstantial with God, the *logos* of nature." In other words,

> Stoic physics sees the world in monistic terms; God is identified with the natural world and with the human mind. Words, thus, are intrinsically real, in a physical sense. Speech is a natural phenomenon. Both the denotations of words, their etymological derivations, and the grammatical structure of language are hence natural.
> (Colish "Stoic Theory" 19–20)[43]

To put it another way, the Stoics laid the foundation for the undermining of the natural signification of language in their unavoidable positing of a relationship between language and logic (i.e., *lekta*). In this they look ahead to the gradual dismantling of Augustinian language theory in the later Middle Ages. Augustine invokes "the doctrine of *lekta* or intentionality in relation to logic" in *De Doctrina Christiana* (II.35) when he explains the use an exegete should make of the classical liberal arts. In examining the discipline of dialectic, he is upholding the Stoic assertion that logicalistic predications are *lekta* behaving within the domain of their own rules and without necessary correspondence to realities outside the mind. Here he is speaking about an "internal cogency or logical possibility" of a proposition, even when it is based on a false premise or otherwise a physical impossibility (Colish 29). For example, he details "two kinds of falsehood, one of which involves things that are not possible, and the other of which involves things that are possible but nevertheless do not exist" (II.35).[44] Yet, as Colish remarks, "[o]ne still ought to 'spoil the Egyptians' and study dialectic, he counsels, for it sharpens the mind and it can be applied just as easily to true propositions as to false ones" (29–30). Augustine departs from the Stoic line of thinking in his distinction between internally cogent logical statements and real being (II.37). But he sees rhetoric (IV.2)—"a neutral art, even though it may provide arguments for falsehood as well as truth and even though it may be a vehicle for lying"—as a device for finely tuning one's critical abilities "to detect and to reject these inappropriate uses of speech as one learns to apply the art of eloquence to the service of truth" (Colish 29–30).

---

[42] *Stoicorum Veterum Fragmenta* I.74, II.140–41.

[43] Cf. *Stoicorum Veterum Fragmenta* I.85, 87, 102, 153–54, 159–62, 493, 495; II.299–328, 526.

[44] "Possumus etiam dividere, dicentes, duo esse genera falsi: unum eorum quae omnino esse non possunt; alterum eorum quae non sunt, quamvis esse possint." This and all further translations of *De Doctrina Christiana* are by D. W. Robertson.

What we are seeing in Augustine's thinking is the gradual disintegration of the unified world comprised of language and reality that is essentially posited by him. The word may be the "verbum mentis," but read properly, and in the light of divine grace, it will lead its reader (its auditor, or seer) to the truth. Yet in proposing the question of lying (as opposed to falsehoods) as being contingent on intentionality—a contingency Augustine finds in the relationship of a logistic *lekta*, and the actuality of speech and language as understood first by the Stoics—he makes possible a further division between language and reality, beyond what is implied in his formulation of a "verbum mentis" in which language cannot lead the user directly to the truth. In reestablishing an ontology of language, predicated on its proper internal rules and therefore self-governance, he also anticipates the further analysis of language by later medieval logicians who are—whether they are fully conscious of the implications of their work—busy at wresting themselves from the sure grip of grammar. However, in doing so they face a new tyranny, that of logic.

The thinking of Abelard, the preeminent logician of his time, presents us with a crossroads in the history of semantics. In him, we also perceive the later Middle Ages' positioning as regards the authority of antiquity in relation to the development of logic as it transformed the ways of looking at language per se. Logic's growing claim to be able to systematize reality implicitly presented its bid for coequal status with traditional metaphysics. Reality was linguistically grounded, moreover, insofar as the logic of the time was thought to be a science of language, called *sermocinalism* after Abelard's distinction between a mere utterance (*vox*) and a word (*sermo*). Around this distinction, Abelard organized his theory of universals; as words—utterances and even inscriptions—are themselves things, so too, in the strict sense of being the combination of *vox* plus *significatio*, as Kretzman writes, words are "products of human arrangements rather than being the products of natural effects" (369).

Reality, in other words, was seen to be more socio-centered than it had been in the past, more contingent upon ethical language. This emphasis on usage found its theoretical focus in speculations about the properties of terms and, significantly, in the syncategorematic aspect of language. In itself the syncategorematic classification, and the larger question it addressed regarding predication, signaled a departure from "Aristotelian-Boethian tradition in that it was precise where the tradition had been vague." The idea of predication, without a doubt, was an "essential part of the subject matter of logic"; Aristotle and Boethius, however, had dealt with it in a manner frequently suggesting "that predicates might be extralinguistic and even extramental entities." Here the way was being paved for the elevation of logic to the status of a science. "This crucial vagueness," on the part of Aristotle and Boethius, became to a degree "the source of the medievals' concern with universals," which "left open the possibility that logic might be essentially a science of reality, resembling or subsumed under metaphysics." One of Abelard's contributions to this "science" was to replace the overly simple concept of utterance, which had held sway since Boethius and after him in the *Dialectica* of Garland the Computist of the late eleventh century, who held that predication can occur only in an utterance and therefore only utterances are predicable; that is, predication obtained to utterances that were the elements of logic. Even so, "recognizing that utterances are physical events which are, as such, of no interest to logicians," Abelard substituted the *sermo* (i.e., signification and utterance both) for the utterance simple (Kretzman 370). Thus logic became a product of mental utterance (*sermo*) and was divorced from the spoken word. To put this another way, Abelard found it necessary to include in the notion of utterance its significative aspect. All the same, he refused to admit that mental entities were elemental within a system of logic; he argued that propositions which were true as terms "could not be verified by an appeal to the status of mental entities." He emphasized the connection between a term and the definition of that term, for the term itself, categorically, had to be included in "the string of terms making up the definition of the term [. . .]." Abelard's sermocinalism was "directed not only against the notion of logic as a science of reality (*scientia realis*) but evidently also against the notion of it as the science of reason (*scientia rationalis*)" (Kretzman 371).

It is this distinction that provided Avicenna and others who followed after him, such as Albert the Great, with a locus of attack within which a philosophy of logic could be truly erected—a philosophy, however, furthered in the later Middle Ages more by thinkers who involved themselves with metaphysics than with logic. In Avicenna's *Philosophia Prima*, logic is the science of reason, for "the relation of this doctrine [logic] to internal thought, which is called internal speech, is just like the relation of grammar to outward signification, which is called speech."[45] Hence it was not logic but grammar that underwrote the sermocinal science; this notion leads directly to the speculative grammar movement (Kretzman 371).

Taken together, the contributions of Abelard and Avicenna to the development of Western philosophy tell us of the tenacity with which grammar as an epistemological system continued to be influential, receded in popularity, and then prevailed again, in the subsequent "philosophy" of speculative grammar put forth by the *modistae* as a way of explaining experience. How did this occur? In the attempts of these two philosophers to create a science of language we witness, particularly in their respective definitions of language, the splitting off of abstractive mental processes from the spoken utterance and as well from the semantic and syntactic linguistic functions. What becomes evident in the writings of both thinkers is the growing importance of mental abstraction as difference, which in turn is grounded in a dialectical split caused by the elevation of reason to a new, more privileged position.

Later medieval poets are also engaged in a two-fold struggle, first of all to envision a world beyond that which was, to put it broadly, sanctioned by Augustine, and second, to develop a linguistic stance toward reality, one that

---

[45] In Kretzman, 371.

transcended the contradictory nature of their inherited grammatical and logical paradigms. Central in this struggle was an ontological assertion on the part of these poets, one which revealed itself as two, contradictory forms. On the one hand, they staked their claim as poets who were unique and preeminent within a literary tradition. On the other hand, they virtually defined themselves within the context of that tradition and the all embracing structure of which the literature was a part—that of Christian, and secondarily literary, *auctoritas*. The classical forebears could variously fall within one or the other category—either under the Scriptural-Augustinian dispensation that, in a sense, revised the pagan texts, "rewriting" them in Christian terms, or else within the category of literature that, in any case, remained subsumed within a larger theologico-philosophical world. Pilgrimage literature (the *Commedia*, the *Canterbury Tales*, *Piers Plowman*), as Julia Bolton Holloway has shown (in *The Pilgrim and the Book* 209), exhibited "the mirroring of God's writing in man's writing [as] the essence of pilgrimage *imitatio Christi*" through "two authorial, intertextual paradigms [. . .] the first of Luke at Emmaus, the second, God himself, the subject of Luke's Gospel [. . .]." Through topoi of modesty and/or ineffability, conversely, poets like Dante, Chaucer and Langland propose a linguistic system that is totally divorced from the reality it purports to describe; in doing so, they create a gulf between themselves and the past of Scripture and antiquity, which essentially posited a unified world. These poets' linguistic systems, outgrowths of the new textuality and logic, called attention to themselves as being the only reality they could in fact ultimately describe. This philosophy of language, never clearly articulated except through the opacity of poetry, provided the subtext of self-naming that these poets adopt as a way of thinking about language per se, a language that had its own being apart from the world and which, through contemplation of its self-referentiality, makes possible the self-realization and self-actualization of the poet who has named himself. For this autocitation exists in order to speak of the world of names, a world that is separate from experience yet a world that, for the poet, is the only possible vehicle with which he or she may coexist and commune with that experience.

Thus it is that both the logicians and the poets, in their respective fashions, have intercourse with the experiential world; they commune with reality, ironically, by engaging and trying to resolve the increasingly vitiated theological and hence increasingly substantial philosophical investigation of a language that will never quite adhere to that which it claims to describe, and, in theological terms, as in the idea of the Word incarnate, a language that will never fully adhere to the world of reality that perhaps in some sense is the product of, is created by, language itself. "In the content, [. . .] even in the forms of thought," Stock observes,

> medievals appear to have consciously imitated their ancient predecessors. Yet, as their imprecisions, misinterpretations, and sources of anxiety demonstrate, they were unlike their forebears in fundamental ways. The roots of these differences are traceable to the conceptual vocabulary, if not to the process of

conceptualization itself, which derived from a few linguistic models [. . .].
(*Implications of Literacy* 530)

The new textuality contributed to a deepening dichotomy between word and truth, just as it implicitly held out the possibility of a language that owed its being only to itself. Rather than merely through its use as a descriptor of the world, this language could provide the realization of the world through its self-contemplation; as we have said, such self-reflection constituted a cognitive procedure that was provided by both logic and poetry. More and more, language had broken off from the world it could hopefully signify in order to form another, coeval world of its own. It was in these terms that the poets of the later Middle Ages could define themselves in relation to the larger world beyond both themselves and the language with which they struggled for the prize of meaning—a meaning that had to be inextricably woven within language's apparently ineluctable self-meditation. And so the vehicle for meaning could but only have been self-naming, and more importantly the manipulation of the current understanding of the process of naming as a fundamental epistemological concern. The rise to preeminence of logic may have provided the ground for this poetry, but it was language—indeed, in *Piers Plowman* grammar itself serves as a metaphor for a larger theologico-philosophical discussion—which provided the very fabric of the poetic discourse.

All of this, finally, allowed later medieval poets to define themselves as individuals apart from literary, theological and philosophical traditions. In short, in the light of *auctoritas*, poets like Marcabru, Dante, Chaucer and Langland were able to effect themselves in their poems as being their own *auctores*, and they were able to speak about their struggle to arrive at this precarious state of individuality, poised as they were between the anonymity afforded by the larger tradition that demanded their subsumption, and the fully realized individuality of the later Renaissance. This crisis, in which meaning could no longer be satisfactorily expressed in either theological (i.e., philosophical, quasi-scientific, quasi-empirical) terms or in the language of poetry (i.e., the neo-mythical and/or quasi-scientific, such as is exemplified by Bernard's *Cosmographia*), most vividly revealed itself in the changing attitude toward textuality as it increasingly came to be associated with writing and reading. "Texts," Stock writes, eventually

> raised the possibility that reality could be understood as a series of relationships, such as outer versus inner, independent object as opposed to reflecting subject, or abstract sets of rules in contrast to a coherent texture of facts and meanings. Experience in other words became separable, if not always separated, from ratiocination about it; and the main field of investigation turned out to be, not the raw data of sense or the platonized ideal of pure knowledge, but rather the forms of meditation about them. This set of changes resulted in a rebirth of hermeneutics as a critical philosophy of meaning, in a renewed search for epistemological order, and in a widespread interest in diachrony, development, and processual evolution. Understanding as a consequence began to emerge from the accumulation of reiterated and reinterpreted experience, even though, as was recognized, the tools of methodological analysis were not given in each concrete set of events; and an

understanding formed of similar elements links the contemporary reader to the past through the preservation of those very written artifacts which originated new patterns of thought and action themselves.
(*Implications of Literacy* 531)

As the physical representation of discourse it had come to mean, the notion of a *text* could have found justification in, before Aquinas, Abelard's rigorous elevation of words as being the only phenomena in which universals may reside; and, in consideration of this, Abelard concluded that words are themselves things in that only they may contain universality. Notably, he further distinguished between *what* words name (*nominare*) and the *way* in which they signify (Kretzman 369). To comprehend the epistemological crossroads we see exemplified in a thinker such as Abelard is to provide the key to reading the poets of the later Middle Ages, whose poems—that is, whose fictions—were instigated by the recognition that the process per se of signification provided the opportunity to write, and to talk about in writing, the ramifications of a supreme language or rather an unparalleled style.

The insistence on the part of the poets that they create an individual poetic authority could only have occurred within a more diverse, dialectically ordered social structure. The dialectic was integrally involved in the very poetics of these authors, and so poetic self-referentiality, inextricably woven into the fabric of the poetry as well as into the linguistic traditions the poetry modulated, acted as both theme and writerly strategy for these ultimately secular texts. *Auctoritas* is a function of intertextuality. To say that intertextuality lies at the heart of the later medieval poet's attempt at self-definition is quite possibly to state the very obvious; for medieval literature, like the larger medieval world of which it is a part, can only take place within the context of a hierarchized authorial tradition. This does not assume, however, that poets since the twelfth century are not capable of creating images of themselves, for these self-depictions depend for their insistence upon, as well as distinction from, the context of *auctoritas* that they consciously hold at a distance.

The hierarchy of authority defining the medieval imagination, which in its time is considered to be immutable and rigidly determined, is not so much the consequence of Christianity's inviolable articles of faith as of the very language out of which the articles evolve. The metaphors of Scripture and the exegetical tradition establish an unalterable field for poetic endeavor in their insistence on images of the *word*, the *book*, and so on; characterized by the field's intertextual nature, the metaphors are the central descriptions of revelation and redemption. Once a proportion is established between God and the word, it will be the *word* (i.e., the *text*, etc.) that will serve as a formal basis from which Christian epistemology will manifest itself and flourish.

Although no one event or even group of events might completely account for the emergence of a singular poetic voice in early twelfth-century Europe, what is clear is that poetry since then has not only possessed such a voice, as the mark of a unique point of view, but that it has been generated out of the impulse to establish an individualized poetic authority. This is not the voice of the Renaissance, when the aim of poets and thinkers alike is to make "a radical break with tradition" (Stock *Myth and Science* 6). Particularly in the twelfth century, the medieval imagination turns back toward the ancient, pagan world, and sees itself as a part of a continuum; people of this period are the "dwarves" who stood "on the shoulders of giants." What sets the twelfth century apart from the later Renaissance is the latter period's energetic repudiation of its more immediate, medieval past. Hence the twelfth century initiates tensions, rather than precluding their possibility, between its near and distant past, its sense of validity resting on Scripture and particularly the thinking of Augustine, and on a newly revised Aristotelianism that had made its way into Europe. Twelfth-century Europe was thus also a contrast to its immediate past; in comparison with it, the twelfth century was a hotbed of contradictory (as well as, often enough, complementary) ideas and discoveries. Instead of denying the past, the task became that of reconciling the new learning to the *auctoritas* of what was already known and could not be doubted.

This turning to the past in order to augment it, by the assertion of a new present, is not only the driving force among theologians and philosophers like Anselm and Abelard, Aquinas and Ockham, but, again, among poets as well. Gellrich notes that while Dante, and after him Chaucer,

> look away from the medieval past, they also look back to the vital commitment of their past in the reading of the Bible, in the challenge to interpretation and change that it poses.
> (247)

Other poets more openly address their Scriptural roots, though, such as Marcabru and Langland who effectively represent the near and far ends of a unique period in Western intellectual and esthetic development. As an early troubadour, Marcabru helped to inaugurate the new poetics. The troubadours go so far as to *name* the individualized poetic voice as a poetic cause célèbre—as the emblem for, the aegis under which verse is to be made. Ironically, in order to break with their past, poets had to name it. In consequence, the poetic impulse included nascent, historically determined discourses—a strategy that helps to explain Dante's crucial exclamation in the Inferno (II.32), "io non Enea, io non Paolo sono."[46]

What must be recognized is that this dynamic could never have been possible without the legacy of Augustine, particularly the Augustine of the *Confessions*, which was never to be fully supplanted by Scholasticism or its descendants. It is in the *Confessions* that we find the most profound expression of a primal link between a text that the "I" of the reader and of the author "reads," and the maker of that

---

[46] Cf. the Introduction.

text. The "I" of a medieval poem may be only a part of a larger textual convention formulaically referring to, even fully discussing, itself in the poem; in this case, the poetic text may be understood to be the dominant factor in the poem (Zumthor "Autobiography in the Middle Ages" 30-32), rather than, say, the "I" of modern narrative that was fully born in Romanticism. As Vance says, in the *Confessions* Augustine failed

> to consummate the logic of autobiography by refusing to allow the "I" of narrative recollection to converge with the converted "I" that is writing [in part because] he finally distrusted any attempt on the part of man to know his true nature by commemorating his existence in the abyss of time and space [. . .].
> ("Augustine's *Confessions*" 9)[47]

As we shall see (in the following chapters), the poets of the twelfth to fourteenth centuries represent a middle stage of transformation, a segue, from an Augustinian world view to a modern one, which is defined by their poetry's budding historicism, fictional values, and a self-referentiality that makes the poets as distinct from their autonomous texts as from the literary tradition out of which these texts emerged. Yet the seeds of this transformation are to be found, of course, in Augustine. His

> poetics of selfhood in the *Confessions* does not really differ significantly from that of any narrator—Virgil, for example—who seeks to inscribe the sundry fragments of individual experience in an order of discourse whose code serves as what we may call the notation of authority. In such conditions the self becomes merely a contingent signifier. The deictic "I" becomes a purely "grammatical" sign pointing to an order of written signs identical with history, to a logos born not of the speaking self but of the divine Other by whom we are originally spoken.
> (12-13)

Whatever the circumstances, in other words, even within a binary category such as fact/fiction, the literary "I" is in some measure subject to the text it is creating in the sense that this "I"'s ultimate terms of self-definition will have to include an understanding of itself as a text, whether or not the understanding is explicitly stated.

Medieval poetic individuality, in the sense we have been speaking of it, can be said to have been a function of the very text in which such an individual may have appeared; that is, the individual is defined by the text. The ultimate measure of the text's "I" is the text itself. Arguably, therefore, we might want to predict that a

---

[47] Compare this with Freccero's and Beaujour's respective remarks in the Introduction.

motif, which can be found in all later medieval poetry, is that of a persona who finds a reflection of himself or herself in his or her text. This dynamic is a function of both the poet's effected inter- and intratextual maneuvers. The genre in which the voice of this individual first consistently shows itself is that of the troubadour *canso*. Thus we can say that textualized self-awareness in the troubadour tradition was compounded, as has already been noted, by the troubadour's *vidas* and *razos* of the thirteenth and fourteenth centuries, which comprised revisionist readings of the original troubadour songs; the impulse of this tradition reached forward in time beyond this poetry.[48] Yet, as has also been mentioned already, such an inter-/intratextual strategy reaches back at least to Augustine. The *canso*, to be sung, was also written down, which provided later commentators with a fixed version that could be invoked to support a revisionist, interpretive gloss or *razo*.[49] Hence writing in and of itself called into being a secular textuality that matched the exegetical tradition as promulgated in works such as *De Doctrina Christiana*. In fact the *canso*—even if first apprehended by an audience through the singing of the *joglar*, within the social interaction of the aristocratic court—contained an especially intricate structure that must to some extent have depended for its full appreciation on the leisurely and therefore careful scrutiny of a literate reader.

This is in part to say that the troubadours mark the transition from oral to written literature, perhaps in more dramatic fashion than their contemporaries, the writers of Romance or *geste*. And at least some of what intellectual and political developments motivated the Romance genre can be said to have inhered in the versifying efforts of the courtly lyric makers (indeed, quite possibly more profoundly). In all circumstances—Chrétien's romances, the *Chanson de Roland*, or the songs of Marcabru—what seems clear is that there was an understood, inherent textual element within and beyond the spoken as well as the written word. All individuals, groups, and institutions could be defined in terms of texts. Again, this was the text as was most vividly defined by the *Confessions*, whose vision of a worldly scroll or *text* was that of a layer of *skin* (*tex*tus, *teg*umentum; cf. above)— this was a world *written* by God. Thus, in the most graphic fashion, Augustine laid the groundwork for a later, fully evolved relationship between the "I" of an utterance and that very text the "I" speaks, writes, and even reads; by doing so, the "I" reads itself as it is defined by its text. This dynamic is rooted in the association of *skin*, that which contains the physical body (as well as the soul) and which covers the *self*, and the text with which the self might both merge within a community and find distinction from that very same community, just as the covering of a book, in the later Middle Ages, was often known as the book's skin (*integumentum*); the book was a place where individual and community could come together. The text represents the discourse that, in turn, essentially defines and orders the community as it is ruled by an ethical imperative.

---

[48] Cf. the Introduction.

[49] Van Vleck's book makes an important contribution in this regard, as does Laura Kendrick's.

Chapter Two

The Poetics of the "I"

As late as the twelfth century, the ideas and esthetics of Augustine continue to dominate the thinking and art of Western theologians and poets. Thus we find the world view and even the language of Augustine very much present in the songs of the troubadour Marcabru. Marcabru's songs are often meditations on the nature of themselves, as songs, on their ability to make meaning and to convey truth. This act of self-reflection is essentially Augustinian in nature. Yet Augustine's influence manifests in other ways as well. In these songs the poet carries on, at times implicitly, an argument between *amors*, true love, and *amars*, false, cupidinous love or lust. In order to arrive at this dialectic, the theology of Augustine is taken up whole. Marcabru condemns the false use of words, a position that reflects contemporary rhetorical theory but one that is steeped in both classicism and early Christianity. "The blame of empty eloquence," as Linda Paterson has written (in *Troubadours and Eloquence* 11), is a pretext for establishing a true eloquence. This topos is traceable to Plato's blame of Isocrates; but Augustine more pointedly asserts in *De Doctrina Christiana* (IV.28), making Christian doctrine the foundation of true eloquence, that

> [i]n his speech itself [a teacher] should prefer to please more with the things said than with the words used to speak them; nor should he think that anything may be said better than that which is said truthfully; *nor should the teacher serve the words, but the words the teacher.*[1]

This same outlook can be found even more forcefully expressed in the imagery of the *Confessions*; as has been discussed in Chapter One, the notion of false eloquence could have been derived from the false skins and garments (i.e., tex*tus*, teg*umentum*, tex*tilis*) of the sinner. Likewise, the question of eloquence is unavoidable when we read Marcabru—especially, for example, when he attempts to combat the propagation of a new, eroticized love, by his immediate forebear Guillem IX.

Be this as it may, the poet is not a pure copy of the theologian. Marcabru draws upon many textual sources in order to establish the ground of his own

---

[1] "In ipso etiam sermone malit rebus placere quam verbis; nec aestimet dici melius, nisi quod dicitur verius; *nec doctor verbis serviat, sed verba doctori.*" My emphases.

literary authority. Although often recasting and hence disguising his sources in paraphrase and allusion, he can be quick to remind us of the root of his authority—in the following case it is the Bible, particularly in the eleventh strophe of his song "Dirai vos senes duptansa."

> Qui per sen de femna reigna
> dreitz es que mals li·n aveigna,
> si cum la Letra·ns enseigna;
> —Escoutatz!—
> malaventura·us en veigna
> si tuich no vos en gardatz!
> (ll. 61-66)

> Whoever obeys the judgment of a woman,
> it's right that evil should come to him,
> just as the Bible teaches;
> listen!
> May bad luck come to you
> if you're all not on your guard against it![2]

Marcabru clearly enjoys and uses the book of Proverbs, and he often cites David and Solomon. James Wilhelm comments (in *Seven Troubadours: The Creators of Modern Verse* 65-66) that Marcabru's subject is often "the Christian exultation that antedated secular joy [. . .] the perennial newness, the *vita nova*, of which Paul spoke." Accordingly, this troubadour tries to unmask "new impostors by restoring the original sacred values to their terminology." Within this (newly restored) religious tone, Goldin observes (in *Lyrics of the Troubadours* 52), Marcabru creates "for the first time the figure of the singer who takes a stand against 'false lovers', the *fals amadors*, whom he identifies as the other poets of the court."[3]

He "uses"—perhaps one could say "glosses"—other sources as well, as diverse

---

[2] My trans.

[3] Van Vleck (160), in discussing this poem, writes that it reverses the usual exegetical procedure: "The literal level of meaning vanishes, or is transformed, when scriptural commentary applies its principles of interpretation to passages whose literal meaning seems unacceptable for moral instruction [. . .]." Borrowing an image from the Song of Solomon, the patristic idea of interpretation was to extract the "honey of meaning" from "the letter of the text" that contained the meaning or honey.
> When the Occitan poets adapt this image to their poetry, they observe that with *amors* the [container's] wax at times becomes as important as the honey, just as *trobar* values form as highly as meaning. In Marcabru's "Dirai vos senes duptansa," *amors* reverses the normal interpretive procedure: she extracts the wax from the honey. After this action, it will be difficult for her to be true in the future.

Ruth E. Harvey (in *The Troubadour Marcabru and Love* 115) identifies line 63 as specifically alluding to misogynist passages from the Song of Solomon, and the entire poem as alluding to Proverbs (especially 6.20-27). Wilhelm (78) cites Proverbs 5.3-4 and 6.32.

as the classical Ovid or the contemporary Abelard. In his song "Bel m·es quan la rana chanta," the Provençal poet attacks the false uses of eloquence by associating a frog ("rana") with the joglar Alegret; Marcabru sees him as a flatterer, whose obsequiousness toward his patron is repugnant. As a symbol of boorish, noisy and finally "false loquacity" (Paterson 39), Marcabru's image of a frog—although mediated by medieval writers like Peter Damian and Arnulf of Orléans—originally derives from the *Metamorphoses* (VI.339 ff.) in which frogs are what boors become through their transformations. All the same, the matter of a classical Ovid has been set within a new context. We can consider Marcabru as strictly up to date in his likely borrowing of Abelard's *sic et non* dialectic to alert us to the danger in its possible misuse. In one song, "L'iverns vai e·l temps s'aizina," Marcabru warns against *Amars*, which can set "a gracious trap" into which the "simpleton" can be lured in his attempt at divining truth:

> Gent sembel fai que trahina
> Ves son agach lo brico,
> Del cim tro' qu·en la racina,
> Entrebescat hoc e no; [. . .].
> (37–40)

> [*Amars*] sets a gracious trap
> When it lures the simpleton into its snare;
> From the top to the root
> It weaves together yes and no [. . .].[4]

It is Augustine, however, with whom Marcabru remains on the most intimate terms. He begins his song, "Per savi·l tenc ses doptanssa," by contemplating the inherent ambiguity in *all* verbal expression and the misuse to which it can be put:

> Per savi·l tenc ses doptanssa
> cel qui de mon chant devina
> so que chascus motz declina,
> si cum la razos despleia,
> qu'ieu mezeis sui en erranssa
> d'esclarzir paraul' escura.
> (1–6)

> I say he's a wise man, no doubt about it,
> who makes out, word for word,
> what my song signifies,
> and how the theme unfolds:
> for I myself take pains
> to cast some light on obscurity [i.e., on obscure language][5]

---

[4] Trans. Paterson.
[5] The bracketed clarification in the present passage was made by Goldin when this book was in manuscript.

Here the peril for the poet is the very language he must use, a language that can easily be misconstrued. Quite possibly the poet's language will never transcend an unavoidable obscurity taken in by the listener/reader and especially by the "false lovers" criticized in this poem's succeeding lines, those "fools" who live in bad faith—who are, keenly, assigned the name (*"nom"*) of *fool* (*"fols"*).[6] Thus the poem continues,

> Trobador, ab sen d'enfanssa,
> movon als pros atahina,
> e tornon en disciplina
> so que veritatz autreia,
> e fant los motz, per esmanssa,
> entrebeschatz de fraichura.
>
> E meton en un' eganssa
> Falss' Amor encontra fina [etc.].
> (7-14)

> [. . .] those troubadours with childish minds
> who worry honest men:
> they scourge and improve
> what Truth itself puts forth,
> always taking pains to make their words
> tangled up and meaningless.
>
> And they put up that false love of theirs
> against true love, as though it were as good.

Yet even as Augustine's diction, temperament and cast of mind are all quite palpable throughout Marcabru's verses, what this poem discloses is his elaboration of a much older rhetorical tradition—one that the poet could easily have discovered in Cicero, as Paterson explains:

> When Marcabru introduces the problem of *paraul' escura*, he may well be thinking of the Rhetorical *causa obscura*: the kind of case "in quo aut tardi auditores sunt aut difficilioribus ad cognoscendum negotiis causa est implicata." His own "case" could be described as obscure both because the subject is difficult—it takes a wise man to perceive the exact truth in it—and because the foolish troubadours are *tardi*. The *De Inventione* says that in such a case the speaker must make the audience receptive in the introduction [...].[7]

---

[6] Cf. ll. 42, 46, 49, 59.

[7] The first citation here is *De Inventione* I.16.20: "in which either the audience is slow witted or the subject is bound up with matters which are fairly difficult to understand." Trans. H. M. Hubbell. Cf. Brunetto Latini *Li Livres dou tresor* III.17.4. The second reference is to *De Inv*. I.16.23. Harvey has noted that, "[d]epending on the interpretation given to 'per esmanssa', this distortion of the truth could be understood as deliberate, achieved by calculatedly twisting the meanings of words, or it could be the result of the

Indeed, Marcabru is precisely following Cicero's precepts, step for step, first by ingratiating himself with his audience through flattery ("Per savi·l tenc . . . ") and a formula for modesty ("Qu'ieu mezeis sui en erranssa . . . "),[8] then by stating the subject of his address ("paraul' escura,") and the reason for it (namely, that false and foolish troubadours have been mixing up the truth—the song's second stanza). He puts forth his subject with simplicity and clarity, as best he can: "E meton en un' enganssa / Falss' Amor encontra fina." There can be no meeting between false and true love. Now he must try to define what he means by their difference, Paterson observes, "as clearly and graphically as possible." This procedure "closely follows the basic pattern of *dispositio* in Classical Rhetoric: introduction, exposition, definition or division, defence of one's own case, refutation of the opponent's case, and conclusion" (16-17), as can be found in *De Inventione* and in the *Rhetorica ad Herrenium*.[9] Of course, a typical education of Marcabru's time would have included the study of Cicero as well as of many other pagan writers.[10]

Throughout his works, Marcabru appears to be quite aware of contemporaneous streams of thought. Just the same, his basic intellectual and spiritual positions are thoroughly grounded in the past. And it is Plato, rather than the rediscovered Aristotle, whom Marcabru finds most compelling. The notion of obscurity in "Per savi," perhaps too facilely attributable to either Cicero or Aristotle, also resonates in Platonic doctrine. This doctrine has been redefined by Paul, and then by Augustine, who hold that the natural world reflects a divine truth, insofar as knowledge of the obscured meanings the physical world contains is understood to be essential to a full comprehension of Scripture. This concept is central to Augustine's pronouncement in *De Doctrina Christiana* (II.16) that "[a]n ignorance of things makes figurative expressions obscure when we are ignorant of the natures of animals, or stones, or plants, or other things which are often used in the Scriptures for purposes of constructing similitudes."[11] Nature, for Marcabru, can be understood in Scholastic terms, but in his songs we find an awareness of

---

illusory opinions of these poets, of their incomplete understanding of the true nature of love" (33).

[8] Cf. Curtius, 84.

[9] *De Inven.* I. 14.19: *exordium, narratio, partitio, confirmatio, reprehensio, conclusio*; a digression is possible before the conclusion (I.51.96). *Rhet. ad Her.* I.3.44: *exordium, narratio, divisio, confirmatio, confutatio, conclusio*.

[10] While the details of Marcabru's education are unknown, Kendrick demonstrates that there is ample circumstantial evidence suggesting such an education. She surmises that "[m]any of the early troubadours whose *vidas* do not mention their Latin studies must, nevertheless, have been lettered. For example, a ruler such as Guillaume IX needed some Latin training, and [in certain of his verses] he prays to Jesus in both 'romans' (the vernacular) and in Latin" (etc., 62). Moreover, "[a]ccording to the chronicler Ademar of Chabannes, Guillaume the Great (the troubadour's grandfather) was 'doctus litteris' from childhood" (201 n. 14). Cf. Curtius, 49.

[11] "Rerum autem ignorantia facit obscuras figuratas locutiones, cum ignoramus vel animantium, vel lapidum, vel herbarum naturas, aliarumve rerum, quae plerumque in Scripturis similitudinis alicuius gratia ponuntur."

Augustine's teachings that, in any event, formed the basis of later theology and philosophy. For Marcabru, and for Augustine,

> nature is a reflection of hidden truth and moral order, requiring wisdom and effort to penetrate its outward form and discover its true significance. This attitude governs [Marcabru's] use of nature imagery: imagery which not only illustrates moral truths, but in some cases, through the use of symbols, reflects the need to probe behind the outward appearance of natural objects to appreciate their true significance.
> (Paterson 31)

Obscure language, in the case of Marcabru, was an enemy to be reckoned with, for the poet's first responsibility was the words that most of all were his representation within his society. Thus the troubadour *canso* often took as its subject the travail of the poet's attempt to create clarity and truth that the poet saw as an ideal *canso*—the *ideal form*. It might be hoped that this form, a form of language after all, could convey the truth—that is, that it could not merely aspire to but instead become the *ideal*. Yet if the *canso* represented the ideal to be achieved, it was, in fact, also seen to be the inevitable failure implicit in any striving toward that end, much like an image in an imperfect mirror. In contemporaneous Neoplatonism, Goldin writes, "the figure of the mirror represent[ed] the decline of the 'great chain' from God the highest to the lowest dregs of things" (*Mirror of Narcissus* 7)—an idea that had been spelled out in Macrobius' *Somnium Scipionis* (I.14.15). Augustine, in *Soliloquia* (II.6.10), uses the mirror to show that "the mother of falsity is the similitude of things which reaches the eyes." Within there is the human desire "to see," as Goldin phrases it, "the whole face of truth; but often we are deluded, thinking that what we know or seek to know is all that is to be known."[12] It was, however, through the failure of language, of poetry, that the ideal could be signified, could be gestured toward. The shaped beauty of the song could serve as the imperfect resonance of an ideal, singular temporality (aspiring toward a celestial timelessness) that had been felt to have been absent in language.

The ideal *canso* of the troubadours engulfs the potential individual; thus it precludes the possibility of the singular voice. Even in its imperfect state, when performed the *canso* "necessarily denied the inflection of a historically particularized individuality," as Patterson has noted (*Chaucer and the Subject of History* 9).[13] Those who partake of this sort of literary experience, Godzich writes, "are there as the necessary correlatives of the *memoria* from which they derive their sense of identity and purpose" (xv–xvi). The burden of the *canso*'s discourse, then, is the need to plumb the obscure world in order to reach deeper, inner truths, while the very music of this discourse that is the poetry, itself attempts a linguistic perfection; it makes a claim for itself as being the ultimate possible

---

[12] In Goldin, 7. Cf. *Soliloquia* II.20.35.
[13] Cf. Zink, 71.

mortal expression of the truth. Even in its time bound, flawed language, which must ultimately fail to create the ideal form of the *canso*, the truth is evoked by the very failure of achieving it—that is, of *naming* it.

The emblem of this dynamic and indeed the epitome of this poetry's discourse is the poet's act of autocitation. The troubadour names himself in his poem and comments on the very writing of that poem, and ponders its future survival. This is the charge of songs such as Marcabru's "Pus mos coratges s'es clartits," "Per savi·l tenc ses doptanssa," "Contra l'ivern que s'enansa," and "Aujatz de chan com enans e meillura." Guillem IX, Marcabru and other troubadours have not constructed the fully elaborated autobiographical voice to be found in Dante, Chaucer or Langland; yet, like their descendants, these earlier poets confront the issue of *auctoritas*. And they do this with great subtlety. What should we think of Peire Vidal's slightly self-derisive contemplation of his own poetic efficacy, durability, and most of all singularity?:

> Ajostar e lassar
> sai tan gent motz e so,
> que del car ric trobar
> no·m ven hom al talo [etc.].
> (1-4)

> I can put together and inter-
> lace words and music with such skill,
> in the noble art of song
> no man comes near my heel [. . .].

For the troubadours, autocitation always served a specific end: theirs was an ongoing meditation on the act of making poetry. Perhaps it is not too farfetched to assert that the *name* they were after—that is, the ideal—was eloquence itself, that which *cannot* be named but which can be softly hinted at through a poetics. Joan Ferrante (in "'Ab joi mou lo vers e'l comens'" 131) comments that Bernart de Ventadorn's verses often bring together certain themes including "the problem of writing a poem" and "the beauty and power of the lady" (118), which can be combined or employed separately to talk about "'the most beautiful truth' as opposed to the foul lie ('lag mentir')" (131). These oppositions are clearly underwritten by Augustinian linguistic theory in which the *littera* are the "lying" containers of beautiful truths. Furthermore, both Bernard and Vidal link the theme of composing verse to that of individual achievement within the poetic, and generally the literate tradition; such achievement distinguishes the poet within the literary, inherited past, the literary river that nourishes him. In fact, Vidal speaks of poetry as the form for the voice of the poet, a form that must by definition subsume that voice—could the ideal of itself be attained. The force of his statement is embodied within a conundrum whose power resides in the statement's commentary on itself. Vidal is saying, I can compose the ultimate song—the absolute song, like language before there was sin, set in timelessness—which must sing only of itself in its formal meditation; however, I can claim for myself the fame for having made this song that in a sense will always "forget" me, for as its maker I have become its mere instrument through which it has been brought into being. In making this song, though, Vidal has invoked a literary-historical time frame. He is looking *backwards* from within a continuum and setting himself up within it by suggesting that he is at the least its equal (e.g., the claim, "no·m ven hom al talo"). If Vidal is not engaged here in full blown self-contemplation, an extended introspection of himself as poet, he is just the same creating, by a kind of self-citation, the very emblem of such an inward journey that must ultimately yield the full, unique voice of self-knowledge and self-acknowledgment.

Vidal and all troubadours name themselves and their competitors, as if to invoke talismanic power, but such naming resides within the context of the craft not only of poetry but of the larger sensibility of the *cortezia* they serve and in which they ostensibly seek to be subsumed. This view of poetry as an adjunct of a more fundamental world view is firmly established in the twelfth century and it persists at least as late as Chaucer. Quite possibly the most emblematic of Chaucer's figures (as we have noted in the Introduction), which suggests the analogy between courtly loving and poetic inquiry—the *makyr*'s epistemology—is the opening gambit of the *Parliament of Fowls*:

> The lyf so short, the craft so long to lerne,
> Th'assay so hard, so sharp the conquerynge,
> The dredful joye alwey that slit so yerne:
> *Al this mene I by Love* [. . .].
> (1-4; my emphasis)[14]

Formalism, as the guiding light of *fin' amors*, here becomes the principle in forging the mimetic artifact; these first lines may hint as well at the likelihood that all knowledge—all modes of apprehension of a world—must not only proceed by way of an artificial, "formed" method, but that knowledge is actually the forms themselves—"knowing" as one with form. It should follow that philosophical ideality (i.e., a notion of a perfect, pristine dimension) as well as the creative, or intuitive impulse, must be amorphous in the sense that such a dimension is inferred by all finite, corporeal, perhaps lapsarian or "fallen" forms that are distinct from this ideal state. These forms are the manifestations or at least the Platonic shadows of the "ideal form." Logically, however, the notion of an ideal form is untenable, especially when *form* is understood in sensible, material contexts such as literal, physical shapes. Yet more abstract and imaginative forms are easily recognizable—courtly mannered behavior, for instance, or literary genres. Such organizing principles as these are also limited, in any event; and mortals only know

---

[14] As noted previously, the lines are a conscious echo of Horace's "ars longa, vita brevis." I should also mention here the ending of Chaucer's poem, where Nature herself cannot bring the birds' debate to an orderly end; the birds, however, must borrow an artificial order from French poets.

these finite forms although they may intuit—they make the attempt to conceive of, *to know*—the ideal, the infinite.

The question of God's active presence in the palpable universe—in other words, ideality perceived as existing in or through the sensible objects of the world—does not involve Chaucer directly, yet there is an underlying philosophical dialogue taking place, particularly in his dream poems. Nominalist thinking of the twelfth, thirteenth, and fourteenth centuries, remained intimately bound up in what was and perhaps still is skepticism regarding a subtle relationship that might exist between imaginative and experiential cognitive realms. Nominalist doctrine emphasizes the particulars of the world landscape but refuses to accept the possibility of a universal ordering of these "things" of the world: the ideal may only be apprehended indirectly—if at all—through knowledge of the individual or perhaps through knowing the instant in time.

The dream *visio*, on the other hand, is for Chaucer the esthetic alternative to this dilemma (as we shall examine more closely in Chapter Four), much in the way that the poetry of the ideal *canso* serves to answer the underlying Christian dichotomy forming the context of troubadour poetry. What is crucial in this dynamic is the very fact that the troubadour or trobaritz serves *cortezia*, that the poet is therefore determined by the poetry as the instrument, the mere scribe or *joglar* the poet despises and with whom the poet fears to be identified (thus, in their verbal contests with each other, poets often smear their competitors with the name *joglar*).[15] Yet among these troubadours there is, finally, a subtle assertion of individuality, of individual will, an assertion of themselves as *auctores*. They must excoriate the *joglars*. They fear being seen as mere performers who are, in a sense, liars, rather than as authors. And most of all they fear being silenced.

The *Minnesänger* Heinrich von Morungen counterbalances the making of verse through which, as he claims, he will attain true worth, with the recollection that when he "[stands] mute in sorrow" he is worth nothing (to his lady): "do ich in leide stuont, dô huop ich si gar unhô" ("Leitlîiche blicke und grôzliche riuwe" 12). Through composition and service, however, the poet may realize himself. In fact, this construct can become the vehicle for the ultimate self-enunciation, as in Walther von der Vogelweide's elegy for Reinmar von Reuenthal, which quotes a line from the dead poet ("'sô wol dir, wîp, wie reine ein nam!'"—"Joy to you,

---

[15] I acknowledge the long line of scholarly opinion that runs counter to my argument, as reflected in this passage from Harvey (quoting M. Stevens in "The Performing Self in Twelfth-Century Culture" 210):
> That a composer should "sign" his songs, referring to himself as the composer, has been understood as a *jongleuresque* practice, "the writer's self-reference being in part the effect both of his uncertain patronage and the conditions of oral performance which governed the dissemination of his art."
> (11).

What I am claiming is meant to refute this opinion. Self-naming was an element within a metapoetry ultimately about language in and of itself. As such, while I do not wish here to discount the oral dynamics of the *joglar*, self-naming was involved with more than the singer's social and political circumstances.

Woman, how pure a name").[16] Here Walther pays homage to his predecessor, but he does so in order to valorize the art of poetry itself. Significantly, Walther is asserting his individuality in terms of a text, an inherited text. Reinmar's text becomes the example of how each of these poets serves courtly song. It is the text that reminds us of the worth of the poet, which resides in his service to a beloved and which can, in turn, be expressed in the terms of devotion to the poetic vocation that is always in pursuit of an ideal or *true* art.

This is the hierarchy of the superlative, and in looking upwards toward the ideal, the individual feels himself as less and less distinct, yet there is no choice but to ascend. Nevertheless, there are ways out of this dilemma. Walther's ultimate self-assertion and his song turn on the very recognition that the art of song comprehends both himself and Reinmar:

> Dêswâr, Reimâr, dû riuwes mich
> michels harter danne ich dich,
> ob dû lebtes und ich waer erstorben.
> ich wilz bî mînen triuwen sagen,
> dich selben wolt ich lützel klagen:
> ich klage dîn edelen kunst, daz sist verdorben.
> ("Owê, daz wîsheit unde jugent" 14-19)

> The truth is, Reinmar, I mourn for you
> much more than you would mourn for me
> if you were living and I had died.
> I want to say this on my honor:
> you yourself I would not shed a tear for.
> I mourn the passing of your noble art.

Walther defines himself within the terms of courtly forms. We know him to be the one who, at least as an appreciative witness, can *name* the art of courtliness as that which sustains him. And in the last lines of his poem he does not fail to align himself with his Other (even as he distinguishes himself from him), in order to suggest his own poetic power. Addressing Reinmar, he foretells, poignantly, a future reunion:

> sô leiste ich dir gesellschaft: mîn singen ist niht lanc.
> dîn sêle müeze wol gevarn, und habe dîn zunge danc.
> (25-26)

> Well, I shall be with you again, my singing is soon over.
> May your soul fare well, and your tongue have thanks.

Through the naming of the Other, then, even in derision, as can be seen in the poetry of Vidal, Walther and others, the poet can achieve self-elevation. The

---

[16] Texts and translations of the German lyrics are from Frederick Goldin's anthology, *German and Italian Lyrics of the Middle Ages*.

name embodies great ethical power. La Comtessa de Dia, for instance, comforts herself in her attempts to win back a lover by noting that her name in itself is an asset in luring him to her: "Valer mi deu mos pretz e mos paratges" ("A chantar m'er de so qu'eu no volria" 29). Here the rewards of naming are obvious. The trobaritz strategy need hardly be deciphered—and in her example we perhaps observe the most convincing evidence of naming as a poetics. There is value in her "pretz" or "worth," an ambiguous term as used here, which perhaps suggests both a kind of intrinsic human and a monetary worth, and surely a worth in relation to her familial descent ("paratges"). Within this tautological ("Valer [. . .] pretz") and virtually untranslatable line, however, the poet has inscribed the notion of *fama*, in ethical terms the good *name* of the worthy lover who in this case is doubly worthy in that she has been ennobled a second time through her longing for the distant beloved. This longing makes possible the bettering of the individual who subscribes to the courtly love experience. The longing, too, informs a poetry that aspires to its ideal. There are a great many ways of manifesting the poet's sense of an individuated self-worth, through naming. Peire D'Alvernhe not only names himself in one of his verses but he systematically dispenses with twelve of his fellow poets over the course of the same number of stanzas ("Cantarai d'aquestz trobadors"). Yet, again, the form is what is important.

Given the expectations of Marcabru's audience, however, and the fact that he will employ naming, as part of a poetics of presence, we also find in his verse, remarkably, a poetics of absence. We have examined this ploy as it is used in Dante's *Commedia* (in the Introduction). Earlier poets, arguably, have shown Dante the way in this. We have also observed Heinrich's conspicuous absence. Other troubadours have made use of absence too. One of Bernart de Ventadorn's songs names no one particularly, yet the poet manages to align himself with the song that comprehends all poets:

Non es meravelha s'eu chan
melhs de nul autre chantador,
que plus me tra·l cors vas amor
e melhs sui faihz a so coman.
Cor e cors e saber e sen
e fors' e poder i ai mes.
Si·m tira vas amor lo fres
que vas autra part no·m aten.
(1–8)

Of course it's no wonder I sing
better than any other troubadour:
my heart draws me more toward love,
and I am better made for his command.
Heart body knowledge sense
strength and energy—I have set all on love.
The rein draws me straight toward love,
and I cannot turn toward anything else.

Bernart concludes his song by turning it back on itself; he will send it to the beloved at whose instigation he has had the opportunity to serve love truly, to serve *cortezia*, and thus to become a better poet and a better man:

> A Mo Cortes, [. . .]
> tramet lo vers, e ja no·lh pes
> car n'ai estat tan lonjamen.
> (57-59)

> To Mon Cortes, [. . .]
> I send this song, and let her not be vexed
> that I have been so far away.

Deriving the meaning of Bernart's discourse in "Non es meravelha s'eu chan" depends upon an equation that was established by poets of his previous generation, which describes a cause and effect relationship between success at making truly great poetry—synonymous with speaking the truth—and having the capacity to love truly. Bernart's a priori assumption is that he sings best of all because he exists for the purpose of serving love; through such service he must thrive. The terms of this love reflect a dichotomy that was thoroughly explored by Marcabru.

In "Per savi·l tenc ses doptanssa"—unlike several of his other songs in which Marcabru names himself—the poet is *not* specifically named. Nevertheless, he manages to assert himself through a first person voice that constantly insists upon itself as being someone who is not foolish, not brutish, not without speech, and so forth. All that he is *not* perfectly describes other poets, other detractors, liars, and for that matter all others who live in a kind of bad faith. The voice does not invoke its owner through naming but—albeit less elaborately than the future Dantean triad "io sol uno" (discussed in the Introduction), and in keeping with what can be called a poetics of the superlative—Marcabru employs a figure to refer to himself *twice* over—"qu'ieu mezeis sui" (5). Thus, subtly yet powerfully, the poet emphasizes himself, and thereby distinguishes himself from all others. In doing so, furthermore, he juxtaposes himself with the notion of light that can plumb or clarify the obscurity of ordinary speech:

> qu'ieu mezeis sui en erranssa
> d'esclarzir paraul escura.
> (5-6)

Ordinary speech is either spoken or sung by the troubadours of the next lines ("Trobador, ab sen d'enfanssa," etc.) who are essentially without true speech and who therefore "worry honest men" ("movon als pros atahina," 8).

Marcabru's point is typical of the thought of his time, in part dramatized by a resurgence of interest in categories as seen in Porphyry's tree that delineates, according to genus and species, the various possible forms of worldly existence.[17] Later in this song, Marcabru finds he cannot even bring himself to refer to such troubadours as human; rather, they are the "dogs" of his world who have been "kept in the dark":

> La defenida balanssa
> d'aquest vers e revolina
> sobr' un' avol gen canina
> cui malvatz astres ombreia, [. . .].
> (55-58)

> The end of this *vers*
> takes its stand and turns
> on a vile people, dogs
> whom an evil star keeps in the dark [. . .].

We have traced Marcabru's construct of obscure speech—versus the clarity the persona can bring to bear on such speech—to Augustine and particularly the Augustine of *De Doctrina Christiana*. As well, we have noted how Marcabru establishes a dialectic; on the one side lies obscurity, the consequence of false love or *amars* (e.g., "qu'ieu dic: que Amar s'aizina / ab si mezesme guerreia," 15-16— "And I say: whoever settles down with Lust / wars against himself"), and on the other side lies *amors* through whose power one can enjoy both insight and eloquence. These poles roughly resemble the Augustinian concepts of *cupiditas* and *caritas*.[18] In light of Augustine, it is possible to say that a basic impulse in

---

[17] Cf. Vance's discussion of this matter in *From Topic to Tale*, 85-87.

[18] I do not wish to imply here that these poles do not also signify systems of value other than the religious, such as having to do with class status. I also recognize that there has been a long standing debate about this point of correspondence between the two sets of opposites, one religious and the other secular; the debate has been admirably summarized and documented in Harvey (23 ff). I believe that my overall argument sustains my assertion here that there is, however, a rough correspondence. And I concur with Harvey (26), as follows.

> That Marcabru should have drawn on the Christian ethic and mythology in order to provide a forceful illustration of the power, purity and qualities of *fin' amor* is not surprising, since the rhetoric and imagery of the sacred was often used to reinforce and colour literary depictions of erotic love in the Middle Ages.

Furthermore, my own argument is indebted to Harvey's subsequent qualification:

> In Marcabru's poetry, *fin' amor* "is profane, but possesses qualities which associate it with Christian love." In his songs there is no discernible difference or conflict between the ideal of profane love and Christian love; on the contrary, these two ideals are integrated in Marcabru's concept of "whole thinking or entiers cuidars, embracing all that is noble in courtly, feudal, Christian and philosophical thought and faith."

Marcabru's verses is to restore an older ontological order that had been disturbed by immediate predecessors like Guillem IX[19] who helped to fashion a revolutionary concept of courtly love that admitted of eroticism; yet this love, resembling Marcabru's *amars*, was understood to be an ennobling force.

What has not been fully examined is the debt Marcabru's ideas owe to a textual tradition that can be credited to Augustine in *De Doctrina Christiana* and particularly to the Augustine of the *Confessions* where Marcabru most closely aligns himself with the Church father. Marcabru's poetry elaborates an Augustinian view of textuality and creativity, the relationship between them, which defines itself in direct relation to the question of love. Furthermore, it is precisely the poem in which the poet does not overtly name himself—when the expectation of the time was that this is what poems *would* do—which names the poet most profoundly. In this fashion Marcabru most becomes his text. Within a dialectical matrix of *amors* and *amars*, "Per savi" discusses Marcabru's struggle to create true eloquence by using the imagery of light and the question of love, and by aligning these values with the success at making verse. Further, we can say that the poet has truly become his text since this notion is embodied in his implicit claim, as demonstrated in what amounts to his signature, the dyad *ieu mezeis seu*.

Marcabru's superlative assertion in "Per savi," that the poet sings best of all, is set in opposition to the fools who cannot understand his song and who emptily mimic the true poet in the noise they produce ("Fols, pos tot cant au romanssa, / non sec razo, mas bozina," 49-50—"The fool, since everything he hears he sings to others, / does not follow reason, he just makes noise"). They are incapable of reason ("razo"), both in the sense of being rational, truly human and perhaps capable of possessing wisdom, and as well in the sense of reason as the word is used to denote the formal properties of eloquence, for the fools are also bad poets *and* poor exegetes (cf. ll. 4 and 50). This conjoining of eloquence and wisdom, as a kind of working definition of true poetry, is in turn used as a measure of the poet's moral worth. "With their Latin letters," Kendrick observes, "the schoolboys who later became troubadours learned exegetical techniques and practiced these on literary texts in a competitive, game-like way [and thus the songs of Marcabru are] rich in criticism of the troubadours for their false interpretations." These interpretations reveal a "linguistic corruption" that, in turn, "is a sign of moral corruption"—an idea Marcabru could have inherited indirectly from Augustine and directly from Isidore of Seville (63, 65).

Yet for Marcabru intentionality, most of all, prescribes the truth, insofar as a speaker's individual will is expressed in the sense of his words—a thoroughly

---

The two passages Harvey quotes here are from, respectively, Leslie T. Topsfield, "*Jois, Amors* and *Fin' amors* in the Poetry of Jaufre Rudel," 303; and, "*Malvestatz versus Proeza* and *Leautatz* in Troubadour Poetry and the *Lancelot* of Chrétien de Troyes," 42. Kendrick also argues that Marcabru associates "'fin amors' or *caritas*," yet, ingeniously, analyzes *amars* to mean "love of art, recollecting Ovid's '*ars am*-atoria'" as well as "burning sexual desire (*am-ars*, playing on the Latin verb *ardeo*, used by the Christian fathers to describe lust)" (18).

[19] In this regard, cf. Wilhelm, 65 ff.

Augustinian idea. Marcabru (*fl.* 1129-1150) is reacting to a poetical climate that is most clearly enunciated in the work of his predecessor, Guillem (1071-1127). Guillem's poems suggest the tendency toward a revision of Augustinian thinking about language and truth; remarkably, his discourse reflects the philosophical inquiry into language, intentionality and objectivity, of the slightly older Anselm (1033-1109). In *De Doctrina Christiana* (I.36) Augustine held that lying was constituted of three criteria: "objective untruth, the intention to deceive, and a misguided sense of what is to be loved and hoped for."[20] Significantly, for Augustine, lying involves an immoral intention that brings together both the hearer of the untruth and the speaker himself; moreover, it involves, intellectually, a wrong attitude toward truth. In sum, we may say that for Augustine—and for Marcabru—lying involves a disassociation of words from the state of being marked by the presence of *caritas*, which reflects, on the part of speaker, hearer or, specifically, interpreter, a defective love of the self and of others too (Colish "Stoic Theory" 31). By the time of Anselm, the machinery of rationality had already been brought to bear on religious or, more to the point, on quasi philosophical tenets, which initiated a rethinking of the issues surrounding language and truth most comprehensively defined in the fourth century. Anselm sought to distinguish among the parts of language more finely, which led him to separate the Latin substantive *grammaticus* into two aspects, one adjectival and the other truly nominal (as discussed in Chapter One). Of major importance is the fact that this distinction also necessitated a rethinking of accepted notions concerning the role of the individual will in human affairs, especially as this related to the issue of language and its power to describe experiential truth accurately, to name the world that existed extralinguistically.

As Colish observes, rather than blindly embracing Augustine's theory, Anselm "[resuscitates] the Stoic doctrine of *lekta* and the logical statements which they constitute" in order to contrast statements that possess "a natural truth" and those that merely possess "an accidental truth" (39). But rather than Augustine's perception of *natural* truth, in *De Veritate*, as we have observed already (again, in Chapter One), Anselm does not directly concern himself with the denotative ability of language to signify an objective truth, nor with non-linguistic natural signs, signs that for Augustine involuntarily denoted things in experience (such as smoke that will signify the fire producing it). Aristotle's distinction between substance and accident, furthermore, particularly obtains to semantic developments under way with Anselm. For he held that, as Colish says,

> [. . .] all statements, in virtue of their semantic coherence, possess an intrinsic truth (*veritas*). This truth inheres in them as a function of their logical and grammatical cogency, whether or not they correspond with anything in the real

---

[20] As paraphrased by Colish, "Stoic Theory," 30. "Inest quippe in mentiente voluntas falsa dicendi: et ideo multos invenimus, qui mentiri velint; qui autem falli, neminem [etc.]" ("Lying involves the will to speak falsely; thus we find many who wish to lie, but no one who wishes to be deceived"). Cf. *Confessions* V.35, X.41.66-42.67.

order [of things]. However, such propositions, while they always possess truth, do not always possess rectitude (*rectitudo*).
(40)

For there to be rectitude, a statement must indicate both a world beyond itself and a "reality" within itself. In other words, it must be "true" objectively as well as coherent, and thereby true (*veritas*), internally. Any cogent statement can signify, yet what ends would such a statement serve? Anselm believes that all significatory utterances possess *natural* (*naturaliter*) truth; that is, in terms of semantics, such expressions are said to be true. This is a revolutionary perception, one that compels him to demote the status of intentionality in Augustine's conception of falsehoods. The later theologian

> omits the intention to deceive as the *sine qua non* or even as one of the necessary components of a lie. [Rather, in] *De veritate*, where he considers lies under the heading of the *veritas enuntiationis*, he confines lying purely to the level of incorrect objective reference. [Thus] his real goal [. . .] is to exalt *both* intellectual and moral rectitude as the criteria of truth in all respects.
> (Colish 40; my emphasis)

What must be underlined here is that, in Anselm's scheme, except for the essences of things, nothing automatically possesses rectitude, and so in human affairs rectitude becomes "a function of the free exercise of human will and judgment," which Anselm prizes more than actions of a reflexive nature (40). Here he has virtually resurrected "the Stoic conception of logical statements as possessing their own internal rules" (41).

We see this issue, the interrelationship of language. language user, and truth, played out to its greatest effect in the fourteenth century (as noted already) in *Piers Plowman*. The poem's persona, Will, is to be viewed in the midst of a yet later struggle to reconcile or otherwise to reestablish a balance between Augustine and—instead of Anselm, or for that matter the later Abelard or Aquinas—Ockham, as well as the speculative grammarians and realists. The realists—in contention with Ockham and others like Robert Holcot—assert the primacy of language as the determinor of what could be held to be actual. The nominalist-realist differentiation was not always a simple matter, however. Anselm was surely a realist; he also agrees with Augustine and the Stoics that "*lekta* cannot legislate for the world outside the mind" (Colish 41).

In the twelfth century, a version of this struggle is depicted in what might be called Marcabru's counter-revolutionary ideology, which he promulgates in reaction to the new courtly love that had been elaborated at least by the time of Guillem. There is no textual evidence to support the claim that courtly love had fully evolved before him—and thus, perhaps, as early as Anselm—but Guillem's songs, Hult comments, "presuppose a codified network of rhetorical commonplaces, verse forms, and technical vocabulary." Indeed, the verses often contain "biting irony" suggesting Guillem is, more than simply perpetuating a tradition, also satirizing it "from the depths of its premises" (309). As the poet and troubadour translator Paul Blackburn observed (in *Proensa* 275), we can see in the work of Guillem that he

> is already bored with [his own] poses of being fated, of being sorcered, of being so dizzy from love that the troubadour cannot tell if he's coming or going or asleep or awake, of being sick and near death from [his] lady's refusals [of his romantic approaches]—even the theme of "the love afar" is there, which we do not otherwise find until Jaufre Rudel sings [of] the countess of Tripoli in the *middle* of the 12 C.

Employing terminology and concepts similar to Guillem, Marcabru's "Per savi" attacks what the younger poet considers to be a false language he finds generally in use all around him—in the courts, on a crusade, among other troubadours.[21]

In Guillem's songs, on the other hand, fundamental assumptions about perception (i.e., Augustinian assumptions), biblical imagery and the Christian hierarchy of values are all invoked for the purpose of delineating and thereby elevating a system of secular, erotic love. In "Mout jauzens me prenc en amar" we find, as Wilhelm notes, "a brilliant expression of mysticism applied to material objects" (54). Guillem praises his lady, and in doing so, by a constant repetition of the word *joy*, he deftly makes of this emotion her very emblem:

> Mout jauzens me prenc en amar
> un joy don plus mi vuelh aizir,
> e pus en joy vuelh revertir
> ben dey, si puesc, al mielhs anar,
> quar mielhs orna·m, estiers cujar,
> qu'om puesca vezer ni auzir.
> (1-6)
>
> I begin, rejoicing already, to love
> a joy that I want most to settle down in;
> and since I want to come back to joy,
> I must go, if I can, the best way:
> for I am made better by one who is, beyond dispute,
> the best a man ever saw or heard.[22]

In this and in the ensuing stanzas "joy," which is an objective courtly reality, and which also denotes for the poet a state of sheer rapture, echoes the liturgical *gaudium* that was

> the favorite word of hymnologists to describe the emotional impact of religious belief or awakening. It occurs again and again in Easter hymns and in poems written in praise of the Virgin Mary. As a result, when William writes in praise of

---

[21] Cf. Peter Makin, *Provence and Pound*, 122.
[22] Trans. Wilhelm.

his own lady, he seizes upon the sacred word and travesties it with the same kind of exultant repetition that one finds more often in the Latin *Carmina Burana*. (Wilhelm 53)

Guillem "echoes" Philippians 2.10, Peter Makin notes, when claiming that "Every joy must bow down before her / and every pride obey / *Midons*," and in the formula, "no-one can find a finer lady, / nor eyes see, nor a mouth speak of [etc.]." Moreover, the "incantatory fifth stanza of this song enumerates powers that were invoked every day in the Virgin and the saints" (102).[23] Here we see only three of many possible examples of the ways in which Guillem remakes a received sensibility into a shape that can express new courtly values. And this *amor courtois* "was not 'religious' in the sense of being part of any Christian ethic; it was a religion in its psychology. The courtly lover did not think of his lady as the Church thought of her, but as the Church thought of God" (102).

Yet at heart Guillem's strategy presupposes a view of language that echoes Anselm's emendation of Augustine, who constructed the parameters of language and truth that affected the European world view well into the Renaissance. Guillem could not have made such novel, and what in some circles would have been thought of as sacrilegious, uses of language had the freedom to believe in a language that could be, in and of itself, either capable of truth or falsehood not been created, inadvertently or otherwise by Anselm's testing of contemporary language theories with the force of logic. The notion that language is in some sense autonomous or independent of the language user is a subtext of Guillem's song, "Companho, faray un vers . . . convinen." Here he weighs the question of what expressions and/or thoughts can be considered as truly possessing—to borrow from Anselm—*rectitude*. The specific question Guillem asks, which will have the greatest impact on what status courtly love can enjoy within its larger society, is whether or not foolish talk can be of any worth at all. For if in a *vers* such foolishness can be found to be worthy, even beautiful, then perhaps courtly love, *amars* rather than *amors*—to borrow this time from Marcabru—can be seen as a noble way of living, and implicitly, therefore, as being capable of redemption:

Companho, faray un vers . . . covinen:
et aura·i mais de foudaz no·y a de sen,
et er totz mesclatz d'amor e de joy e de joven.
(1-3)

My companions, I am going to make a *vers*
that is refined, and it will have more foolishness than sense,
and it will be all mixed with love and joy and youth.

How can such foolishness, such lack of sense, be refined, be fitting, except in that it is mixed up with love and joy? Guillem tells us that only those who are noble

---

[23] Cf. the *Te Deum* and the Psalm *Confitemini Domini* from the Vulgate (in Makin 102 and 324 nn.).

will understand and have an answer to this question:

> E tenguatz lo per vilan qui no l'enten
> o dins son cor voluntiers qui no l'apren;
> greu partir si fai d'amor qui la trob'a son talen.
> (4-6)

> Whoever does not understand it, take him for a peasant,
> whoever does not learn it deep in his heart.
> It is hard for a man to part from love that he finds to his desire.

Here he proves his point, and furthers argument in favor of erotic if not courtly love (indeed, the remainder of this song is thoroughly salacious—as is a considerable amount of his oeuvre)[24] by invoking the Pauline and later Augustinian argument for exegesis that prescribes the *proper* (*"convinen"*) reading of a text, so that the truth will out, despite what the words may signify on the surface.[25] Guillem's attitude about language and communication emphasizes, though, the ambiguity of expression, and furthermore the possibility of a new kind of expression, one that demonstrates the divorce of word and intention. His own expression is the very sign of the hairline fracture Anselm left in Augustinian cosmology whose coherence depended upon the idea of a seamless communion between language and truth, even if it was a language that had been made obscure.

Reading Marcabru, and then looking back at Guillem's "fractured" language— "totz mesclatz"—what the bawdy story teller is arguing for becomes more significant, inasmuch as Marcabru will later favor a kind of expression in which language embodies the individual will, or, that is to say, in which language and intention are reunited in the Augustinian spirit. In "Per savi," for example, Guillem might easily be included in that group of troubadours who are essentially without speech ("Trobador, ab sen d'*enfanssa*," 7—i.e., as in the Latin *infans*; my emphasis),[26] who thus, in making meaningless noise, "worry honest men" ("movon als pros atahina," 8), and who twist beyond recognition the teaching of the *auctores* ("e tornon en disciplina / so que veritatz autreia," 9-10; note the binary nature of "*autreia*" suggesting *auctoritas* as well as *slander* or *detraction*). In other words, these false speakers take the very words of the inherited past and make them tangled up and fractured ("e fant los motz, per esmanssa, / entrebeschatz de fraichura," 11-12); and in doing so they equate their false love with the true ("E meton en un' eganssa / Falss' Amor encontra fina," 13-14).

[24] Cf. Kendrick, 122 ff.
[25] Cf. Kendrick, 65-66.
[26] Cf. Kendrick, 17-19.

Again, the basis upon which either Guillem or Marcabru validates his claim about love and language is the poetry itself, which significantly must, in turn, represent them; their modes of self-enunciation are their poetics, respectively. In "Per savi" self-enunciation takes the form of the poet's actual statement of poetics that comprises the burden of the poem's opening lines. Marcabru's prescription for poetry is to have the theme of the poem unfold as each word is taken in and comprehended ("devina," 2) by the listener or reader. What is implied is that, to understand his poem, which means to appreciate his view of how poetry ought to proceed, is to understand Marcabru, the author of the poem. In this metapoetical statement, it is the poet himself who will demonstrate the art of true poetry by making the effort to achieve, in words, a clarity of vision ("qu'ieu mezeis sui en eranssa / d'esclarzir paraul' escura," 5-6). The "I" in these troubadours' poems ultimately understands itself as a text, just as these poets define themselves in light of their *vers* that serves as the vehicle by which they may judge others of their society, and by which they may finally set themselves apart from those others who are false in love, lacking in wisdom, and as implied, who use language unwisely and immorally. In "Companho, faray un vers . . . convinen" Guillem writes, "[. . .] tenguatz lo per vilan qui no l'enten" ("whoever does not understand [the song], take him for a peasant," 4), and in "Per savi" Marcabru retorts, "La defenida balanssa / d'aquest vers e revolina / sobr' un' avol gen canina [. . .] c'ab folla cuida bobanssa" ("The end of this *vers* / takes its stand and turns / on a vile people, dogs [. . .] all pompous with their dumb ideas," 55-57, 59).

This association of the poet with the text takes place within the broader framework of a meditation on naming that mirrors previous and current thinking about the role of names in thought and more largely in theological affairs. What either of these poems can show us is that their authors treat them—and therefore we can guess how they approached all poetry—as the forums in which their assertions can be vindicated and perhaps redeemed. If the poem is true to itself, then, the ideas it presents will also ring true. This textual connection accounts, in part, for the almost constant ploy to be found throughout much of troubadour verse of self-referentiality. Often manifesting at the ends of poems, self-reference both poetically and rhetorically provides closure, a roundness to the poetic discourse. It also emphasizes the fact that the discourse is rooted in a certain philosophy and poetics of the self, as we have seen in Marcabru's inward turn that concludes "Per savi," particularly in the use of the word "revolina." Guillem's "Pus vezem de novel florir" ends first with a call to all noble persons to read the poem correctly, followed by a brief review of precisely how the discourse was carried out, and then the comment that indeed Guillem is pleased with what he has made, for it is worthy:

Del vers vos dig que mais en vau
qui ben l'enten e n'a plus lau,
que·l mot son fag tug per egau,
    comunalmens,
e·l sonetz qu'ieu mezeis me·n lau

bos e valens.
("Pus vezem de novel florir" 37–42)

Concerning this *vers* I tell you that it is worth more if one
understands it, and gets more praise;
and all the strophes are built exactly
on the same meter,
and the melody, which I myself am happy about,
is fine and good.[27]

Furthermore, Guillem proposes that his very song represent him to others, when he is unable to do so:

Mon Esteve, mas ieu no·i vau,
sia·l prezens
mos vers e vuelh que d'aquest lau
sia guirens.
(43–46)

Let my *vers*, since I myself do not,
appear before her,
Mon Esteve, and let it be the witness
for my praise.

While Marcabru's intentions are to wage war on the values of Guillem, in order to restore society and poetry to a proper balance, both poets reflect a contemporary, gradually changing, attitude toward language. As I have been saying, language was coming to be understood as capable of being either a mental construct in and of itself, or a medium, perhaps the cement that holds society together as a vibrant whole. Again, we can locate the most dramatic shift in the way language was viewed in the writings of Anselm, who elaborates a conception of what language is through the critical recognition that language can, in a sense, enjoy its own internal cogency or logic; and this language can also signify a world beyond the language per se, a world that becomes the arbiter of the language's *rectitude*. For Augustine, the palpable world had to be "read" or interpreted in order to arrive at the truth of it, because it was at best an imperfect reflection of the real. For Anselm, this imperfect reflection becomes the standard for measuring the worldly power of any given statement. Augustine's view of words and statements was that, even as they were a part of a world, a world as an imperfect reflection of the divine truth, they were nevertheless derived from the world they sought to represent; they were in keeping with that world, intrinsically of a piece with it. Here again we find a connection back to the ancients. For Augustine's, and Anselm's, ideas are much like those of the earlier Stoics who viewed words as being "[automatically correlated] with the material and corporeal realities for which

---

[27] The first two lines of the translation here represent Goldin's emendation of his published translation, when this book was in manuscript.

they [stood]" (Colish "Stoic Theory" 19). With Anselm, however, the hierarchy of natural speech is transformed. Augustine's speech was natural in its "automatic correlation" to the manifest world, yet his doctrine never fully recognized an integrity to language in and of itself, an integrity separate from the world the language aspired to signify. Conversely, as we have seen, Anselm calls *natural* that speech which need not signify any reality other than itself (even as he ascribes to language a *rectitude* that takes the capacity for actual, objective reference as its criterion for validation, where such rightness is the function of human will and judgment).

Marcabru is surely, if unconsciously, echoing the Stoic distinction between the articulate human voice and the meaningless, inarticulate sounds made by animals, when in his songs he sets himself apart from the others (troubadours and joglars) who are without mature speech, perhaps without any speech whatsoever (as in, "Trobador, ab sen d'enfanssa"). At best, they, make sounds that would approximate true discourse but are finally meaningless, like the sounds of animals, (for these others are the "gen canina"). Marcabru's point, of course, is in keeping with Anselm's belief that a decision made of one's own free will is superior to a reflex action (*De Veritate* 4–5).[28] Likewise, for Marcabru true eloquence can only result when an individual is engaged in a fully reflective process. It is then that individuals can be said to have songs of their own, songs possessed of *razos* (i.e., rationality in the sense of argument or theme), harmony and poetic integrity. We find *razos* especially contrasted, Paterson writes, in Marcabru's depiction of a bluejay as "an image of pride and discord" (in "Quan l'aura doussana bufa"), which draws on a tradition that saw the jay as a gossip and "imitator of other bird's songs." As well, those cries were ugly (36–37):

Quan l'aura doussana bufa,
E·l gais, desotz lo brondel,
Fai d'orguoil li ramel,
Ladoncs deuri' hom chausir
Verai' amor ses mentir
C'ab son amic non barailla.
(1–6)

When the gentle wind blows,
And the jay beneath the twig
puffs itself up with pride and disdain,
and the branches are shady,
then one ought to choose true, undeceiving love,
which causes no strife with its lover.[29]

What is perhaps clear in the poetic discourse of Guillem, Marcabru and other troubadours is not simply the recognition that language can be possessed of

---

[28] Cf. Colish, "Stoic Theory," 40.
[29] Trans. Paterson.

plenitude, clarity, and thus can be truly glorious, but that there is another possibility, which is that language can be empty, even tragically narcissistic and self-involved, so that it is no longer capable of conveying truth in the sense that Anselm speaks of *rectitude*. Such a language, for Marcabru particularly, will set its user beyond the pale of courtly (*lege*: human) society, and so the language is not only ultimately useless but pernicious too.

As has been touched upon already (in Chapter One), what Anselm initiated, in effect, by raising an intellectual system to a level commensurate with a moral one, was the contemplation of a language that could be untrue or rather irresponsible vis-à-vis objective reality. He accomplished this when he "[obliterated] the distinction between lies and falsehoods drawn by" Augustine. Anselm assigned *rectitudo* to the classification of *accident*, while he spoke of "the semantic or natural *veritas* of propositions" (Colish 40).[30] Anselm also distinguished, as has been said, between mere reflex action and intentional act. How, therefore, might language mediate a relationship between the objective world and individual decision-making? Marcabru's *trobar naturau*, as if consciously comprehending both Augustine and Anselm, includes what is within as well as beyond the pale, in the sense that Marcabru "is concerned with what is in harmony with nature and outside it, 'segon natura et estiers'" (Paterson 29-30). It is precisely this harmony that is at stake in Anselm's presumption. Ironically, perhaps, we see this most acutely in his attribution of the term "natural" (*naturaliter*) to any statement that might possess an "intrinsic truth" (*veritas*), a decidedly internal, "logical and grammatical cogency" (Colish 40) even when such cogency does not coincide with anything in the real world. This sort of statement can be made unintentionally, just as a statement possessing rectitude may require intention. In these terms, then, Marcabru most profoundly seeks to restore an older order that reaches back in time to before Anselm, while the poet necessarily employs the terminology and concepts that he probably shared with the nearly contemporary theologian.[31]

---

[30] All the same, this distinction "should not be [interpreted as] Anselm's apparent neglect of ethics" (Colish 40).

[31] My point here and as it develops in the next pages is especially important to my overall argument, and it is also a controversial one. I hope to move the debate about *trobar naturau* closer to a resolution. Harvey, for instance, writes that *trobar naturau* is Marcabru's "concept of natural composition [which] involves philosophical, moral and artistic considerations." The synergy, if you will, of Marcabru's world view and textual praxis will be taken up shortly. But let us begin this discussion now, just the same, with Harvey's subsequent remarks. She says that Marcabru's *trobar naturau* "may be understood as a conscious attempt to express, partly by means of nature symbolism used in the tradition of biblical exegesis, a spiritual and moral message derived from the divinely-established, harmonious order which is discernible in nature by those who possess the 'whole' way of thinking" (34). Here she cites A. Roncaglia's essay, "Riflessi di posizione Cistercensi nella poesia del XII secolo," which locates *trobar naturau* within contemporaneous philosophical and theological contexts, and, "*Trobar clus*: discuzzione aperta"; regarding Marcabru's use of nature imagery and symbolism, she also cites the third chapter of Topsfield's *Troubadours and Love*, as well as Paterson, 28-41. In contrast, and

Marcabru especially locates these language problems within the social sphere. *Trobar naturau* includes rationalism and intellectualism in its vision of the world (Paterson 29–32), but it sees this rationalism as a necessary component in a world harmony. Similarly, John of Salisbury saw rhetoric as a necessity in any system of thought that might accurately comprehend society and its larger sustaining world. The *Metalogicon* proclaims that "[r]hetoric is the beautiful and fruitful union between reason and expression. Through harmony, it holds human communities together."[32] In *Entheticus*, John restates Cicero's view of rhetoric (in *De Officiis* I.50), which has its roots in Posidonius and Isocrates; in the poem reason and speech, acting in conjunction with each other, create the foundation for manners

---

in all fairness, I offer this heavily documented passage from Van Vleck, concerning the medieval Provençal word *naturals*:
> [A]fter Roncaglia's study of the term, especially in "'Trobar clus'—discussione aperta," [. . .] it is no longer satisfactory to associate Marcabru's *trobar natural* [sic] primarily with "the moral symbolism of colours and natural objects, trees, plants, animals, insects and birds" (Topsfield ["The 'Natural Fool' in Peire d'Alvernhe, Marcabru, and Bernart de Ventadorn"] 1155). Of special interest for understanding the term *naturals* are Roncaglia's citations [in "'Trobar clus'—discussione aperta" 46, quoting *Scolia Vindobonensia ad Horatii Artem Poeticam*, ed. J. Zechmeister] from medieval Latin rhetorical theory, where the "natural" and the "artificial" are two types of word order or narrative sequence: "Naturalis ordo est, si quis narret rem ordine quo gesta est; artificialis ordo est, si quis non incipit a principio rei geste, sed a medio, ut Vergilius in Aeneide" ("The natural order is when someone narrates a thing in the order in which it was done; the artificial order is when someone does not begin at the beginning of the thing done, but in the middle, as Vergil did in the Aeneid"). The "natural order," then, is historical—structured by the idea that an event to be told has a beginning, an order, and an end. [Yet] most troubadour's *joi natural* persistently shows itself to be the opposite of "natural" in this sense, for it is anti-historical.
> (141)

But Von Vleck is already taking us far afield, and I will try to address her concerns later on. Here, though, I must return to Harvey, in order better to position my current discussion, who also cites R. N. B. Goddard's doctoral thesis, "The Early Troubadours and the Latin Tradition," which, according to her description (211–12),
> situates Marcabru's use of the term and concept of *natura* in the broad context of contemporary philosophical interests and movements but, while he concedes that the expression *trobar naturau* may be used by Marcabru in this quasi technical sense, he casts doubt on the interpretation [of previous] scholars of "nature" and "natural" as terms always loaded with a particular learned significance. He argues that in Marcabru's works "natural" can often be translated simply as "instinctive, innate, inner," that he frequently employs nature imagery to negative effect, to evoke sterility and discord, and that Marcabru's songs, rather than demonstrating a particular debt to the exegetical and mystical traditions, more probably dimly mirror these scholastic preoccupations.
> (260–66)

Obviously, I hope to show that there was something more than a dim reflection.

[32] Pp. 7, 13 ff.; paraphrased in Curtius, 77.

and society.[33] John is of course partaking of an old tradition. Augustine before him, a trained rhetorician, viewed discourse and textuality generally as central in his cosmology. Similarly, he held that language was integral to all meaning, intrinsic to the unfolding of world events (albeit it was seen by him to be opaque, in the Pauline sense of vision in a dark mirror). Centuries later, Isidore constructs his *Etymologarium* predicated on the belief that the "intrinsic meaning of an object [could be discovered] through often hypothetical etymology" (Paterson 31); his procedure was a direct outgrowth of Pauline typology as well as the Augustinian notion that the objects of the world contained hidden meanings, meanings capable of being deciphered; this belief had led to interpretation of Scripture and all literature of Latin antiquity "in the light of supposed symbolic meanings" they contained (31). And, according to Isidore, words possessed a natural hidden force that could be disclosed through etymology. [34]

The idea of world unity, implicit in the notion that experience can be decoded and elucidated, which meant that there was a harmony among the world's elements, was revealed in the language of Occitan and particularly in the use of that language. The troubadour manipulation of language discloses an opportunism, and it also suggests that the poet's attitude toward language was like his or her attitude toward the world. Marcabru defined this epistemological construct most profoundly in his ability to exploit the philosophical view that a fundamentally intimate relationship existed between language and the manifest world; moreover, he did so in order to talk about poetry and, ultimately, about himself, the poet who was at least as worthy, at least as noble, as the poem he created.

If the "major innovation Augustinian rhetoric offers is the valorization of desire, or will," as Sarah Spence contends (in *Rhetorics of Reason and Desire: Virgil, Augustine, and the Troubadours* 114), then will becomes the "motivating force of persuasion"; in a model of discourse in which will must be present in both speaker and listener, so that the language of the discourse may have an effect, we can note an inherent relationship between language and will, on the one hand, and, on the other, "a dialogue of powers in which reason is balanced by faith and will." Consider the rich pastoral scene of a song such as "Bel m'es can s'esclarzis l'onda," in which Marcabru insinuates himself among the many birds—each possessing its own language—with the poet capable of singing better than any of them. He sings best of all because of a "joyful understanding":

[33] Eloquii si quis perfecte noverit artem,
    Quodlibet apponas dogma, peritus erit.
Transit ab his tandem studiis operosa juventus
    Pergit et in varias philosophando vias,
Quae tamen ad finem tendunt concorditer unum,
    Unum namque caput Philosophia gerit.
    (in Curtius, 77)

[34] "Etymologia est origo vocabulorum. cum vis verbi vel nominis per interpretationem colligitur [. . . .] Nam cum videris unde ortum est nomen, citius vim eius intelligis." *Patrologia Latina* LXXXII.105.

> Bel m'es can s'esclarzis l'onda
> E qecs auzels pel jardin
> S'esjauzis segon son latin;
> Lo chanz per lo(s) becs toronda,
> Mais eu tropo miels qe negus.
>
> Qe scienza jauzionda
> M'apres c'al soleilh declin
> Laus lo jorn, e l'ost' al matin,
> (1-8)
>
> It pleases me when the wave grows bright
> and each bird in the garden
> rejoices according to its own language;
> the singing gushes from their beaks,
> but I compose better than any.
>
> For joyful understanding taught
> me to praise the day at sunset
> and my host at sunrise (to count my blessings) [. . .].[35]

Marcabru has deftly aligned his ability to sing—to compose poetry—with the natural cycles of the sun; thus the confirmation of his poetic powers is effected, not merely by his bald assertion that he is the poet par excellence, but by comparing himself with nature in which he derives a joyous comprehension of the world. He is suggesting that his own cycles of composition, his very intention to make poetry, are as true as the cycles of the day and night, the seasons, and so on. In this poem the season is spring, a fact that is especially significant. The nature opening is part of an ancient literary tradition. Yet it should be noted that Marcabru stands out within it, and particularly so among his contemporaries, in his use of the topos to instigate a trenchant investigation into the relationship between the world and himself and, more importantly, between the world and his ability to compose verse. In that verse, as we have seen, he establishes a dialectic. Harvey asserts that his

> use of the nature opening [. . .] refers to the moral state of the world as the mainspring of his poetic inspiration, rather than to the mood of the season alone. He represents the natural world as being in conflict with the spiritual state of man, and this is particularly clear in those poems which contain a spring opening. [. . . .] While there may be an initial harmony with spring, with the natural world [. . .] the corruption of the rest of the world conflicts with the natural *ambiance* and this discord is the subject of [the poem's] remaining stanzas [. . .].
> (44-45)

We need only return to "Per savi" to realize the full import of Marcabru's strategy:

---

[35] Trans. Paterson.

> Per savi·l tenc ses doptanssa
> cel qui de mon chant devina
> so que chascus motz declina,
> si cum la razos depleia, [. . .].

Here we see that the true reader, who we must presume possesses the joyful wisdom that understanding of the natural world and one's place in it brings, will be able to "divine" the structure, rationale (*razos*) and purpose of Marcabru's song. There is no doubt ("ses doptanssa") about this, for the poet is in step with the progression of the world's events—as we see precisely in his song that represents him: wise persons will appreciate how each word unfolds ("declina"), much as the day and night are disclosed naturally according to the declination of the sun, as we see in "Bel m'es can." Humanity experiences, Spence writes, a "necessary distance from God and truth" (109), but rather than be frustrated by it, Marcabru adopts the fundamentally Augustinian position of *De Doctrina Christiana* in his realization that the "gap provides necessary room in which [a] divine spark can occur" (Spence 109). The poem's Pauline echo, from I Corinthians[36] ("paraul' escura"), moreover, is used to full effect as both poet and reader—indeed, as all members of a society essentially defined by their joyful wisdom—engage in an Augustinian struggle to tease out ("d'esclarzir") from an opaque and symbolically rich language the transparency of the truth. This struggle also finds a parallel in Jerome's dictum that, in translation, the spiritual meaning of a text should be "extorted"—"*exprimere*"—from the *littera*.

To elucidate the truth, finally, is for Marcabru to restore a unity in the world, a unity that has been threatened by all misusers of language who create the fractures in discourse and perception and thus cloud the truth. In "Lo vers comens quan vei del fau" he attacks these misusers of language, the "buzzing, petty troubadours who [would] confuse the truth" ("menut trobador bergau / entrebesquill," 9–10). And when Marcabru writes in "Doas cuidas ai, compaigner" that "In two ways of thinking, I am anxious to distinguish the broken from the whole" ("En do cuidars ai conssirier / A triar lo frait de l'entier," 9–10),[37] he is elaborating his "theme of imprecise and corrupting use of words [as] bound up with [his] concept of 'dos cuidars', the 'entier' and the 'frait', the right and illusory ways of thinking" (Paterson 10). He is attacking other poets who are "[incapable or who simply refuse] to distinguish good love from bad, truth from what is false, and their fault is clearly bound up with the way they express themselves in song. Bad love results in bad poetry" (Harvey 33).

Such a perception of this fractured language, a language lacking the capacity to denote objective reality, yet which might seem to be capable of doing so, is akin to Anselm's postulation of a *naturally* occurring language that is "natural" despite the fact that it does not comply with any objective truth. Such speech is in some sense false; that is, in its lack of objective reference, ironically perhaps, it suggests that

---

[36] 13.12
[37] Trans. Paterson.

the natural world exists in opposition to truth, and if so then the use of this language will sow confusion and doubt. Marcabru's task—to restore truth and certitude, to reassociate these values with the workings of the phenomenal world, a world from which he derives a "joyful understanding"—drives him to compose his songs. The desire to accomplish the task is driven by his intention based on his consideration of the world, and on its inspiration. To accomplish this task is to return to the Augustinian vision of truth as discourse, to the unity embodied in the notion of a world text.

Certain basic assumptions underlie a poem like "Per savi." Viewed in their context, the poem represents the later Middle Ages' shifted and enlarged apprehension of time, the society's conception of *auctoritas* within an overall hieratic framework, and the developing claim for individual poetic authority in the light of a specifically *literary auctoritas*, on the part of the poets of that society. Marcabru's poem represents the cultural nexus of an older, dying culture, and a newer, literate culture in which we witness the individual poet's struggle for singular recognition. The poetic "I" of medieval Provençal verse is deeply ambiguous; Marcabru is an exemplary courtly man, and he is also an individual creator and observer. The songs he writes are precisely *about* his struggle to solve the palpably binary nature of his existence. They convey the sense of that struggle through both their discourse and their poetics. Furthermore, the poems display the intersection of the two intellectual streams that provide the language and thus the thought processes of a "modern" culture, in which individuals define themselves as much *against* the past and hierarchical authority as from within it. Particularly the thinking of Aristotle, Cicero and Quintilian, as they are appropriated in the twelfth century, presides over the birth of the literate and modern world of individuals who feel compelled to *inscribe* themselves within the collective text of their society.

At its deepest level, Marcabru's song "Per savi" reveals an anxiety over the possibility of being kept silent; or rather, it concerns itself with the question of whether or not the poet will be able to speak, to sing, to utter an existential truth. At the poem's surface, therefore, its discourse takes up the question of poetic form that is the manifestation of the broader and generative form of *fin' amors*. The poem asks and also answers the question for itself. The new poetry is an authentic language, a language capable of conveying a true assessment of the changing experiential landscape.

The binary oppositions that form the matrix of this discourse are several: love versus lust, poetry versus mere metrics—and, perhaps at the root of these opposites, *razos* versus chaos or disorder. In invoking *razos*, moreover, the poet comprehends a debate about whether or not narrative is a discourse capable of conveying truth: the nature of time,[38] the empirical validity of history, and the ontological validity of the literary impulse, are all thus also invoked in the poetic attempt at speaking or singing the truth—that is, at rendering an accurate verbal description of reality. Interpretive strategies common to exegesis, according to Allen (in *The Friar as Critic* 42 ff.), were appropriated by writers of fiction. As Gellrich comments, however, purely literary endeavors in the later Middle Ages did not simply replicate, mirror and otherwise repeat the inherited "matter" of Scripture and antiquity—an operation that was "[grounded] in the Platonic and Augustinian concept of imitation" (25)—but rather the rewriting of the past in the hands of poets like Dante, Chaucer and Langland, was constituted of "a new kind of interpreting, one that no longer allow[ed] for the straightforward validation of meaning in an 'old book', the sequence of events, or the voice of a speaker." The "convention of imitation" was usually undermined "by casting the narrator in the role of copyist or reporter" (26). What Gellrich calls the inherited "book of culture"—essentially defined by the Church Fathers' exegetically sanitized versions of Scripture and pagan myth—

> leaves no doubt that it is a true account of the cosmos, history, nature, and the afterlife. Medieval fictions, in contrast, specialize in doubt, and while they also delight in religious values, they remain basically different from, if not opposed to, the myth of the book of culture.
> (48)

What constitutes the opposition here is a recognition to be found in Plato's *Phaedrus* as well as the *Republic*, yet which can also be found in Boccaccio's *De Genologia Deorum*—that fiction has a sense of how it creates illusion, and that it operates based on the presumption that those who read it will embrace its untruths (Gellrich 48).[39] A poet like Dante understands literature to be for the sake of his reader in the sense that his "poem is less an allegory of history than a reflection of the reading process, with all its limitations in the uncertainty of meaning and the temporality of understanding" (Gellrich 24). Thus fictional narrative procedures of this sort are significations that destabilize logocentrism as never before "in the pages of the grammarians and exegetes, and the question about locating the authority of meaning in an origin or text is postponed indefinitely [. . .]" (24). We clearly witness such a destabilization in obvious ways, such as the profoundly unreliable narrator to be found in the greater part of Chaucer's work. Chaucer's persona is a "mere" reporter who warns us of the questionable accuracy of his narrative due to the fallibility of both perception and memory.

The destabilizing force is what a modern reader would quickly identify as the element of play. In *Homo Ludens* (179), Johan Huizinga noted that the Middle

---

[38] Perhaps the various forms of time—diachronic, narrative, retrospective and eschatological, and atemporal—as discussed in Chapter One. Cf. Le Goff, 78–79.
[39] *Phaedrus*, 275AB (cf. Gellrich 33 and n. 6); the *Republic* II (cf. Hazard Adams, *Critical Theory since Plato*, 22–23; and Gellrich, 47 and n. 31). Regarding *De Genologia Deorum*, cf. especially Boccaccio on poetry, 63 (and cf. Gellrich 47).

Ages

> [. . .] had inherited its great culture-forms in poetry, ritual, learning, philosophy, politics, and warfare from classical antiquity, and they were fixed forms. Medieval culture was crude and poor in many respects, but we cannot call it primitive. Its business was to work over traditional material, whether Christian or classical, and assimilate it afresh.[40]

It is in the context of a tension between the authority of the past and the contemporary maker of text that we ought to read a poem like the *Commedia*, because the allegory at the heart of this work, Gellrich comments,

> [. . .] consists in the structure of temporal distance between the originary *liber* of God, envisioned in the sky at the end of the poem, and the book of written efforts to explain the experience of its meaning. The allegorical sign is constituted not by a desire to represent its referent—to have ontology—but rather by the impossibility of the sign to coincide with the full significance of its origin or end. The understanding, therefore, that the allegorical mode occasions for Dante is the recognition of the continuing desire for recovering the *volume* with which he began—both his memory and its image of God's presence. For the determination to move through the limits of language in time, to struggle with meaning, was another medieval way of realizing the desire for God.
> (165)

The parameters of what amounts to Dante's meditation on ontology and epistemology, a discourse as much philosophical as theological, will presently be taken up at length. For now, all we need to note is that there is an inherent "playfulness" in all narrative, which may be distantly signified by the Anselmian terms *natural* and *true*, insofar as narrative will always invite acts of judgment and interpretation. One sign of this emerging aspect of play in the later Middle Ages, grounded in the dialectical impulse, is of course a separation insisted upon by the individual poet, between himself or herself and both his or her own text and those texts of the past.

The fundamental charge of Marcabru's poetic enterprise is this separation. His budding narrativity is evident first of all in the pose he adopts in relation to his society. There is a pitched battle taking place between himself, the poet, and those who love falsely and who are untrue in the very language they use. As a poet, Marcabru is steeped in the rhetorical tradition. His diction consistently resonates earlier Latin meanings that are the conveyors of that tradition. "Per savi" is built out of such terminology, and the poem is precisely organized according to the structure of medieval *dispositio*; "the ideas in [the poem are] clearly arranged, [. . .] the Rhetorical structure [coinciding] with an especially strong concern to clarify, define, and argue his ideas on love" (Paterson 18-19). Marcabru's songs, in fact, are definable both in terms of medieval rhetoric and dialectics, while the power and

---

[40] Cf. Gellrich, 49.

ingenuity of his *trobar naturau* is like contemporary Scholasticism's understanding of the phenomenal world; for instance, there is a similarity of temperament, as well as point of view, between Marcabru's *trobar naturau* and Hugh of St. Victor's development of natural theology. As Copleston writes,

> Hugh contributed to the systematic advance of natural theology by giving *a posteriori* arguments both from internal and external evidence. As regards the first line of proof, it rests upon the experiential fact of self-consciousness, the consciousness of a self which is "seen" in a purely rational way [. . .]. (*Medieval Philosophy* I.197)

Of special importance is the fact that dialectical procedures, which might be structured according to the precepts of rhetorical *disputatio*, let us say, gave rise to poetic forms like the *partimen* (such as, for example, "Amics Marchabrun, car digam" by Marcabru and Ugo Catola). As it "came to dominate the trivium" in the twelfth century, Glynnis Cropp points out (in "The *Partimen*" 95), dialectics "had the special task of being used to distinguish true from false, in contrast with rhetoric, which could be used on behalf of both." Hence, in its examination of dialectics, the *Leys d'amor*, for instance, reveals the peculiar cast of Augustine and Cassiodorus both. Augustine had written, "Qui enim disputat, verum discernit a falso"; and Cassiodorus similarly claims, "Vera sequestrat a falsis."[41] Likewise, the *Leys d'amor* sharpens the powers of discernment.

> Dialecta ensenha tensonar, contendre e disputa e far questios, respostas e defensas la us contra l'autre e mostrar per dreyta razo e per vertadiers argumens la vertat e la veraya oppinio de la questio moguda.
>
> Dialectic teaches one how to argue, contend, dispute and to compose questions, answers and defence in opposition to one another and to show by sound reasoning and by truthful argument the truth and the correct opinion about the question set.[42]

Dialectics had once been "viewed as a snare set to trap the believer," according to James J. Murphy (in *Rhetoric in the Middle Ages* 46); thus Hilary of Poitiers' *De Trinitate* celebrates truth for its innate resistance to "marvelous devices of perverted ingenuity" as were contained in Arian logic (VII.1).[43] But dialectics came to be regarded as the means for arriving at truth, which in turn allowed for the manipulation of others through the ability to prevail in dialectically structured argument. For example, Peire de Corbiac's thirteenth-century encyclopedia offers the following, as a definition for dialectic.

> Per Dialectica sai arrozonablemens a pauzar e respondre e falsar argumens, sofismar e conduire, e tot gignozamens menar mon aversaire ad inconveniens.

---

[41] In Cropp, 110, n. 13.
[42] [T].I, p. 81, ed. Anglade, *Las Leys d'Amors*; in Cropp, 95, and 110, n. 14.
[43] In Murphy, 46.

> Through dialectic I know to present a case and reply and falsify arguments by reasoning, to use sophistries, to conduct and lead my adversary quite cunningly into discomfiture.[44]

For his part, Marcabru "attributed to the troubadour the legal role of 'investigator, defender and inquisitor' in the enquiry into the truth about love" (Cropp 95). Note, for instance, these lines from "Al son desviat":

> Qu'ieu sui assatz esprovaire,
> Deffendens et enquistaire, [. . .].
> (43-44)

> For indeed I am investigator,
> defender and inquisitor, [. . .].[45]

The point here is that the poetic form of the *partimen* invites a poet "to discriminate between right and wrong (*lo dreit* and *lo tort*), to choose the better alternative" (Cropp 95). This act of discrimination is intentional, and it pertains to the manifest world that language can signify so that there is, as Anselm says, *rectitude*. Through such rhetorical and cognitive procedures, then, we can say that the discourse of a poet such as Marcabru, grounded in recent developments in dialectics, embodies a nascent assertion of individual poetic authority within the confines of a poetics that makes a convention of the individual singer. This singer, however, is understood to be a part of the larger text that comprises the song, one which subsumes the singer under its aegis.[46] In other words, the struggle to assert the individual is mirrored in the intellectual movements of the time.

---

[44] In Paterson, 26-27; cf. Cropp, 110, n. 15.
[45] Trans. Paterson.
[46] In this regard, cf. especially Zumthor, "Autobiography," 30-33.

Chapter Three

The Poet As Text, the Text As Name

Up to now, we have noted that the works of three later medieval poets—Marcabru, Dante and Langland—represent critical turning points in the development of the poetics of authorship; and we have examined some of the context of their works, so that we have begun to see how they are, in fact, these pivotal moments in a literary history. These works represent the modulations of ideas current in their respective times; their inflections, I believe, were calculated, were effected quite consciously. The ideas involved the positing of a relationship between epistemology and ontology, between, to be specific, signification and self-knowledge. Yet these poets did not merely reflect their intellectual milieux, but rather, the poets contributed to a wider intellectual awareness and perhaps set out the terms for further inquiry. Poetry was an important form of signification, to the extent, indeed, that it could even be viewed as "scientific"—whatever this term could mean at any given moment, inasmuch as its status underwent continual change over centuries. These poets realized, moreover, that the concept of textuality was at the heart of a great and ongoing enterprise involving several, often binary, problems: how could later medieval thinkers distinguish among grammar and logic, history and fiction, group and individual, language and being? The notion of *text* could be used as a metaphor, one that might be employed to make one's way through these problems, yet it often served as something much greater. The question of *presence* was important to the intellectuals of the later Middle Ages, and no less so to the poets whose esthetics exploit and nurture contemporaneous theories about presence and absence in the world at large and specifically in language, including theories regarding the possible relationship between presence in and of itself, or absence in and of itself, in linguistic expression and in the reality beyond it.

We see this textual dynamic uniquely at work in Dante, who can be viewed as *the* pivotal writer within the historical development of the poetics of authorship. He is pivotal because in the *Commedia* his persona takes his name as well as his vocation as poet. More than this, the persona is on a pilgrimage toward a truth that will have to be described in mere language. Even poetry, arguably language's most exalted phenomenon, cannot relate the full truth of the pilgrim's experience. "Language fails" at the *Commedia*'s terminus, writes Glenn C. Arbery (in "Adam's First Word" 42), "but in its failure it addresses the Light in whom its failure is meaningless; by means of that address, the reader's mind necessarily turns toward the divine completion of its own language-borne conception." Furthermore, like its predecessor, the voice of Marcabru's lyrics, the Dante-figure engages in an extended contemplation of language, of its very nature, and of verse particularly, its strengths and shortcomings. Here, then, we behold a fictional personage, whose very fictionality is derived from a philosophy of language, and possibly from a philosophy of history as well, which this very figure is in the process of enunciating. In other words, the poetics of authorship is once again intimately involved in the phenomenon of metatextuality, but which flourished with the spread of literacy because of the increased opportunity for abstraction and reflection a written text provides.

After Dante, the authorship trope develops in two directions. The differences between Chaucer's "Geffrey" and Langland's "Will" are taken up at length in Chapter Four. For the present, they can be understood within the context of this chapter's focus—which will be on the interchangeability of poet and text—a two-way communication to which, I believe, the later medieval poet was enormously sensitive. Even so, these two fourteenth-century poetic figures may best explain this focus, as we find it most crucially explored in Dante, because they allow us to place it within a historical continuum. Of the two, Will helps us to see the overall evolution of the authorship trope, inasmuch as another level of signification, that of theme, has been added by Langland to this figure; in his case the theme is that of *voluntas*, as noted previously. We will also see how Langland's poem, its machinery, operates as a deeply subtle criticism of allegory. *Piers Plowman* ultimately deconstructs itself; and in doing so it is implicitly commenting on the nature of allegory, and indirectly on language itself. Geffrey, all the same, also merits our attention. Chaucer uses his persona so that he, too, may talk about allegory—and, clearly, the roundness of this character, like so many of Chaucer's creations, signals the modern turn away from allegory and toward modern narrative and poetics generally. There is one instance in which either Geffrey or Chaucer himself directly comments on the Chaucer corpus—namely, in the Retraction to the *Canterbury Tales*; there is also another instance in which, without a doubt, it is Geffrey, and not this figure's author, who is challenged to defend Chaucer's works—in the Prologue to the *Legend of Good Women*, when they are being attacked by Cupid. These texts contain retrospective, authorial views that reveal an ambivalence toward allegory and a penchant for metatextuality. Chaucer and Langland, finally, in their different ways, look back on medieval poetics, but they are also looking ahead.

The legacy of Augustine determined that the concepts of writing and text would comprise the chief metaphor for truth in the Middle Ages. The Book, as image, was a primary instance of this metaphor. Its "idea," Gellrich writes, "is perpetuated in a sense of writing as a metaphor of the 'system of signified truth'" (44).[1] Writers of the later Middle Ages can assert themselves as individual *auctores* through their manipulation of this metaphor. Hence, their "fictions" are integrally, inherently, bound up with the notion of textuality, for textuality must

---

[1] Cf. 29–44, 96–101 ff.

become their ultimate subject; in the metaphor of the text lie the profoundly theological and/or philosophical issues that center themselves around the issue of signification. It was inevitable that, through a self-imposed identification with a *text*, poets would announce themselves as unique, and this was particularly true in the later Middle Ages when poets purported to speak to their audiences from the poets' very own texts; in their alignment with the issue of textuality, they made the claim that they were *the* unique text sine qua non.

They were *authors* who spoke to us in that they were themselves *texts*. On the face of it, this idea may strike the modern reader as absurd. But the power of symbolism is not to be underestimated. The fundamental poetic assertion of textuality mirrors its larger Christian world. For in the Middle Ages, as Howard Bloch has said (in *Etymologies and Genealogies* 60), "words always refer to the Word."[2] Words are the attempt to recover the divine abundance after the Fall, as follows from the sense of the relationship of part to whole established by Augustine for whom creation was, as Gellrich writes,

> a concatenation of utterances proceeding from the first Word. [. . . .] Although the primordial creation is a moment of profound differentiation, the created world and words of Augustine endure not a breach but an expansion from their origins of meaning.
> (120-21)

Augustine's expression of a sentiment such as can be found in the *Confessions* (XI.8)—that the eternal reason "is your Word, who is also the Beginning, because he also speaks to us" ("Ipsum est verbum tuum, quod et Principium es quia et loquitur nobis")—provides the basis of the traditional source for the identification of author with his text; his authority for this conception is the received notion of the Word incarnate. Furthermore, particularly in the *Confessions*, he employs the strategy of textual self-commentary. For instance, just as the distinction between divine and human discourse is being made, he parallels his own act of writing

> with the creating *Verbum*: while there is nothing similar in essence between them, the first nonetheless is profoundly involved in the second by virtue of the differentiation they both carry out. The strategy through which the text comments on itself occurs at various points when Augustine speaks of *haec verba*, but it is particularly emphatic in the interrogative mood, with which the chapter closes: "By what word of yours was it announced that a body might be created, from which these words might be created?" ("Ut ergo fieret corpus unde ista verba fierent, quo verbo a te dictum est?").
> (Gellrich 120)

---

[2] Cf. Gellrich, 121.

Through such an alignment, medieval authors also make possible their emergence from a textual tradition as entities distinct from it, and from their own "new" texts as well, which they are at the moment creating.

After Augustine, we see the way for this assertion prepared in the development of dialectical thought, which in its ability to atomize systems makes possible the fundamental bifurcating transformation of poetry into double voiced discourse, a human discourse that will eventually lead to, as William McClellan writes (in "Bakhtin's Theory of Dialogic Discourse" 485), "the structural complexity and heterogeneity" of a work like the *Canterbury Tales*. Chaucer's works, in many respects, are a far cry from the *Confessions*. Yet in Augustine's thought, and in later treatises on dialectics, we can locate the ground for the eventual differentiation that occurs. We can also find the split in the earlier period of the troubadours. The differentiation entails the poet standing back from his or her text.

Poets like Marcabru, Dante, Chaucer and Langland establish themselves as readers and commentators, and of course as the authors of their texts. Using Bakhtin's theory of dialogic discourse as a model for reading medieval texts, McClellan has analyzed Chaucer's texts in a way that can demonstrate their filiations with seminal works like the *Confessions* as well as with other contemporary or near contemporary writing. The "Clerk's Tale," for instance,

> is one of the tales where Chaucer was experimenting with multi-voiced narrative discourse. The combination of vari-directional discourse and the decrease in objectification of the narrative voice results in a mode of discourse where several different narrative voices participate in the tale's narration. These heterogeneous voices can conveniently be identified as the Petrarchan voice of moral allegory, the clerkly voice of humanistic pathos, and the nominally Chaucerian voice of grotesque parody. These different voices are not, however, completely autonomous voices. Although the tendency toward the radical extreme of complete splitting has progressed sufficiently to make these different voices distinctly identifiable, they are only relatively autonomous. They are still intertwined with each other; they form a conceptual bond; that is, they constitute a dialogic relationship.
> (483)

Fourteenth century narrative possibilities, such as we see in Chaucer, exhibit the tension between past and present to the extent that there is a struggle for a unique point of view that must emerge out of a world view that insists upon homogeneity. The effect of such writing, Gellrich comments,

> is to see the past and present from a different perspective, and that difference compares with the objectivity sought by scholars in the renaissance who wanted to separate themselves from medieval tradition by understanding the past in its own right before [Christological] time put meaning upon it. Medieval fictions certainly brought about no Copernican revolution. But the difference of myth from fiction

figures prominently in the separation of "Middle Ages" from "Renaissance" [...]. (50)

Fourteenth-century nominalism is a mark of this shift toward modern historicization—just as it is a contributor to further changes in narratology. The same can be said for an increasing reliance, among intellectuals, on empiricism as it came to apply to a budding physical science. So too, fiction writing might also have contributed to alterations in the modes of signification. We see this transformation serving as the fabric of Chaucer's writing. But Marcabru, Dante and Langland are the pivotal poets whose works exhibit intellectual developments that will include what we may call a "poetics of the text." All four of these poets align themselves with their texts in progressively complex, subtle and powerful ways. The development of fictional narrative poetry makes possible the creation of figures or characters who represent the poet, and who therefore are at a remove from their author-signifiés as a part of the poetic texts. Yet they are used to maintain a link with their authors; this maneuver is most readily discernible in the fact that these figures bear the names of their authors and are often portrayed, to one extent or another, within the contexts of many of the events of the authors' real lives. That is to say, we know something of the lives of Dante and Chaucer; we know little if anything about Marcabru, and a poet like Langland presents a slightly different problem, as we shall see.

By the fourteenth century, especially but not exclusively as concerns an increasingly popular dream vision genre, the author's act of "signing" his or her text took a wide variety of forms, as George Kane first demonstrated in *Piers Plowman: The Evidence for Authorship*, such as overt naming, cryptograms, anagrams, codes of alphabetic numbers, "acrostics and syllabic disarrangement with punning effect," at times employing macaronics (54). This naming could, moreover, extend to other real personages in the poet's life. A rondel by Eustace Deschamps is a good example of how subtle and clever such signatures can be:

Les noms sarez du seigneur et servent
*Cou*vertement en ce rondelet *cy*
Maiz diviser les vous fauldra ainsi:

Une silabe prendrez premierement
Du second ver et la fin autressy:
Les noms sarez du seigneur et servent
*Cou*vertement en ce rondelet *cy*.

En reversent prendrez subtivement
En derrain ver troiz petiz mos de li:

> *A ce eust* bien un autre defailli.
> Les noms sarez du seigneur et servent
> *Cou*vertement en ce rondelet *cy*,
> Mais diviser les vous fauldra ainsi.[3]
> (my emphases)

Kane writes of this poem that its "essence [. . .] is the technical ingenuity applied to compliment" Deschamps' patron, Coucy, who is signified by the combination of the first and last syllables of the poem's second, seventh and eleventh lines. But Deschamps' true poetic mastery is revealed in his ability "covertly [to name] patron and poet together" in a poem whose subject is such naming. Deschamps succeeds in aligning himself with his patron, within "an exacting lyrical form," while in doing so he associates himself with that form (68), which is his text—note Deschamps' signature in the poem's tenth line, his name embedded in the poem in reversed syllabic order.

Kane claims that the "poem has, in effect, no other meaning"—or we may presume no other purpose—than to signify Coucy and his poet (the "seigneur et servent" respectively). This judgment is needlessly reductive, however, as it misses an important goal of this poem. The poem's first line announces a submotif that establishes a logical pretext for the clever acts of naming, one which, I believe, would not have gone unnoticed to a contemporary audience. Both Deschamps and Coucy are elevated in stature precisely because they are *named*, and, again, the entire poem is a discussion of how naming occurs, of how language functions. Furthermore, we should note that the poem is self-reflexive; the poem's naming is being presented as an integral part of a particular genre, the "rondelet," which has been pressed into the service of a rather cool discussion about how exactly the poem goes about signing both its author and his patron (in so doing, implicitly signing itself as the agency of such naming)—but as a subtext of the rondel form. The signatures covertly ("Couvertement") insinuate the purpose of the poem, the poem's ultimate end, which is also, we are left to conclude, the poem's instigation. In other words, it might not be too farfetched to say that the poem is about the act of naming; the discourse of the poem suggests that its very genre, in this instance the rondel, has been created for, or at least is presently serving, the act of nomination. Deschamps' poem is particularly powerful for its ability to encapsulate the linguistic and epistemological theories of his time in a few circular, well turned and symmetrical lines, which offer a polish, an esthetics of finish, which in turn suggests perhaps a benign and airy innocence, even a pseudo-childishness. Yet, at the same time, the poem not quite secretly carries out a serious and penetrating examination of language forms, a demonstration of how language works. What is more, the implication is that the architecture of language either mirrors or can be used to structure human society, to promote and advance certain individuals while, it might occur to the poem's readers, language can also

---

[3] *Oeuvres*, 1880, iv, p. 114; in Kane, 68.

be the downfall of others.

Indeed, the poem indulges in detail concerning the ways of linguistic signification, which brings to mind Robert O. Payne's observation (in "Late Medieval Images" 250 ff.) regarding Deschamps' friend, Chaucer. In Deschamps' rondel constructed personae are deeply, textually embedded. Chaucer's *House of Fame* carries on a discourse concerning the dynamic of language and idea, as being grounded in the physicality of experience. The character of the eagle establishes the basis for one of Chaucer's ongoing preoccupations: not merely an author's ability "to speak" with his present audience, but with future readers as well. The issue of what constitutes a sentence, a word, a syllable—all of which is raised by Deschamps in his rondel—is echoed in Chaucer. Or perhaps Deschamps was echoing Chaucer. One poem is decidedly more comical and irreverent than the other, yet this difference may be exactly unimportant to the poems' shared agenda:

> Loo, this sentence ys knowen kouth
> Of every philosophres mouth,
> As Aristotle and daun Platon,
> And other clerkys many oon;
> And to confirme my resoun,
> Thou wost wel this, that spech is soun,
> Or elles no man myghte hyt here;
> Now herke what y wol the lere.
> "Soun ys noght but eyr ybroken,
> And every speche that ys spoken,
> Lowd or pryvee, foul or fair,
> In his substance ys but air;
> For as flaumbe ys but lythted smoke,
> Ryght soo soun ys air ybroke.
> But this may be in many wyse,
> Of which I wil the two devyse,
> As soun that cometh of pipe or harpe.
> For whan that a pipe is blowen sharpe,
> The air is twyst with violence
> And rent; loo, thys ys my sentence;
> Eke, whan men harpe-strynges smyte,
> Whether hyt be moche or lyte,
> Loo, with the strok the ayr tobreketh;
> And ryght so breketh it when men speketh.
> (I.757–80)

Speech here, for Chaucer, is a natural sign, much in the vein of Augustine's set of semiological distinctions. In fact, Augustine employs the example of smoke as a natural, unintentional sign of fire in *De Doctrina Christiana* (II.1. through II.3; cf. Chapter One). Chaucer makes the analogy for sound as speech by positing that "flaumbe ys but lyghted smoke" (769).

As Augustine would have had it, the notion of speech being defined by the eagle, if it is to be likened to natural signing, embraces the concept of unintentionality. Lack of intention is perhaps at the heart of Chaucer's humor in this first book of his poem, for in one sense, to speak unintentionally cannot help but be an act devoid of decorum, judiciousness, purpose, dignity, and otherwise importance or profundity; and in the world of human affairs (versus, say, the world of animals such as an eagle, or of gods such as angels) to speak unintentionally is to forego the possibility of making meaning or in any sense being truthful. Thus the act of human speech in the postlapsarian world, and more so perhaps the act of making poetry, Chaucer is telling us, is fraught with the greatest risks. On the one hand, there is the possibility of uttering less than the full meaning experience proffers to the seer. On the other hand, one risks uttering falsehoods, banalities, and by extension blasphemies.

In any case, it is within this framework of the rehashing of current language theory that Chaucer is able, as Payne puts it, to "[manipulate] his self-image as narrator not (insofar as we can tell) for any overt psychological revelation, but to help try to define the poetic process [and therefore his poetic process]" ("Late Medieval Images" 251). It must be added that this process is one that has been made into an emblem by Chaucer, an emblem standing for the very poet who has gone to great lengths to create it, as well as to create a larger symbol system in which utterances and therefore *formal* utterances such as poetry become representations of their authors. This strategy on the part of poets like Chaucer and Deschamps partakes of the same tradition that produced a larger preoccupation with names and naming, which by extension included the notion that all particles of speech, even the letters that made up the very words of such speech, were reflections and thus in some measure representations of their divine and natural origins; that is, even letters, besides contributing to the signification of one or another meaning within a word or group of words, also signified to a degree their own ontological ground in that they bore the mark or were somehow suffused with the essence of their origins in Adam's speech of the world before the Fall.

Letters, like words, maintained a "natural" connection with the past; it was possible to trace them to their divine source. John of Salisbury in the *Metalogicon*, for example, believed that "the very application of names, and the use of various expressions, although much depends on the will of man, is in a way subject to nature, which it probably imitates" (I.14). The study of grammar was also, for John, "an invention of man"—even as it "imitate[d] nature, from which it derive[d] its origin" ("naturam tamen imitatur, et pro parte ab ipsa originem ducit"). And, as it followed that words and names bore the cachet of their origins, so too could letters, which for Isidore of Seville (according to John) were "the indices of things, the signs of words" (*Metalogicon*. I.13). Interestingly, Isidore goes on to qualify his perception when he observes that in them "there is such a power that they speak to us without voice the discourse of the absent" ("dicta absentium sine voce loquantur"; I.13).[4] The question of absence is an important one, which must be explored at some length. For the moment, we might only say that it is possible to read both Deschamps' and Chaucer's poems as containing the *presence* of their

---

[4] Cf. Gellrich, 103.

authors, even when these authors are absent from the scene of reading; in lieu of themselves, they have constructed poems that are their emblems, poems that in effect name them and therefore bring them into being. In a sense, then, it can be said that these poems strive to declare, for their poets, an ontological ground.

Of course, the role of absence in the thinking of intellectuals and poets of the Middle Ages presumes the construction of an ontological hierarchy which accounts for the phenomenon of language and which allows for a unity of experience precisely in that the language of contemporary human affairs came to be palpably linked to a historical continuum, to say nothing of a link with the more fundamental continuum of truth itself, in both a pre- and postlapsarian world. Such a philosophical outlook affords poets like Chaucer and Deschamps a ready made vocabulary, a set of metaphors and other cognitive tools they can readily bring to bear on their fascination with poetry and how it is both connected to and separated from them. Just as the word, even the letter, represents an immanent truth as well as a historical origin, so too the poem can be constructed so that its discourse will come to include an annunciation of its origins, its terms of existence, and, particularly, its very capacity to serve as the emblem of its author.

Both Deschamps' "silabe" (l. 4) and Chaucer's perception that "spech is soun" (l. 6), at their deepest levels, hearken back to the Augustinian dichotomy of phenomenal meaning and ultimate meaning, which is embodied in the image in the *Confessions* (XIII.15) of the angels' silent syllables. Addressing God, Augustine says of the angels that they

> have no need to look upon this firmament of ours or read its text to know your word. For ever they gaze upon your face and there, without the aid of syllables inscribed in time, they read what your eternal will decrees. They read your will, they choose it to be theirs: they cherish it. They read it without cease and what they read never passes away. For it is your own unchanging purpose that they read [. . .].

Augustine records in the *Confessions* the death of his mother, which suggests for him the silent will of the Divine. The "tumult" of the "flesh" ("tumultus carnis") has been silenced, as well as "every tongue and every sign" ("omnis lingua et omne signum"). Not even a "veiled parable" ("aenigma similitudinis"—literally, "obscurity of a similitude") interfered in their final conversation (IX.10). Thus, Augustine has confronted "outright," in Gellrich's words, "the irony of speaking and writing about silence"; and so he must seek

> a means of avoiding further confused wandering in the *regio dissimilitudinis*. He recognizes fully the separation between the text that the angels read "without the

syllables of time" ("sine syllabis temporum") and his own noisy, distracted reading. But he is led irresistibly toward that Book, toward the discourse that Ambrose, like the angels, read *in silentio* and that he now reads with Monica. (118)

As for Chaucer, he compounds this fundamental Augustinian dichotomy with Aristotelian notions of substance and accident to conclude, perhaps, that the last, best hope for communication lies in *poesis*. Our speech is likened to breaking wind (especially when implicitly compared with that of angels). Yet Chaucer's ongoing meditation throughout his corpus is more broadly on the nature of the past, the efficacy of the specifically literary past to bear the burden of the truth, the dichotomy of books and writing versus first hand experience. This essentially philosophical problem is most sharply drawn in the opening lines of the Prologue to the *Legend of Good Women* (which will be examined in Chapter Four). It is a great and multifaceted question of which the present discourse with the eagle is a part—a question raised finally for the purpose of staking an ontological claim for poetry, for specific poems, and ultimately for the poet who is the maker of such formal, poetic language. Chaucer must win a place for himself in the pantheon of poets through the ages. His best hope of doing so lies in the trenchant exploration of the possibilities for communication which his own and all poetry affords. Chaucer's motives and methods are not unlike those of his contemporary Deschamps; they can be used to construct a background for discerning some of the extended meanings of his rondel—and in them we can appreciate the even larger theological, philosophical resonance having to do with the question of whether language can serve ontology.

Literary signatures of the sort we find in Deschamps may seem to be relatively trite, as merely pointing to their author, simply for the purpose of assigning authorship. Yet what is the full import, for instance, of the phrase that introduces Langland's name in the line, "'I have lyued in londe', quod I, '*my name is Longe Wille*'" (my emphasis), in *Piers Plowman* (B XV.152)? The three words, *my name is*, contextualize Langland's signature. Kane rightly observes that a "common feature of signatures," such as Deschamps' "*Cou . . . cy*," especially, "is their obscurity." He writes that Langland's phrase "apparently" keys his entire signature, yet the phrase is somewhat opaque (note the possibly puzzled arrangement of *Longe Wille* to indicate, in transposition, *Wil*l*iam Lang*land). The phrase's "full meaning would be denied, it must seem, to anyone initially ignorant of the poet's surname" (Kane 69). On the other hand, the statement's direct assertion, its claim to provenance of a particular *name*, would have held a fascination for Langland's audience; the character speaking his name, who is overtly signing himself in this manner, what is more, would have had the effect of a close identification on the part of his audience.[5] Signatures could be grounded in larger, weightier matters that entered into and affected their reception. Underlying

---

[5] Cf. Middleton, "William Langland's 'Kynde Name'," for a thorough and brilliant examination of this issue, especially as it pertains to Langland's social context.

the signature's claim of a particular name was an ontological claim.

While self-naming had occurred prior to him (there is the example of Cynewulf mentioned in the Introduction), the autocitations of Marcabru signal the proliferation of authorship poetics. Marcabru names himself in several of his poems, has his poem's voice—the poem's persona—proclaim itself as "Marcabru." Thus the persona is understood under the aegis of its author. Dante's persona does *not* proclaim itself as the poet "Dante," though it is quite evident that this is the persona's name; the protagonist of the *Commedia* is actually named by Beatrice (Purg. XXX.55). Langland goes out of his way to name himself by explicitly proclaiming, "my name is Longe Wille." Despite the differences in methods of self-naming among these three poets—there is of course the progression of method culminating in Langland and Chaucer—when taken together, these differences reveal a common weltanschauung founded in the two fundamental wellsprings of the European intellectual and textual tradition, the Judeo-Christian and the Greco-Roman. As in these later medieval poets, the interweaving of classical and Christian streams can be located in Augustine's *De Doctrina Christiana*. At the end of the work's second book, subsequent to a discussion concerning the nature of signs, Augustine finally asserts that all signs will ultimately indicate the truth of the divine; in other words, all texts are ultimately univocal. Yet as much as Augustine, therefore, provides an intellectual foundation for the later medieval poetics, this poetics will also be influenced by Aquinas in the thirteenth century, who inherits Augustine's basic distrust of figurative language. In *De Sacra Doctrina* (art. 9), which echoes Dionysius, Aquinas observes that such language, in principle, must lead us away from the truth. Even so, the human condition is such that we pursue intellectually constituted truths through things known by the senses, those things from which metaphors and other figures are drawn, since all knowledge must stem from the senses. Employing the idea of dissimilarity, Aquinas concludes that such figures are a kind of necessary evil; hence, figures that are constructed to signify divine things should, by their nature, be only remotely connected to these things.

While Augustine's construction of univocity posited a world of *presence*, which could be deeply felt, Aquinas is invoking what is essentially a doctrine of *absence*, which emerges in his notion of dissimilitude and is predicated on the belief that, in our attempts to understand God, we come not to know Him but rather to see more clearly what he is not (*Summa Theologiae* Ia.1.9). This position is in keeping with Dionysian mysticism, which holds that there is a *via negativa* according "more closely with that which is ineffable." In order that humanity not attempt a comprehension of the divine in terms of worldly images, an ultimately futile attempt, Scripture uses "unlike images" that will not easily allow for comparisons, since what the "Invisible, Infinite and Unbounded" is not is what we learn of it, which is "more in accord with Its nature."[6] Thus, what Dionysius calls "'inharmonious dissimilitudes' or negative images do not risk the identification of sign with signified"—which is always a danger in Augustine's construct of univocity—"because an 'unseemly image' cannot be mistaken for that which surpasses all comparison" (Gellrich 112).

In short, what we find in all three of these thinkers—Augustine, Dionysius and Aquinas—is an acute sensitivity to the forces of absence and presence. This sensitivity, arguably, is rooted in what Auerbach (in *Mimesis* 7) has called the "foregrounded" meaning in classical mythology, a meaning that is *present*, versus the relative *absence* of meaning in the ellipticality and consequent mystery of the Bible. In Homer, for instance, we find "externalized, uniformly illuminated phenomena, at a definite time and in a definite place, connected together without lacunae [and with] thoughts and feelings completely expressed [. . .]." In contrast, biblical accounts externalize "only so much of the phenomena as is necessary for the purpose of narrative"; only the "decisive points" are made explicit, and so "time and place are undefined and call for interpretation," as do thoughts and feelings. What confronts readers of Scripture, then, is an essential mystery.[7] Exegetical practices, however, constituted an attempt to fill in the lacunae left by Judeo-Christian sources, in order to explain, in typological terms, the actions described therein. In this manner, conformity and unity could also be achieved in order to invoke a peculiarly Christological power. What amounted to a rewriting of religious history meant that the literature of this tradition that comprehended, as Gellrich puts it, "the essential secrecy and mystery of divine meanings, and an appreciation of their absence," would be rendered into an entirely new form, a form of presence deriving from the other sensibility reflected in a text like the *Odyssey* whose "'foregrounded' style of myth seems to be of a piece with the immanence of divinity in signs—the logocentric presence of meaning" (123).

It is ironic that, while medieval exegetes undoubtedly knew the difference—the presencing of classical literature, the mystery of Scripture—there might be no sign of such knowledge in their writing styles; one affect could slide "into the other, the earlier mythological form of signifying [leaving] its mark on the course of the medieval hermeneutic project" (Gellrich 123-24). This early tradition influences the thought and esthetics of the later Middle Ages when we see, within the texts of poets and theologians, an essential dance taking place between the contingencies of absence and presence. Dante, taking the thought of Aquinas into account, is a good example of this tension that, when understood, especially illuminates the Dantean triad, "io sol uno." Within this figure, the author of the *Commedia* is absent in name yet powerfully present as a poet. When read in the light of Aquinas' ideas about absence and presence generally but especially as they concern themselves with the question of language, the figure reveals Dante's sure grasp of the relationship between verbal expression and ontology. We have seen how Aquinas draws upon Augustine and Dionysius in his discussion of metaphor, which

---

[6] Trans. Eds. *Mystical Theology*, 25; in Gellrich, 112.
[7] Cf. Gellrich, 123.

in turn is determined by the larger perception that worldly reason cannot hope to describe the mysteries of the divine; regarding the Trinity, reason will never capture its *esse*, for it can only "manifest" (*manifestare*) Christian doctrine.[8] Yet in order to appreciate the Dante-Aquinas relationship fully, a brief discussion about the context of their shared ideas will be necessary, particularly as pertains to current theories about language. This discussion, in turn, will help to elucidate not only Dante's but also Marcabru's, and Langland's, pivotal roles in the development of the authorship trope as they developed within the intertwining Greco-Roman and Judeo-Christian traditions.

In the philosophically based insistence on studying the "how" of language signification, instead of the "what" that language signified, a group of later theologians, the *Modistae*, asserted that there was a separation between language and the world it attempted to describe; they sought to place language in a category unto itself. We have already examined (in the Introduction and Chapter One) how, prior to the twelfth century, this philosophical tendency can be traced back to Anselm in his use of the term *naturaliter* to designate statements that may not accurately reflect reality although they might possess an internal cogency, a kind of "truthfulness" (*veritas*), in and of themselves. Language could be seen to be self-consistent, as a consequence of progressive advances in dialectics and logic. After Aquinas, Thomas of Erfurt and other *modistae* continue the study of language. They establish the basis for perceiving language as self-sufficient by placing it squarely in the provenance of the phenomenal world—that world of human rather than divine affairs. Also, in the thirteenth century, Roger Bacon advances the idea that there is a single grammar—that is, Latin—and that this grammar is subject to physical forces and human comprehension; grammar is "one and the same according to the substance in all languages" (in Gellrich 105). In the next century, Thomas furthers Bacon's ideas; he appropriates the terms of Scholastic logic, which set form and matter in a contrastive relationship with one another, so that he can talk about language per se. Looking intensely at language as an entity unto itself, another of the *modistae*, Siger of Courtrai, found it possible to differentiate elements within language in novel ways. To be precise, Siger elevated the noun to a place of greater importance than the verb. He also made a formal distinction between a word's material appearance, its *dictio*, and its class, its *pars orationis*. Furthermore, he found there to be a difference between being, *essens* or *ens*, and understanding, *intelligens*. Lastly, he differentiated between *essens*, being-in-motion, and *ens*, being-at-rest. His decisions were based on a comparison of potentiality and actuality, which in turn was predicated on assumptions about language that he linked to natural and historical origins in the prelapsarian world.

---

[8] *Summa Theologiae* Ia.1.8, 2; cf. Gellrich, 66.

These assumptions were not unlike those of Augustine. All the same, Siger was able to make some novel observations.

In his *Summa Modorum Significandi*, Siger writes that the noun "is the mode of signifying substance, permanence, rest, or being" ("modus significandi substantiae, permanentis, habitus seu entis"). In other words, the noun is more clearly and directly rooted in the prelapsarian origin of language than is the verb. The verb, according to Siger, is a "mode of signifying becoming or being" ("modum significandi fieri seu esse")."[9] That is to say, the verb resides more in a state of activity and temporality, and, in the sense that its temporal quality causes it to be relatively transient, in comparison with the noun, the verb possesses less *presence*. Siger concludes that, in the ranking of being, nouns precede their verbs, as ontologically prior—we might presume that verbs are derived from their nouns— since his reasoning is that action (*esse*) follows being at rest (*ens*).[10]

After Siger, Thomas elaborates a further hierarchization of linguistic elements; he turns his attention to pronouns, claiming that the first person pronoun (i.e., "I") is greater than the second person (i.e., "you"), and so on. In Thomas' *Grammatica Speculativa* there are two possible modes of signifying, which derive from the active and passive forms of understanding, being and verbal moods, as delineated by Siger. Yet hierarchical superiority and ontological priority of signification had been most clearly defined by Hugh of St. Victor in the *Didascalion*, in his stipulation that all language descends from the divine Word. (Hugh, like Thomas after him, identified discourse with presence.) For Thomas, hierarchy became a function of what he called *propriety* (*proprietas*); he writes that "every active mode of signifying comes from some property of the thing [signified]" ("omnis modus significandi activus est ab aliqua rei proprietate").[11] *Proprietas* is a principle that he can apply to all elements and particles of a language, and which ultimately subsumes the possibility of human convention to what occurs naturally. As Gellrich shrewdly comments, in Thomas' thinking grammar "is imitating nature, which is in turn imitating it" (107). However, the force that invests each with the sense of plenitude is *presence*. Thomas writes that, in the demonstrative pronoun, a thing is signified by means of the "property of presence" ("proprietate praesentiae") (200–01).

The growing interest in grammar underwrites a consonant development in poetry: namely, the various uses of authorial personae, which are, more or less, present in their poems in a variety of forms. And no matter the incidental form, the authorial persona could be, and in fact was, seen in terms of its being a grammatical entity, and by extension a position within a discourse. What are the hallmarks of the relationship between grammar and poetry? What is its medieval history? In Anselm, as has been demonstrated (in previous chapters), we first see a critically new alignment of language per se with nature. This alignment also divorces the decisive criterion, in Augustine's thinking, for determining

---

[9] *Les Oeuvres de Siger de Courtrai*, 95, 108; in Gellrich, 107 and n. 33.
[10] *Summa Modorum Significandi*, 108.
[11] Ed. and trans. Bursill-Hall, 136–37.

falsehoods—the criterion of intentionality. Anselm's terminology, his changing concept of what is *natural*, drives a wedge between intentionality and the judgment of what is true or false. Now a statement can be true according to whether or not—let us say, grammatically, or else syntactically—the statement makes sense; such coherence need have nothing to do with the world beyond the statement; conversely, in Anselm's thinking, a statement may be a falsehood insofar as it does not accurately describe the experiential world. "My chair," as Anselm would have it, may not really be "upside down," and in fact I know this to be true by virtue of the fact that I am able to sit in it as I write this passage, while I am quite free to assert that "my chair is upside down," and in doing so I am using language to denote a falsity even though my statement (i.e., "my chair is upside down") is perfectly understandable; my statement, however, defies belief predicated by objectivity. Centuries later, Thomas of Erfurt feels free to prioritize various grammatical elements based on a *natural* hierarchy. The ground for his argument has been prepared by Anselm in his initial separation of intention and objective reference.

Thomas' distinction becomes important when we turn to Dante's autocitational triad, "io sol uno" and before him, to a lesser extent, Marcabru's "ieu mezeis seu" (as has been discussed in the Introduction and Chapter Two). These poets are employing words that act as pronouns would—inasmuch as words stand in for the kind of first person insistence we see later in Langland, whose dreamer will *overtly* claim for himself, in his own words, his actual name: "'I have lyued in londe,' quod I, 'my name is Longe Wille'." Thus we find a shifting tendency toward utilizing the proper noun instead of the pronoun, when citing oneself; as well, and here more importantly, in a theory like Thomas' we are seeing the endorsement of first-person citation, when he privileges the first person over the second, and the second over the third.

The effect all three poets have, by employing pronouns to represent their personae, is that they insert themselves into their texts. They are invoking their own presences, albeit, oftentimes, through the sense of absence effected by pronouns—since, grammatically, unlike nouns, pronouns have meaning only in relation to them. Hence, as he modulates the troubadour tradition of naming, Dante insists on his *presence* in his text through, paradoxically, employing a poetics of absence that is not to be confused with emptiness. He carries out this strategy at every level and in all aspects of his poem. Both his poetics and theology are based on the presence-absence conundrum, which is most acute, most illuminated, as it were, in Paradiso XXXIII when he "sets the possibilities of significance," as Arbery comments,

> into a ceaseless motion, like the circling of the stars moved by divine love. Both the text and the created world it imitates are fundamentally written, never self-present; their meanings always center on the God who is always conceptually beyond them, therefore always "present" only to the sign of the human answer. (43)

Marcabru's *ieu*, Dante's *io*, and even Langland's *I*—like Thomas of Erfurt's *ego*—are richer and more powerful than a lyrically anonymous address to a reader or listener, a rhetorical posture corresponding to Thomas' second grammatical person, *tu*. By the time of *Piers Plowman*, a poem that can be viewed as the vertex of the poetics of naming—author, persona and theme have been brought together within a single linguistic embrace that also includes a meditation on the nature of language. Langland's elaborate "signature" takes into account its own textual dimensions because it includes a discussion about, moreover, how its poem works. This self-meditation is epitomized in two corresponding phrases—phrases that also bridge two finished versions of the poem and which, when taken together, especially considering their chronological progression, disclose Langland's rewriting of Will as a more substantial character, indeed as someone who has something to say about the act of writing and no less so than from within the poem out of which he is emerging.[12] At one point, the poem states that "Grammer" is the "ground of al" (B text, XV.370), and at another, that "god" is "the grounde of al" (C text, III.353). I will have occasion to say more about this alignment of language and the divine (in Chapter Four). For now, we need only observe that the poem is built around Langland's persona. As a figure, Will represents human intentionality allegorically; he is in search of Truth, and he must struggle to understand the language that may hopefully serve that truth, including the language of poetry and ultimately of the poem *Piers Plowman*.

The linguistic "ground" of Langland's poem is abundantly fertile. It has been nourished by intellectuals and poets who have preceded it. Common to all later

---

[12] My argument presumes that the C text is the most fully realized version of Langland's endeavor, since it represents his final revision (incomplete though it is), and since, as Derek Pearsall writes in the Introduction to his edition of the C text, in that version we see Langland's "single-minded concentration on essentials [representing] the work of a man who knows what he is doing" (11); all the same—in light of my remarks in the Introduction and those of Vance et al., condoning multiple text critical approaches to the study of medieval literature—I must consider *Piers Plowman* as a poem that to a degree will always be in flux. Pearsall also writes (in "Editing Medieval Texts" 99-100) that "Langland's whole life seems to have been a prolonged and continuous act of composition," that his poem "[exists] in a state of continuous evolution," and that "[o]ne can be sure that if Langland saw the Kane-Donaldson B text, the first thing he would want to do would be to revise it." In short, I want things both ways, yet such a procedure should not foreclose on the possibility of an intimate reading of Langland's poetic and philosophical tendencies. I have not included the Z text in my examination, since it derives from a presumably early, and single witness, and since it does not include passages relevant to what I need to show primarily: the relationship between B and C, and I take the B text edition by A. V. C. Schmidt and the C text by Pearsall to be sufficiently authoritative. I also recognize, as Pearsall, says (in his Introduction), that all these editions are no doubt "merely interim statements in a continuing process of discovery" (1).

medieval poets is the understanding that moral integrity is a necessity if there is to be truthful perception and the proper use of language. Also, these poets view language as separate from themselves and as having a life of its own. Within this understanding, which evolves into a fully blown discourse, each of the poets insinuates himself. Yet another element is also injected into the discourse, one that emerges out of the linguistic dynamic—that element is the question of authorship. The issue of authorship is linked to the search for the truth; therefore, looking for one, according to the equation of the poetry, will lead the reader to the other.

The *modistae* specifically located the "discipline" of linguistics as functioning somewhere between "being" (*essens* or *ens*) and "understanding" (*intelligens*). Their construct reflects a central preoccupation among poets contemporary and nearly contemporary with them, who strove to achieve an ontological fullness through their capacity to understand their world. Since it is through the personae of these poets that the drama of this struggle is carried out, it should not be surprising to find that, for the poets, the power to understand and indeed to be redeemed was self-centered. The voice of a poem, to be identified by the listener-reader, will both lay claim to the poem's assertions while seeking its own distinction from them; that is, the voice will, in a manner of speaking, seek its own integrity. As in the Anselmian separation of objective reference and verbal coherence, by extension the poetic voice is distinguished from the poetic discourse. This distinction also reflects the original breach of language and intention that Anselm had instituted.

The use of a proper noun, like that of the first person pronoun, is the crystallization of the poet's attempt at autonomy and centrality, which, if achieved, will invest this author's, the persona's text, with a profound sense of presence. In Langland this poetics is brought to full flower, since the sine qua non in assessing autonomy and distinction is individual volition—which we see portrayed in Will. Hence the presence of the individual *voluntas* becomes the theme of *Piers Plowman*, as the poem progresses, and in fact the poem can easily be viewed as the testing ground of Langland's ideas about precisely how salvation is to be accomplished for the autonomous individual of later fourteenth-century England. Not only do we see the roots of Langland's vision in earlier theologians and philosophers, but of course in earlier poets. We see the origins of the issues Langland raises as they are centered in thinkers like Aquinas, Siger, Thomas of Erfurt, as well as Ockham; we also see these issues in the poetics of Marcabru where the question of intentionality is first raised, echoing Anselm's ideas, and then later on in the poetics of Dante. In Thomas of Erfurt, the conceptualization of the first person pronoun goes right to the heart of the poetics of all three poets, first of all because, like all the *modistae* and for many thinkers before them, what holds Thomas' attention is the *modus* of language rather than the *object* of language's reference. Likewise, Marcabru, Dante and Langland, are interested in aligning themselves with their texts, as they locate themselves or we can say as they insert themselves into their respective discourses. The discourses thematically characterize these texts. Just as what is important for Thomas is the way in which language, in and of itself, actually *works*, so too the preoccupation of the poets' discourses is with the very making of poetry and, furthermore, with the viability of poetic and by extension all linguistic expression. In the later Middle Ages both the philosophers and poets, then, are involved in an examination of self-referential systems, which they are able to separate from the world they describe, and perhaps even enact, as autonomous. Furthermore, both groups seek to ground their projects ontologically, as if poetry could be viewed as a kind of reality. From their perspective, the world of the poem is of at least equal importance with the world beyond it, that world to which it, as a minimum, purports to refer—and, too, with a philosophy of language that might enjoy the status of being a "scientific" discipline of thought unto itself.

The prioritizing of pronouns typifies this issue, for it raises the question of *presence* in language as well as in the world at large. We can recall that for Thomas *proprietas*, as a function of meaning, becomes peculiarly crucial in the case of pronouns, since, although a pronoun can only as it were stand in for a noun, it nevertheless indicates the thing the noun describes by dint of the "property of presence" ("proprietate praesentiae").[13] Of importance is the fact that he finds six indications of *presence*, the five senses as well as the intellect. This observation generally parallels the epistemological concerns that fuel the poetics of authorship of Marcabru, Dante and Langland, for these poets can only truly *be*, in their poems and in the world, if they can rightly *know* and therefore *speak* or *write*. Thomas does after all make distinctions between sensual presence and intellectual presence; there are "different modes of certainty and presence" ("diversos modos certitudinis, et praesentiae").[14] Yet even though he constructs different categories of perception, what is constant for him is that linguistic expression can convey presence; he conceives of "spoken or written utterance as a property of the presence of meaning" (Gellrich 108).

It is in distinguishing among relative degrees of *presence* that Thomas privileges the grammatical first person, which he uses as a metaphor to help his reader conceptualize these distinctions. And although he might not apparently construct a hierarchy of presences in an expression such as "the grass is growing in my garden," spoken by someone who might actually be holding a bunch of grass in his hand—where obviously what is being demonstrated (*demonstratur*) is not what is being signified (*significatur*)—Thomas surely does, all the same, create a set of priorities when he likens these different presences to a hierarchy of personal pronouns. We can conceive of what is "actually established or present, as is demonstrated by the pronoun *ego*, to the less certain and present [. . .] demonstrated by the pronoun *tu*" ("contingit enim rem esse praesentem et certam, et maxime certam vel praesentem, et sic demonstratur per hoc pronomen *ego*, vel non maxime esse certam et praesentem, et sic demonstratur per hoc pronomen *tu*, et alia similia"), and so on down the line.[15] In Thomas' view, and in Hugh of St. Victor's before him, "discourse" enjoys a fundamental identification with *presence*.

---

[13] *Grammatica Speculativa*, 200–201; in Gellrich, 107–08.
[14] *GS*, 200–201; in Gellrich, 108.
[15] *GS* 200–201; in Gellrich, 108.

Yet, as Gellrich comments, "this factor means that, for Thomas and the other *modistae*, the *modus essendi* is just as much defined by, as it defines, its *modus significandi*" (108).

This same impulse is clearly operating in the poetry of Marcabru, in his unqualified assertions that he can sing best of all poets, that he is the one who can use language to its fullest, truthful potential, and in his claims, like those of other troubadours, that his language and his written texts are the representations of him— that they indeed *speak* for him. This position, at once philosophical and poetic, is carried on after Marcabru, as it is elaborated and enriched, until it is fully evolved in a poet like Langland. Dante, Chaucer and Langland present far more complex versions of the troubadours' poetics of authorship, but they never depart from the recognition that the discourse which embraces the issue of metapoetry will ultimately best define their more overt philosophical and/or theological themes, and, more, that such discourse will most profoundly enunciate themselves, they who are *auctores* of texts that have, through such self-assertions, marked off a territory distinct from literary and theological traditions. At bottom, here is the import of Marcabru's railing against eroticism, for the act of *true* loving will bring eloquence with it. Marcabru makes himself present, most explicitly, by mentioning himself in his poetry. Presence is enacted more deeply through his discourse on the nature of morality and its relationship to the possibilities for eloquence. On the deepest level, we sense Marcabru's presence in an ongoing discussion of the means to knowledge, which leads him to a consideration of the issues of language and self.

In "Per savi" wisdom belongs to the person who can perceive ("devina") the way in which his song presents meaning, how each word unfolds ("chascus motz declina") to reveal the poem's theme or reason ("si cum la razos despleia"). What Marcabru and all wise persons seek is the illumination that is a property of clarity ("d'esclarzir paraul' escura"), which brings the understanding of truth and which in turn will show the way to living an upright life, the life of "joy, patience and restraint" ("Jois, Sofrirs e Mesura"). This is a likely description of how truthful poetry might operate or "decline" (again, "declina"). Thus the epistemological question is bound up in the issue of poetry itself; and so is the question of the individual as someone who can know and act autonomously through the use of language that, at one and the same time, can be viewed as capable of either falsity or truth depending on who uses it (as has been examined in Chapter Two). For Love ("Amors," rather than "amars"), "by its word [. . .] action and [. . .] look, / comes from a true heart / when it gives its promise and pledge" ("Segon dich, faich e semblanssa, / es de veraia corina / car se promet e·s plevina"). As we have noted already, contrary to what occurs in many of his other poems, Marcabru does not employ his own name in "Per savi"—but the question of naming is within the poet's reach; a person might befoul love's gifts, he continues, and "whoever does not hasten to [Love] / bears the *name* of fool" ("ab sol que·l dos no sordeia, / e qui vas lieis no s'enanssa / porta *nom* de follatura"; my emphasis).

By the time Dante finishes the *Commedia*, the epistemological issue has become more fully evolved. The dual question of what constitutes knowledge and how we know things had always impelled Dante. Appropriately, then, in the *Commedia* a reader encounters a literary persona who is a virtual witness. The term *virtual* is most suitable here, because the Dante-figure will speak of the physical ability *to see* as *virtù*. The word is almost as fecund for us today as it was in Dante's time. *Virtù*'s range of meaning extends from the ability to negotiate the physical world, to the comprehension of ideas per se, to spiritual truths, to a moral integrity and/or stature. In *De Civitate Dei* (XV.22), Augustine had used the term *virtus* to indicate "rightly ordered love."[16] For several hundred years prior to the *Commedia*'s inception, the mechanics of sight had been the subject of a rigorous investigation on the part of medieval intelligentsia.[17] And, as Patrick Boyde comments (in *Perception and Passion in Dante's* Comedy 61), "anyone who studied philosophy in the late thirteenth century would have known the opening paragraph of Aristotle's *Metaphysics*, where the Philosopher observes that 'we take pleasure in the senses for their own sake, and above all in the sense of sight, preferring it to all the other senses because it is the principal source of knowledge'." This inquiry would contribute to the eventual formation of modern physics. Yet the very title of a treatise by Peter of Limoge, *Tractatus Morales de Oculo* (1275-1289), illustrates the difference between pre-modern and empirical science—that is, during Dante's life the physical and the moral were viewed as aspects of the same thing. Dante's work contains an abundance of themato-imagistic cruces that exemplify the issue of poetry, epistemology and morality; in the larger context of our discussion of authorship and epistemology, his exploitation of the Italian word *virtù*, and the cachet it brings with it, demonstrates this interrelationship.[18] What the *viator* in Dante's poem sees, and, more importantly, how he sees, are finally expressed as a struggle to know. This effort is characterized by the weighing of experiences as provided by the five senses and memory against simple faith and divine grace. Sight, the chief physical sense, is both like and unlike vision, the analog of grace.

At sunset, at the center of the *Commedia*, Purgatorio XVII, the pilgrim is climbing up the mountain of Purgatory through the smoke of the third terrace; as

---

[16] "Nam et amor ipse ordinate amandus est quo bene amatur quod amandum est, ut sit nobis virtus qua vivitur bene. Unde mihi videtur quod definitio brevis et vera virtutis ordo est amoris [. . .]" ("We must, in fact, observe the right order even in our love for the very love that is deserving of love, so that there may be in us the virtue which is the condition of the good life. Hence, as it seems to me, a brief and true definition of virtue is 'rightly ordered love'"; trans. Henry Bettenson); in Peter S. Hawkins, "Divide and Conquer: Augustine in the *Divine Comedy*," 480-81, n. 10.

[17] By far the most important, comprehensive, and brilliant study of this undertaking is by David C. Lindberg, *Theories of Vision from Al-Kindi to Kepler*. See also, Judith S. Neaman, "Magnification as Metaphor"; and, Linda Tarte Holley, "Medieval Optics and the Framed Narrative in Chaucer's *Troilus and Criseyde*."

[18] Cf. my article, "Visionary Science in Purgatorio XVII and Paradiso XXX."

he climbs, sunlight makes its way through a mist. This is, markedly, a re-visioning of the sun, and it is both poignant and elegiac. The light is fading, almost totally gone. Strategically, at this moment the pilgrim calls upon the reader's power of imagination, and aligns it with his own, and sets it against the ebbing, tangible world—for when that world is gone, how does one "see"?:

e fia la tua imagine leggera
in giugnere a veder com' io *rividi*
lo sole in pria, che già nel corcar era.
(7-9; my emphases)

then your imagination will be quick
to reach the point where it can see how I
first came to see the sun again—when it
was almost at the point at which it sets.[19]

Dante's use here of "*rividi*"—"saw again" *(ri-vidi*: literally, to have "seen again")—is set in opposition to "*imagine*"—"imagine" (in the sense that Dante uses this word, in an appeal to his reader's imagination)—specifically to evoke two texts, a past text that is philosophically central to Dante's poem, the *Summa Theologiae*, and a particular future text by Dante himself, Paradiso XXX. The nexus of these texts is Purgatorio XVII, where, as noted by Italo Borzi (in "Il Canto XVII Del *Purgatorio*" 363), "through the speech of Virgil Dante expounds the theory of love that represents the fundamental problem of his philosophical thought [. . . . This theory will lead him finally to the] infinite love [of God. . . . The road Dante will travel is] part poetical and part ideological."[20] Prudence Shaw (in "Paradiso XXX" 191) has described Paradiso XXX as the beginning of the end of Dante's journey—an end marked by sheer visual brilliance. The canto will synthesize imagistic, philosophical and theological issues raised in the *Commedia*'s middle canto, Purgatorio XVII, and thus will bring together preceding and engendered texts. A dualism in Thomas Aquinas' ideas about knowledge, as typified in the differences he specifies between sight and vision, is elaborated through the interrelationships of these texts. In both pagan and Christian traditions the analogy between light and thought or knowledge enjoyed the widest use—and perhaps more so by the time of Dante and Aquinas. Chenù writes (in *Toward Understanding Saint Thomas* 171-72) that the analogy

---

[19] In this section of my discussion I am deeply indebted to Professor Mandelbaum for his commentary on the *Commedia* generally and specifically for his glosses of Purgatorio XVII and Paradiso XXX. I am also grateful to Paul Spillenger for his careful reading of my analysis of these cantos and his helpful comments, especially for pointing out some lapses in translation. Last but not least, I must thank George Economou for his careful reading of this section.
[20] My trans.

represents an inheritance that men of all civilizations have drawn from. The manner, however, in which philosophers avail themselves of its resources varies in the extreme. Aristotle, Dionysius, Avicenna discover these resources each according to the horizon of his own insight, while the Christian Middle Ages increase their action twofold in the case of the "light" of faith. Things are carried to the point at which this image finally becomes entirely conceptualized, with the result that, henceforth in philosophic parlance, the word itself refers directly to that which was compared to it. The word no longer implies a metaphor; *de plano* (outright), it designates the mind. Such a devoiding of the figurative power of words is the normal and accepted outcome of Saint Thomas's philosophical style.

A similar association between sight and concept existed at least as early as Plato. As Ong observes, "[t]he term *idea*, form, is visually based, coming from the same root as the Latin *video*, to see, and such English derivatives as vision, visible, or videotape. Platonic form was conceived of by analogy with visible form. The Platonic ideas are voiceless [. . .]" (80). In the *Commedia* Dante wants to test the integrity of material existence, just as he would want to reach essential immateriality and behind it the divine; in short, his strategy aims at developing a dichotomy in Aquinas' thinking about knowledge.

Sight, for instance, is mediated by spirits of sight, according to the science of Dante's time and as is discussed in the *Convivio* (III.9.7-10); the agency of sight, then, is *non*-physical, so that the act of seeing a three dimensional world is contingent upon a power that derives from yet another dimension or dimensions. Indeed, there can be more than one kind of sight, and so in the *Commedia* we find a pattern in which a concern for the sensual powers of the *viator* discloses a progression from the physical and mortal to the non-physical and divine, which mirrors a major theme of the poem, that of conversion through perception.[21] Yet this theme also leads to the question of poetry. Dante is ultimately able to portray Aquinas' construct, of the material/non-material universe, by bringing the question of making poetry—the question of, finally, an amorphous but decidedly poetic imagination—to bear upon the Thomistic dichotomy. Dante wishes to celebrate a unified world of theology and poetry. In this regard, the relationship of the *Summa* is crucial to an often subtle and complex communication between Purgatorio XVII and Paradiso XXX. The key passage in Dante's parent text deals with the struggle to arrive at the Aristotelian concept of vision through likeness, by way of categories—that is, briefly, we see an object in that its form resides in our soul (*ST* I.85.2). In the spirit of Plato, Aquinas' diction here tellingly links the verbs *videre*

---

[21] Cf. Shirley Adams, "The Role of Sense Perception in the *Divine Comedy*." Other recent studies of Dantean vision in the *Commedia* include: Rebecca S. Beal, "Beatrice in the Sun: A Vision from Apocalypse"; Luigi Blasucci, "Discorso teologico e visione sensibile nel canto XIV del Paradiso"; Anthony K. Cassell, "Santa Lucia as Patroness of Sight: Hagiography, Iconography, and Dante"; G. C. Di Scipio, "Dante and St. Paul: The Blinding Light"; Edward Hagman, "Dante's Vision of God: The End of the *Itinerarium Mentis*"; Susan Noakes, "Dante's *Vista Nova*: Paradiso XXXIII.136"; and, Emilio Pasquini, "La metafora della visione nella *Commedia*."

and *intellegere*, as if to assert the evolution of natural knowledge out of two kinds of activity. One activity remains within the agent, such as seeing or understanding ("ut videre et intelligere"), and one passes over into a thing outside; each activity is produced in accord with a form. Thus, "what is understood is in the one who understands by means of its likeness" ("quod intellectum est in intellegente per suam similitudinem"); and, so, "what is actually understood is identical with the intellect as actualized" ("quod intellectum in actu est intellectus in actu"). In Purgatorio XVII, this natural knowing is to be coupled to the divine through the querying of the origin of any sensible form that might reside in the imagination when no external thing is present. Aquinas had written that "with natural reason we only come to know God through images in the imagination"; however, "the same is true of the knowledge we have through grace" ("per rationem naturalem in cognitionem divinorum pervenire non possumus [. . . .] nisi per phantasmata, similiter etiam nec secundum cognitionem gratiae"). Even so,

> By grace we have a more perfect knowledge of God than we have by natural reason. The latter depends on two things: images derived from the sensible world and the natural intellectual light by which we make abstract intelligible concepts from these images. [. . . .] The light of grace strengthens the intellectual light and at the same time prophetic visions provide us with God-given images which are better suited to express divine things than those we receive naturally from the sensible world.
>
> [P]er gratiam perfectior cognitio de Deo habetur a nobis quam per rationem naturalem. Quod sic patet: cognitio enim quam per naturalem rationem habemus, duo requirit, scilicet phantasmata ex sensibilibus accepta, et lumen naturale intelligibile, cujus virtute intelligibiles conceptiones ab eis abstrahimus [. . . .] lumen naturale intellectus conforatur per infusionem luminis gratuiti; et interdum etiam phantasmata in imaginatione hominis formantur divinitus, magis exprimentia res divinas quam ea quae naturaliter a sensibilibus accipimus, sicut apparet in visionibus prophetalibus [. . .].
> (*ST* I.13.3)

Yet faith, which is necessary to the attainment of grace, "lacks the element of seeing"; hence, faith "fails to be genuine knowledge, for such knowledge causes the mind to assent through what is seen [. . .]" ("Et sic in quantum deest visio deficit a ratione cognitionis quae est in scientia, nam scientia determinat intellectum ad unam per visionem [. . .]"). All the same, faith may be necessary to knowledge of the divine, as it may perhaps be a prerequisite to truly prophetic visions ("visionibus prophetalibus").

Aquinas is trying to chart a progression from physical sight, to imaginative "sight," to divine knowledge that somehow eludes empirical procedures such as those predicated on sight, understanding and imagination. Dante plays out this resultant dialectic of the material-immaterial through a likely metaphor for revelation; first the act of seeing the sun and the question of *how* a reader might be able to imagine such a thing are delineated at the beginning of Canto XVII, in order to link the imagination and physical sight. As well, the second act of seeing that occurs may connote a "second," suprasensory, imaginary or otherwise intelligent "vision":

> Ricorditi, lettor, se mai ne l'alpe
> ti colse nebbia per la qual vedessi
> non altrimenti che per pelle talpe,
> come, quando i vapori umidi e spessi
> a diradar cominciansi, la spera
> del so debilemente entra per essi [. . .].
>
> Remember, reader, if you've ever been
> caught in the mountains by a mist through which
> you only saw as moles see through their skin,
> how, when the thick, damp vapors once begin
> to thin, the sun's sphere passes feebly through them [. . .].[22]

This is the place where the imagination will be linked with physical sight (again: "e fia la tua imagine leggera / in giugnere a veder com'io rividi / lo sole in pria, che già nel corcar era"). To be sure, the entirety of Purgatorio XVII is nothing less than a paean to the imagination that is frequently invoked in the words "imagine" (6, 21, 31), "imaginar" (43), "imaginativa" (13) and "fantasia" (25). All of these terms are philosophically grounded in Aquinas' assertion (above) that the mortal imagination can at times serve as the vessel for images that are "divinely formed," so to better express divine things of the kind often conveyed in prophetic visions.[23] As Mandelbaum asserts, however, Dante's usage reveals an ontological claim for the *poetic* imagination or fantasy:

> while Aquinas would hardly have qualified poetic fictions (or fictions within a fiction—as Dante's are here) as "prophetic visions," Dante does conjure that possibility both here and, implicitly, in the fiction of which these fictions are a part.
> (*Purgatorio* 345–46)

In considering this *fictio-visio* context, then, it is especially important to note that words out of the Latin root *videre* occur in signal fashion throughout the canto—in "vedessi" (2), "veder" and "rividi" (8), as we have seen already, in "veder" (46, 130) and "vede" (59), distantly in "visione" (34), more distantly in "vista" (52), and even in a word like "viso" (41, 68, 107; i.e., "face," especially the forehead where sins are inscribed, each to be lifted off with the brush of an angel's wing as the pilgrim makes his way upward [68]).[24] There is also "apparivan" (72),

---

[22] For similar discussions of this passage, cf. Mazzotta, *Dante, Poet of the Desert*, 267; and *Dante's Vision and the Circle of Knowledge*, 166 ff.
[23] Cf. Pasquini, esp. 144–45, 151.
[24] On this use in Paradiso XXX, cf. Joan Ferrante, "Words and Images in Dante's *Paradiso*: Reflections of the Divine," 124.

"sentiva" (74), "sai" (93) and "comprender" (103). And there are the varied uses of the Latin original *virtus*, which first appears in "la mia virtù quivi mancava" ("my power of sight was overcome" Purg. XVII.54); "virtù " substitutes for words like *sight*, or *eyes* (compare this with Par. XXX.59-60: "che nulla luce è tanto mera, / che li occhi miei non si fosser difesi"—"that even the purest light would not have been so bright / as to defeat my eyes").

Although the Dante pilgrim continually bemoans what seem to be his own perceptual, mortal limits, his use of *virtù* progressively transforms him and extends those limits. In his attempt to climb up to the fourth terrace, it is not long before he is moved to exclaim, "O virtù mia, perché sì ti dilegue?" ("O why, my strength, do you melt away?" Purg. XVII.73). Then, shortly, Virgil's commentary makes an epistemological leap to: "Quinci comprender puoi ch'esser convene / amor sementa in voi d'ogne virtute" ("From this you see that—of necessity—/ love is the seed in you of every virtue" 103-4). Other word play leads to the same Thomistic knot in which the corporeal somehow becomes the vehicle for the spiritual—a theological construct that is emphatically put forward through a delicate and subtle, greatly removed rhyme bringing together the rays of light, the ability to think about their meaning, and the ability to utter the resultant thought. *Raggi*, in "li ultimi raggi che la notte segue" ("the final rays of [sun]light before the fall of night" Purg. XVII.71), is meant to imply, I believe, *reason, ragione,* as embodied, moreover, in the verb *to discourse, ragionare*, which is shrewdly employed at the canto's end:

L'amor ch'ad esso troppo s'abbandona,
di sovr'a noi si piange per tre cerchi;
ma come tripartito si ragiona,
tacciola [. . .].
(136-39)

The love that—profligately—yields to that
["different good" Dante will meet further on in his journey]
is wept on in three terraces above us;
but I'll not say what three shapes that love takes [. . .].

The association of reason and speech, Curtius has noted, was an "antique ideal [of] rhetoric as the integrating factor of all education" (77). This association is evident in the twelfth century, most notably in the popularity of Martianus Capella's *The Marriage of Mercury and Philology*, which has long been regarded as the schoolbook most widely used in the period.[25] The particular conjunction of the image of light rays, and both reason and discourse, has precedent in none other

---

[25] Cf. Henry Osborn Taylor, *The Classical Heritage of the Middle Ages*, 49.

than Marcabru's trope, "d'esclarzir paraul' escura," which we have already examined extensively. And, incidentally, the conjunction brings to bear upon Dante's pun the assumption on the part of later *modistae* that *presence* resides in discourse (cf. above). Nearly concomitant intellectual developments in the universities may help to account for the figure, such as the influx of Averroism generally and specifically "Arab natural science and a 'metaphysics of light'" (Curtius 56). While in Dante's time there may have been a false etymology to account for the association of light and reason or, alternately, discourse, actual etymology reveals a difference ("raggi" from the Latin root *radix*, "ragionare" from the Latin *ratio*). This difference, however, might not have prevented the literate Dante, who was capable of both auditory and visual punning, from making the connection. In fact, after Dante there is a long tradition of this association. The figure, and indeed this intellectual association, exhibits a great tenacity, as evinced in writing as late as the seventeenth century. The Spanish poet, Gracián, like the earlier Marcabru, employed the negative version of the Dantean construction to emphasize darkness and obscurity. Gracián speaks of an "eclipse del alma"; immediately likened to a "paréntesis de mi vida," this trope implicates discourse as the medium for knowing by employing the rhetorical term *parenthesis* as a metaphor, which in turn can suggest that, again, *presence* is a function of such discourse.[26]

Previous to the composition of the *Commedia*, Dante had aligned both reason and discourse with the powers of the sun and its materialization in its rays of light. The song, "Amor che ne la mente mi ragiona"—which is a part of the *Convivio* resurrected in the Purgatorio conversation between Dante and Casella who starts to sing it—begins by proclaiming that Love *discourses* in Dante's mind; the discourse is about his beloved. The song's second stanza (ll. 19-23) creates a parallel with the sun, which in a sense, like the discourse that *speaks* of his lady, "never *sees* / a thing so noble as in that moment / when it lights the region where she dwells" ("Non vede il sol, che tutto 'l mondo gira, / cosa tanto gentil, quanto in quell'ora / che luce ne la parte ove dimora / la donna").[27] She is, says Dante, "the lady of whom Love makes me speak" ("di cui dire Amore mi face"); and indeed, "every intelligence above beholds her" ("Ogni Intelletto di là su la mira"). Just as the sun can *see*, so can the intellect *behold* the beloved of whom Dante *speaks*. Perhaps even more closely anticipating the Purgatorio passage, several stanzas later Dante further elaborates this topos of the weak intellect that can barely express, that can barely comprehend the truth of his beloved's beauty, which was established early in the poem:

[. . .] se le mie rime avran difetto
ch'entreran ne la loda di costei,

---

[26] Cf. Curtius, 415.
[27] My emphasis. This and the further translations of the *Convivio* are taken from Goldin's *German and Italian Lyrics of the Middle Ages*.

di ciò si biasmi il debole intelletto
e 'l parlar nostro, che non ha valore
di ritrar tutto ciò che dice Amore.
(14-18)

if my verses are not adequate
that undertake the praise of her,
let the infirm intellect be blamed,
and our speech, which does not have the power
to recount all that love speaks forth.

He proclaims that "Divine power descends into her" ("In lei discende la *virtú divina*"; my emphasis), much as the sun's rays descend to earth to illuminate the world. The implication here is that the rational intellect—which determines the ability to discourse—and one's physical powers of sight are, on a Platonic scale, perhaps alike although not as powerful, not as penetrating or comprehensive as the supernatural powers afforded by the bestowal of grace. The song "Amor che ne la mente mi ragiona" also anticipates a Pauline echo that is crucial to the relationship between Purgatorio XVII and Paradiso XXX, the recounting of the blinding light, on the road to Damascus, which brings Saul revelation. The song continues its elaborate analogy:

Cose appariscon ne lo suo aspetto
che mostran dé piacer di Paradiso,
dico ne li occhi e nel suo docle riso,
che le vi reca Amor com'a suo loco.
Elle soverchian lo nostro intelletto
come raggio di sole un frale viso:
e perch'io non le posso mirar fiso,
mi convien contentar di dirne poco.
Sua bielta' piove fiammelle di foco,
animate d'un spirito gentile
ch'e creatore d'ogni pensier bono;
e rompon come trono
l'innati vizii che fanno altrui vile.
(55-67)

In her aspect things appear
that image the joys of Paradise,
in her eyes, I mean, and her sweet smile:
Love leads them there as to his realm.
These things overcome our intellect
as a ray of sunlight eyes that are weak;
and because I cannot gaze on them continually
I must be content to speak little of them.
Her beauty rains down flames of fire

alive with a gentle spirit
that is creator of all good thoughts;
and like a thunderbolt they shatter
the inborn vices that make us vile.

For Dante, the confluence of "raggi" and "ragiona" in Purgatorio XVII helps to delineate how it is that the intellect can become the mediating force between spirit and body, one which, in its capacity for abstraction or, that is, for the non-palpable, mimics or perhaps mirrors the truly divine experience. Dante can see the rays of the sun, and can as well understand the idea of divine light even if he cannot (yet) experience it. Other ghost rhymes with Paradiso XXX make this clear, such as "[O]cchio" (48) and "occhi" (60), and "raggio" (106), which denotes the "light that [has made] apparent the Creator to the creature" ("Lume é là sù che visible face / lo creatore a quella creatura" [100-1]); here "raggio" represents the ultimate in Thomistic teleology—that is, how the divine may be apprehended by a mortal. In this context "virtute" (57) denotes the pilgrim's new (divine) knowledge when, concomitantly, he finds himself in a state of levitation due to an agency that "[sormante] di sopr'a mia virtute" (that surmounts, is "beyond the power that [was] mine"). Furthermore, the poem's culmination in Paradiso XXXIII contains the same set of rhymes.

Of course, the thematically critical passage in Purgatorio XVII, which makes all that ensues in the poem possible, is Dante's apostrophe that grows out of his recognition of the possible depth of imaginative experience:

> O imaginativa che ne rube
> tavolta sì di fuor, ch'om non s'accorge
> perché dintorno suonin mille tube,
> chi move te, se 'l senso non ti porge?
> Moveti lume che nel ciel s'informa,
> per sé o per voler che giù lo scorge.
> (13-18)

> O fantasy, you that at times would snatch
> us from outward things—we notice nothing
> although a thousand trumpets sound around us—
> who moves you when the senses do not spur you?
> A light that finds its form in Heaven moves you—
> directly or led downward by God's will.[28]

Doctrinally, these lines come right out of Aquinas, as we have seen (and right out

[28] Mandelbaum uses "fantasy" and "imagination" interchangeably to designate "that internal sense or power that retains sensible forms drawn from external things through the 'outer' senses" (*Purgatorio* 345, n. for ll. 13-18).

of the Platonic tradition as restated in Augustine's ideas about sight and understanding, about illumination). But also evident here is the general, experiential manner in which Dante has come to sympathize with, to understand the very instigation of Aquinas' pursuit; for it is out of a state of rapture, in which the normally sensible world would fall away, that his persona can acquaint himself with an "inner" light.

Thus Aquinas' basic dialectic is firmly entrenched by the time a reader turns to Purgatorio XVIII. In Paradiso XXX the play of sensible and divine light is adumbrated in a direct response. The light in Paradise is sumptuous and dazzling; Dante writes of it employing forms of the verb *to see* no fewer than 16 times, and he often uses the words "vista" and "occhio-i," the noun "palpebre," and the adjectives "visible" and "visivi," as well as the verb "Mira"[29]—which may have been anticipated at the start of the *Commedia* (Inf. II.8) in the line, "o mente che scrivesti ciò ch'io vidi" ("o memory, that set down what I saw").[30] Beatrice, furthermore, speaks a succession of three sentences that begin with the imperatives "Mira," "Vedi" and "vedi" respectively (128-31).[31] Such repetition and alliteration suggest, as Ferrante has put it (in "Words and Images in Dante's *Paradiso*" 124), "the 'vita nuova' that the vision in each case [each imperative] heralds," particularly in the rhyming of *vidi* with itself (XXX.95-99), which focuses on the concept of vision and "also connects Beatrice, the sight of whom started Dante on the journey to God, with the God to whom she has now brought him"; *vidi* is the only self-rhyme in the Paradiso apart from *Cristo*.

Overall, these lines from Purgatorio XVII and Paradiso XXX crystallize the question of the individual's capacity, his spiritual and intellectual depth as well as volition—that is, the question of an individual's resolve—to make poetry that can comprehend a truth beyond linguistic expression. The question of resolve was not unrelated to theories about cognition. In Dante the epistemological aspect of the poet's struggle is more fully explored than in Marcabru. But so too is the question of the individual will, which we see dramatized broadly in the frequent exhortations of the pilgrim's various guides to continue his journey. That journey finally leads to a splendor that is almost more than can be beheld and is of course much more than, as the poet-pilgrim tells us, he can report to us. His vision, as well as his resolve, and ultimately his ability to speak of his experiences, are all determined by his faith. Much as Marcabru establishes a link between the

---

[29] Di Scipio, 156, n 7. Cf. Pasquini, 134-35, 138-39.
[30] Cf. Pasquini, 135. In passing, let us note Chaucer's Proem in Book II of the *House of Fame*: "O thought that wrot al that I mette, / And in the tresorye hyt shette / Of my brayn [. . .]."
[31] Shaw, 211.

individual poet and the question of knowing, which is fully explored by Dante, in turn, the link Dante establishes between faith and volition will be fully developed by Langland. In this light we might better understand what takes place in the *Commedia*; we particularly need to comprehend the inter- and intratextual relationships Dante has created there, such as the special communication between this Purgatorio and this Paradiso canto. Poetically, Dante is attempting a critique of experience, one which he would like to have reach beyond Aquinas' phenomenology.

What is remarkable is that Aquinas can be seen to be Dante's doctrinal *and* poetic source. Aquinas writes, for instance, that "the stronger our intellectual light [is] the deeper the understanding we derive from images, whether these be received in a natural way from the senses or formed in the imagination by divine power" ("quod ex phantasmatibus vel a sensu acceptis secundum naturalem ordinem, vel divinitus in imaginatione formatis"). Revelation provides a "divini luminis." Yet "Faith is a sort of knowledge" ("fides cognitio quaedam est"); but (again) because it "lacks the element of seeing faith fails to be genuine knowledge" ("Et sic in quantum deest visio deficit a ratione cognitionis quae est in scientia").[32] In response to Aquinas' explanation of how understanding takes place, Dante creates something new. Purgatorio XVII invokes the question of knowing the nonsensible and even the divine, when the sun has almost wholly set; Paradiso XXX, where Dante first apprehends the celestial Rose—finally, a rose of light—occurs when the sun is about to rise. Thus Dante strives to resolve the dialectic beyond Dante the reporter's, the witness', retreat into his topos of ineffability when confronted by Godly things.

This pivotal relationship is unique, ultimately founded deep in the linguistic fabric of Dante's doctrinal sources: Aquinas, and *his* source, Augustine. In trying to find a way out of Aquinas' epistemological dilemma, the dilemma of how to know the divine with only the tools of perception (i.e., the Aristotelian aspect of Aquinas), Dante can only name the unnamable through a poetics of intense linguistic "play." He employs strategies like alliteration, rhyme and repetition. He uses neologisms. More pertinent to this present focus is Dante's telescoping of Latin syntax and morphology in the simpler Italian.[33] Along these lines, however, we find an even subtler and truly penetrating play, which has everything to do with Dante's loaded use of the word *virtù*—a key to a finer, almost subliminal procedure that is grounded in polysemous punning.

Aquinas speaks of how knowing—and its necessary adjunct, *mental* knowing, by which the *sign* of the object is apprehended (or, as Augustine calls it, the "verbum mentis")—unavoidably means consciousness of both good and evil. And Aquinas is paraphrased in Purgatorio XVII as follows.

Lo naturale è sempre sanza errore,
ma l'altro puote errar per malo obietto

[32] *ST* I.13.3; cf. above.
[33] As Ferrante has examined at length.

o per troppo o per poco di vigore.
(94-96)

The natural is always without error,
but mental love may choose an evil object
or err through too much or too little vigor.

The authority for Thomas' assertion derives from Augustine, who is quoted in the *Summa* (I.1.12) in the general context of the author's discussion of grace as that capacity to bestow divine knowledge. He writes that Augustine says in his retractions, "Non approbo quod in oratione dixi; Deus, qui non nisi *mundos* verum scire voluisti. Responderi enim potest multos etiam non *mundos* multa scire vera" ("I do not now approve what I said in a certain prayer, 'O God who hast wished only the *clean* of heart to know truth . . .' for it could be answered that many who are un*clean* know many truths"). Thomas then adds to Augustine the explanatory phrase, "scilicet per rationem naturalem" (i.e., "by natural reason") (*ST* I.12.3; my emphases).

It remains for a poet, rather than a theologian, to appreciate the depth of Augustine's diction, and to profit by it. Here Dante finds the opportunity for semantic expansion in Augustine's use of "mundos" (as in, "multos etiam non *mundos* verum scire"—"many who are not *clean* know many truths"). In Augustine's Latin *mundos*, as in the Italian *mondo*, there are two meanings for this word: "clean," and "world" or "universe."[34] Therefore, privileging the term *mondo* as the end rhyme that will link the canto's first two tercets, Paradiso XXX begins with a description of a world in shadow:

[. . .] e questo mondo
china già l'ombra quasi al letto piano [. . . .]
(2-3)

[. . .] and now our world
inclines its shadow to an almost level bed. . . .

Such a world presages a subsequent paraphrase of Paul's witnessing and conversion (first indicated, by the way, in Inferno II. 28-33) of later lines:

Come sùbito lampo che discetti
li spiriti visivi, sì che priva
da l'atto l'occhio di più forti obietti,
così mi circunfulse luce viva,
e lasciommi fasciato di tal velo

---

[34] Charlton T. Lewis, *A Latin Dictionary*, 1175. Alexander. Souter, *A Glossary of Later Latin to 600 A.D.*, cites for *mundus* as an adjective: "clean from (some filth)," and for *mundo*: "cure, heal; blot out (sins), purify (the sinner)." J. F. Niermeyer, *Mediae Latinatatis Lexicon Minus*, also cites for *mundus* as an adjective: "3. *lavé d'un blâme, innocent* — clear of guilt, innocent."

del suo fulgor, che nulla m'appariva.
(46-51)

Like sudden lightning scattering the spirits
of sight so that the eye is then too weak
to act on other things it would perceive,
such was the living light encircling me,
leaving me so enveloped by its veil
of radiance that I could see no thing.

Saul's life was, in a sense, still in shadow, when he was blinded by a uniquely strong light on the road to Damascus (Di Scipio 151-52):[35]

Factum est autem, eunte me, et appropinquante Damasco media die subito da caelo circunfulsit me lux copiosa: decidens in terram, audivi vocem dicentem mihi: Saule, Saule, quid me persequeris? . . . . Et cum non viderem prae claritate luminis illius, ad manum deductus a comitibus, veni Damascum.[36]

And it came to pass, as I was going, and drawing nigh to Damascus at midday, that suddenly from heaven there shone round about me a great light: And falling on the ground, I heard a voice saying to me: Saul, Saul, why persecutest thou me? . . . . And whereas I did not see for the brightness of that light, being led by the hand by my companions, I came to Damascus.[37]

Likewise, Dante's pilgrim speaks of a veil of light that can blot out the ordinary light of the world, which derives from Paul's "da caelo circunfulsit me lux copiosa."[38] This image turns on the verb for apprehension, "appariva" (51; above). Arguably, the earlier distant rhyme of "raggi" and "ragiona" foreshadows

---

[35] It is worth noting, as Cassell (76) reports, that Guido da Pisa's *Espositiones* (written 1327-28) makes a connection between Saint Lucy, who is identified with, as Cassell puts it, "prevenient and illuminating grace," and the biblical passage. Furthermore, Cassell observes:
> Lucia's association with infirmities of the eyes is clearly Guido's main motive for expanding on the conversion of the Apostle who was "three days without sight" (Acts 9:9). The sinful Saul, soon to be Paul, is "lumine ocolorum privatus"; the infirmity and the cure of Paul's sight, the physical signs of his spiritual sin and conversion, link the wayfarer's protest "Non Paolo sono," his reluctance and distress, to Lucia's appearance as *gratia illuminans* in the canto [i.e., Inf. II].

[36] Acts 22.6-11, from *Biblia Sacra iuxta Vulgatam Clementina*.

[37] *The Holy Bible (Douay-Rheims Version)*, 161-62.

[38] But note Thomas (*ST* I.13.2 and *contra*): ". . . for Dionysius says, 'It is impossible for the divine ray to shine upon us except as screened round about by the many-coloured sacred veils' [*De Caelesti Hierarchia* I. Patrologia Graeca 3.121]"; and, *Sed contra*: "St. Paul says, 'God has revealed to us through his Spirit [I Corinthians 2, 8, 10] a wisdom which none of this world's rulers knew' and a gloss says [Interlinear Gloss from Jerome. PL 30.752] that this refers to philosophers."

this revelatory development.[39] Yet, finally, discourse and reason (*ragione, ratio*) must belong only to the clean of heart. The pure, Dante suggests, will experience a second sight, a revision—even a *vista nova*. Alive to both the range and register of his terms, however, he could also be recalling Thomas' citation of Matthew. In speaking of the word *visio*, Thomas wrote in the *Summa* that

> Any term may be employed in two senses; one in keeping with its original imposition, the other with common usage. This is apparent in the word visio, the initial reference of which was to the act of the sense of sight. This term, in view of the special nature and certitude of the sense of sight, is extended in common usage to the knowledge of all the senses . . . and it is even made to include intellectual knowledge, as in Matthew 5, 8: "Blessed are the clean of heart, for they shall 'see' God."
>
> De aliquo nomine dupliciter convenit loqui; uno modo, secundum primam eius impositionem; alio modo, secundum usum nominis. Sicut patet in nomine visionis, quod primo impositum est ad significandum actum sensus visus; sed propter dignitatem et certitudinem huius sensus extensum est hoc nomen, secundum usum loquentium, ad omnem cognitionem [. . .] intellectus, secundum illud Matt. 5: Beati mundo corde quoniam ipsi Deum videbunt.
> (*ST* I.67.1.3c)[40]

The dynamic of sight, reason, discourse and spiritual purity, is foreshadowed by Dante in Purgatorio X where it has been abundantly particularized. Here, the pilgrim comes upon a sculpted wall with three examples of humility, prior to his encounter with the prideful souls. Marilyn Migiel comments that, although Virgil has pointed them out (ll. 101-02),

> the pilgrim has difficulty deciding what it is that he sees, and says to Virgil, "Maestro, quel ch'io veggio / muovere a noi non mi sembian persone" ("Master. . . what I see moving toward us does not seem to me persons") (Purg. X.114), but then in a more severe outburst, "O superbi critiani" ("O proud Christians") (X.121-29), Dante presents his inability to see as the result of a scene which is in reality confused: in short, it is the proud who are blind, unable to integrate themselves into Christian society, and therefore render themselves unrecognizable as men.
> (151)[41]

Dante has in effect spoken to the reader several lines earlier (97-98), by explaining the purpose of the bas-reliefs: "[. . .] io mi dillettava di guardare / l'imagini di

---

[39] The Pauline theme is reprised, moreover, at the very end of the *Commedia* (Par. XXXIII.141-42) when the seer's mind is "struck by light that flashed" ("la mia mente fu percossa / da un fulgore"); then, force fails his "high fantasy" ("l'alta fantasia qui mancò possa").
[40] *Biblia Sacra iuxta Vulgatam Clementinam.* Cf. *ST* I-II. 77. 5 *ad* 3.
[41] Cf. Beal.

tante unilitadi [. . .]" ("[. . .] I took much delight in witnessing / these effigies of true humility [. . .]"). This previous address becomes the agency by which the question of "who it is who really sees, and who on the other hand is responsible for the visual confusion," is clarified.

> If the pilgrim has trouble figuring out what the "text" of the body says, the fault lies in the inability of the text to communicate virtue properly; the fault of the text is, interestingly enough, also called blindness, in accordance with a theology of humility which associates pride with blindness and humility with clear vision. (Migiel 151-52)

The intertextual message embedded in this complex of texts—the testimonies of Paul, Matthew, Augustine, Thomas, and the pilgrim in Purgatorio XVII, Paradiso XXX and XXXIII—is that only the good, whose sins have been removed, who are now pure, may know a divine and clear light. The diction of the Paradiso cantos and perhaps their imagery are anticipated in Purgatorio XVII; they are grounded in a dualism that is introduced through imagery in Dante's observation of the sensible light of the stars:

> Già eran sovra noi tanto levati
> li ultimi raggi che la notte segue,
> che le stelle apparivan da più lati.
> (70-72)

> Above us now the final rays before
> the fall of night were raised to such a height
> that we could see the stars on every side.

In this "re-seeing" of the sun another truth emerges; lights appear through the rays of another (sun)light. The implicit, ultimately Thomistic meaning of an apposition like this is that the sight of the divine is a moral sight, the virtue enjoyed by the purified. Here is the thematic context in which Dante, in Paradiso XXX, counterpoints Purgatorio XVII's paradox of fully sensible starlight in a night sky, when the sun has yet fully to disappear, with his playfully double use of *vidi* to enact the absolute Godly radiance:

> O isplendor di Dio, per cu' io *vidi*
> l'alto trïunfo del regno verace,
> dammi virtù a dir com' ïo il *vidi*!
> (97-99; my emphases)

> O radiance of God, through which I saw
> the noble triumph of the true realm, give
> me the power to speak of what I saw!

In Purgatorio XVII the sun is seen again ("rividi") as the light of the stars overtakes it. Likewise, in Paradiso XXX there is a twice-seeing ("vidi . . . vidi"). And even if Dante does not have the power ("virtù") to speak of what he sees (he does, however!), he nevertheless has clearly been given a vision that is possible because of both his purity and his "understanding."

The poet Ezra Pound might have been thinking of this moment when he wrote that artists are the antennae of their race (in *The A B C of Reading* 73); artistic imaginings may lead to scientific beliefs. Paul Ricoeur writes (in *The Rule of Metaphor* 257-313) that in the use of metaphorical expression we extend the frontiers of meaning and thus extend the reach of human knowledge. And here we might recall Hans's stipulation (as discussed in the Introduction), that artistic activity allows the employment of "the furrows of [a] predictable range [of experience] to get outside of those furrows of predictability and, in going outside of them, [to enlarge] the field of some of the furrows" (90). Perhaps this is, in a fashion, what Dante has in mind. The bas-reliefs in Purgatorio X, for example, raise the question of a mortal poet's limitations. The sculptures are Godly art, of course. Yet they are art. Rather than a prideful emendation of Aquinas, what we can find asserted in the very presence of the sculptures is that, as Migiel writes, they are

> in fact a most effective way of presenting the necessity of the expression of humility. Humility is given life here in a medium which is otherwise silent, a medium which in its cold stoniness could remind us of tombstones, which conceal rather than reveal. Clearly, this association was present to Dante, who notes in Purgatorio XII.16-24 that the images of the proud were like tombstones. Not only do the images immediately communicate their message, but that message is immediately available to the interpreter.
> (150-51)

Dante was at least indirectly influenced by new Aristotelian texts, particularly the *Nichomachean Ethics*. As a result of these texts, "[h]umility came to be defined as a mean in opposition to extreme exaltation or deprecation of the self" (156). Francesco Tateo argues (in "Teologia e 'Arte' nel canto X del *Purgatorio*") that—rather than a "mortification of one's person" as conceived of by theologians, particularly as Aquinas might have understood it, which was a "deprecation of the self"—for Dante

> [h]umility is the awareness of human limitations (just as pride is blindness, unawareness of those limitations); and it is precisely the sense of human containment that renders man equal to himself, a creature worthy of the highest divine acknowledgment. [42]

It is the ability of art, of poetry, through its inherently artistic tensions, tensions founded on ambiguity of expression, which makes possible both the realization of mortal limits and the promise of transcendence of these same limits through divine

---

[42] Trans. Migiel, 153.

aid, that is, through grace. Thus it can be said that through the reportage of the pilgrim-witness he creates, Dante attempts a universal unification through poesis. In doing so he will deny that he has the power authentically to name his experience in Paradise; perhaps, though, he has quietly spoken that name in the sense of, not only Paul's vision (in I Corinthians) that is merely sight in a distorted mirror, but, more graphically, in the sense of the parables that end, "let those who have eyes to see, see."

Dante does not actually name himself in the *Commedia* but has others do it for him. In this sense we can speak of him as absent in his poem—in comparison with both Marcabru and Langland, who do specifically name themselves. However, Dante is profoundly present throughout his writing—and his presence deepens as the poem unfolds—by virtue of his poetic ingenuity; though he is not self-named, he is just the same signified through a construction like "io sol uno" as well as through the naming by other characters in the poem. Beatrice actually calls the pilgrim "Dante" (Purg. XXX.55);[43] she speaks his name aloud. As a poet, the sense of Dante's presence, indeed, increases exponentially with the departure of Virgil, his precursor. Mandelbaum has noted that when Dante is alone, he remembers Virgil the most ("Taken from Brindisi" 233; cf. the Introduction). Thus, the older poet's absence is emphasized through the strength of Dante's language of memory. More to the point, Virgil's exit marks the transformation into a full scale autobiography, where Dante's name will for the first time be invoked. "As Vergil disappears," Mazzotta writes,

> the poem actually seems to take on what might be called an Augustinian literary form. [. . . .] Dante explicitly recalls both Boethius and Augustine's autobiographical focus in the *Confessions*. [. . . .] The pilgrim voices his contrition and goes into a brief recapitulation of his past from the 'vita nuova' (Purgatorio XXX.115) to the new encounter with Beatrice.
> (*Dante, Poet of the Desert* 187)

Yet Dante invokes his presence, more profoundly, by bringing to the fore of the *Commedia* the issue of discourse itself, its possibilities and its dangers, which he examines in the context of a larger epistemological discussion. Discourse is symbolized in the first part of the poem by Virgil's mentoring and Dante's inclusion into the "bella scola" (Inf. IV.94) made up of the West's great poets. As well, it is first and foremost dramatized in the conversations with his various guides, which represent spiritual as well as intellectual unions. These

---

[43] Cf. Holloway's discussion of Beatrice's naming of Dante, and its parallel in *Piers Plowman*, to be examined in the next chapter.

conversations are carried on as vehicles for alternate, in a sense absent, "intertextual conversations" Dante enjoys between himself and others. In the case of Purgatorio XVII and Paradiso XXX, for example, it can be said that Dante "discourses" with Aquinas, Augustine, Paul, and quite possibly Dionysius, Aristotle and Plato.

The *Commedia* finds its contrast in the fourteenth century English poem *Piers Plowman*. Like the earlier Marcabru, Langland invokes presence in his poetry by specifically naming himself. He also presents us with a newly poetic and philosophical development. He aligns his name with the thematic crux of *Piers Plowman*, which involves the individual's capacity to direct his or her own journey toward salvation. The poem further asks how that journey is determined by knowledge; once again, and most importantly, the poem asks whether or not that journey can be comprehended by discourse—because for Langland *journey*, *discourse*, *knowledge* and *salvation* are all represented repeatedly by images of texts and books. This conceptualization is no longer merely that which was bound up in the Augustinian book, however, nor is it that hypothesized by the Scholastics or Aquinas. Rather, Langland's understanding of the book as symbol shows how symbolism can be pushed to its extremes, by the nominalist point of view, as was most comprehensively developed by William of Ockham (to be discussed in the next chapter).

Dante's poetic authority is ultimately asserted by the fact that, symbolically, he triumphs over his "father poet" Virgil; Dante the pilgrim continues on into Paradise while Virgil the pagan must turn back from making that ultimate journey. Subtextually, too, Dante "triumphs" over Aquinas through a uncommonly poetic "resolution" of Thomistic doctrines. In like fashion, Langland "triumphs" over Ockham and other thinkers of his time—the later *Modistae*, the *Moderni*. So, in a different fashion, does Chaucer. These poets transcend their respective circumstances, specifically through their philosophical meditations on language and reality. In *Piers Plowman* the transcendence is depicted quintessentially in "triumphs" over other characters Will the pilgrim encounters on, as in the *Commedia*, his own journey toward salvation. For Dante, self-enunciation is linked to the thematics of the persona's poem. In Langland's work, we see a final stage in the development of the authorship trope, as the poem's theme and its persona are seamlessly fused into a single entity. This fusion occurred—perhaps it can be said that it was first attempted—in the *Roman de la rose*, but in this encyclopedic, earlier allegory, the persona was merely an allegorical figure. Langland's Will, on the other hand, not unlike the Dante persona, is fully drawn. He is a flesh and blood individual with whom a reader can easily identify. Thus, as we shall see, Langland's persona is fully present.

Chapter Four

Poetic Voice, Poetic Text, Thematics and the Individual

In *Piers Plowman* the overwhelming preponderance of proper nouns—names—incidents in which things or characters are named, and the like, attest the theologico-philosophical currents of the poem's time. In the B and C texts, for instance, there is an astounding number of names of individual personages (approaching three hundred, respectively), of which the greatest majority represent allegorized, personified concepts. Lavinia Griffiths reports (in *Personification in Piers Plowman* 3) that in each of these versions "over 80 inanimate and abstract nouns from a number of lexical and grammatical categories become persons (and a considerable quantity beyond that are turned into horses, trees, castles, etc.)."[1] By Langland's time, "literate culture [had] opened an epistemological space," in the words of Britton J. Harwood (in Piers Plowman *and the Problem of Belief* 21), "between sensory experience and [. . .] the 'non-visualness . . . of the sheer idea'."[2] As well, nominalist views, professed by thinkers like William of Ockham and Robert Holcot, brought to a critical mass what had already been a progressively focused meditation on language—a language that had come to be identified by theologians with the processes of nature. This identification arose as early as Anselm (as we have seen in the previous chapters), in his recognition that any given utterance contained a natural (*naturaliter*) cogency that inhered in a statement regardless of the statement's objective truth or falsity. Anselm's recognition modified Augustine's description of what was natural and true. Both men held that naturalness could be the criterion of a kind of truth, and both separated that criterion as distinct from other means of determining knowledge and truth. Anselm was a philosophical realist; by no stretch of the imagination can he be viewed as any kind of nominalist. Yet the inquiry into the nature of language, which he set in motion, was premised on language's autonomy; the effect of that recognition, moreover, was the elevation of the natural world to a greater status than it had previously enjoyed. Nature, too, could be unique and independent. Ockham, a nominalist, initiated a "patient and remorseless" application of principles of logic to the contemplation of statements, as Ernest Moody has put it (in *Studies in Medieval Philosophy, Science, and Logic* 431), which eventually led to the emergence of Newtonian science more than three hundred years later.

---

[1] Griffiths cautions that these are only estimates. "It is difficult," she writes, "without the availability of a concordance, to catalogue all the occurrences of personification in the poem, or to note preferences for one syntactic form over another" (n. 2).
[2] Harwood is quoting from Eric Havelock, *Preface to Plato*, 229.

Ockham's criticism of alleged proofs of theological beliefs was "merciless" (432). Even as language remained a distinct entity, with Ockham, it acquired an inertia neither Augustine nor Anselm could have foreseen.

The fourteenth century's conceptualization of the divine deepened with Ockham; however, it took on new limits, and the same can be said for individual human potential. His critique of his received theology and philosophy focused on the illogicality of postulates that accept the possibility of speaking about theological truths yet fail to demonstrate how such statements might be made; the ultimate criterion for ruling out this possibility is *intuitive knowledge*, what the Chaucer persona in the Prologue to the *Legend of Good Women* refers to as seeing "with ye" (11).[3] Ockham's form of nominalism set the individual adrift in his or her moral life, lacking any surety in absolute truths, with the assumption that the will and intelligence were finite and ultimately weak, and with the perplexity that is a given in such a circumstance; logically, for example, God could withhold grace from an individual despite the fact of his or her good works, or could command a person to hate or to disobey Him.[4]

This complex of beliefs gave rise to a wealth of great literati—Chaucer and Langland, but also the *Pearl* poet, and the author who composed the mystical "Cloud of Unknowing." The fact is that, in the face of what for Ockham became a severely limited mortal world, one in which God could do anything including withhold grace, the best a *viator* could do in striving for salvation was simply to do his or her best. This mortal responsibility is typified variously in the fourteenth century, explicitly in Langland's Will or Chaucer's narrator in the *Canterbury Tales*, implicitly in other of Chaucer's poems. Indeed, figures like Will and Geffrey deeply resonate what we can take to have been their authors' beliefs.[5]

The shared concern of theologians from Anselm's time to the period characterized by what became known as the *modistae*, and even later the *moderni* of the fourteenth century, involved the attempt to describe the role and significance of the noun in the dynamic of language, especially in relation to a reality beyond the dynamic proper. Inevitably, the *moderni* involved themselves with the role of the name. Within this particle of language resided the greatest possibility for language to reflect reality, it was thought, because nouns, and proper nouns (and, secondarily, pronouns) were, in some of the most radical, philosophically realist inquiries, viewed as containing the full plenitude of being (as has also been discussed in the previous chapters). As nouns and pronouns functioned within their utterances, their language was understood to have been as ontologically full as any mortal language could be. Or, rather, we can say that particularly these parts of speech could be understood as possessing immanence. Therefore, they were capable not only of fueling the phenomenological processes of linguistic

---

[3] My discussion throughout this chapter focuses on Chaucer's G text that I consider to be the later, revised version of the Prologue.
[4] *Commentary on the Sentences* III, q. 8, *Ockham: Philosophical Writings*; in Moody, 435-36.
[5] Cf. my essay, "Ockham, Chaucer, and the Emergence of Modern Poetics."

expression, but of ordering such expression as first of all proceeding from a source within them.

The issue of the noun speaks directly to the fundamental conceptualization of *Piers Plowman*, to Langland's uses of personification and to what we shall come to understand was his critique of, and attempt to undo, the poetic and otherwise epistemological form of inquiry known as allegory. These related stratagems are of a piece with Langland's ideology. Thus, as Coleman writes (in Piers Plowman *and the Moderni* 19), pertinent to any examination of *Piers Plowman* is the recognition that "[t]he way in which the *moderni* understood language as signifying reality shows us how [. . .] as theologians [they dealt] with the language of Scripture as signifying historical reality." "History," Frank Kermode has said (in *The Sense of an Ending* 56), "is a fictive substitute for authority and tradition, a maker of concords between past, present and future, a provider of significance to mere chronicity."[6] The twelfth-century expansion of the Aristotelian corpus included the *Sophistical Refutations*, which was of great importance to a seminally nominalist work, Peter of Spain's *Summulae Logicales*; the *Summulae*, in turn, concerned itself with what Peter considered to be the primary elements of propositions—nouns and verbs. Augustine had linked signs to real and true signifieds. Aristotle, and Boethius, had recognized that, through the significative function of substitutive nouns, things in themselves could come into being within the confines of statements about these things.[7] This shared view was succinctly expressed, for example, in Boethius' assertions that "nomen est vox significata" and, in commenting on Aristotle's *Categories*, that the work seeks "de primis rerum nominibus et de vocibus res significantibus disputare."[8] This traditional idea of language was elaborated in the early nominalism of Peter Abelard, who overemphasized the significative capacity of the Scriptural word.

All of these critical turns in the intellectual history of the Middle Ages set the stage for the fourteenth-century *moderni* to "[press] the methodology of speculative grammarians and logicians onto issues of dogma" (Coleman 22). The adoption of the basic position of earlier thinkers like the speculative grammarians resulted in a linguistic realism, since the *moderni* were virtually following Peter of Spain who viewed terms as physical and who thus endowed words, as Coleman puts it, "with material and formal causes usually reserved for substances." In propositions, words substituted for things whose physical characteristics were attributed to their signifying words (199 n. 16). This resulted in a further vitiation of the discipline of theology, as speculative energy continued to spread into a newer discipline of philosophy that comprehended questions of language and logic. Perhaps such a change could be better understood as the inability of theology to withstand purely abstractive procedures that also relied on rationalism in a denial of mysticism; the common medium between the two, the rational and the mystical, was language.

---

[6] Cf. Middleton, "Narration and the Invention of Experience," 120.
[7] Cf. *Soph. Refut.* I.165a.6-13.
[8] *In Categorias Aristotelis Libri Quattuor; PL* 64.159a-294c, espec. 159a-61c; in Coleman 21, 199 nn. 13 and 14.

The role of logic per se in this process, however, should not be underestimated:

> Instead of grammar, logic and theology remaining separate but interrelated disciplines, they were merged under the conceptual rubric of Logic. Theology was, so to speak, dragged down by the "scientific" methodology of the logicians. All knowledge was resolved into propositions. Rational dialectic with its emphasis on argumentation by means of the soundly argued sophism analysed the parts of speech in the proposition. This methodology intruded into all other fields of knowledge and invaded the realm of theology with dramatic consequences because of the belief that all knowledge, thought, language, could be broken down into the terms of propositions.
> (22)

As Paul Vignaux has said, "[b]eginning with the logic of language, the nominalist consciously [set] up ontological problems."[9]

A counterpart of this emphasis on language was the deepening conviction, Coleman observes, that the mortal individual "was exalted in the realm of nature, to the point of working his own salvation through the exercise of his free will" (23). Again, it is possible to see the origin of these views in Anselm's observation of the *natural* machinery of linguisis as well as in nominalistically literal readings of Scripture. By the fourteenth century, though, the properties of statements had become integrated into a more complex vision in which language, human will, and salvation through divine grace, existed in an interactively existential structure. In fact the new theology, more than before, came to be concerned with moral issues, especially after the thirteenth century and particularly in England.[10] These issues centered around the necessity for humanity's "conformity to God's reward or justification and acceptance" (Coleman 24), which in a thinker like Holcot is embodied in the claim that to do one's best naturally ("ex puris naturalibus") facilitates the bestowal of Grace upon the individual ("Facientibus quod in se est Deus non denegat gratiam").[11] In the thirteenth century, Aquinas had distanced himself from Aristotle by linking the rational appetite (*appetitus rationalis*) with the Christian will (*voluntas*). In the fourteenth century, as we see expressed in *Piers Plowman*, pivotal theological and philosophical concepts become the sense of obligation and merit on the part of the individual. Now the focus is on the *viator*, and his or her possible reward. Ultimately, the question being asked is, can there be a *natural* act that is a prerequisite for salvation? Langland asks this question, and so too does his contemporary, Chaucer; the question is also being pursued by the nominalist *moderni*. For the natural act might be that which is distinct from human actions that unfold with the aid of divine grace.

---

[9] *Philosophy in the Middle Ages*; in Coleman, 22.
[10] Cf. Damasus Trapp, "Augustinian Theology of the Fourteenth Century," 146–274, espec. 149; in Coleman 23–24.
[11] *In Librum Sapientie Salmonis*, 28 B and 120 fol. clxxxiii.ra–va; in Coleman 24 and 200 n. 25.

It is within this theologico-epistemological construct that the ways in which reason and conscience were conceived of, in the latter half of the fourteenth century, intersect in the poetry of Langland and Chaucer, in *Piers Plowman* most definitively. In that poem Langland avers, "'wot no man . . . who is worthy to have'," since, as Coleman has keenly noted,

> worthiness for reward is to be understood so that God's free will as well as the free will of men might survive intact. A reconciliation of the wills, like a reconciliation of the two orders of justice, finds its unity in Christ. The poem, then, is an elaborate gloss on John 1:17—"for the law was given by Moses but grace and truth came by Jesus Christ." Through Christ, justice and mercy are reconciled. (195)

This conception of reconciliation represents a decided shift in how the workings and effects of divine grace were conceived of, a shift away from what was generally held to be true in the previous century. The new alternative, also expressed in Langland's poem, can easily be viewed as the ethical expression of its time. According to Dante in the *Commedia*, Thomistic philosophy sees the realms of the senses and imagination as distinct from faith and grace; these realms are alternative points of departure for acquiring knowledge of the world and furthermore for expressing that knowledge. Such a poeticized theology receives a total renovation in *Piers Plowman*. This fourteenth-century epic's ideas about knowledge, language and reality embrace the thinking of Langland's contemporaries the *moderni*. Not only Ockham, of course, but other grammatico-logistic theologians such as Holcot, Thomas Buckingham and Adam Woodham, all caused a reaction and radical turn to orthodoxy (Coleman 23). Chaucer's work reflects this turn as well in the epistemological wrangling typical of his dream poems' respective narrators and other characters, most of all in the Prologue to the *Legend of Good Women*; all of his poems, however, privilege the role of witnessing events in the process of what was, according to Ockham, the acquisition of *intuitive knowledge*. In the work of both poets the personae are reporters of events; they are witnesses—as was the Dante-figure in the *Commedia*. Both Dante and Langland, in Middleton's comparison of them (in "Narration and the Invention of Experience" 101-102),

> make the "I" the narrative subject, a center of "sense-making" for the poem. He does, suffers, and interprets as well as reports its actions, simultaneously composing and reading them as personal history, a "horizontally motivated" narration. This individual *historia* constitutes his own counterpart to the world's salvation history—that universal design which he can know in the books of philosophers [. . .]. His effort is thus active and practical as well as receptive and contemplative and effectively supplants the purely visionary as a center of narrative interest.

Chaucer's persona in the Prologue to the *Legend of Good Women* must also weigh the worth of knowledge derived from books versus what he can gain through first hand experience. This scenario—the poet-reader who must ascertain the truth—is the basic formative impulse for the first person narratology of all three poets.

Edwards comments that

> Chaucer's achievement in devising his narrator consists in aligning the traditional function of authentication with a notion of textuality. The narrator of the dream poems refers not to a private experience but to a poetic tradition that has shaped his experience and provided the materials for recounting it.
>
> (*The Dream of Chaucer* 49)

Yet when we come to Will in *Piers Plowman*, while we surely discover a character who aligns himself with a textual tradition through quotation, allusion as well as more subtle forms of self-positing, what we also find is a character who, as he moves in and out of his dreams and within them, as he speaks with one or another interlocutor, presents us with a dizzying array of properties and associations. This amorphism contributes to the poem's overall effect that has too often been taken for a disunity. And as Middleton notes, there is a difficulty in making the normal "distinction [. . .] between literal and allegorical meaning, between narrative and symbolic 'levels' of description. There seems to be an unusually large gap between the two: one does not easily translate into the other, and they seem not to be describing the same work" (91). In a similar vein, Rosemary Woolf (in "Some Non-Medieval Qualities of *Piers Plowman*" 91, 86) has written about Langland's "indifference to the literal level of his allegory [that is] tenuous and confused."[12] As for the persona, Will, which has been taken often enough for an everyman type of allegorical figure,[13] Lawton has mentioned this figure's inconsistency as a character made up of "a bewildering number of attributes [. . .] some contradictory [. . .]" ("The Subject of *Piers Plowman*" 11).[14] However, Jill Mann (in *Langland and Allegory* 8) qualifies these judgments in a significant manner when she says that

> Langland's allegorical fiction never leaves the world of concrete reality behind, but subsumes it, in the awareness that its role is more important than to be merely a source of metaphor. He uses the ambivalent grammatical status of his personifications to establish a bridge between his allegorical fiction and the realities of fourteenth-century society, in a way that has important implications for his poem and for his view of the world.

---

[12] In J. A. Burrow, *Langland's Fictions*, 2.
[13] Cf. Burrow, who provides a concise review of the salient features of Langland's critical reception
[14] In Burrow, 90.

Indeed, what finally holds the poem together is its trenchant meditation on language, indirectly and directly—and more so than in the work of either Chaucer or Dante—which is ultimately accomplished through Langland's poetics. As Griffiths observes, the poem's many

> transformations, the sudden materialisings and collapses of people and places, which are effected by changes in the signifying properties of the names in the narrative discourse, are part of the dream-like "kaleidoscopic" quality of *Piers Plowman*, and they are part of its quality as "anti-narrative," its tendency to subvert the ordinary conventions and forms of narrative representation.
> (106)

This quality is punctuated and intensified by the poem's numerous authorial signatures. Middleton writes that they

> typically occur at the joinings of sections, as one venture yields to another, and, with remarkable regularity, in close association with the characteristic disruptions of the narrative: they show the "I" in the act of repeatedly transforming rather than finishing his project. With an increasing fullness in each successive revision of the text, they present Will primarily in the guise of an active inquirer and writer ("here is wil wold wite") so as to ally the two activities.
> (120)

Furthermore, the signatures perform this organizing task ever more systematically from one revision to the next, which yields "a broader kind of enabling and textual competence as a ground of the 'truth' of the work." To be sure, these signatures underscore Langland's acts of revision. They

> are disposed through the work not only [. . .] sporadically to foreground the poetic and intellectual aspirations of Langland's project, but systematically to mark and display the critical points of genesis and transformation of that project, realized as a succession of critical turning points in the author's life. The moments of signature become narratively pivotal events that render biographical and poetic self-awareness synonymous.
> ("William Langland's 'Kynde Name'" 41–42)

Here, then, we must not assume that subjectivity in later medieval poetry need necessarily be made manifest through linear story-telling. Our ongoing consideration of contemporaneous philosophy and theology will allow us to understand how the subjective is necessary to all narrative and its relationship to historiographical and scientific impulses, albeit this narrative can take many forms. Dante had "made possible a poetic celebration of the discrete mortal historical self"; he centered his poem on "the subject's understanding as a being in historical time." But for Langland "the value, autonomy, and cultural authority of personal history as a genre, and the status of a serious fictive work centered upon it" was "always at issue." Again in contrast, Dante's "temporal acts acquire particular clarity as he assumes personal authority for them among souls whose every moment in eternity is spent in recognizing and taking upon themselves the authorship of their own life stories" ("Narration and the Invention of Experience" 103-104).[15] Langland's Will also assumes this kind of "personal authority" yet the "clarity" of this assumption is wrapped up in a poetics that is more deeply metatextual. As we shall see, Langland's narrative—and Chaucer's in a different fashion—examines its own narratology as a part of its overall epistemological enterprise. Even so, the narratives of all three poets are possible because of a subjectivity they are each embracing.

The remainder of this chapter will compare Chaucer's and Langland's narrative procedures and their ultimate significance to the authorship trope. However, before embarking on in depth analyses of them and their ultimate significance within the parameters of an investigation into the poetics of authorship, we need to recall previous remarks (made in the Introduction) about subjectivity—in order to issue a caution against construing such subjectivity, within the context of the fourteenth-century narrative, too narrowly. Subjectivity must be thought of according to the conditions of this time and particularly in relation to the period's philosophical movements. To do so is to arrive, finally, at an appreciation of the central importance of language as an object of contemplation within this narrative, and of how philosophy of language, as understood by Chaucer and Langland, was a structuring agent of it. Patterson writes, we must not "assume that subjectivity comes into existence only as an effect of specifically modern systems of subjection [. . .]." To assume so

> ignores a great deal of historical evidence to the contrary but, more important, posits selfhood as by definition beleaguered and ineffectual. But if we can understand that subjectivity is a human characteristic that has always been part of our history, albeit in different configurations and with different powers and values, we can also recognize that it has often been experienced as being set in some form of opposition to both the past from which it emerges and the social world within which its destiny is shaped. It is of course true that human self-consciousness has been reified into the concept of a wholly autonomous individual, a concept that has in turn been transformed into a fully fledged ideology of individualism. But this impeaches neither the fact of subjectivity itself nor its capacity to act within the world.
> (*Chaucer and the Subject of History* 12)

In one arrangement or another, we see the emerging autonomy of the self vying for equal or perhaps greater status with, variously: an autonomous divinity, an autonomous nature, and an autonomous language; this last the poet knows as intimately and intuitively as he might know himself. The reactions to the truths posited by previous thinkers, Ockham and others, are central to Langland's vision,

---

[15] Cf. Patterson, *Chaucer and the Subject of History*, 11.

and to Chaucer's—but especially Langland's and most of all in his poem's concerns for epistemology and grammar. Indeed, his extended grammatical metaphor[16] is crucial to understanding how he finally viewed his poem, its intentions, philosophy and esthetics. This metaphor will ultimately lead to the realization that "[l]anguage is for Langland," as Mann has said,

> not merely a mirror of reality, it is a mirror of *more* than reality. It not only names the objects that make up our physical life, it also names the invisible qualities which animate the physical world and constitute its hidden dynamics. And it does more than name: its generative capacities, its transformational powers are the index of the world's multiplicity, multiplicity of dimension, relationships, potentialities. Medieval philosophy was as familiar as twentieth-century philosophy with the notion that language structures our experience. But whereas in the twentieth-century this tends to create unease, to imply that we are imprisoned in language, barred by it from contact with reality, Langland responded to the idea with excitement and enthusiasm. For him, the structure of language is not a distortion, but the sign of an extra dimension of meaning. (23-24)

From the point of view of the history of philosophy, ironically, we can say that these fourteenth-century figures needed to construct a world vision that contained two fundamental aspects, the *potentia absoluta* and the *potentia ordinata* of God. Respectively, the one was designed to express the absolute freedom of God within a world of necessity, the other to indicate divine power in its aspect relative to humankind and the possibility for the exercise of the individual will toward the achievement of salvation, all according to the Divine covenant. This ultraconservative response was a consequence of the dismantling of miraculous thinking that, in 1277, resulted in the papal condemnation of the Paris arts faculty, an event brought about by advances in philosophy that included rationalism as a central procedural tenet of current theology. Duns Scotus (c. 1265-1308) had approached theology as a science that he held must be as mathematically exact as geometry; so too, succeeding theologians "felt their inadequacy as scientists when it came to knowing and demonstrating properties of the divine essence which they knew only as a general idea, not as a distinct object of knowledge" (Coleman 18). In defense of logic and philosophy, Ockham and others chose to make a stand within the realm of language, by pursuing the question of whether or not it could contribute to the establishing of truth or falsity in the demonstration of principles. This in a sense became their "geometry." Yet there was, perhaps, a cost to be paid in this "retrenchment." Just as the three-in-one paradoxical nature of the Trinity was irreconcilable,[17] God's "primacy and unity" could not be demonstrated. Consequently, the

> realms of experience and faith were split as they never were for thirteenth-century thinkers. This meant that logical analysis applied more to the workings of God in

---

[16] Cf. Chapter Three, and below.
[17] Cf. the Introduction.

the world as it is (the *ordinata*), than to God's nature *per se*.
(Coleman 19)[18]

As we have seen in the *Commedia*, Dante diverges from Aquinas' doctrines in relatively conservative ways. We have examined this attempt to establish poetic thought and language as an entity unto itself and subsequently to integrate the poetic processes into an all embracing, theologically grounded epistemology. Langland and Chaucer perpetuate such a claim for poetry. Also, Dante also places the heathen emperor Trajan and Ripheus in Paradise (Par. XX.121-24) despite the Thomistic doctrine of the supremacy of Grace in the machinery of knowledge and salvation (i.e., Dante's claim for the pagans was based on their good faith apart from other circumstances). In the fourteenth century there is an even greater accommodation to the idea that the individual will, which can manifest itself as faith, can achieve salvation through good works performed naturally. In the C text of *Piers Plowman*, Langland, having elaborated the Trajan story more emphatically than Dante before him in order to show the importance of following natural law, gradually settles into a position similar to Wyclif.[19] Langland has done so, moreover, after having taken up the more radical views of Ockham or Holcot. We can say in hindsight, from the point of view of the development of philosophy as a discipline that would someday be considered as distinct from theology, that Langland has traveled great lengths beyond what was possible in the thirteenth century. Taking the latter portion of the C text to be his ultimately evolved position on these matters, it is possible to conclude that he at last held there to be a concord, necessary to salvation, between individual deeds and divine grace, which was attainable through the agency of faith. This doctrine is espoused in C's later passus by Liberum Arbitrium, whereas earlier in the poem a more extremely "modern" position had been proposed by figures who represent "the more intellectual faculties" (Coleman 252). In any case, what needs to be underlined here is that Langland's theology is clearly at odds with Dante and Aquinas.

The same can easily be said for Chaucer. His poetry suggests that he found himself right in the middle of the nominalist-realist debate that had been rekindled by Ockham and cast in a contemporary light by others Chaucer knew or could have known such as Holcot, Ralph Strode, Thomas Bradwardine and Wyclif. In this light, it hardly seems coincidental that Ockham, the nominalist, and Chaucer, who is fervently interested in the philosophy of language, place great emphasis on the importance to epistemology of *experience*. To be sure, Chaucer's poetry never asks absolutely Ockhamist questions, even though it was written during a time

---

[18] Cf. Scotus, I *Sent*. d. 17 q. 1; and Ockham, *Quodlibet* VI q. 1.
[19] Coleman *Medieval Readers and Writers*, 251. Cf. B XI.140-59, C XII.86-7, B XII and XV, and C XIV and XVII throughout. Yet, as William Kamowski asserts (in "Langland and Wyclif on Theology," p. 1 in ms. sent to me), "[t]he once popular notion that Langland was a Wycliffite has now been put to rest." Kamowski's convincing paper cites, in support of its thesis: Bowers, "Piers Plowman and the Police"; Pamela Gradon, "Langland and the Ideology of Dissent"; Lawton, "Lollardy and the 'Piers Plowman' Tradition"; and Christina von Nolcken, "*Piers Plowman*, the Wycliffites, and *Pierce the Plowman's Creed*."

when people like Holcot were being strongly persuaded by what Ockham had had to say; and Chaucer's friend Strode, a realist and Ockham reactionary like his associate Wyclif, took up a number of anti-realist positions after 1375.[20] But even when no philosophy is openly espoused, Chaucer's vocabulary clearly partakes of the nominalist controversy. As already noted, there are ubiquitous discussions in his poems concerning the nature and significance of experience—how its very force can present the hope of genuinely knowing, of genuinely *being* in the world. These discussions argue for situating Chaucer within the sphere of the controversy.[21]

Chaucer's discourse, moreover, furnishes us with a fundamental insight into his poetics. The degree of attention he paid to the question of, particularly, first hand experience as a conduit for arriving at truth, is of extraordinary importance in trying to understand what I believe was his major literary innovation, the persona, especially as this persona developed from poem to poem; this development charts his experiments with and ultimate turn away from allegory, that medieval poesis par excellence. It is no accident that in each successive poem his persona, increasingly, resides outside any allegorical framework.[22] Keeping Ockham's ideas in mind, what becomes strikingly clear is that Chaucer employs his persona to carry on an implicit criticism of allegory as both a poetic and epistemological form.[23]

---

[20] Cf. David Lyle Jeffrey, "Chaucer and Wyclif: Biblical Hermeneutic and Literary Theory in the XIVth Century," 111; and, J. A. W. Bennett, *Chaucer at Oxford and at Cambridge*.

[21] And many scholars have done so, for example: Morton W. Bloomfield, "Fourteenth-Century England: Realism and Rationalism in Wyclif and Chaucer"; Holly Wallace Boucher, "Nominalism: The Difference for Chaucer and Boccaccio"; John Gardner, *The Poetry of Chaucer*, 298 ff.; Jeffrey, "Chaucer and Wyclif: Biblical Hermeneutic and Literary Theory in the XIVth Century"; Stewart Justman, "Literal and Symbolic in the *Canterbury Tales*"; J. Mitchell Morse, "The Philosophy of the Clerk of Oxenford"; Russell Peck, "Chaucer and the Nominalist Questions"; Jay Ruud, "Chaucer and Nominalism: The 'Envoy to Bukton'"; Geoffrey Shepherd, "Religion and Philosophy in Chaucer"; David C. Steinmetz, "Late Medieval Nominalism and the 'Clerk's Tale'"; Robert Stepsis, "*Potentia Absoluta* and the 'Clerk's Tale'"; P. B. Taylor, "Chaucer's 'Cosyn to the Dede'"; and, David Williams, "From Grammar's Pan to Logic's Fire: Intentionality and Chaucer's 'Friar's Tale'." Ruud (211) especially argues that Chaucer's attention to detail results from the influence of Ockham's emphasizing of *intuitive cognition*.

[22] There may be some question as to the persona's fundamental role in Chaucer's earlier poems when the distinction between allegory and a less determined sort of logico-rhetorical structure is not as subtle as it was eventually to become; but I believe there can be no doubt of Chaucer's decision to move beyond a strictly ordered allegorical framework (as I shall define this, below) in his late and monumental works, *Troilus and Criseyde* and *The Canterbury Tales* (here individual tales may be allegorical, but the frame of the tales surely is not), and, arguably, in the Prologue to the *Legend of Good Women*.

[23] On Chaucer's persona, cf. among others: Lisa Abshear-Seals, "Boccaccio's Criseida and Chaucer's Criseyde"; Donald Baker, "Dreamer and Critic: The Poet in the *Legend of Good Women*"; Dorothy Bethurum, "Chaucer's Point of View as Narrator in the Love Poems"; Sheila Delaney, *The Naked Text: Chaucer's* Legend of Good Women; Maureen

It is within this nominalist-realist context that we can also comprehend Langland's intense poetics of naming, a poetics that at least matches the vast array of personages in Dante's *Commedia*. The number of proper names in Langland's poem reflects its unusually intense, animated quality, which we see in the three dimensional characterization of personified abstract qualities such as Reason, Conscience, and Truth (they need only be compared with previous and succeeding counterparts, such as in De Meun's and Lorris' *Roman de la rose* or Bunyan's *Pilgrim's Progress*). "In *Piers Plowman*," notes Griffiths, "personification is not just an incidental rhetorical ornament, but a master trope [. . .]" (105). As Mann says, furthermore, "[w]hereas other allegorists work on 'Platonising' principles, penetrating the veil of physical experience to reach the transcendental reality behind it, Langland shows us abstractions as inextricably embedded in concrete individuals" (8). Even Dowel, Dobet and Dobest are, arguably, memorable within the limits Langland sets for them, although these terms do not readily adhere to clearly recognizable forces in the objective world existing beyond the purview of Langland's poem—that is, they are what Middleton calls "coined terms" ("Two Infinites" 171). We shall explore, shortly, their existence within the poem as grammatical anomalies. As poetic figures, moreover, our conclusion respecting them can only be that, within themselves, they provide a unique integration of Langland's concern to establish a discussion about the making of poetry. This discussion is intimately connected to his conception of the availability of salvation to the individual. Of course, I have already tentatively advanced the notion of such an integral relationship—one suggesting that poetry possesses the power of redemption—as operative, albeit in less determined forms, in the works of Dante and Marcabru, those predecessors of Langland who fundamentally develop the later Middle Ages' poetics of naming.

Beyond the instances of Langland's allegories we can also appreciate his poem's unusually animated energy in the many levels of consciousness through which a reader views "reality" within the poem, as in the persona Will's frequent dreams, the multiple levels of dreaming, and dreams within other dreams. These dreams interweave, in terms of points of view and perception and as pertains to

---

Fries, "The 'Other' Voice: Woman's Song, Its Satire and Its Transcendence in Late Medieval British Literature"; Greetham, "Self-Referential Artifacts: Hoccleve's Persona as a Literary Device"; Michael B. Herzog, "The *Book of the Duchess*: The Vision of the Artist as a Young Dreamer"; Jeffrey, "Sacred and Secular Scripture: Authority and Interpretation in the House of Fame"; Lisa J. Kiser, *Telling Classical Tales: Chaucer and the* Legend of Good Women; Lawton, *Chaucer's Narrators*; Robert O. Payne, *The Key of Remembrance*; "Late Medieval Images and Self-Image of the Poet: Chaucer, Gower, Lydgate, Henryson, Dunbar"; and "Making His Own Myth: The Prologue to Chaucer's *Legend of Good Women*"; Gale C. Schricker, "On the Relation of Fact and Fiction in Chaucer's Poetic Endings"; John Stephens, "The Uses of Personae and the Art of Obliqueness in Some Chaucer Lyrics" Parts I, II and III; and, Richard Waswo, "The Narrator of *Troilus and Criseyde*." My essay, "Ockham, Chaucer, and the Emergence of Modern Poetics," analyzes the influences of contemporaneous intellectual theories on the development of the Chaucer persona.

their thematic contents, with the pilgrim's waking states in which, ostensibly, the drama of the poem unfolds. The dream vision genre is fully exploited by Langland in ways we might presume never occurred to Dante, who in comparison with Langland hardly makes use of the relationship between dreaming and waking. In hindsight, from Langland's point of view, we see the dream vision as a mere vehicle in Dante's hands, as a context for his overall discourse. How, then, might Langland fully exploit and portray the dynamic between these two states of consciousness? Langland's poem "seems somehow reiterative rather than progressive," as Middleton phrases it ("Narration and Invention of Experience" 92). The linearity of Dante's narrative exists in relation to this dream vision structure, which Langland turns into a rather free wheeling and seemingly discontinuous accumulation of multiple and at times enigmatic subnarratives. As for the earlier Marcabru, he did not really concern himself with dreams and the questions of perception within the confines of different states of awareness.[24] Nevertheless, a growing popularity of dream poetry suggests its proportional relationship to a concomitant development of a poetics of naming, and a relationship, too, between the two and a changing theologico-philosophical landscape. The "animation" that deeply characterizes *Piers Plowman* finds a parallel in contemporary beliefs about language and particularly the hope for the efficacy of language, which, in extreme cases, when driven by the forces of rationalism, led to the logical conclusion that words could contain reality—that they could contain *being* and, therefore, that they could enjoy at least an ontological parity with the things of the world beyond language. In *Piers Plowman* dreams are also at least as interesting, espouse at least as complex, profound and provocative beliefs, and are at least as vivid and in terms of plot as important, as anything that occurs during the dreamer Will's waking moments.

In other words, we might say, in sum, that this poem's language itself comprehends an animated quality in its capacity to contain being. For Langland, more so than for Dante or Chaucer, the dream *visio* was integral to his philosophy and his poetics. As I have been suggesting, in one sense we can read *Piers Plowman* as a poem that makes its strongest statement through its poetics, which represents not only the culmination of the development of a poetry of naming but ultimately the undoing of the very poetic form *Piers Plowman* inhabits. Langland is, of course, interested in availing himself of the inherent grace and power of the dream vision genre, just as he is writing a poem of pilgrimage, and, more, composing an allegory. He is intent, though, upon employing these "genres" to achieve new ends. He wishes as much to demonstrate his vision as to state it directly; thus his poetry, a poetry of indirection, ultimately expresses its author's world vision through subversions of various poetic forms. In Langland's view, we might presume, these forms have become stale, even obsolete. Chaucer shares this point of view but his poetics and the discourse of his persona address this situation

---

[24] Burrow's first chapter, "A Gathering of Dreams," is a comprehensive survey and evaluation of the dream genre. See also: Steven F. Kruger, *Dreaming in the Middle Ages*; and, A. C. Spearing, *Medieval Dream Poetry*.

in a considerably more understated manner; we will be principally noting the subversive effects of his persona, its comical "feebleness" particularly. All the same, both poets are interested in subverting traditional poetic forms, with a single-minded and unswerving intention not to be found in Dante.

Therefore, regarding *Piers Plowman* and the Prologue to the *Legend of Good Women*, one question that invites examination is the possible significance of the respective dreamers' waking states—beyond the mere exigencies of the stories themselves and aside from those values embodied in the poems' dreams—since their dream sequences comprise the vast majority of their poems.[25] Especially in *Piers Plowman*, the phenomenon of dreaming and its connection to language, knowledge and poetry, take us to the very heart of the poem's critical "problems" and its power. This phenomenon is operative especially in its relationship to the manner in which the poem proceeds, in all three versions, as an allegorized set of dream visions.

We will note at some length, however, that in the C version's autobiographical fifth passus, which is unique to this revision of the poem, the insertion of the awakened Will and what he says to Reason and Conscience not only considerably alter the significance of the dreams in and of themselves but of the poem as a whole, when seen as being one instance in the greater context of a dream vision tradition. On the other hand, once readers realize that the poem is an allegory, they will also admit that its allegoresis is, in the final analysis, maddeningly equivocal (certainly for modern readers) in terms of its possible "meaning." Hence, problems of interpretation attendant upon any close reading of *Piers Plowman* must be met by setting the poem within the dream vision genre's literary history, precisely because Langland departs from generic expectations in singular ways. In fact, his originality can be described especially in terms regarding what might be viewed as the radical attempt to dismantle his very own dream vision architecture, insofar as prior to him the dream vision form had lent itself to the allegory process. Langland's attempt, a success in large measure, is to set *Piers Plowman* apart from all other dream visions by creating a poetic machinery that implodes; in so doing, the poetic structure calls attention to and thus implicitly comments on itself. By extension, moreover, the implosion—or perhaps the better term here would be deconstruction—of the poem comments in large on the nature of the poetic imagination. And it is this connection, to a radical poetics, a poetics that is characterized by a self-awareness as both dream vision and allegory, which discloses most fully the significance of the Langland persona.

We can make considerable headway in understanding the nature of Langland's poetic enterprise by studying his persona; in this regard, the following extended

---

[25] I am taking the Prologue to be a poem in and of itself, because of its relative similarity to Chaucer's other dream poems, as distinct and possessing a unity apart from the "legends" that follow it.

comparison of "Will" with the contemporary "Geffrey"—and briefly with "Dante"—will divulge the philosophical and poetic background of these "poets," which in turn will allow us to appreciate the alternatives Langland and Chaucer created for themselves in response to that background. To understand Geffrey we must also see this figure within the context of its functioning according to the dream vision expectation as that expectation is modified and undermined by Chaucer; and perhaps as we may see Geffrey at work, even if not so named, in *Troilus and Criseyde* and the *Canterbury Tales*. This persona is explicitly named in some of Chaucer's poems and signed in others, in a number of ways. In the *House of Fame* the figure is given Chaucer's proper name (729); furthermore, as Sheila Delaney points out (in *The Naked Text* 31), this persona also worries that "no wight have my name in honde" (1877). Clearly, having a particular name is significant for both Chaucer and Geffrey. This evidently intense interest in naming would suggest that Geffrey will appear so named in each of Chaucer's successive poems. In the *Troilus*, though, the narrator goes unnamed. We know, however, who he is, because he exhibits certain characteristics—there is especially his weak will and equally weak wit—which seem, ironically, to hinder him in telling his tale; these characteristics, to one extent or another, inhere in all of Chaucer's narrators. There are other reasons, as well, for recognizing the persona. Delaney notes that in this poem

> an occasion could have been invented, or a narratorial name included with those of Gower and Strode at the [poem's] end. In any case, the pronounced authorial self-consciousness in *Troilus* is not expressed in naming. Nor is it in the *Legend [of Good Women]*—not, at least, directly. There is a fair amount of naming in the *Legend*: various sources and authors are named throughout, and the naming of Alceste is an important feature of the Prologue: she names herself (F 432, G 422), she is named by Cupid (F 511, G 499), and the Narrator acknowledges her by name (F 518, G 506). Moreover, though the Narrator is not named, his previous works—which also happen to be the works we recognize as Chaucer's—explicitly and profusely are both named and evaluated. What seems to happen is that personal self-referentiality is displaced onto Alceste, while the poet himself exists as maker of his works and as object of a critical discourse. Whatever his personal fate, the poet seems to realize that he will live as the author of works that, unlike so much medieval literature before (and even after) him, will not be untitled or anonymous; in short, his name (albeit here suppressed) is going to have a function—the one, I suggest, that Michel Foucault has called an "author-function."[26]
> (31-32)

Chaucer will refer to himself, through mention of his literary achievements, twice more in his writing—in the Man of Law's Tale and in the Retraction of the *Canterbury Tales*. The significance of this late development in his career has much to do with our investigation into the Prologue to the *Legend of Good Women*, and

---

[26] Cf. the Introduction.

thus I will have more to say about it in due time. Here I first must circumscribe our discussion in order to focus solely on the issue of presence and absence through explicit self-naming rather than on the more broad and multiple strategies of autocitation.

We must note initially, then, that the Chaucerian strategy in which the persona is named by an other has been employed by both Dante and Langland.[27] As has been discussed, Will refers to himself as "Longe Wille"—close enough to "William Langland" although this persona's self-description is not absolutely explicit. One thing that the vast array of *Piers Plowman*'s authorial signatures points to is Langland's choice precisely *not* to name himself explicitly. Such indirection is, generally speaking, a departure from the expectation that an author will name himself or herself directly. Yet Langland's authorial strategy does not take the form of absence such as we find in Dante.[28] Even so, there is a strong parallel between the *Commedia*'s protagonist, who late in the poem is first actually called "Dante" by Beatrice (Purg. XXX.55), and the first actual naming of "Wille" by Lady Church (C I.5). The parallel between these later medieval poems and the *Consolation of Philosophy* is striking, although both Dante and Langland reverse the Boethian process, as Middleton explains:

[Lady Philosophy] shows the grieving and dispossessed subject [i.e., the Boethian narrator] that in reality he has lost nothing of value: his alienation from his story and worldly identity is the aim of her philosophy. That alienation is the starting point of Dante's and Langland's poems: in both, the direction and amplitude of the narrative effort gradually return the subject to the full possession of his worldly history, enabling him to know it profoundly as—*and because*—he has made it. What the *Consolation* ascribes to Fortune and defines as radically unknowable, these two great fourteenth-century poems present as the germ of modern autobiography, developing in the interstices of an encyclopedic display of universal knowledge.
("Narration and the Invention of Experience" 102)

In the Prologue to the *Legend of Good Women* Chaucer undermines the Boethian tradition by a reversal in which his persona names Alceste, who serves as an intercessor much like Beatrice and the other female figures.

Furthermore, even as textual evidence tells us that Langland was called William or Wilhelmus, in his poem his persona is never called by these names but rather by the name *Will*.[29] In C's fifth passus, Will's debate with Reason becomes profoundly important when we consider what *will* had come to mean; in Langland's time the human *will*, as Bowers points out, could be viewed as an antithetical force to *wit* (177),[30] while *wit* was almost indistinguishable from *ratio*. Unlike

---

[27] Cf. Kane, *The Evidence for Authorship*, 26–51, 56–57.
[28] Cf. the discussion of Dante, especially in the Introduction and in Chapter Three.
[29] Cf. Bowers, 177.
[30] Cf. *Oxford English Dictionary* XII.201, "wit" I.2; Alexander, *Theories of Will in the History of Philosophy*; and Gilson, *History of Christian Philosophy in the Middle Ages*; in

Chaucer's persona, or Dante's, whenever Langland's dreamer is called by his name we must read a special import into the event itself—although the question of wittedness arises in a pointed manner in the characterization of the Chaucer persona (as in the Prologue where the narrator cannot mount a credible defense of his own writing against Cupid's accusations). On two occasions it is clear that Will is being named specifically in order to establish a relationship with Reason or Wit, as Bowers observes:

> While Skeat maintains that Will is first named in the B-text after Reason has delivered the sermon that "made Wille to wepe water wiþ hise ei3en" (B V.61), there is some doubt that this is anything other than the collective *voluntas* of the people. Yet the Dreamer is certainly the one later named Will by the figure Thought, who has taken him in search of Wit: "Wher Dowel and Dobet and Dobest ben in londe / Here is Wil wolde wite if Wit koude hym teche" (B VIII.128-29). In the B-text, Wit's sermon represents the first expansion upon the teachings of Holy Church since Passus I, placing important emphasis on the internal rather than external reality of the good life. The C-poet, knowing that the action would eventually focus upon the Dreamer and his inner quest, inserts the personal allegory of C V and uses it to signal future difficulties by pitting Will against Reason, the faculty that should be his partner and guide, in an informal but recognizable debate.
> (179)[31]

It is the addition of what Skeat called the "personal allegory," the directly autobiographical passage in C V, which allows for the great forcefulness that a fourteenth-century reader must have felt in coming upon the name Will and in marveling at the fantastic configuration of signifiers other than, and including, the explicit name. This great semiological puzzle coalesced around the poem's persona.

Yet what, or who was this figure? We know, of course, that Will was meant to be seen as a poet. In modern times the Chaucerian persona, also a poet, has been far more widely admired. While both figures may confront themselves with their own activity of making poetry, and while they are confronted by other characters, often in humorous ways, we tend to derive greater enjoyment from Geffrey because of Chaucer's literary realism generally, and especially because of what to a modern reader is this persona's obviously ironic status. Both personae, however, emerge from the same traditions. And there are more similarities. Not only are both personae, first and foremost, identified as poets, but they are poets who are concerned with the act of recording their respective experiences, with being able to achieve revelation on some cognitive level or other through the possible reflection *makyng* might afford. Both also concern themselves with what are the meanings and uses of texts, books, and stories. We can include Dante in these descriptions.

Bowers, 177 n. 33.
[31] Skeat II.71. Cf. Kane, *The Evidence for Authorship*, 59. Bowers' citations to the B text here and elsewhere refer to the Kane and Donaldson edition.

Just the same, Geffrey and Will display other attributes apart from Dante. For instance, these later English poets cannot adequately defend themselves in their poetic roles, as poets, against the accusations of those who can see no use in their verse making—an activity which, furthermore, allows both of their authors to bring into their poems or stories the issue of poetry's, and by extension language's, suitability and effectiveness. Langland and Chaucer were undoubtedly aware of a tradition as old as Western letters in which poets complained that the buffoons of their respective societies received the better treatment; Curtius writes that "medieval poets too had every reason to emphasize the value and dignity of their art and to defend it from reproaches" (473).

Where the conceptualizations of the two English personae most obviously part company is in the fact that Will is clearly, if he is nothing else (he surely *is*, however), an allegorical representation of *voluntas*, while Geffrey, just as clearly, does not serve any obvious allegorical function in Chaucer's poems, which accounts in part for the realistic sense we have of this character. We feel, so to speak, that we need not see past Geffrey or rather *through* him to some didactic value for which he might be standing in; he does not seem to be carrying out some mission for his poet. Nevertheless, we need not see Will in this fashion—even if this is so very easy to do, and we should hesitate before presuming that we understand him in the way readers did in his own time. Perhaps it is fair enough to assert that a certain contemporaneous reception of Will is often presumed by the modern reader, and therefore categorical condemnation of Langland's supposed lack of creativity or vitality may follow; or rather, modernity has trouble recognizing his lack of literary realism, when he is judged by standards that have evolved in a later era.

Recent critical theories, on the other hand, make possible new forays into Langland studies, and there is now a new appreciation of *Piers Plowman* based on its metatextual dimension. These theories implicitly invite an examination of Chaucer's use of dreams, how he uses the dream vision genre to help to define his persona and to instigate an epistemological discussion that will include a focus on the making of poetry. Such an examination will, in comparison with Langland, tell us much about this "allegorical" poet's metalinguistic, metapoetical, and ultimately self-enunciatory intentions. Ultimately, these intentions and writerly maneuvers, on Langland's part, will lead us to our deepest appreciation of the authorship trope that, in its medieval incarnation, became fully developed in *Piers Plowman*. As for Chaucer, his persona suggests how its author was striking out in new literary directions—but this figure cannot be fully comprehended, either, without setting it beside Will.

Particularly in Chaucer's dream poems, there is an underlying philosophical dialogue taking place, which unites in a single poetic vision the interrelated motifs of authorship, dreaming, language, and the possible perception of reality. As we have noted (principally in Chapter Two), Chaucer makes the attempt to reconcile a discrepancy between the principle of formality, and knowledge—an essentially epistemological problem that is most vividly addressed in the opening of the *Parliament of Fowls*, which draws an analogy between formalistically determined courtly love that occurs within the realm of experience, and artful writing; by extension, the capacity truly *to know* the world is held to be a likely possibility through the act of writing that must also take place, for the author, as an experience:[32]

> The lyf so short, the craft so long to lerne,
> Th'assay so hard, so sharp the conquerynge,
> The dredful joye alwey that slit so yerne:
> Al this mene I by Love [. . .].
> (1-4)

As he has at his disposal only the forms of postlapsarian language, and the artful uses to be made of them, how can the truth be told, Chaucer is asking, considering that Truth is an ideal state, considering that the truth exists, ultimately, beyond all physical and/or temporal structures—beyond all experience? Hence, the poet is left with a mere gesture. That gesture, in its very failure, the failure of the poet's language, is meant to indicate the ideal truth beyond that language.

As we have said, the dream *visio* is at heart an esthetic and philosophical response to this predicament. The dream state's miracle-like texture, if at times a sharpening force, may also blur or otherwise undermine differences between particularity and abstraction, time and eternity—the feasible as opposed to the supernatural. Yet the dream vision poem eventually returns to these distinctions, from within the *visio* context, because it recognizes a paradoxical truth that resides in the imaginative literary impulse, a truth that exists separately from the sensible, factual world. Thus in the Prologue to the *Legend of Good Women* Chaucer confronts the conundrum of knowing through literature as opposed to first hand, material experience:[33]

> But Goddes forbode but men shulde leve
> Wel more thyng than men han seyn with ye!
> Men shal nat wenen every thyng a lye
> For that he say it nat of yore ago.
> God wot a thyng is nevere the lesse so
> Thow every wyght ne may it nat yse.
> Bernard the monk ne say nat al, parde!
> Thanne mote we to bokes that we fynde,
> Though whiche that olde thynges ben in mynde [. . .].
> (G 10-18, F 10-18)

The philosophical and problematical relationships between memory and the

---

[32] Cf. the Introduction and Chapter Two.
[33] In this regard cf. Payne, *Key of Remembrance*, 93 ff.

factual present, the *auctoritee* of books (history and imaginative literature) and experiential reality, are eventually resolved in Chaucer's Prologue through the narrator's intuitive epiphany that a dream may afford: in the dream state alone, we are told, will humanity be able to solve the riddles of nature such as, for example, the possibility of communication between man and beast. The marvelous qualities of dreams, and nature as well, will be celebrated through the joy readers find in the poem's narrator when he listens to and understands in his dream, as if with a new mind, the singing of birds:

> This song to herkenen I dide al myn entente,
> *For-why I mette I wiste what they* [the birds] *mente*,
> Tyl at the laste a larke song above:
> "I se," quod she, "the myghty god of Love" [and so on].
> (G 139–42; my emphasis)

Here a reader bridges the real and surreal, in witnessing the unfolding of events leading to the God of Love's savage and comical indictment of Chaucer's persona, a topos that finds an apt parallel in the dreamer Will's ineffectual defense against Reason's charges of "ydelnesse" in C.V, as well as the defense of Geffrey's actions cleverly brought about by the goddess Alceste. But to appreciate what transpires, the reader needs to remain cognizant of the fact that Chaucer's narrator is dreaming. Although Alceste and Cupid, and the Chaucerian persona, become real enough for the sake of momentary dramatic success, in the back of a reader's mind it is never quite forgotten that all which is being viewed takes place through the persona's fantastic vision. This awareness is the result of the Prologue's enchanting quality, since it is possible to understand through the memory of one's own dreams, which informs one's reading, the magical quality of dreaming. The dream *visio*, then, moves readers precisely because of its unreal nature. However, when they partake of its fantasy they also intuit, or derive, a sense of unity out of a contradictory actuality—that is, the experiential as well as literary "reality."

The introduction of the gods Cupid and Alceste into an existential equation, in fact, is announced by the fictive birds in the narrator's dream;[34] they are precisely like the birds he would encounter on his walks through the countryside in his worship of the daisy. And after all they are the same birds. One realizes this duplication in part because the settings and actions of visionary and waking states are closely aligned, although what the birds say and do are altered by dream consciousness. It is a wondrous and lovely scene. Nevertheless, and perhaps paradoxically, a more serious note is sounded at this juncture in the poem.

This same dream circumstance becomes the vehicle by which Chaucer's persona and the gods take up the problem of epistemology itself; it is because all that finally occurs in the Prologue happens within a *dream* framework that the very *real* problem of how *to know*, by way of a cerebral process like literature, may be discussed and synthesized. Literature enjoys a kinship with dream consciousness

---

[34] The birds in the F text do not introduce Cupid and Alceste.

insofar as, like dreaming, it is once removed from the experiential, perhaps physical and certainly objective reality that is its very "matter." Certainly, the problem of *matiere* is the basis, though not necessarily the crux, of the God of Love's argument against what Chaucer has accomplished in his translations of poems that become the *Romaunt of the Rose* and *Troilus and Criseyde*: Chaucer has "lat be" the "corn" and written the "chaff" of old "apreved storyes." This confusion is, again, paralleled in Will's misprisions and misquotings of scripture when defending himself against Reason.

In Chaucer's poem, the answer the dream state allows will preclude philosophical dogma. The dream vision itself, therefore, becomes emblematic of an imaginary, intuitive process that may engage the complexity of "truth"; the dream vision represents, moreover, as Chaucer understands, language's idealized potential for which literature may strive: literature, like truth, is a complex affair, and if we try to make less of it than it is, if we try to simplify it, we will be lost in what becomes meaningless language. Exactly and disjointedly so, the God of Love misreads Chaucer's translations. Likewise, Langland's Reason thinks the making of poetry is not a proper occupation. The Chaucerian narrator is accused of crimes against love. Confusion ensues, in consequence, to be sorted out by Alceste who, like the daisy and rather than Cupid, is a symbol of love. As Payne has said, Alceste becomes a figure, a poetic embodiment, the "apotheosis" of the daisy the Chaucer persona had been worshipping earlier in the poem (*Key of Remembrance* 106),[35] as part of its author's revamping of the French *margerite* lyric genre; as the deified flower, she also exists as an inscription, a symbol of intelligence.[36]

---

[35] William Quinn (in *Chaucer's Rehersynges: The Performability of the* Legend of Good Women 58) comments that the "idealized" Alceste also "mirrors the comic distortions of her court."

[36] Keeping in mind my remarks about the opening lines of the *Parliament of Fowls* and about Alceste as a daisy, I must mention Patterson's commentary—with which I am only in partial agreement—on the Prologue and on Alceste specifically, as she is used to define the narrator:

> The poet's fervent experience of daisy worship [. . .] fends off appropriation by the authority of literary tradition and especially by the courtly rivalry between the flower and the leaf ([F] 188-96). Chaucer takes pains to stress the independence of his daisy worship from the cultic practice of courtly game. His experience is prior to these social forms; an event that took place "er swich stry was begonne" (196), it is represented as presocial if not pretextual, an instinctive, unmediated, almost prelapsarian affinity between man and the natural world. Yet once he enters the world of the dream—the traditional locale for courtly poetry—just this feared absorption into contemporary social and textual form occurs. The heliotropic calling of daisy to sun that he celebrated while awake is now refigured as the sovereignty of the tyrannical God of Love over his sacrificial consort Alceste. What was before an instinctive symbiosis here becomes hierarchy, and the "gladly desire" that moved the poet is now absorbed into "the craft of fyn lovynge" (544).

(*Chaucer and the Subject of History* 237-38)

I am assuming, here, an equivalence between the philosopher's striving for a world unity

To overstate the case, let it be said that the God of Love perceives what Chaucer has written, and in fact the phenomenon of *traductio* itself, through nominalist eyes. The irony in this circumstance is that he is a god who remains an icon for ideality in its interactivity with the phenomenal world. To return to the larger philosophical problem this situation implies, by definition the God of Love is a contradiction in terms, for the nominalist question precludes ideality's capacity, paradoxically, to manifest itself. This contradiction is perhaps made most vivid through his iconographical status, since he can see, as the narrator takes pains to point out; he says of Cupid: "And al be that men seyn that blynd is he, Algate me thoughte he myghte wel yse" (G 169–70). Cupid's capacity to see is meant as an ironic counterpoint to the question of first hand experience, seeing "with ye," which had been taken up at the poem's start. As Sarah Stanbury Smith has emphasized (in "Cupid's Sight" 95), not only had tradition depicted Cupid as blind, but so had Chaucer—in the *House of Fame, Troilus and Criseyde* and the Knight's Tale—with the exception of the god's characterization in the Prologue. Therefore, the God of Love, symbolically, possesses clarity; yet in a typical Chaucerian paradox he is portrayed as myopic, cognitively. In other words, if the ideal cannot manifest itself in the actual world, the world of *potentia ordinata* (except perhaps through one's faith in the ideal, but never through experiential evidence of it), then how will the ideal be known through literature? The poem's persona is being asked for the impossible when the God of Love misinterprets the *Troilus* and the *Romaunt of the Rose*. Even in a dream this seems to be a bit much.

For many thinkers of Chaucer's and Langland's time, however, an awareness of the limitless ideal, the immortal, is still an actual possibility. Hugh of St. Victor had said that the whole sensible world is like a book written by the hand of God.[37] One then only needs "to read" the book, an imaginative act Chaucer is exercising in his writing of the dream poems and the *Troilus*. Conversely, the God of Love is incapable of *reading* Chaucer's translations correctly; thus he prefers them rewritten to suit his own sensibility. The question of misreading is underscored by the fact that the poet-translator-narrator has talked specifically about his practice of translating literature into vernacular English. Thus Cupid is being set in opposition to him, as representing tradition and authority, against the individual poet who is contemporizing old *matiere*; in this sense, Copeland writes, "Chaucer invents his own authorship out of [convention]" (195). Yet regardless of the particular language, the very fact of translation presents Cupid with a wealth of interrelated difficulties. These problems, as they are taken up in the poem, also

---

and *intelligence* that may serve as an emblem for such a unity; intelligence may also be perceived, however, as being the way of achieving knowledge of unity, or as being the paradigm of that knowledge. In the daisy-Alceste figure we may also see, because of its idealized beauty, the paradigm of that striving for unity. See Appendix A.

[37] "The entire sensible world is, so to speak, a book written by the hand of God. [. . . .] All visible things, visibly presented to us by a symbolic instruction, that is, figured, are proposed for the declaring and signifying of things visible" (*Didascalion, PL* CLXXVI.814). Hugh of St. Victor died in 1141; nevertheless, his thinking influences others in the fourteenth century.

serve to locate Chaucer as distinct from, but in relation to, both a philosophical and otherwise literary tradition with which he very much wishes to be associated; as well, they serve to show the wider social and ontological implications of the linguistic, indeed of the literary, act. Cupid yearns for a static universe, while the narrator thrives when there is change, as typified in the change of form and thereby of meaning that occurs with translation; for translation, as we have said, is essentially metaphorical.[38]

Hugh's method of knowing the world body, in which writing itself becomes a form of "reading" the world, is not an altogether new notion in the fourteenth century, though Chaucer occupies himself with it often enough. We have noted how this way of knowing surfaces through Chaucer's analogy, in the opening assertion of the *Parliament of Fowls* ("The lyf so short, the craft so long to lerne") which sees love as a truth to be attained through the struggle for craftsmanship.[39] Like the skill in loving that helps to define courtly love, Chaucer's "craft" or *makyng* becomes the agency by which human beings may establish a vital relationship with their environs, with the natural world and God. Therefore, also, readers often find the perversion of skyl or craft—humanity out of step with nature—a disorder such as occurs in the Prologue when a fowler is cursed by Spring's birds for betraying them:

> Now hadde th'atempre sonne al that releved,
> And clothed hym in grene al newe ageyn.
> The smale foules, of the seson fayn,
> That from the panter and the net ben skaped,
> Upon the foulere, that hem made awhaped
> In wynter, and distroyed hadde hire brod,
> In his dispit hem thoughte it dide hem good
> To synge of hym, and in here song despise
> The foule cherl that for his covetyse
> Hadde hem betrayed with his sophistrye.
> This was here song, "The foulere we defye" [. . .].
> (G 116–26, F 128–38)

Although nominalist epistemology emphasizes the importance of the physical, the *potentia ordinata*, Chaucer might reasonably have included words as part of this natural, phenomenal world. Augustine's notion, to offer another example of miraculous thinking, is that words, perhaps even literature,[40] are signs indicating

---

[38] Cf. Chapter One, and Reiss, 102–103.
[39] As in Horace's "ars longa, vita brevis." Robinson's note to this first line indicates its origin with Hippocrates (cf. Skeat, *Early English Proverbs* 57.135). Cf. J. M. Manly, "Chaucer and the Rhetoricians," 8; Everett, 1 ff.; the Introduction and Chapter Two.
[40] P. B. Taylor (315–16 nn. and 325n) writes that "Augustine, in *Soliloquia* II.16, explains that the feigning of art is pleasing rather than deceiving [. . .]. In *De Mendacio* Augustine lists eight categories of lies; but in *Soliloquia* II.18 he distinguishes between those who will to be false and those who are capable of being true. He excludes from opprobrium the artist's will to imitate truth."

the knowledge of God, making truth pleasing, plain, and effective.[41] On the other hand, recalling the problem of palpability in and of itself as being devoid of human power to abstract or to draw any universal or class distinctions from what can be discovered in such a sensible world, "words" must also be the names for these things of the world and are therefore at variance from the physical universe (i.e., they are apart from these material instances).

Chaucer is composing a literary realism in verse, within a complicated philosophical context, which departs radically from the verse forms and thus the thinking of his contemporaries. No one, certainly, can equate the *Canterbury Tales* with *Pearl*, or with *Sir Gawain and the Green Knight*, a work like the *Temple of Glas* or with *Piers Plowman*. Yet we may observe that none of these works is "philosophical" in the same manner as are the writings of, for instance, Ockham, Bradwardine, Holcot, or Strode. Furthermore, although poems like *Pearl* and *Piers Plowman* are perceived to be allegorical by nature, they do, just the same, include dramatic and otherwise tropic material not to be found in a work such as, say, Boethius' *Consolatio*, even as this Boethian tract contains a drama not to be found in any of Ockham's work. And, conversely, dream visions such as *Pearl*, or Machaut's *Dit du Vergier*, Froissart's *Paradys d'Amours*, Deschamps' *Lay de Franchise*, and so on, do not take up the questions we see Chaucer grappling with in his own dream poems, problems the *Consolatio* certainly engages. In one of its aspects, the dream *visio* genre remains celebratory. Chaucer will use the panegyric mode, such as the Prologue's praise of the daisy, as but an entrée into his real discourse that, of necessity (if not at least tangentially, as in the *Book of the Duchess*) mounts a philosophical inquiry. Questions in regard to nominalist or other schools of thought might not have interested Chaucer in themselves; nor, most likely, were they of special interest to the authors of these other "imaginative" works (i.e., Deschamps, Froissart, et al.). Yet probably like them, Chaucer had access to a branch of nominalism in the Stoicism of Macrobius' commentary on the dream of Scipio Africanus, which asserts that "every word has a true meaning" (*Somnium* 20.1); words, as it were, may possess their ontological realities after all. The point is that for Chaucer there is a confusion, or at least a disagreement within fourteenth-century thinking, a plethora of divergent philosophies ranging throughout the time and place he inhabits.

Although Chaucer puts forth, at the beginning of the *Parliament of Fowls*, a

---

[41] *De Doctrina Christiana* IV.11.26. Earlier in *De Doctrina Christiana* Augustine writes: "Rerum autem ignorantia facit obscuras figuratas locutiones" (II.16.24). Hence words, as being the beginning of any potential figuration, figuration's Ur-forms, would seem to be contingent upon at least one's knowing the "things" of the world, which are the source, it appears here, of knowledge.

rather sophisticated notion of the relationships among art, life, and love (and perhaps intelligence), we as readers nevertheless re-discover in this poem his ingenuous, perhaps bumbling narrator who has been and will continue to be the poet's alter ego throughout the Chaucer corpus. This persona acts as a foil as he is set against Chaucer's philosophico-esthetical dilemma—that is, the contradictions comprising the background against which his characters live in the poems, having to do with the possible values of words and their relationship to things, and generally with the possibility for knowledge, for truth in language, especially in poetry and translation.

As Russell Peck has observed (in "Chaucer and the Nominalist Questions" 745), Chaucer

> is profoundly interested in the moral implications of nominalistic questions. Dorigen will gladly leave the fine points of disputation to the clerks [viz her complaint to "Eterne God" in the Franklin's Tale,]; after all, she has the conclusion. Chaucer, for the most part, is her opposite. He seems to prefer the questions and will leave the conclusions to the clerks (or rather, the clerks to their conclusions). Though he may not be interested in whether we can know with certitude only individual things, he is profoundly interested in how we know individual things. And though his concern may not be with the questions about whether universals exist in creation or only in our heads, he is always interested in those generalizations which fill people's heads and which exist there exclusively insofar as they matter to that individual.

Chaucer's various examinations of this same nominalist versus anti-nominalist theme through characters and plots in all of his poetry are thrown askew, to one degree or another, by his narrator, thus producing what Diomede in the *Troilus* calls an "ambage" or, in this case, a wanted ambiguity: "That is to seyn, with double wordes slye, / Swiche as men clepen a word with two visages" (V.898-99). These "two visages" of language, and more to the point, of poetry, are what gets Chaucer's persona into trouble with the God of Love in the Prologue, because this supernatural god can only understand literature in ideological terms. Yet the ambiguity is desirable because Chaucer the poet's literary realism recognizes the hesitancy of conflicting philosophical dogmas which are themselves exegeses of human, fallible situations. Moreover, ambiguity operates even when the persona is merely one who may report events while he cannot, he claims, understand them, as in the *Troilus* in which the narrator tells his tale of erotic love and betrayal even though, he dutifully reminds us, he has never experienced such a love for himself and so he may not pass judgment on the events transpiring in his poem.

In Chaucer's dream poems, furthermore, as any writer of this genre must realize, the problem of an ambiguous reality is compounded by the addition to the poetic terrain of the psychological dream dimension. Dream consciousness may violate at will the strictures of rationality and sensibility, more so in order to demonstrate the unique, pristine but ineffable absolute that underlies and otherwise engenders, ironically, an imperfect state of world affairs. In fact this is one purpose most dream visions serve, in a variety of fabulous, fantastic, and to one degree or another allegorical constructs. In a poem like *Piers Plowman* abstract values can more easily and deeply be investigated as such, precisely because of the dream visions that present them for consideration as apart from the viewer, or that serve as an unreal, contrastive backdrop for them; in either situation, the abstractions exist at a distance from the viewer in which there can be some perspective. Further, because the reader will never quite forget he or she is reading a poem within a dream framework, the poem, by virtue of its own structure, will therefore never escape its allegorical orientation as a result of, simply, this very same structure that insists upon the distinction between experience and imagination. Such bipartism might work against the unified vision that is the ideal of the poem's method of discovering and describing the world—the poem's, as it were, potential or kinetic epistemology. However, in terms of Aristotelian principles of mimesis, Chaucer's inclusion of philosophical themes within a framework in which dream and reality share more than a coincidental similarity of setting and plot, such as occurs in the Prologue, indicates his choice to abandon an allegorical impulse, as Kemp Malone asserted (in *Chapters on Chaucer* 96), for the more viable "fusion" of literary realism. Perhaps the re-creation of experience in art will not lend itself to polemical (i.e., philosophical) and otherwise allegorical exegesis.

Chaucer's dreams are actually valued by modern readers precisely because they have gone far in abandoning what can be viewed to be burdensome apological frames, since allegory reduces the possibility of semansis in the sense of such meaning being an accurate reflection of the sensible, real, synthesized world. Angus Fletcher has pointed out (in *Allegory: The Theory of a Symbolic Mode* 5 n.9) that because they tend to be anatomical, or otherwise depend for their success upon principles of enigma (i.e., the inclusion of a formal obscurity that results from mysterious, so to speak, elements of a poem or plot), allegories tend to subvert the poet's capacity to create textures consonant with the more complicated reality of living, those actual complexities of life and love alluded to in the opening lines of the *Parliament of Fowls* and elsewhere.

> The whole point of allegory is that it does not need to be read exegetically; it often has a literal level that makes good enough sense all by itself. But somehow this literal surface suggests a peculiar doubleness of intention, and while it can, as it were, get along without interpretation, it becomes richer and more interesting if given interpretation. Even the most deliberate fables, if read naïvely or carelessly, may seem mere stories, but what counts [. . .] is a structure that lends itself to a secondary reading, or rather, one that becomes stronger when given a secondary meaning as well as a primary meaning.
> (7)

Although an allegory's virtue is its ability to sustain a consistent "secondary meaning," Fletcher's comment makes clear that such a duplicity, almost by definition, will not readily lend itself to the mirror-like unity, the distillation of intellect and experience which in fact constitutes esthetic realism, something closer to the metonymic versus the metaphorical impulse. On the other hand, Chaucer perceives the problem of re-creating complexities in a poem that might satisfy the demands of *imitatio*. Truly, it is because Chaucer, his persona, has achieved a "wholeness" in a poem such as *Troilus and Criseyde* that he becomes subject to Cupid's displeasure in the Prologue, and will therefore have to write the legend of women who were "true in love" as penance.

As Lisa Kiser observes (in *Telling Classical Tales* 82), the most significant shortcoming

> in the God of Love's reading of the *Troilus* is his failure to perceive the poem's complex expression of the relationship between pagan secular love and Christian caritas [. . .]. In short, his thought is dominated by a rather simple-minded conflation of pagan and Christian love, both of which he sees as the same virtue.

Again, considering the comedy Chaucer creates, we might remind ourselves of the matter of the legends he resuscitates, which Robert Frank has recognized (in *Chaucer and the* Legend of Good Women 26) is particularly violent and uncharacteristic of an idealized courtly love the God of Love is supposed to but does not represent. The legend genre, though, is especially appropriate to assuage him because of its didactic nature. Kiser rightly notes, as well, that the

> *Legend* is also a poem about the difficulties inherent in Chaucer's role as a teller of others' tales, one who has obligations to his sources and also to the new and different audience [here, of course, the audience must include the God of Love] for whom these sources were to be adapted.
>
> To present his views on the uses of classical fiction, Chaucer finds it necessary to include several other issues in his poem [i.e., in the *LGW* entire] as well. He reacts to certain traditional theories of art, he comments on allegorization (one of the commonest ways in which medieval poets made classical texts confirm Christian truth), he reveals to us many fourteenth-century assumptions about literature's usefulness to everyday life, and he betrays his beliefs about the act and purpose of translation.
> (26)

All the same, it is because the God of Love thinks in a simplistic, polemical, and perhaps allegorical fashion (as many fourteenth-century readers of religious sermons and other exemplary literature might have done), that he has misunderstood Chaucer's translations.

> In the simplest terms, allegory says one thing and means another. It destroys the *normal expectation* we have about language, that our words "mean what they say." When we predicate quality X of person Y, Y really is what our predication says he is (or we assume so); but allegory would turn Y into something other (*allos*) than what the open and direct statement tells the reader. Pushed to an extreme, this ironic usage would subvert language itself, turning everything into an Orwellian newspeak.
> (Fletcher 2; my emphasis)

In the sense that allegory "destroys" our "normal expectation" for discourse, we might conclude that the proclivity of dream visions is toward allegory because they are indeed dreams, not real; yet they make use of reality's very space in order to establish something other out of it, some new meaning from this same ground. This is a problem of poetics. As we shall see, it is worked out in a novel and radically different fashion by Langland. By modern standards, allegory is understood as a form of thought and/or expression that might naturally subvert reality, as it forsakes language's full semiotic power. As a case in point, Northrop Frye has said (in *Anatomy of Criticism* 312), "Boethius' *Consolation of Philosophy*, with its dialogue form, its verse interludes and its pervading tone of contemplative irony, is a pure anatomy, a fact of considerable importance for the understanding of its vast influence." The *Consolatio* does not need to appeal to readers on grounds of drama (although it certainly makes that attempt); for if anything is true of it, it is that the *Consolatio*'s metaphoric vitality is so shaped and directed as to create meanings that are nothing less than ideological, nothing short of unqualified polemic.

If Boethius' work is popular in Chaucer's time, however, this is because it affords a certain matrix in which logical functions take precedence. Unlike Shakespeare's or Henryson's version of her, for instance, in Chaucer's *Troilus* we find Criseyde's ultimate betrayal of her lover agonizing because, on one level, it defies logical dicta. It is as if fourteenth-century readers were intent upon working out the subtleties of nominalist and realist doctrines extant in literature like the *Consolatio*. Yet this is in fact the case, precisely so because Boethius' poem takes the form of an "anatomy" (as Frye termed it). What such a structure will not allow is the "uncertain" tropism and simulacrae (a hypersemiotic, multiplicity of meaning) that occur more and more throughout Chaucer's career within his poems' narratives and as pertain to the characterization of his persona as well. Writing of the *Canterbury Tales*, Leicester remarks that "the voice of the textual working we call 'Chaucer' shares the Derridean desire to escape knowledge and certainty, to reach a point of not knowing any longer where he is going because of the constraints such 'knowledge' imposes" (413). If we were to change the form of some of Chaucer's imagery, in Rosemund Tuve's words (in *Elizabethan and Metaphysical Imagery* 101), we as readers would "stop looking to think, to condemn, to marvel, exult, pity, or judge." It is because we instead suspend such judgments, participating in language and characterization themselves, that we know an experiential reality in the poems. In turn, Chaucer would have us condemn or praise by virtue of tensions he establishes between personalities and situations, which depend for their vitality upon shaped meanings that avoid a one to one, unreal or fantastic deciphering of imagery on the part of the reader.

Yet the dream vision that so readily—and here it is assumed "dangerously"—lends itself to an allegorical epistemology, may also achieve an effect of quite another order. As stated, readers of the *visio*'s sequence of "events" will eventually be brought back to the realization that what occurs in the dream state is merely a fantasy, a dream. A reader cannot avoid this reflection, even in the Prologue. Yet to know the miraculous—the dream—so might the logic run, means that the dream sequence suggests a principal, unifying God-force behind an imperfect and sensible world: the dream is itself a psychological miracle implicating the fantastic, allowing the reader who indulges in such a state of mind a helpful machinery in his or her exegetical search for the divine. This inclusion of the imaginary is readily perceptible in poems like *Piers Plowman*, but such a dynamic is more deeply embedded, and more powerful because it is more subtly present, in a work like the Prologue. After all, the dream poem is in turn a creation of the miraculous world by way of the hand and an almost Coleridgean imagination of the poet; of course, as Payne has said, the Prologue's focus is directly on the poet and his striving to "make" truth in his poetry (*Key of Remembrance* 93 ff.).[42]

In part, this is Chaucer the *makyr*'s meditation, based on the assumption that dreams, like words, have their ontological realities, even when words are names sequent to, instead of concomitant with, the things named (a sentiment he might have found expressed in Dante's *La Vita Nuova*: "nomina sunt consequentia rerum").[43] By logical extension, imaginative and historical literature seem also to be real, suggesting truth in themselves and beyond their own instances of being—beyond themselves as well.[44] In other words, literature may partake of a protean nature—art as the product of the creative impulse. Chaucer points to this phenomenon in his preoccupation with the viability of adherence to tradition and *auctoritee*, as an epistemological method, his way of knowing the world. Set against such a construct of knowledge is the real, experiential world. Hence, the Prologue to the *Legend of Good Women* begins with this very discussion, finding in mind-sustained memory a unifying force (here is the opening passage in full):

> A thousand sythes have I herd men telle
> That there is joye in hevene and peyne in helle,
> And I acorde wel that it be so;
> But natheles, this wot I wel also,
> That ther ne is non that dwelleth in this contre
> That eyther hath in helle or hevene ybe,
> Ne may of it non other weyes witen
> But as he hath herd seyd or founde it writen;

---

[42] As stated, the Prologue's dream sequence is, in its setting and emotional structure (such as, e.g., the worship of the daisy that occurs in both dream and waking states), so very like reality that the problem of limited semansis, which occurs when allegory distances primary and secondary literary interpretations from one another (i.e., *un*like settings between dream and experiential reality), is reduced to its minimum so that the poem may be said to approximate, to a greater degree, the natural synthesis of philosophical contradictions—the gestalt of the real, natural world experience (i.e., the intellectual-sensibile dynamic), which philosophical speculation disrupts, intrudes upon, as it were—occurring in God-ordered nature. On Chaucer's relationship to the allegorical tradition, see Appendix B; and Lawton, *Chaucer's Narrators*, xiv and 12.

[43] *Cap*. 13.

[44] In my argument I am of course presuming the medieval world's confusion in which imaginative literature is taken, to a degree, to be synonymous with written history.

> For by assay there may no man it preve.
> But Goddes forbode, but men shulde leve
> Wel more thyng than men han seyn with ye!
> Men shal nat wenen every thyng a lye
> For that he say it nat of yore ago.
> God wot a thyng is nevere the lesse so
> Thow every wyght ne may it nat yse.
> Bernard the monk ne say nat al, parde!
>   Thanne mote we to bokes that we fynde,
> Thourgh whiche that olde thynges ben in mynde,
> And to the doctryne of these olde wyse
> Yeven credence, in every skylful wyse,
> And trowen on these olde approved storyes
> Of holynesse, of regnes, of victoryes,
> Of love, of hate, of othere sondry thynges,
> Of which I may nat make rehersynges.
> And if that olde bokes weren aweye,
> Yloren were of remembrance the keye.
> (G 1-26)[45]

The poem begins by outlining precisely its own and Chaucer's prevailing and very workable strategy: literature as a viable world force will be set against the trial of present experience, even when that experience occurs within the poem-sustained dream frame. Furthermore, Chaucer's poetry will be put to a test by his own persona's artlessness—though we may easily concede the simpleminded reading of the poetry by Cupid, and, if Alceste is not at least artless in her defense of Chaucer, she does not really, either, invoke his poems' fundamental virtues. But the controlling philosophical stance is Chaucer's.

Readers view the events of the dream poems and *Troilus*, however, if not always through the eyes of the narrator then at least through what is going on, so to speak, from over his shoulder. As Payne points out in connection with the Prologue (to one degree or another his remarks obtain to the narrator we meet in each of the poems in the sequence—whatever that precise order might be), Chaucer's whole discussion

> is framed in that troublesome defensive irony—the self-revealing pose of naïveté—which provides him simultaneously with a sub-liminal awareness of the limitations of human certainty, and with a prearranged escape from having to face up finally to the profundity of the aesthetic problem which his poetry constantly raises.
> (*Key of Remembrance* 96)

---

[45] Note Chaucer's verbal echo of Ockham in his phrase "For by assay there may no man it preve"; Ockham, and here Chaucer, allow that there is a heaven and hell, that is, that there is a divine order—and both men also realize the futility of speaking seriously, in the sense that their words could be ontologically full, about such divine existence. Without experience, without *intuitive cognition*, there can be no proof. Cf. Andrea Tabarroni, "Mental Signs and the Theory of Representation in Ockham"; and below).

Payne goes on to say that our participation in the poem through the agency of the persona's point of view, or at least as a result of this tangential connection with the narratorial machinery, involves us in one of a number of the poems' "paralyzing system[s] of ironies" (109).

To return to the discussion of form and ideality for a moment, we need to bear in mind the nominalist thinking of Ockham and his followers, which raises a key contradiction. On the one hand, nominalism proclaims that all knowledge resides in the "things" of the world, unordered by any universality mortals might know. But as Peck suggests, Ockham tends to "subordinate questions of intellect to questions of will," thus shifting the nominalist focus:

> Just as God's ordained power (*potentia dei ordinata*) ties the contingencies of the world to God's Will, so are the mental structures created by men within their intellects instigated by voluntary choices which give them meaning. (746)[46]

In light of Ockham's point of view, it might be possible to conclude that Chaucer's translations are the result of the poet's or translator's will, his inclination as well as his ability to engage the semiosis of language in order to make cognitive choices. Again, an allegorical structure, almost by definition, to a great degree circumscribes "choosing" in this manner. But reaching further for a form, beyond allegory, means the poet may effect a truly—in the modern sense—literary meaning, hopefully to resurrect or to intimate the immanence if not the presence, at least on the metaphysical level, of the ideal. The warrant for the poet, then, is to be like God, or rather, to discover the real that resides in multi-meaningful figuration, and to convey this same tropism. Paradoxically, the God of Love either cannot understand or simply will not tolerate Chaucer's deified project(s) in which the poet seeks to invest words, literature, with ontological substance—the excuse or the reason for being.

Further, because Ockham "places the efficacy of the will at the center of his epistemology," his views are all the more "compatible with Chaucer's strongly Boethian orientation. Knowing, for Ockham, becomes a combination of desire, perspective, choice, and judgment" (Peck 746). P. B. Taylor has speculated (in "Chaucer's 'Cosyn to the Dede'" 318) about the source of Chaucer's nominalism: the concept that

> universal ideas have ontological reality in words is an aspect of philosophical realism, and [as stated] Chaucer knew its most persuasive expression in *De consolatione philosophiae*. [Yet] nominalism, which posits that particulars precede the idea of a universal and that words are without real referents may have become known to Chaucer through Boccaccio, if indeed the *Decameron* was known to

---

[46] *Reportatio* III, q.10–12.

Chaucer, for Boccaccio's epilogue stresses the indeterminacy of intent over word and word over effect.

Assuming that Chaucer had not seen the *Decameron*, it must nevertheless be conceded that even if a unity of philosophical point of view is not derived from Chaucer's poems, it is at least possible to read there the discrepancy of points of view being demonstrated through characters and situations. This diversity is as it should be, because these characterizations are derived from language's signifying power. They are the creation of language and so they implicate language as being a creative force. The medieval mind, Stewart Justman contends (in "Literal and Symbolic in the *Canterbury Tales*" 200), understood symbols as a reality in the sense that analogies were neither arbitrary nor verbal. In the medieval tradition

> an analogy can pass for a literal identity [. . .]. The bread of the Eucharist was not just a symbol of Christ's body, an analogy for it; it was Christ's body. Again, St. Paul says, "as the body is one and hath many members; and all the members of the body, whereas they are many, yet are one body: so also is Christ [1 Cor. 12:12]." But this is not merely an analogy for merely illustrative purposes. In fact it is not an analogy. Paul means it: "Now you are the body of Christ" (1 Cor. 12:27) [. . .]. For another medieval ideal of the perfect symbolic body, we may look to Dante. In his ascent through Paradise, Dante sees souls which form the symbols of eagle and rose. In each case the symbol literally is the larger community. The symbol of the eagle stands for law and literally embodies law, in that all the souls that make it up have taken their proper places. To the modern reader, the rose may signify transfigured sexuality. But the great transfiguration that has made the rose is also an actual display of something much like what we understand by "sublimation," the redirection of will according to "law" and in the mode of symbols. In each case the symbol is more than a symbol. It is itself real. It is a claim for the reality of analogical thought.[47]

In the *Canterbury Tales*, some of which were being composed during the period in which the G version of the Prologue to the *Legend of Good Women* was also being written, certain characters are clearly using language to attest the idea that words are more than merely "verbal." Rather, the words

> are real, formal acts [e.g., the power of oaths in the *Friar's* and *Summoner's Tales*, the Pardoner's rhyme of "swere" and "totere," and so on]—a contract with reality. On the other hand, though, we have the Reeve's statement, "when we may nat doon, than wol we speke" (A 3881); Symkyn's challenge to the clerks, "Lat se now if this place may suffise, / Or make it rowm with speche, as is youre gise" (A 4125-26); the absurd verbal dilation of the *Nun's Priest's Tale*, as opposed to the brevity within it [and so forth]. In these cases, words are vain, inauthentic fictions that stand for nothing.
> (200)

---

[47] Justman cites Joseph Mazzeo's notion (in "Universal Analogy and the Culture of the Renaissance" 302) that the analogies were "nothing arbitrary or verbal."

Taylor's commentary is appropriate here, in his attempt at reconciling the two Chaucerian aspects: There is the idea

> that Chaucer the poet is a Boethian realist while Chaucer the [. . .] reporter [. . .] is a confused nominalist. In general, [. . .] Chaucer's emphasizing of nominalist views on language are found more often in comic and satiric contexts than in serious ones, and considerations of linguistic realism occur in serious contexts. Sometimes it is difficult to distinguish one from the other.
> (318)

In the Prologue to the *Legend of Good Women* it is indeed, often enough, difficult to make such distinctions; but they are there. The Prologue makes a claim for figuration, for the reality of symbols and "analogical thought," as Justman terms it, just as there is an understanding of the psychological and philosophical necessity in the experiential present. It is the tension that Chaucer establishes between these divergent viewpoints which in fact unifies the poem. His meditation is at the same time humorous while it is considering serious, linguistic and philosophical alternatives; and he uses this double edged sword in striking an esthetic unity in the poem.

What is important to see here is that Chaucer is interested in demonstrating a breach of faith in the known lapsarian world, in the discrepancy between intent and deed (Taylor 318-20). The Prologue demonstrates conflicting philosophical points of view with which Chaucer was familiar. He develops his persona through the successive dream poems in part because the dream state demonstrates the resolution of these philosophical opposites; in this the dream state is akin to language when language is not limited and thus being abused—when it is meaningful—and in this Chaucer departs from the mere, conventional dream *visio* mode. According to Ockham, "insights of faith, though they cannot be proved by reason, are not therefore contrary to reason, but simply go beyond it" (Peck 747). Of course, there is as well the knowledge of experience. But because of the "mind's capacity to manipulate words and images in the shaping of its state of being, the boundaries of man's interior reality are open to almost limitless variation" (747).[48] Chaucer's narrator in the dream poems, therefore, strikes a pose, for the sake of the matter being presented by and through him, which depends upon Diomede's *ambage*:

> Though the *ficta* of the mind have no independent reality outside the mind, they form the basis of man's deductions. The nominalist idea that the mind and its knowledge are an ongoing imagistic-linguistic process is appealing to Chaucer.
> (747)

In all likelihood, a principal source of Chaucer's interest in the relationship between language and perception was the *Consolatio*, where Philosophia's therapy

---

[48] Ockham's insistence upon the primacy of faith to higher understanding, a faith partially determined by an act of will, is in keeping with St. Anselm's *fides quaerens intellectum* and *credo ut intelligam* (Peck 747n).

is largely an elaborate word game that utilizes words and images to break down other words and images, and then uses words and mental pictures to construct a psychological dwelling place (747n).

This idea of an "ongoing imagistic-linguistic process" forms the basis of Chaucer's claim for the efficacy of literature vis-à-vis tradition. Holcot, Chaucer's contemporary, noted that despite humanity's double incapacity of weak intellect and weak will we still can achieve our final end if we do what is in us to the best of our ability. This sentiment echoes Ockham's belief that God cannot be known in Himself or as a single concept proper to Him, but only as in a concept that is predicable of Him (i.e., creation, especially the mortal mind).[49]

These existential descriptions of mankind certainly obtain to the narrator we meet in all of Chaucer's poems, but especially in the dream poems and then, especially, in the Prologue. Chaucer's posturing through his persona as being a bit obtuse reveals for us the philosophical and theological dynamic, in conjunction with a meditation on esthetics, which is deeply embedded in the other characters of the poems and in the action of the poems themselves. And, as Kiser points out, in the *Legend of Good Women* Chaucer's esthetical problem is brought under control through a contrast with the God of Love who is as obtuse as the poem's narrator (though this manifests quite differently since he is a god and not a poet) in his accusations against what the persona has translated. It is the God of Love's inability to make a distinction between exemplary literature and that which may be paradoxical, and thus perhaps *truthful*—more so because of the force of *traductio*—which Chaucer has brought into being. The God of Love has a hard time separating "wheat" from "chaff"; he cannot distinguish between language—*traductio*—and the *matiere* that language treats—*auctoritee*. However—keeping Holcot's view of humanity's double incapacity in mind (cf. above)—it is because of Chaucer's

> characteristic refusal to be self-congratulatory [that] we do not get a "corrected" interpretation of the *Troilus* from the *Legend*'s narrator, even though he is given a chance to respond to the accusations of his deified (and reified) reader [i.e., Cupid]. Instead, the only remark we get from him is the reminder that authorial intent ought to be weighed in the literary Last Judgment over which the God of Love presides (F 471-74, G 461-64). Neither articulate nor forceful, the intimidated narrator only weakly asserts his innocence in response to the charges brought against him. Finally, Alceste is left with the responsibility of defending him, which she does with shrewdness and skill.
> (Kiser 83-4)

Alceste as dream figure exists barely beyond an allegorical pale; yet she is not

---

[49] See Heiko Oberman, *The Harvest of Medieval Theology: Gabriel Biel and Late Medieval Nominalism*, 241-48; and Peck, 750.

merely allegorical in intention because of, among other things, her striking resemblance to the real daisy. She resolves the discrepancy between ironic narration and a philosophico-esthetical problem, embodied here in the indictment of what Chaucer has written (Cupid's "[. . .] in pleyn text, it nedeth nat to glose, / Thow hast translated [etc.]" (G 254-55); and, earlier (G 85-87), Chaucer's own remark: "For myn entent is, or I fro yow fare, / The naked text in English to declare / Of many a story ").[50] But note that she only resolves the problem within the context of her own figuration, at Chaucer's hand (as well as in Chaucer's dream), and therefore we view the indictment of translation by the God of Love, who is the representation of a simple minded version of nominalism, from within the dream vision mode (in the point of view of Alceste) as well as in terms of the objectively real and experiential (the poem's narrator who relates to us both his dream *and* his feelings about how one may "know" the truth—either through books or through experience or, we are left to conjecture, through a combination of the two).

Chaucer as persona may therefore claim to be making no judgments upon what he sees taking place around him in his poems,[51] but because he begs his own question, he prepares readers to pass judgment, to condemn or celebrate as if they were free to understand all of the implications of the poems' events and discussions. Readers feel this way, however, not because of the poem's allegorical structure, but exactly as a consequence of the poems' narrator putting them off their guard. Because they are told, and because they see the bungling narration of the persona, they tend to take what he says and does as false. Therefore, readers jump to conclusions of right and wrong based on a polarity the poems' persona has in effect established for them. Readers make decisions, that is, within the narrator's choice of context, though they often tend to forget this.

Recalling once again the opening to the *Parliament of Fowls*, we can now say that Horace is paraphrased by Chaucer in order to bring together the strands of a complex discussion in the dream poems and in all of his work; Chaucer's is a progressively trenchant meditation on knowledge sustained in literature and in other life experience as well, knowledge that is to be measured against a religious and philosophical ideal. Rhetoric itself, then—or certainly the question of

---

[50] My reading of the poem, here, is emphasizing the leitmotif of Cupid's displeasure with the act of *traductio* itself. This I understand to be a decidedly nominalist view of all art and, underlying this attitude, a mistrust of language itself.

[51] "For, as to me, is lefer non, ne lother" (G 66-75). The narrator's analogy between "corn" and "chaf," and flower and leaf, makes clear his valuation within a larger discussion, in the poem entire, of the value of both *auctoritee* and *traductio*. He would of course prefer the "corn"—in other words, the matter of the old approved stories that should be brought to life, once again, in English. This problem of the matter of old stories is, as has been discussed, the substance in part of Cupid's indictment. Nevertheless—to the original point—beyond the persona's adherence to one symbol or figure (such as the daisy, or the "corn") over another, he does not take sides in the larger philosophical debate (a debate that has more to do with the phenomenon of translating than with that of the matter to be translated).

figuration in poetry, which for Chaucer perhaps underlies the concept of *translatio*—becomes *the* metaphor in a poetic search for a truth that may be viable in all spiritual, mental, and experiential states of being. And in the Prologue Chaucer seizes the opportunity to write, particularly here where he may turn his innovative hand to established forms such as the dream *visio* and *margerite* genres, what should be understood as a palinode to this poetic form (beyond Ovid, Froissart, Machaut, Deschamps). Frank adds his commentary to that of a long line of critics regarding the Prologue's conventionality.[52] But he rightly observes that in the Prologue the appearance of orthodox conventionality is misleading, especially so because the poet's "explanation and defense of what he is about to do [is] not merely conventional. True, the Prologue has all the conventional furniture" (12), even if these formulae are employed for a new purpose. The term *palinode* must be used advisedly, although, as Robert Estrich stated long ago (in "Chaucer's Maturing Art" 329-30), the G prologue to the *Legend of Good Women* certainly makes best use of dramatic humor and irony which we recognize, moreover, as a predominating quality of the later Chaucer and "in line also with the steady development of the poet away from the clichés of medieval courtly-love poetry."

Some of these clichés are of course necessarily bound up in allegorical values, even when Chaucer finally eschews the dream genre's allegorical determinism, most notably in the Prologue as well as earlier in *Troilus and Criseyde* and later in the *Canterbury Tales*. Because the dream vision allows the poet to wed real and surreal states of consciousness, Chaucer manages to include in *his* examination the problem, to designate it so, of civilization's historical—and therefore Christological, and moral—impulse. Yet it is Chaucer's secularity that becomes the force by which he may reconcile the miraculous nature of religio-historical knowledge with that of the tangible, real terrain he is a witness to in his everyday world.

The world "text" Chaucer reads is composed of sensible "things," but as Hugh of St. Victor's remark intimates (i.e., that the sensible world is like a book written by the hand of God), through the power of cognition the mysterious force that orders the palpable world body may also be known. Allegory reflects the presence of the mysterious through enigmatic duplicities of meanings, while it seeks to establish a context for logical thinking within an esthetic mode. Interestingly, however, as this logic was elaborated to its ultimate ends by Ockham and others, the weaknesses of allegory were revealed. Of many esthetic epistemologies, allegory is the form that attempts to reconcile the factual with the supernatural through a reinvention of a world experience often dismantled by philosophical attempts to "explain" such experience. But poetically framed inquiries invoke the supernatural because, like language (and dreaming), the imagination must be God-induced, even if this contingency cannot be empirically established. Ockham understood this problem. As Andrea Tabarroni explains (in "Mental Signs and the

---

[52] Starting with G. L. Kittredge, *Chaucer and His Poetry*, 2; and J. L. Lowes, *Geoffrey Chaucer*, 126.

Theory of Representation in Ockham" 208),

> for Ockham, intuitive knowledge does not necessarily require the presence of the object, but can also logically exist (*de potentia Dei absoluta*) in the absence, or even given the [postulated] non-existence, of the object. The difference between the two types of knowledge is therefore purely epistemological. Intuitive knowledge is the necessary and sufficient condition for an evident judgement of existence or non-existence, and thus for all contingent propositions concerning the object in question, while abstractive knowledge does not guarantee any evidence.[53]

Logic such as Ockham's need not concede, due to its very nature, the existence of the less material, supernatural, dream-like and often enough literary, world elements. This discrepancy is played out in the debate between Chaucer's narrator and the Prologue's God of Love. *Traductio*, or *makyng*, the imaginative acts of "reading" the world or God's text, are questioned because they are abstractive, interpretive, imaginative ways of being-in-the-world, performed in compliance with Jerome's translation principle, "non verbum de verbo, sed sensum de sensu exprimere."[54] Likewise, dreaming is an interpretive act in its rendition of reality. Alceste, naturally, who finally is real *only* through her figuration in a dream, in a literary work, in the Prologue, "settles" the issue.

Smiling and mollified, the God of Love, also Chaucer's figure, concedes that, after all, Chaucer may restore the unified world, may reestablish order by writing the "wheat" and letting go of the "chaff" in the forthcoming legends of women true in love. We as readers know the connection between love and imagination; and *we* restore the unity by reading Chaucer's text of the buffoonery of dream-induced gods. This text is a reflection of the complex book of the world from which it derives—a book whose "narrative," as Gellrich states, "is the 'history' of mankind from creation to the ascent to the celestial city" (22; cf. 211).

The nominalistic idea, in Peck's words (above), that the "mind and its knowledge are an ongoing imagistic-linguistic process," forms the basis of Chaucer's meditation on the authority of literature within a nominalist world that had come to rely on experience alone. When we "read" the world landscape, however, we may also realize historical and imaginative dimensions beyond the physical present. Reading is, indeed, humanity's ennobling epistemological virtue, and through the act itself reading also becomes an experiential action.

That such reading is especially of a written text, moreover, and that Chaucer may have sensed that there was a relationship between literacy and the emergence of individual authorship, is underscored by Chaucer's revisions in the G Prologue. Caroline Eckhardt (in "The Art of Translation in *The Romaunt of the Rose*" 52) asserts that Chaucer's actual translation of the *Roman de la rose* into English— which in part has inspired Cupid's wrath—"increases the first person vocabulary of the poem."[55] The Prologue is about the writing of verse but it especially focuses

---

[53] Cf. *Ord.*, *Prologus*, q.1, vol. I, pp. 31-33, and *Rep.* II, qq. 12-13, pp. 256 ff.
[54] *Epist.* 57; *PL* 22.571; cf. Chapters One and Two.
[55] In Edwards, *The Dream of Chaucer*, 51.

on translation and its relationship to authority, and, at that, translation into English, such as is keyed by the narrator's declaration:

> For myn entent is, or I fro yow fare,
> The naked text in English to declare
> Of many a story, or elles of many a geste,
> As autours seyn; leveth hem if yow leste.
> (G 85-88)

This pursuit of the meaning of translation parallels Chaucer's gradual shifting of emphasis from the act of reading, as author, of "many a story" of the *auctores*, to the act of writing. Delaney has charted this shift:

> In moving through Chaucer's work, we observe a development in the figure of the Narrator. The Chaucerian Narrator is always both reader and writer, yet the balance of these functions is not constant. In the earlier dream-visions, the readerly function dominates as the Narrator confronts and absorbs various discourses, texts, and experiences. In some cases a specific text is named and summarized: Ovid's *Metamorphoses* and *Heroides*, Virgil's *Aeneid*, and Macrobius's commentary on the *Somnium Scipionis* are among them. This text provokes the Narrator's dream, which, when recorded, becomes the poem at hand. The narrative stance, then, is a passive or receptive one at the start of the poet's career. Over a period of about eighteen years, however, it shifts very perceptibly toward an active and self-conscious authorial position. The balance inclines progressively toward the writerly function, until in the *Canterbury Tales* we are very little aware of the Narrator as reader or scholar. Instead, we are invited to see him primarily as writer and artist, his ostensible sources no longer books but people and experience [. . .].
> (13-14)

Delaney also notes that the Chaucer persona moves from being named "Geffrey," as in the *House of Fame*, to "Chaucer," as in the Prologue to the *Legend of Good Women* (by implication), the Man of Law's Tale (by specification), and the Retraction (by implication again). The "bumbling, scholarly, versifying 'Geffrey' no longer exists. Instead, we have 'Chaucer' [. . .] the formal, dignified patronymic that will survive through history and set the poet apart from any other Geoffrey" (33); Chaucer will become an individual author among the great *auctores*.

In a similar vein, the G version clearly places greater emphasis on reading than on listening, on writing than on speaking. In G, there are a great many verbs that call attention to the act of declaration: verbs like *answer*, *say*, *tell*, *devise*, *hear*, *write*, *renounce*, *translate*, and *work* (*wrought*); these terms can be oral or written in nature. Yet Chaucer also substitutes *make* for *say*, in underlining the duality the narrator ascribes to the *Troilus* when he finally does get around to talking back to Cupid, although feebly. In a typical Chaucerian turnabout, though, he can only manage to deny an intention to say what he has, in fact, written in his own poem: a true lover

> [. . .] oghte me nat to blame,
> Thogh that I speke a fals lovere som shame.
> [Lovers]oughte rathere with me for to holde,
> For that I of Criseyde *wrot or tolde*. . . .
> (G 456–59; my emphasis)

The passage is punctuated by the two verbs "wrot" and "tolde." It is fitting that here in the Prologue, considering the play of opposites we find in Chaucer's other works, there should be a motif emphasizing verbal expression precisely when Geffrey is being physically confronted about his writing and can find nothing worthy to say, out loud, about it. This difference would be even more evident if Chaucer's audience knew two versions of the Prologue, which is what Quinn argues: that the F Prologue is a performance text whose phraseology is predominantly of "direct address" (27); that the G Prologue is for reading silently, "revised to satisfy [Chaucer's] concern that [. . .] readers, by virtue of their being able to review the text in hand, would be more technically demanding," and so the story line would be more consistent (39–40)—which means that some passages are reduced and/or shifted to another place within the narrative while others are amplified, such as occurs in G's fifty-five line expanded indictment of Chaucer by the God of Love (44).

To be sure, Cupid "exhorts Chaucer to *reherce*," observes Copeland, which was then the job of a "*compilator* who gathers together the opinions of others rather than setting forth his own" (196). Whether or not Cupid is supposed to be insulting to Chaucer by demoting his status from author is not clear, I think. Just the same, this passage is deleted in G where, instead, "the God of Love exhorts him to 'let be the chaf, and write wel of the corn' (G 529)." All in all, considering the revisions and "significant omissions of G, it is clear that Chaucer as translator affirms his claim to *auctoritas* and underscores the auto-exegetical force of his *Prologue*" (197), in great measure because he is both *scriptor* and *auctor*, in an imagined world, like the actual world Chaucer inhabited, a world that is increasingly privileging writing and reading over speaking and hearing. The text of the world has become a fixed, written text; it has become the evidence of a divide between the divine and the mortal, which can only be bridged through faith or through the exercise of the individual will, which requires faith. The emblem of this hiatus is the *mis*reading of the Chaucer corpus by the Chaucerian characters—Cupid, Alceste, and even the Prologue's narrator—god and mortal alike.

Yet through the Prologue's comedy human nobility is recalled in the various misreadings—Chaucer's speakings and writings, his translations, his "ear" or two of original "corn." This comedy serves a serious purpose. In Chaucer's hands, misreading, rather than reading, also is meant to signify the efficacy of all artistic endeavor. Art may most authentically describe the truth, Chaucer seems to be saying, in its gesture toward that truth, a gesture that takes the form of human expression's ultimate failure at truth's transcription.

This transcription is carried out through the Chaucerian persona that is unique in all of literature ultimately because this figure contains a central paradox its author has intentionally built into it. As a narrator, the persona lacks sufficient wit to tell his story properly. Ockham and others, we have noted, could at times view wit and will as virtually synonymous. Chaucer dramatizes this dyad. It is likely that he embraced the Ockhamist idea of the liberty of the will, which was nothing less than a moral ground where human dignity, goodness and responsibility could exist;[56] therefore the will was more important than thinking, even as wit and will were intimately intertwined. In a poem like the *Troilus* the narrator, not without sympathy for his tale, tells us that he "weeps" as he "writes," perhaps in part because he is merely "the sorwful instrument,"[57] who wonders whether he will have both wit and will enough to carry out his task of rehearsing the lovers' tragedy. But at the same time, typically, Chaucer has his persona wrestle with weighty philosophical problems that provide the backdrop for his narratives. And, when they have to do with love, the persona will confess, he cannot speak from first hand experience; he is not as worldly as he perhaps ought to be. He is, indeed, as A. Blamires has put it (in "A Chaucer Manifesto" 30), a "poet manqué." Chaucer would have it no other way. While what Chaucer's Geffrey does and says is at times even hilarious, it is also sober, wise and complex.

Out of the disruptions the narrator helps to cause, Chaucer fashions an esthetic and philosophically consistent poetry. As has been argued, his strategy is precisely to invent a *dis*unity; he carries this through by essentially abandoning allegory. This forging of a new poetics, moreover, is effected in conjunction with his awareness that his poetry is predicated by the authorship trope. For example, in the Prologue Chaucer has Alceste, who is busily defending his poetry, invoke the trope first in her mentioning of Dante, at a crucial moment:

[. . .] thus seyth Dante;
Whoso that goth, alwey she mot nat wante.
This man to yow may wrongly ben acused,
There as by ryght hym oughte ben excusid.
(G 336–39)

Dante had the temerity to write into *his* script his persona's acceptance into the *bella scola* made up of Virgil and the other great poets of antiquity. Chaucer must now be more subtle; he must mention Dante in passing, yet in his own defense. Essentially, Alceste is making a point to Cupid about what she sees are

---

[56] *Quod.* III, q. 13.
[57] Cf. I.7, I.10.

questionable connections among truth, literary value and intention. Here, indeed, she also employs the most common troubadour topos used to define oneself as set over and against all others in the court; the Prologue's narrator is portrayed by her as a truth teller who must move through a treacherous world of jealous liars. She says that there is

> [. . .] many a losengeour,
> And many a queynte totelere accusour,
> That tabouren [. . .] many a thyng
> For hate, or for jelous ymagynyng [. . .].
> (G 328-31)

These lines resurrect an earlier stage of the authorship strategy in which the poet is singled out, claiming for himself the mantle of eloquence within a barbarous society. Dante turned the society into a welcoming one, as the sheer virtuosity of his verse, describing the embrace of the great poetic authorities of the past, whispered the fact that he was the greater poet. As for Chaucer, his comedy, set in verse that is equally elegant and powerful, reverts back to the fundamental configuration of the authorship trope—the individual poet who is, symbolically at least, an outsider standing apart from a tradition whose greatness he acknowledges, and who wants that tradition, such as is graphically demonstrated in the case of Dante, to pass through him. Of course, in Chaucer the tradition has, in the guise of the gods, turned upon him.

For Chaucer, this new configuration, derived from his predecessors, is bound up in his ongoing contemplation of and innovations within the tradition of poetic form. This, in turn, is contingent on Chaucer's world view. What becomes obvious when looking through the nominalist lens, moreover, is that his persona vitiates the potency of the allegorical form[58] and distinguishes between poetic form and philosophical formulation. As a figure, the persona comprehends three, interrelated, nominalist assertions.

The first assertion arises from Ockham's critique of postulates that accept the possibility of speaking about truths yet fail to demonstrate how such statements might be made; the ultimate criterion for ruling out this possibility is that of experience. The second assertion stems from Ockham's rejection of the thirteenth century's and Aristotle's notion of species; it is one thing to know an object by experiencing it sensually, while it is another to know of it in the abstract. Ockham's ideas are a renovation of what had been proposed by Duns Scotus, who had allowed for abstract

---

[58] Fletcher (in "Allegory in Literary History" 1.46) has noted that the "symbolic mentality" of the Middle Ages
> denied the more immediate puzzles presented by the senses. The flight [via allegory] from the limited toward the infinity of the Divine Being kept its balance only, if at all, by asserting that man's world was closed and finite. Ockham's principle of parsimony was invented, it seems, to stem this iconographic tide, since scholastic thought, at first rationalizing, ends by absorbing the medieval compulsion to turn relations into icons.

knowledge based on the concept of separately existing entities that were likenesses of any directly apprehended object.[59] Ockham's "razor" eliminated any intermediary entities between the intellect and the object of knowledge. Any sign could therefore only be rememorative (Tabarroni 209); echoing this idea, Chaucer writes of the "keye" of "remembrance" (G 26, F 26). Ockham refused, on the basis of logic, to grant that the names of entities (or other representations) in and of themselves were ontologically grounded. This epistemological construct is typified by Geffrey, a fictional personage, in Ockham's terms a *name*, and a figure bearing his author's name, who describes what he sees, hears and feels. Geffrey is witness and reporter of his experiences, and he is virtually obsessed by the question of whether experience can adequately convey the truth of existence. As if to make sure that the reader does not miss the philosophical point, he is presented as being either mentally slow or else reluctant to live at the center of the events he is reporting.

Why reluctant? The question of mental acuity brings us to the third crucial tenet of Ockhamism, one that is of paramount significance in what will shortly be our attempt to comprehend *Piers Plowman*: that is, the role of *voluntas* in the attempt to achieve salvation. The very credence Ockham placed in the structure and force of logic compelled him to conceive of a universe of radical contingency, which meant there had to be a division of the universe into two worlds—the one a world of God's potential power, the other of actuality—one of God's will, the other of the individual's will. Thus the central nominalist question became one of causality—whether or not there could be a demonstrable causal relationship between these two worlds. Because God's enactment of miracles is logically possible, the furnishing of absolute proof of causal transactions becomes impossible.[60]

As has been mentioned, nominalists could view wit and will as virtually synonymous. And Ockham had said that free, individual will was knowable evidentially, through experience, since "a man experiences the fact that however much his reason dictates some action, his will can will, or not will, this act."[61] Hence Chaucer embraces the Ockhamist idea of the liberty of the will, which existed within the world of *potentia ordinata* or rather actuality; this idea was nothing less than a moral ground where human dignity, goodness and responsibility could exist.[62] To be sure, the will could be more important than thinking, even as wit and will were intimately involved with one another—an idea, again, demonstrated in the *Troilus'* narrator who "weeps" as he "writes" because he is merely "the sorwful instrument" for telling the poem's tale.

In these lines Chaucer is also addressing what is, basically, an Ockhamist question, that of authorial intention. The Prologue to the *Legend of Good Women*, furthermore, adds a particular account of what Chaucer has written. Other than the Prologue, only his Retraction to the *Tales* contains this sort of in-depth literary self-reflection (the Man of Law simply catalogs Chaucer's works). The Retraction

---

[59] *Quod.* I, q. 13.
[60] *Sent.* II, 8-5.
[61] *Quod.* I, q. 16; Moody 434.
[62] Cf. *Quod.* III, q. 13.

is one last signal, one final key to the code of reading, for those of us who, like Cupid, have a problem keeping straight the literary "wheat" and "chaff." The key—to use this rich term from his and then Payne's famous phrase "the key of remembrance"—is forged out of the rumination, at the Prologue's start, about knowledge. In old age, then, Chaucer looks back at his work as a poet—from within his own writing—as is implied by the Prologue's passing allusions to the *senex amans* theme in the *Roman de la rose* and in the *Troilus* through Pandarus, where, in both cases, there is some resemblance to the Chaucer-figure Cupid calls an "old fool" (G 249-62).[63] All three—the *Troilus*, Prologue, and Retraction—foreground a meditation on the nature of fiction. In the Retraction, Chaucer repudiates those works that the modern world most prizes for the synergy they present of ostensible fiction and actual, experiential truth. He comments, significantly, that

> if ther be any thyng that displese [my readers], I prey hem also that they *arrette it to the defaute of myn unkonnynge and nat to my wyl, that wolde ful fayn have seyd bettre if I hadde had konnynge./* For oure book seith, "All that is writen is writen for oure doctrine," and that is myn entente.
> (my emphasis, 1082-83)

Here we find, once again, the typical Chaucerian ploy of equivocation. Is this Chaucer speaking or his persona? In the Prologue the answer is clearly that both are speaking. The Prologue is poetry that, on its surface, is meant to be taken as playful. In the prose Retraction we should not underestimate the speaker's dependence on the explanation that, if Chaucer has sinned in what he has done, this is due to his "unkonnynge" and "nat to [his] wyl." Using the excuse of his "unkonnynge," he "retracts" several of his works, not least among them the *Canterbury Tales*. In the words of David Williams (in "From Grammar's Pan to Logic's Fire" 90-91), Chaucer is taking back the work

> he is in the very act of disseminating. The paradox of an author denying what he is simultaneously saying, or unwriting what he is writing, suggests in the Chaucerian context a [literary] realist theory of fiction in which two intentions are operating at the same time—an intentional representation and a communicating one—the one put forward, the other withdrawn. But the relation of these directions is binary, like the ontological relation of universal to particular, and as poetics it suggests a theory of fiction, primarily representational, in which the intention to communicate is variously absent and present.

Fiction merely represents. Inhering in the fictional text, a text of particulars, is the nominalist recognition that communication is limited and that the will is fallible although one must exercise it as best as one can. Yet what is it to say that fiction is

---

[63] In this regard, cf. Quinn, 44. Delaney, 37, argues for Chaucer seeing himself at about age fifty-four as middle aged. However, Chaucer's self-mockery could easily include seeing himself as old, as failing in his powers.

"mere" representation? The textual illustrations of real life, flesh and blood authors are in one sense fictions, but they merge the unreal and the real; in Ockhamist terms, they bridge the gap between faith and experience. Both the Prologue's indictment and the Retraction's disclaimer were versions of topoi that came down through time to Chaucer from Ovid.[64] These topoi, however, have become suffused with the textures and ideas of the fourteenth century's nominalist-realist debate—in Chaucer's work, and in Langland's, as we shall now discover.

No less than Chaucer's, we have noted that Langland's innovative skills worked to undermine traditional expectations of various literary forms such as the dream *visio*, the poem of pilgrimage, and allegory. Like Chaucer, Langland, his contemporary, reflects the upheavals of his time—social and political, theological and philosophical, and esthetic. *Piers Plowman* has frustrated, as well as pleased, readers because it has resisted adhering to what at first appear to be the poem's set literary forms. This resistance is in fact the measure of its originality, of what in fact is its revolutionary poetics. The resistance allows for an identification of its innovative energy, an energy that in itself is a reflection of the changing fourteenth-century landscape.

While Chaucer turns his back on the allegorical tradition, and in so doing sends it up in a spoof that has ultimately serious purposes, Langland, just as seriously, achieves literary power by methodically dismantling poetic structures from within. Considering the wide range of theological and philosophical thinking in the fourteenth century, and the concomitant range, in England alone, of poetic voice and genre, it is reasonable to assume that an innovator like Langland should have approached the problem of generic expectation from quite a different direction than had Chaucer. In their time, England produced an extraordinary variety of poetry, and literature generally. *Cleanness*, *Pearl*, *Sir Gawain and the Green Knight*, *Piers Plowman*, Chaucer's dream poems, *Troilus and Criseyde*, and, last but not least, *The Canterbury Tales*, are all contemporary to each other, and we may safely assume they were all popular.

These poems attest, of course, not only a wide range of literary taste and novelty, but the divergence of values between their own period and ours. Especially to a twentieth-century sensibility, there is a world of difference between Chaucer's literary output and that of, say, Dame Julian of Norwich. Richard Rolle, if we are to judge by the number of extant manuscripts and other records in the fifteenth century, was enormously popular, more so than his contemporary Chaucer. Apparently, the *Form of Perfect Living* was more compelling for fourteenth-century readers than was the *Canterbury Tales*. All the same, to gauge

---

[64] As has been argued by Copeland, 195; and by Michael Calabrese, *Chaucer's Ovidian Arts of Love*, esp. 8-9, 17-19, 115, and 126.

these two works by such a narrowly drawn criterion as this comparison must miss the point; Chaucer's audience was surely less clerical, more secular, and perhaps more sophisticated. In *Piers Plowman* we see a poem that in all likelihood could reach out to many different kinds of reader, some of whom might have more readily enjoyed Rolle than Chaucer, or vice versa. Yet what is interesting about Langland, in this context, is not so much the matter of his poem as his method of treating that matter.

Both Chaucer and Langland confront the issue of allegorical thinking, deeply rooted as it is in Christian theology since Paul and Augustine. Again, Chaucer has ostensibly rejected the received poetic forms of his time—and in so doing he has staked out an ontological claim for poetry, in the Prologue to the *Legend of Good Women* and elsewhere; thus he has chosen to fashion what the modern mind comfortably designates as esthetic realism. Langland, however, has decided to develop a poem whose very machinery presides over the essential Christian question of the efficacy of language, in making a claim for poetry as a solution to this problem. Moreover, Langland manages this in more explicit fashion than is possible for Chaucer, not least because *Piers Plowman* overtly links the question of specifically Christian salvation with the act of writing. The philosophy of language, as it has come down to him in the Christian tradition, provides Langland with an alternative poetic strategy. Employing a discourse that in comparison with Chaucer's is more obviously philosophical and apparently didactic, Langland recognizes that the resolution of knotty theological and philosophical issues can take place only through a language that can demonstrate its own undoing (a decidedly postmodern notion). Therefore, we find in *Piers Plowman* a cogently self-reflexive intent to make use of irony in the construction of poetic genres, which will most eloquently demonstrate their own integrity of expression by dint of their ability to unravel or rather to deconstruct themselves. From this perspective, it is fair to call Langland's method a poetics of self-cancellation; time and time again it demonstrates its own impossibility, and perhaps this represents the final possibility of an artist's self-enunciation within the *presence-absence* textual matrix that is also a part of the tradition Langland has inherited (and that has been discussed previously).[65]

Chaucer's is a profound discussion of the ultimate confounding that language and poetry cause in their quest for absolute truth, whereas Langland's poetry is a demonstration of that deeply problematic, deeply Christian perception that language and poetry will inevitably only lead back to themselves, and that the only hope of describing truth lies in the gesture poetry can make in its inevitable failure adequately *to name* the absolutely real—to say the truth. Chaucer's gesture is oblique, and thus is peripheral, in contrast to Langland's gesture that is central. Hence, we might want to reconsider the canonical status of works like the *Canterbury Tales* and *Piers Plowman*, as our own critical standards both widen and are transformed—for in obvious ways Langland's poem lends itself to the kinds of critical analysis that have become popular since the advent of structuralism.

[65] Cf. the Introduction, and Chapters Two and Three.

Indeed, to view the poem as a demonstration of its own poetics is to be able to loosen many of what have been widely recognized are the poem's critical knots. The poem's attempt at poetic self-reflexivity occurs, furthermore, in order to make a clearly theologico-philosophical statement.

Langland's epistemological concerns become crystal clear when we place his poem within the intellectual context of its time—more so than for Chaucer, Dante or Marcabru. We have seen how immensely important linguistic paradigms were for thinkers contemporary with Langland as well as those before him. Well within the embrace of the Augustinian textual and autobiographical tradition, in which language per se has been foregrounded, Langland has resorted to linguistic metaphors that are of crucial importance to any attempt at understanding his complex, subtle and powerful poetic structure. They point to the ultimate meaning of his poem, which is conveyed by a self-reflexive commentary on the nature of poetry and its various generic forms. This poetic investigation, finally, leads full circle to where the poem essentially begins, with the theological question of free will and its relationship to salvation.

This question is stressed in the use Langland makes of one particular "genre," that of self-naming. Like the typical Chaucerian gambit, *Piers Plowman* opens with a description of the Fair Field of Folk, in a dream; as Laurie Finke has observed (in "Truth's Treasure" 57-58), Langland poses the question of how to interpret that dream. For Langland, the question ultimately becomes whether or not the dreamer as pilgrim can exercise the *will* to interpret and to communicate what he experiences. In several passages of *Piers Plowman* it is implied that interpretation and communication are the key activities for anyone who holds out the hope of salvation. But we are explicitly told this through the inclusion of the C text's autobiography, a passage that immediately highlights the issue of self-evaluation and redemption by virtue of the attention the passage, first of all, calls to itself. The form this calling to attention takes is of a textual nature. The C passage disrupts an expectation that has been previously established in the poem's last version, the B text. Thus the discourse in B, which had been firmly set within its own chronology, is displaced and deferred by Langland's new discussion of his persona Will's identity as a poet and what that can mean for him in terms of his own personal salvation. We are told this symbolically in the metaphor of the plough, which would have been for both Chaucer and Langland immediately apprehended as signifying the poet's pen. Ploughing was understood as a form of writing; in fact, in some fundamental fashion it was the very act of writing, where the field of the pen signified the text or book.[66]

---

[66] In this section of my discussion, I am trying to demonstrate the analogous relationships between writing and pilgrimage—the source for the ploughman as pilgrim is Luke 10, which calls upon disciples to preach and therefore to harvest, to be laborers worthy of hire, and between writing and education—the sources for which are similar to pilgrimage, especially in that both pilgrimage and education involve preaching; thus preaching, an orally based discourse, is equatable with writing and otherwise literate discourse. Cf. Holloway, 79-81. Appendix C discusses ploughing as a metaphor for writing, as well as ploughing's

Particularly in the C text, the poem's final revision, the issue of self-writing is most vividly at work, and then most conspicuously in the "autobiographical" Passus V, but elsewhere too. In these passages, the Langland persona seeks to establish a complementary relationship between the question of the uses one can make of language, such as poetry, and the exercise of the individual will within a world of conditional and absolute necessity. Indeed, this complex of forces is most graphically depicted in the C text's ninety-one line expansion of a discussion in B concerning, Coleman writes, "heavenly reward, measurable hire, and illicit worldly mede." The passage crystallizes two pursuits: philosophico-theological truth, and the truth of the poetic vocation. Both are founded in a shared epistemological assumption. Thus this passage

> best comes to terms with the [contemporary] understanding of just reward according to the covenant operating in the *ordinata* [i.e., the created world]. It is also in keeping with [contemporary] interests in logic and grammar that Langland should interpolate a grammatical explanation of mede in terms of right relation, and thereby give us some insight into what an audience for the poem was expected to understand.
> (*Piers Plowman* 88)

Grammar, which as a primary forensic tool had still been enormously popular in the last several centuries, in Langland's time remained as a vehicle by which new perceptions and beliefs might be conceptualized and articulated. In a discussion of the seven arts, C III has in effect retroactively created a penetrating echo, originating in B XV;[67] the earlier passage deplores the fact that, in the present state of society's decline, "Grammer, the ground of al," now "bigileth" children (370). In the C text (III.353) the earlier perception is reiterated, in order to establish interrelationships among language, knowledge and salvation, in a reprise that now proclaims "god [to be] the grounde of al":

> 'Relacoun rect,' quod Consience, 'is a recorde of treuthe,
> *Quia ante late rei recordatiuum est,*
> Folowyng and fyndynge out þe fundement of a strenghe,
> And styfliche stande forth to strenghe þe fundement
> In kynde and in case and in þe cours of nombre.
> As a leel laborer byleueth þat his maister
> In his paye and in his pite and in his puyr treuthe
> To paye hym yf he parforme and haue pite yf he faileth
> And take hym for his trauaile al þat treuthe wolde;
> So of holy herte cometh hope, and hardy relacoun
> Seketh and suweth his sustantif sauacioun,
> That is god the ground of al, a graciouse antecedent.
> And man is relatif rect yf he be rihte trewe:
> He acordeth with Crist in kynde, *Verbum caro factum est;*

---

secondary associative network.
[67] As has been mentioned in Chapter Three.

> In case, *Credere in ecclesia*, in holy kyrke to bileue;
> In nombre, rotye and aryse and remissioun to haue,
> Of oure sory synnes to be assoiled and yclansed,
> And lyue as oure crede vs kenneth with Crist withouten ende.
> (343-59)[68]

Langland's strategy here is to come full circle, through these like sentiments, linking together issues of language, knowledge, and salvation.

It is important to see here that such linkage especially pertains to the issue of the exercise of one's individual will, and whether or not such action will result in the ultimate reward of salvation; exercise of volition obtains to the activity of writing. For Langland, late in a twice revised long poem, and more pointedly than in either its A or B versions, this relationship is clearly established through an identification between the author, William Langland, and the poem's persona, a figure that exists as both an allegory within the action of the poem, and as a fully drawn character, about whom we learn much in the way of personal details in the uniquely autobiographical passage, C V. Not only is this passage in itself new with C, but it has been prepared for by a greatly expanded discussion of the nature of reward and free will in the two passus leading up to it. Indeed, this renovation of the A and B texts is sufficient unto itself to tell us of Langland's interest in self-enunciation. Self-assertion, however, is not for Langland an end in itself. Rather, it is employed in order to examine profoundly ontological and epistemological issues of the time, which in turn, in their discussion, serve to deepen and commemorate the individual author within as well as beyond his text. And it is the very mode of the actual signing of the author's name in the poem—the signing changes from one version to the next—which amounts to powerful evidence of Langland's intentions.[69]

Dante, earlier, was intent on defining himself in terms of the philosophical issues of his day, particularly in an implicit relationship with Thomas Aquinas. Langland's intellectual dialogue is conducted between himself and, alternately, Ockham, Holcot or other theologian-philosophers in part or wholly under the sway of Ockham's ideas. In this manner, similar to Dante, at one and the same time Langland wishes to assert his individuality as a poet and by extension to legitimize poetry as an act that can lead to salvation. This of course is an attitude not only common to Dante but to Marcabru as well. All the same, like his forebears, Langland strives to have himself be subsumed into a larger discussion of individual conduct, truth and salvation; he wishes to be subsumed, that is, into the essential discourse of his text. Here we see another instance of the inherently tautological nature of autobiography, also operative in Dante; the composing of the text occurs within the life that has yet to be completed and which is being influenced by that

---

[68] This passage and the grammatical metaphor generally has been examined by: Amassian and Sadowsky, 457-76; Harwood, 19 ff.; Mann, 19-21; and Middleton, "William Langland's 'Kynde Name'," 41 and 61.

[69] Cf. Kane, *Evidence for Authorship*, 61-65; and Middleton, "William Langland's 'Kynde Name'," 17 ff.

composition.[70] Furthermore, the subsumption into a text of pilgrimage, in which a protagonist experiences travail and frustration in his attempt to arrive at his destination, underscores not so much the possibility for understanding the human plight as it does the struggle to exercise the human will.[71] This intricacy, in Langland's poem, particularly as the questions of volition and understanding intertwine, provokes and satisfies; furthermore, it is through such a complex that we will finally know and appreciate the poet, the person who has set all of this in motion. As Patterson comments, however, "[t]he promise of a self-present meaning offered by writing is constantly deferred: rather than providing access to an unambiguous, self-identical meaning invulnerable to historical change, writing offers instead only mediation" (*Chaucer and the Subject of History* 20).

Comparing *Piers Plowman* with the *Commedia*, Middleton identifies the connection between the direct or indirect naming of their respective personae and their poems' very different structures, and the implications regarding the question of history versus fiction that will ensue from such a comparison:

> If the anagram of Will's name in his meeting with Anima initiates the final progression of [*Piers Plowman*]—a penultimate turning point much like that experienced by Dante when for the first time in the poem the poet hears his own name in the first syllables Beatrice addresses to him—then the Lond of Longyng, to which that later signature alludes narratively, may be understood as Will's *selva oscura*, encountered, like Dante's *nel mezzo del cammin de nostra vita* (midway in our life's journey). While Dante's self-confrontation initiates his poem, however, Langland's merely alludes by echo to the beginning of his, proclaiming a second "coming to himself" halfway through its and his life's duration.
> ("William Langland's 'Kynde Name'" 52)

Langland, it is being suggested, was in middle age when composing his B text, his poem's first major revision, in which he "[overlays] a second narrative order on his first [and proposes, like Dante,] to understand through cosmic vision his own position in time, developing the deep correspondences between biography and redemptive history" (52–53).[72]

---

[70] Which was discussed earlier. Cf. the Introduction; and Freccero, 264.
[71] Cf. Freccero, 29 ff.
[72] Middleton's surmisal compares Dante's life and Langland's (and we can add Chaucer's Prologue to the *Legend of Good Women* that I believe reflects his feelings about growing old):
> Like Dante's thirty-three years on the Good Friday of the Jubilee Year 1300 on which the poem begins, Will's age at this critical and extended self-confrontation halfway through his poem is specified explicitly—twice, in fact—in the B text. It is forty-five years of age: [. . . .] the traditional boundary between *juventus*, the middle term of life's three ages, and *senectus*, [which] marks what ought to be a turning point from limitless projects to a vision of their end. Ymaginatif rebukes Will for spending these years "medling" with "makynges" [. . .].
> (53)

We will discuss this encounter shortly.

Another motif germane to this discussion, which is different in all three texts of *Piers Plowman*, is Langland's treatment of minstrelsy. Minstrelsy is the only occupation that is treated variously in each version of the poem.[73] Thus, as I have been arguing, it is valuable and perhaps even essential to consider all variants of Langland's poem, as part of a larger poetic experience that we can posit as being the real poem we call *Piers Plowman*—the A, B and C texts together constituting the hypersign we understand to be the expression that is more than the sum total of the poem's parts. All the same, the writing is not only the map of its author's life; in some sense it is the life. Hence, the aggregation of the poem's earlier and last versions points to the role the poet plays in relation to the central factor in the poetic process, a process that in ways is utterly paradoxical, as has been aptly described by Gottfried Benn: "Here is the mystery: the poem is already finished before it begins; only the poet does not yet know the text. The poem absolutely cannot be different from what it then is, when it is finished."[74] This understanding of poetry, in which text and author can be two aspects of the same phenomenon, may account for the treatment of Minstrelsy in the C text as being of an essentially transformed nature from that which we find in either or both A and B. George Economou (in "Self-Consciousness of Poetic Activity" 189) observes that, while the earlier texts differentiate between "minstrels who guiltlessly 'geten gold with hire glee' and those 'lapers and langelers, Iudas children', who could work if they wanted to," C simply presents the idea of "one bad class of minstrels, those 'That wollen neyther swynke ne swete'."[75] In C, the view of minstrelsy is more distilled. As well, this last revision

> moves from its one-class definition to a view that distinguishes between the original class of minstrels and "godes mynstrales" (C VII.100), a phrase deriving ultimately from Franciscan tradition. The B-text, between passus X and XIII, begins to show a severe judgment against all but the most pious kind of minstrelsy, while at the same time tending to disassociate the dreamer from the vocation. Still, in its identification of Hawkin as a minstrel, the B-text appears to persist in its preoccupation with minstrelsy, possibly even contributing to the connection between Hawkin and the poet so many readers see. But it is in the C-text, with its explicit separation of God's minstrels from the body of everyday minstrelsy and entertainment, that we find the clearest expression of the poet's "conscious assimilation of himself to a minstrel" along the basic line of development found in all three texts: "first, an honest, plausible, idealistic entertainer and ultimately an apostolic-Franciscan *ioculator Dei*."
> (189)[76]

---

[73] As Donaldson has observed, *Piers Plowman: The C-Text and Its Poet*, 136-55; cf. George Economou, "Self-Consciousness of Poetic Activity in Dante and Langland," 189.
[74] Quoted in Maria Corti, *An Introduction to Literary Semiotics*, 84.
[75] Cf. Donaldson, *Piers Plowman*, 136 ff.
[76] Passus VII.100 in the Pearsall edition of the C text. Economou has quoted Donaldson, 155.

Significantly, the autobiographical section in C is related by a Will who is fully awake. In his persona, Langland has wedded his discourse on volition to a recognition, furthermore, that inherent in humankind there is a creative aspect; this aspect can manifest as playfulness and even as verse making. Therefore the notion of play, and of poetry largely, is to be explained within an otherwise alien, binary context: idleness versus work. The question being asked, then, is whether or not the exercise of an individual's will is contingent upon the desire to work, to work in a way that suggests the *lack* of playfulness. And, it is suggested, if poetry is to be legitimized as a serious endeavor, on a par with sober work, then salvation may be possible by way of unusual, otherwise less than serious, or rather willful, means.

Of course poetry, the act of its composition, is ultimately to be seen as a means toward salvation. This "quest" for salvation is "finally profoundly affected and directed by [a] crucial encounter with Imaginative," which Economou points out is "a vivid example [. . .] of self-consciousness fourteenth-century style" (190-91). This "is a figure," John Burrow writes (in *Langland's Fictions* 93), "of considerable authority, representing the mind's capacity to see beyond the present moment and take longer views." The figure can also mean vivid self-representation, according to Joseph Wittig (in "*Piers Plowman* B" 272-73).[77] In the B text, Will's vocation as poet is challenged by him (in a manner not unlike Cupid's condemnation of Chaucer's works); in C, the challenge is deleted, its purpose fulfilled by the new autobiographical passage that has been constructed out of this dialogue.[78] Be that as it may, the making of poetry as a worthwhile endeavor is what is fundamentally being questioned in both texts. Middleton comments that Will's "is a compromised activity in its essence, [without] distinctive integrity and institutional situation of its own, [lacking] the authority of clerical didacticism." What at bottom is being disputed here is Will's standing, his status as an author. His "questionable mode of life [cannot] authorize him to compose a testimony uniquely worthy of serious attention" ("Narration and the Invention of Experience" 115). But *makyng*, arguably, fulfills Will's search for wisdom. "If he could get his answers elsewhere," Economou remarks, "the narrator would give up his 'werke' and go to church to do his more conventional duty." Will insists upon verse-making as valuable, as serious, which is "indeed remarkable, all the more so when we consider that after Langland arrived at his view of himself as one of God's minstrels, they became superfluous" (190-91). A relationship is established between human will and human imagination, not unlike what Dante develops in the *Commedia*. And so "the concept of acceptable forms of work must be expanded to contain the calling of poetry when it is specifically committed to serving God" (191). Chaucer portrays an opposition between imaginative knowledge and knowledge acquired through the process of reason, in the Prologue. Cupid can be read as an attack on the imagination, one readers

---

[77] In Burrow, 93.
[78] B XII. Cf. Middleton, "Narration and the Invention of Experience," 113 and 282, n. 21.

might have been all too quick to think of as impelled by reason, perhaps a kind of right reason, instead of blind inflexibility. Similarly, Langland's poem also emends or redefines a narrow, received notion of reason that otherwise cannot quite serve to elucidate the machinery of salvation.

> Just as Will's admission that he has wasted time (and his resolution a few lines later not to waste it further) in his closing speech of the autobiographical passage foreshadows Imaginative's claim that he has taught the narrator-dreamer not to waste time some nine passus later, the unique connection between these two parts of the poem is also probably partially based on a rather subtle but unmistakable connection between their personified interlocutors at the conclusion of the passage's opening paragraph. We have already read there that Reason, "Romynge in remebraunce," reproached the conscious narrator for his past and current attitude towards work. Considering that part of Imaginative's function, represented by the scholastic *ars commemorativa*, operates through memory, we can see that Reason and Imaginative resemble each other in their vivid representations of experience to the narrator in both dream and non-dream states. Indeed, their similarity is symptomatic of a much deeper connection [. . .].
> (193)

What is the deeper set of associations? In the latter half of the fourteenth century, Anselm's writings enjoyed a renewed interest. Harwood suggests that "the causative power of language underlies one of the most puzzling appearances of 'reson' in the poem [Passus B XI], one that introduces in effect the conception of 'rectitudo' developed by Anselm [. . .]" (35). We should now recall what he had to say about statements—that they possessed *rectitude* when they were intrinsically coherent but also only when they signified the truth of the real world. Further, Anselm applied this notion to physical events in the world; the harmony of nature, for example, is due to a "rightness."[79] Later, Aquinas reprised this idea when he wrote that "res naturales dicuntur esse verae, secundum quod assequuntur similitudinem specierum quae sunt in mente divina"—"'Truth of thing' is caused by the First Being, just as the 'truth of intellect' is caused by the First Truth."[80] This harmony is the result of necessity; yet, as made abundantly clear by thinkers since Ockham, necessity is qualified by free will. In *De Voluntate* Anselm had distinguished between the willing of the useful and the willing of justice; the former will always inhere in the instrument of action, not the latter.[81] As Harwood notes (referring to B XI.369-75),

> Because God has created all things capable of attaining their end, the affection for the useful in brutes adheres to the divine plan by instinct. In human beings, however, justice, or the rectitude of the will, which a person chooses or not, mediates between the ultimate rule of the divine plan and a person's own affection

---

[79] *De veritate*, Cap. 5. I am indebted to Harwood, 35-36, for making this association and the following associations concerning *rectitude* and *will*.
[80] *ST* I.16.1; Harwood, 35.
[81] In Harwood, 35.

for the useful. Aware of his sins, Will grows angry because only humanity has been permitted to lose this rightness; it is only humanity that "Reson" no longer rules.

All the same, "'Reson' as that rightness is a metonym as well for the idea, or 'ratio', thought to exist in the divine mind, inflecting human rightness." And so, deriving originally from Anselm, Langland is possessed of the idea that there is a "truth of the will [. . .]." Finally, this "'rectitudo voluntatis' receives the name 'iustitia' when one wills to preserve it because of itself" (35–36).[82]

What was an assault on the narrator's verse making by Imaginative (in B.XII) turns into, in the C text, a "more broadly based attack" on the manner of the narrator's working, by Reason. Reason's diatribe has "preempted" that of Imaginative, which has been deleted. The result is Will's "proposal of a commitment and hope in his making, just as Imaginative's attack had resulted in a definite, though weaker, defense of it" (Economou 193).[83] This commitment is signaled early in the C text in the metaphorical use made of grammar (cf. above). There is an analogy being proffered between "relacion rect and indirect aftur" (C III.341) and divine versus free will, between Anselm's *rectitudo* when language realizes its full potential that includes objective reference, and his idea of naturalness, *naturaliter*, when language merely possesses internal cogency. Will, who is a *natural* man, must align his will with the divine in order to be *right*. He can possibly do this with language, through poetry. As Amassian and Sadowsky comment, "in a kind of cosmic grammar, indirect man, lacking case agreement, or faithfulness, with God the antecedent, would be unable to inhere in God's will, thus thwarting God's and his own" (469).

Thus far, we see Langland following the line of argument posed by Anselm and Aquinas after him. The ensuing lines in the poem, however, could only have been written in the later fourteenth century. In the earlier passage (III.341-59), Mann observes, "God is the substantive [and] man takes the place of the forms grammatically dependent on this antecedent" (e.g., ll. 354-55: "And man is relatif rect yf he be rihte and trewe. / He accordeth with Crist in kynde [. . . .]"). Yet Langland turns this analogy inside out. "[L]ike all grammatical relationships," this relationship to the divine "turns out to be reversible [. . .]." Ultimately, humankind becomes the substantive while God becomes the modifying adjective (Mann 20):

> Ac adiectyf and sustantyf is as y her tolde,
> That is vnite acordaunde in case, in gendre and in noumbre.
> And is to mene in oure mouth more no mynne
> But þat alle maner men, wymmen and childrene
> Sholde confourme hem to o kynde on holy kyrke to bileue
> And coueyte þe case when thei couthe vnderstande

---

[82] Cf. Aquinas, *ST* I.22.1; Anselm *De veritate* Cap. I, XII.
[83] Cf. Skeat's gloss for "made of" in line 5: "For ich made of tho men as reson me tauhte."

> To syke for here synnes and soffre harde penaunces
> For þat lordes loue that for oure loue deyede
> And coueytede oure kynde and be kald in oure name,
> *Deus homo*,
> And nyme hum into oure noumbre now and euermore.
> *Qui in caritate manet in deo manet et deus in eo.*
> Thus is he man, and mankynde in maner of sustantyf
> As *hic et hec homo* askyng an adiectyf
> Of thre trewe termisones, *trinitas unus deus*;
> *Nominatio, pater et filius et spiritus sanctus.*
> (III.393-406)

Now mortals are represented by the noun and the divine by the adjective; humanity is the substance, God the accident, its "thre trewe termisones" representing the Holy Trinity. As Mann says, "The quality of divinity is grounded in man's substance. And it is the philosophical understanding of grammar that shows how humanity and divinity can be distinct and yet one" (20). Thus the difference between the early and the later sections of this passage about grammar and truth coincides with the difference between the *potentia absoluta* and the *potentia ordinata*.

The poem's allegorized interlocutors such as Imaginative, Reason, and Conscience—what they have to say to Will—also allow us entrance into *Piers Plowman*'s deeper meanings. Finally, however, it is the unique insertion of a parity between God and language (i.e., grammar) which provides a critical link to Langland's self-identity, within his very poem, as a poet; this link takes us to the very heart of the poem. We see Langland as someone who may provide a workable description of truth and self-revelation, albeit with the aid of a fallen language. We have seen this equation elsewhere, in the balance between the natural world and the language of Marcabru's verses. Troubadours could suggest that they possessed the ability to create poetry, as it were, *ex nihilo*, in the same way as there was a creation of the world. Spence observes that "most of the early troubadours start their poems with a word that emphasizes the distinction between their role in the work, and their role in the world"—for example, Guillem IX's use of "farai." "So too the troubadours emphasize their power over standard topoi, most notably the *Natureingang*" (120-21). In Dante, also, we find a version of this parity. As Freccero writes, regarding the centrality of formalism in the *Commedia*,

> [i]n a culture which called its central principle "the Word," a certain homology between the order of things and the order of words is strongly implied. This is another way of stating Kenneth Burke's "logological" principle. If theology is words about God, wherein linguistic realities are used to describe a transcendent divinity, then "logology" is the reduction of theological principles back into the realm of words. What ensures the possibility of the reversal is the central tenet of

Christianity, the doctrine of the Word, according to which language and reality are structured analogously.
(260)[84]

This poetic tradition is uniquely manifested in the fourteenth century. Language and secondarily poetry, for Chaucer, provide the matter of his poetic discussion in which the possibilities of expressing the truth are weighed within the confusion that language also causes in the human striving toward that truth. For Langland, however, the truth is posited as being the language itself—a language, moreover, which will be perceived as emptied of its content. This is a language he will literally inhabit. Within such a construct we may profitably find a comparison with Chaucer's attempts to talk about the problems as well as the hopes for language to enunciate the truth. In Chaucer, the problems come to be identified with his persona, who as a poet is seen nevertheless as standing apart from the poetry he has written—while in Langland there is the suggestion that the poet is in fact his very language and therefore his poetry, without distinction from Will. The grammatical analogy in C III (above) provides a forum for a protracted examination of how human reason and conscience affect the capacity for individual choices in the world; these abilities help to determine the vocation of writing, a choice that in the C text Langland has finally and unequivocally made as his work, a choice that will lead him to the truth of salvation existing beyond the vicissitudes of language, thought, and the reality of the created world, the *potentia ordinata*. In conjunction with other critical passages revised in the C text, C III establishes the basis for the direct assertion of the efficacy of poetry made by Will, to Reason and Conscience, in the autobiographical addition, C V.

The nexus of these concerns inscribes the fundamental world vision of the poem—most eloquently expressed by the ultimate terms of Will's search: Dowel, Dobet and Dobest. And if there is a paradox in this equation, it is that these are truly enigmatic terms. Dante's treatment of Augustine's *Confessions*, in the *Convivio*, focuses on his life as a progress, which went from bad to good, and then from good to better, and finally from better to best ("lo quale fu di [non] buono in buono, e di buono in migliore, e di migliore in ottimo").[85] As we have said, what interests Dante is the central paradox of the "Divine tautology": I am I, but I was not always so—which finds a corollary in Benn's observation on the making of poetry: "the poem is already finished before it begins" (above). For Langland, the paradox of a journey to a fully realized *I* is dramatized in the enigma of the states of being, Dowel, Dobet and Dobest, as these terms come to be considered in and of themselves, as terms, and moreover as terms that both further and undermine the poetic matrix in which they exist. On the one hand, as terminology they fulfill the demands of allegory, that the meaning of an allegory depends upon and gains power through enigmatic elements within the allegorical dynamic.[86] On the other

---

[84] Burke, *Rhetoric of Religion*, 1–7.
[85] Cf. the Introduction and Chapter One.
[86] As defined by Fletcher, above.

hand, these terms do not readily serve a primary requisite that allegory mean something on its literal level, for even if a reader could quickly deduce the burden of these portmanteau words, they still would not be, strictly speaking, readable as components of the syntactical formulations in which they are to be found. Their "application keeps changing as the poem goes on," Middleton notes; yet to observe this fact is merely to perceive the symptom of their influence on the poem as a whole. Contrary to normal expectations for allegory, we find that

> Dowel, Dobet, and Dobest are not personified or hypostatized abstractions taken from the stock of English common nouns; rather, they are coined terms using several parts of speech. Interpreters of the poem, like many of the allegorical speakers within it—including the arch-interpreter Will himself—have assumed that since "allegory is saying one thing and meaning another" the words do not mean what they say.
> ("Two Infinites" 170-71)

Indeed, the allegorical value of these terms derives from the fact that, with respect to syntax, they are impossible.[87] The impossibility is precisely the point. The ultimate terms of Will's search are syntactically and grammatically anomalous, and, like the eventual illogicality of so very many of the allegorical motifs in *Piers Plowman*—such as, in a most profoundly, apparently unreasonable moment, the tearing of the pardon—Dowel, Dobet and Dobest are the terms by which the poem attempts its own unraveling. They are central to the poem. As a part of Langland's larger project to write a poem about the act of interpretation itself, particularly through the act of writing, *makyng* or *fynding*, the use he makes of the three terms requires no simple translation but rather a process of "decipherment" through which readers can possibly apprehend the terms' metapoetical function in their role as "a major structural device." Chaucer's comedies of misinterpretations and confusions over the truths of texts and experiences find, at the very least, an adequate comparison in the many attempts in *Piers Plowman* to explain concepts, terms, definitions, and not least of all the three lives. However,

> [w]hile there is no lack of capsule definitions of the Three Lives in the poem, none of them appears to fit all the uses of the triad. Moreover, the terms stick thornily in virtually every sentence in which they are used, conspicuously at odds with the ordinary syntax surrounding them, like creatures from another world than that of poverty and practical moral precept—and so they are.
> (Middleton "Two Infinites" 171)

In Scholastic terms, as Clergy's analogy in the banquet scene (in the B and C texts) indicates, based on grammar, an analogy cannot be "referential, but purely formal." Any "meaning" to be derived from these anomalies must take grammar as its basis. Their function in the poem, then, is to "order the progressive form of the search for perfection, rather than characterize its object." Thus (to step back a

---

[87] David Mills, 195. Cf. the brief discussion of these terms in Chapter One.

few paces, for a moment, from this search for perfection Langland portrays) the relationship between grammar and pilgrimage will reveal the poem's overall matrix.

> The grammar of the three terms suggests that Langland coined them in an attempt to show intellectual or spiritual relationships in their essential, changeless aspects, independent of the temporal circumstances into which they may be translated. By drawing a complex metaphor from the realm of intellectual rather than sensory reality, Langland has created in his triad an explanatory instrument which is free as is poetically possible from the merely contingent. The use of the Three Lives as an organizing device is an attempt to purify allegorical language—a medium highly vulnerable to misunderstanding and misuse—of its most immediate rhetorical appeal, and hence one of its most slippery qualities. They represent an effort, visible everywhere in *Piers*, which perhaps can never totally succeed: to make human language eschatologically adequate, valid beyond the narrow base in the world and experience upon which the terms of its metaphors rest.
> ("Two Infinites" 171-72)

The "attempt to purify allegorical language" on the part of Langland, as Middleton has it, must finally lead to the undoing of the essential allegorical impulse. The poem, which immediately states that it will begin a process of self-decipherment, as the attempt is made to divine the meaning of the dream of the fair field of folk, then proceeds to unfold one or another allegory that depends on (not unlike the situation in Chaucer, or Dante, for that matter) a dreamer who can fathom the meanings of what takes place and who, as a poet, can record the truth of these events. The problem for Will, and for us as well, is that any of the meanings proffered are absolutely equivocal. Thus, finally, only the surety of grammar, whose rules provide language with, in a sense, meaning, allows Will any respite at all from the enormity of the confusion he perceives in all that he witnesses. Yet even here grammar may not serve him "truly"—when, that is, he is asked to consider the meaning of terms like *Dowel*, *Dobet* and *Dobest*, and so he must embark on his ultimate journey. It is not that these terms do not mean anything at all; in contrast, they are denotatively empty while, at one and the same time, they retain the power of multidimensionality. Recalling the situation Chaucer repeatedly presents us with, we can say that these terms provide the ground on which nominalist and realist thought can merge.

A discussion of the process by which poetry is created, and generally the recognition on the part of the poet of the efficacy of aligning his will with that of God's, was of course an important aspect of *Piers Plowman* prior to the C revision. But it is in the C text that the full implications of Dowel, Dobet and Dobest, and their relationship to *makyng*, are made clear. Economou comments,

> If it is possible that a revision in an earlier part of the C version of the poem helps in part to explain the deletion from C XIV of the defense of making that occurs in B XII, it is possible that the way the B text was completed also helps explain the revision of a passage such as the one with which this same passus, C XIV, opens. The writing, which mostly means the rewriting, of *Piers Plowman* incorporates poetic activity into the subject matter of the poem. What was written in B, especially from this very point in the text on, becomes part of the personal experience the narrator-dreamer brings to bear on his subsequent treatment of his continuing quest, the ongoing nature of which will be confirmed by the identical conclusions of B and C when Conscience announces his intention to seek out Piers the Plowman. Thus, the accomplishment of B in its explorations of Dowel, Dobet, and Dobest influences the removal of a passage that predicates its justification of making on the condition of acquiring knowledge about those three lives; it also influences the rewriting of the lines that introduce the figure that has already initiated the acquisition of that knowledge in the previous version. (191-92)

As Lorraine Kochanske Stock points out (in "Will, Actyf, Pacience, and *Liberum Arbitrium*" 475), to "[embrace] the life of spiritual upward mobility in Do wel, Do bet, Do best" requires individual *voluntas*, "the free will." This idea "is repeatedly suggested and endorsed by Langland, [and] is demonstrated by the renaming of the soul, or *Anima*, as *Liberum Arbitrium* in Passus XV of the C Text." The invention of the three terms, in representing a path of spiritual ascent, can be seen to have precipitated the exchange of terms that designate the soul. The making of poetry is to be seen as conditioned by a state of free will; we view the spiritual journey in a like context.

Bowers' comprehensive treatment of *Piers Plowman* demonstrates convincingly the intent on Langland's part to make of Will the figure of *voluntas*.[88] In order to accomplish this identification, Langland must invest in his poem the theme of language as the most important step on the pilgrimage towards redemption. The poet assiduously casts the greatest sacred historical events as "miracles" of either

> speech or writing. Wit interprets the act of divine creation as a linguistic process under the control of God: "And al at his wil was wrouȝt wiþ a speche, / *Dixit & facta sunt*" (B IX.32-46). The word of prophecy in the Old Testament is fulfilled in Christ (B XIX.80-82 [cf. C XXI.80-82]), and because the Virgin "conceyued þoruȝ speche" of the Holy Ghost, the Incarnation is also transformed into a linguistic act: "*Verbum caro factum est*" (B XVIII.129 [cf. C XX.133]; V.499 [cf. C XII.142]). Just as Moses had received the Old Law through the letters engraved upon the Tablets (B V.566-91), Christ inaugurated the New Law by saving the adulterous woman through the characters he wrote in the dust: "Holy kirke knoweþ þis, þat Christes writyng saued" (B XII.76-84). Even the first act of salvation is described as a result of language, when the gates of Hell are broken with the uttering of the words *Rex glorie* and Christ marshals a phalanx of texts against the speechless Satan—"I may do mercy þoruȝ my rightwisnesse and alle my wordes

---

[88] My discussion over the next pages is deeply indebted to Bowers.

trewe" (B XVIII.389 [cf. C XX.431]). Langland never misses an opportunity to look beyond the evocative and even the hieratic powers of language to elevate it as the supreme instrument of God's work on earth.
(192-93)

Furthermore, Langland aligns the human activity of writing with Genesis' "Faciamus hominem ad imaginem nostram" (1.26) in B IX.42. In this vein, we must note that the first instance of Dowel is represented by "Christ's verbal miracle at Cana," to suggest that "the use of language must somehow be involved in living the good life and repairing man's divine image" (Bowers 193). Linguistic imagery abounds throughout the poem. There are, also, the "lele wordes" and blossoms of "buxom speche" on the Tree of Charity (B XVI.6-7; cf. C XVIII.9-11).

The linguistic context especially obtains to the three Do's, within the parameters of an argument for a right use of language. A person who practices Dowel is "meke of his mouþ, milde of his speche"[89] and "trewe of his tunge," according to Thought. Dobet, likewise, is described as someone who is "lovelich of speche," and someone who has not only preached to people but who has also translated the Bible (B VIII.78-95; cf. C X.76-89). The meaning of Dobest, Wit says, is a right economy of speech, without wasted words "that spire is of grace, / And Goddes gleman and a game of hevene" (B IX.101-02). Later, the Holy Ghost metes out the gifts of grace; the first of the blessings is to go to those who aid fellow Christians through preaching and instruction. Thus, Bowers asserts, "definitions offered by Thought and Wit are really elaborations of a lesson given much earlier by Holy Church herself. When Will asked the question of central importance to the whole poem—'How may I save my soul?'—she explained that the surest treasure was Truth" (193):

> Who is trewe of his tonge, and telleth noon oother,
> Dooth the werkes therwiþp and wilneth no man ille,
> He is a god by the Gospel, agrounde and olofte,
> And ylik to Oure Lord, by Seint Lukes wordes.
> The clerkes that knowen this sholde kennen it aboute,
> For Cristen and uncristen cleymeth it echone.
> (B I.88-93; cf. C I.84-89)

The crucially significant, interlocking threesome, the alliterated *words*, *works* and *will*, is first suggested in this passage (Bowers 193). In order to be saved, Holy Church stipulates, there must be a true speech along with true works and good will toward others. Thus, as in Thought's defining of Dobet, clerics must spread the gospel. However, in such an injunction the core problem of signification is unavoidably evoked.

> [B]eneath the placid surface of her advice lurk problems that Langland would discover later when he began to plumb deeper. Cannot a man speak true words

---

[89] As cited by Bowers, 193.

arising from a false will? And cannot a well-intended cleric write a long allegorical poem but lose the merit of his work through the inability of his audience to understand its hard meaning?
(194)

There are numerous instances of Langland's use of *exempla* in order to further a claim that there can be a useful literary endeavor; this is so when the source of one's words is divine inspiration and hence when they are valuable to a Christian reader. There are the writers of saints' lives, Cato, the angel of annunciation who appeared "[t]o pastours and to poetes" (B XII.148-50; cf. C XIV.92). As the Holy Ghost points out: "Although men made bokes, God was the maister, / And Seint Spirit the samplarie, and seide what men sholde write" (B XII.101-02; cf. C XIV.46-47). Plato is called a poet; Lady Scripture lauds the "patriarkes and prophetes and poetes," for they denounced wealth and praised poverty (B X.175, 337-39; cf. C XI.121).

The linguistic question, of course, centers on the act of writing. Note Will's investigation of writing in his discussion of Solomon and Aristotle:

Maistres that of Goddes mercy techen men and prechen,
Of hir wordes thei wissen us for wisest as in hir tyme—
And al Holy Chirche holdeth hem bothe in helle!
And if I sholde werche by hir werkes to wynne me hevene,
That for hir werkes and wit now wonyeth in pyne—
Thanne wroghtte I unwisly, whatsoevere ye preche!
(B X.381-86; cf. C XI.218 ff.)

Considering the ambiguity inherent in the events that Book (i.e., the Bible) reports in the Harrowing of Hell scene, it is reasonable to conclude that

Langland has generated such an atmosphere of doubt concerning even moral literature that his poem cannot take for granted the merit of its own existence. He is therefore acutely aware of the need, if not always the means, to justify that existence.
(Bowers 195)

The ultimate means at Langland's disposal for justifying the existence of his poem is—and it perhaps presents an important paradox—to engage in a formal meditation on the nature of poetry and language by writing into his text the very undoing of that text. In the 1960's, A. C. Spearing noted (in "Verbal Repetition in *Piers Plowman*" 722) the existence in Langland's poem of textual echoes, including (important to the present discussion) intratextual echoes, especially in the poem's final revision where "thematic recurrence" is key to the evolution of Langland's ideas: "verbal repetition plays an important part in the rhetoric of *Piers Plowman* and [. . .] its use is consistently intensified in the C-Text of the poem."[90] One

---
[90] In L. K. Stock, 461.

theme, that of hunger's relationship to bread, which was examined by Spearing, is used in the C text to unify the poem by linking together three pivotal passages that in turn point toward Dowel, Dobet and Dobest as the ultimate expressions of the pilgrim's truth. Significantly, the first of these passages is in Passus C V, where Will confesses to his slothful life as a clerk:

Non de solo," y sayde, "for sothe *viuit homo,*
Nec in pane et in pabulo, the *pater-noster* wittnesseth;
Fiat voluntas dei—þat fynt vs alle thynges."
(86-88)

These phrases crop up again, first in the C text's banquet scene, Passus XV, in which Pacience instructs *Activa Vita* on the nature of being patient. Finally, *Liberum Arbitrium* defines charity for Will and Actyf, echoing these phrases, in XVI. Much in the vein of the Chaucerian persona, Will thoughtlessly mouths the phrases from Matthew 4:4, "Non de solo vivit homo nec in pane et in pabulo," and from the third petition of the Pater Noster, "fiat voluntas tua," which, as Kochanske Stock asserts, "betrays his ignorance of their specific content and biblical contexts." Later, Pacience and *Liberum Arbitrium* "correct Will's misperceptions." The point here is that

> each repetition or thematic recurrence of this pair of verses serves to rewrite the all-important revelation of the narrator's self that Langland conspicuously interpolates into C Passus V. The result of this series of revisions or reinterpretations [of what, in some broad sense, can easily be construed to be misreadings] is the gradual emergence of one of Langland's most important triads which corresponds to the formulas Do wel, Do bet, Do best.
> (461-62)

The parallel with these terms is achieved by an inverse progression that includes Will's *acedia* or sloth, which in the fifth passus correlates with Dowel.

> *Activa Vita*'s positive recharacterization in Passus XV as a foil for Will's inactivity proves that. Furthermore, the positive example of Pacience, whose role is expanded and refocused in the C Text's Passus XV, suggests that to "Do bet" is to be patient. Langland's exploration of the theme of patient poverty throughout the B Text, the coverage of which is increased and intensified in the C Text, attests to his admiration for and advocation of that virtue. (475)

These scenes are "glosses of one another" (468). If they do nothing else, the scenes at least present us with a paradigm of interpretive and/or writing strategies, which leads us to the contemplation of Will as the poet adumbrated in C V, a passus that recasts the entirety of Langland's final revision in order that it center around the activity of *makyng*. Thus the poem is at heart self-reflexive both in its focus on the activity of writing poetry—that is, of producing itself—and by extension on the capacity to discover significance in either poetry or any other form of expression. Laurie Finke (in "Truth's Treasure: Allegory and Meaning in *Piers Plowman*" 57) shrewdly comments that "*Piers Plowman*, at times, seems almost an allegory of the impossibility of discovering either significance or truth within language, whether one searches for divine or merely for human significance." Finke also has maintained (in "Dowel and the Crisis of Faith and Irony" 129) that language may serve as "a vehicle for classification (of ways of life, or mental powers), a means of imposing order (the law), [or] paradoxically, a means of disorder and deception"; these uses, more often than not, are indistinguishable. Yet—although created in the image of the Logos—the language of fallen humanity "is capable of only an imperfect parody of it." Hence, what becomes plausible is that "[t]he more human language strives to represent the world, the more it is trapped and frustrated by its own failure to assure referentiality" ("Truth's Treasure" 57).

Language may provide a definition of itself as ultimately failing to do what it should—that is, to signify truth. As has been observed, however, this failure of language can also be placed in the service of, as occurs in poetry, a fundamental gesture toward the truth that is otherwise beyond language's denotative ability. This is the case in Chaucer's constant reversion to the theme of textuality versus experience, two methods of knowing the world, and more importantly in his self-enunciatory strategy of naming himself as the author of his own poetic works that are both attacked by others and humorously and feebly defended by the Chaucer persona. The fundamental poetic gesture finds its most stable ground in the act of self-interpretation. Chaucer's persona does a bad job of self-exegesis; through this machinery, though, we not only contemplate more than before the depth of these literary works Chaucer's figure is a part of; we also gain an appreciation of the multi-layered discourse of the present poem that, perhaps innocently on the surface, is engaged in a deeply philosophical struggle. It is precisely the philosophically determined level of discourse that profoundly causes the present poem's effect on its reader.

I have also mentioned the almost painfully baffling actions of Criseyde in the *Troilus*, and how, at a time when among theologians the value of logical procedures was being given perhaps its greatest test by the *moderni* as well as by their detractors, Chaucer strikes a balance within this controversy. Spearing's well known accounting for the popularity of dream poetry (in *Medieval Dream-Poetry* 74) misses the point: In the later Middle Ages

> [a] fiction might be seen as an allegory or parable, in which case it could be said to convey the truth in a veiled form [. . .]. Or again a fiction might claim to be a true history, an account of what really happened as set down in authentic sources. But there was no way of saying that a fiction possessed an imaginative truth or validity even though it did not correspond to any literal truth [. . .]. In these circumstances, to present a literary fiction as a dream—one imaginative product as an analogue or metaphor for another imaginative product—offered a medieval poet an extremely useful way out of his dilemma.

Truly, Criseyde's character resists any univocal interpretation of the sort Cupid demands in the Prologue to the *Legend of Good Women*, and this is because of Chaucer's deep sensitivity to the intellectual currents of his day; as well, his was an intellect that could grasp the ultimate implications of those currents. As for *Piers Plowman*, an allegory that will simply defy the demands of univocity, Finke writes that its "resistance to interpretation" of the sort Chaucer's Cupid would prize, "inheres in its own interpretations of its difficulties," for at its deepest levels the poem is engaged in a discussion of its own poetics. This discussion, moreover, must lead to the contemplation of language as a viable force in the world, which for Langland will explicitly mean as a force for salvation.

> The dreamer's question "How may I save my soul?" leads him [in the B Text] to search for Truth (Passus I-VII), for Dowel (Passus VIII-XIV), and finally for Piers himself (Passus XV-XX). These quests become, in one sense, the search for a transcendental signified that would legitimate all the human signs of the mundane world, the world of the "fair field" and the "half acre." Indeed, the promise of a truth in, behind, or beyond the poem's language, and with it the possibility that Will's dreams actually mean "something," is from the beginning of the poem both proffered and withheld.
> (Finke "Truth's Treasure" 57-58)

Will tells us in the opening tableau of Langland's poem,

> [Ac] as I biheeld into the eest an heigh to the sonne,
> I seigh a tour on a toft treiliche ymaked,
> A deep dale bynethe, a dongeon therinne
> With depe diches and derke and dredfulle of sighte.
> A fair feeld ful of folk fond I ther bitwene [. . .].
> (B Prologue 13-17; cf. C Prologue 14-19)

We are to take his vision here as figurative, in that Will is seeing "representations of things [. . . .] signifiers—tower, dungeon, and field—that seem to mean more than the poet tells us about them, that seem to point to other signifiers" (Finke 58). Will sees—that is, he beholds ("as I biheeld")—the scene that is very much like what he might have been able to find in a state of waking. Compared with the Chaucerian dichotomy, Langland's equivocation of meaning is at least as intense and profound; the

> simplicity of the physical scene shades into the ambiguity of interpretation. The reader, like the dreamer, is compelled to ask, "What my it [by]meene?" The scene, in short, demands a gloss, an interpretation, additional text to explain the poetic utterance. The space that exists between the images of the tower, dungeon, and field and what they signify becomes the figural space of interpretation. It can be bridged or filled only by the attempt to understand it, by reading or creating a text that comments upon the text.
> (58)

With its complex internal echoes and its constant, at times relentless, intention to appeal to texts and authorities beyond itself for verification, validation and eloquence, *Piers Plowman* is a poem that foregrounds and otherwise privileges the act of self-interpretation, an act that may arguably be a quality of any literary text. Chaucer's act of self-interpretation may be, to an extent, an act of self-unraveling; but it never finally appeals to an authority beyond itself, even as it seeks to subsume others' texts within its own discourse through echoes, explicit sententia and the like. In Langland's hands, however, textuality (inter-, intra-) finally becomes the desirable discussion, as predicated on the Pauline and Augustinian linguistic and textual metaphors for revelation and salvation. Will aligns the virtues of natural, "kynde knowyng," with what knowledge and understanding can be achieved through "craft," when he seeks from Holy Church an explanation of the vision he has beheld at the start of his journey:

> "Yet have I no kynde knowynge," quod I, "ye mote kenne me bettre
> By what craft in my cors it [truth] comseth, and where."
> (B I.138-39; cf. C I.136 ff.)

Yet the answer Holy Church offers Will "simultaneously postpones the dreamer's inquiry and widens its perspective until it encompasses—or attempts to encompass—everything, including the divine" (Finke 60), as in B I.150-60 (cf. C I.146 ff.):

> And alle his werkes he wroughte with love as hym liste,
> And lered it Moyses for the levest thing and mooste lik to hevene,
> And also the plante of pees moost precious of vertues:
> For hevene myghte nat holden it, so was it hevy of hymself,
> Til it hadde of the erthe eten his fille.
> And whan it hadde of this fold flessh and blood taken,
> Was nevere leef upon lynde lighter therafter,
> And portatif and persaunt as the point of a nedle,
> That myghte noon armure it lette ne none heighe walles.
> "Forthi is love a ledere of the Lordes folke of hevene,
> And a meene, as the mair is bitwene the kyng and the commune [...].

What is important to see here is that, in this passage's virtual proclamation of language's inadequacy, the poetry achieves its greatest eloquence; in other words, here poetry is "most full of speech." The effort to "explain the mysteries of the divine" results in the accumulation of

> a series of highly antithetical images. Yet the allegory [of the passage] circles around the idea of God's highest expression of love and truth—the Incarnation—by calling that love "hevy" and light as "leef upon lynde," "triacle," and "portatif and persaunt," able to pierce any armor or wall. The same phrase, "For hevene myghte nat holden it," is used to describe both the Incarnation and Lucifer's fall from heaven. This passage is characteristic of the poem as a whole: language does

not progress toward an illumination of truth but falls into the deferral of its own
rhetoric. Each sign produces the next sign in a repetitive sequence that never
arrives at anything but the next trope. The more the poem's language attempts to
describe the divine, the less referential—and the more reflexive—it becomes.
(Finke 60)

We can observe this same sort of equivocation in another key scene, the harrowing of hell sequence, where "words themselves become dramatic acts, participants in the central act of salvation." In this scene, "resignification of linguistic signs" is an absolute necessity, in order that there be a "transformation of everyday language into the *verba arcana* of salvation" (Finke "Dowel and the Crisis of Faith and Irony" 134):

And as Adam and alle thorugh a tree deyden,
Adam and alle thorugh a tree shul turne to lyve;
And gile is bigiled, and in his gile fallen [. . .].
The bitternesse that thow hast browe, now brouke it thiselve;
That art doctour of deeth, drynk that thow madest!
"For I that am lord of lif, love is my drynke,
And for that drynke today, I deide upon erthe.
I faught so, me thursteth yet, for mannes soule sake;
May no drynke me moiste, ne my thurst slake,
Til the vendage falle in the vale of Josaphat,
That I drynke right ripe must, *Resureccio mortuorum*.
(B XVIII.358–60, 364–71; cf. C XX.397 ff.)

In his address to Lucifer, Christ has completely succeeded in manipulating signifiers; they come to mean their contraries: life and death, grace and guile, and so forth (Finke 135). The question of text and meaning—or, alternately, language and truth—is of course epitomized in the pardon scene, whose symbolic values most vividly elaborate the philosophical issues at the heart of *Piers Plowman* and simultaneously resolve them if only in opaque terms.

Piers's tearing of the pardon implicitly underscores his recognition of how inadequate human language is to comprehend the divine Logos. As he rejects the terms of perfection offered by the *Visio* and the pardon, he transforms the *Visio*'s language to propose a very different notion of perfection. He rejects the largely economic definition of virtue (do well), suggested by the image of plowing, by divorcing the sign from its signified. (126)

The plow, symbolically the pen, is transformed by Piers into prayer and penance, spiritual endeavors: "Of preieres and of penaunce my plough shall ben herafter" (B VII.120; cf. C IX.174 ff.). And "whete breed" (B VII.121 123) becomes tears:

The plowman who up until now has occupied himself solely with the physical needs of the folk ceases to concern himself with such necessities as food and turns

> to asceticism, identifying himself with God's holy hermits. Like them he abandons the world, placing his trust in a power his experiences cannot confirm. By way of authority he cites Luke's parable of the birds who are fed in winter though they neither sow nor reap. The parable's command, "ne soliciti sitis" ("be not solicitous"), replaces dowel as the poem's definition of spiritual perfection. For Piers dowel gives way to dobet when he turns his back on the world and sets out on a journey whose goal he perceives but obscurely.
>
> (Finke 126–27)

Yet Piers has only gained for himself "the world's scorn rather than its understanding." He is not readily understandable by the folk (a likely parallel to Chaucer's character Cupid in the Prologue to the *Legend of Good Women*), because his conversion has been

> cast in a language that does more to obscure meaning than to reveal it. Piers deliberately describes his transformation in a parable, the narrative form Christ frequently used. Since a parable is primarily a "similitude," usually between the physical and spiritual realm, it requires and act of interpretation to distinguish the "carnal sense" from the spiritual, hidden sense.
>
> (127)

What we are witnessing in all of these passages are various characters who have recourse to the essential paradox inherent in all attempts at expression, which leads readers, and Will as well, to the recognition that the very act of questioning—rather than any answer that might be elicited—is what is most important. Through the questions, Will can possibly come to know the divine, and to invoke *presence*.

> At the moment of his rebellion Wille looks at his experiences, at the discourse that surrounds him and by which he defines himself (as scholastic philosopher, as dialectician), and perceives only absence. [. . . .] Wille responds to this situation by poetically creating himself, assuming the ironic personae he has fashioned for himself—rebel, sinner, penitent, pilgrim, witness. His roles are the trappings of rebellion.
>
> (Finke 133, 134)

In the B text's banquet scene, Clergy describes Dowel and Dobet as "two infinites, / Whiche infinites with a feith fynden out Dobest [. . .]" (XIII.127–28; cf. C XV.136). Middleton has explained that, according to Priscian in the *Ars Minor*, an *infinite* is usually used in "sentences as the object of a wish or command: *volo legere*, 'I want to read'."[91] In the same fashion, "each of the Three Lives is in

---

[91] Middleton 175–76. "[C]oniungitur autem frequentius voluntativis verbis [. . . .]"; *Institutiones Grammaticae*, XVIII.40.

turn the 'object,' both òf the imperative to pilgrimage and the desire of Will, who is also the will, the voluntative capacity personified" ("Two Infinites" 176). Will's desires are "infinite" in the sense of being incomplete, unfinished or unsatisfied. In the same way it can be said that in "Clergy's definition Dowel and Dobet, like Will himself, become pilgrims to [a] 'finite', seeking their own perfection in Dobest." More significantly, there is another meaning offered by Priscian for *infinite*, one which "enforces the association of these two Lives and Will the pilgrim through a metaphor of asking and answering." Yet the meaning also points to the central concern of Langland's poem as it is conveyed by his meditation on language:

> The second grammatical sense of the word is utterly unrelated to the first, referring to a pronoun rather than a verb, and Priscian makes no attempt to connect them. They are for his purposes as unrelated as a monkey wrench is to a chimpanzee, or an oyster to a cloister. Yet it is the business of the poet to see or make occult resemblances between things unlike to the merely discursive intellect, and in Priscian's discussion of the "infinite" pronoun Langland found in an accident of terminology further substance for his theme.
> (176)

To the Scholastics, the cachet of the term *infinite* was Boethius who had to use the word in order to translate the Aristotelian term into the Latin *nomina infinita*. As, literally, meaning "indefinite noun," in the *Categories* it refers to negative predicates such as *non-albus* or *non-homo*.[92] Thus *infinite* can suggest emptiness and indirection; and it acts not unlike the anomalous three Do's.

> They are only words whose grammatical form gives to the search for perfection the comforting illusion that the quest is orderly and comprehensible. They are the necessary fiction underlying any cognitive pilgrimage. [As Pacience would say,] the terms Dowel and Dobet are not the treasure itself, a healing substance Will sees, but the "bouste," the precious and fragile vessel of linguistic form, which contains and transports meaning.
> (Middleton 180, 181)

The human cognitive faculty, arguably, processes information in a linear or rather serial fashion, in increments. The three Do's reflect this process. As "coined verbal nouns" they are "the fictive terms which give progressive form to Will's pilgrimage"; in doing so, their "reassurance of intelligibility" fulfills the journey (181).

Piers Plowman will always return to the contemplation of its own poetic, generic form; and, in this examination, it will demonstrate the very limits of that form. This is the poem's linguistic gesture, which we find enunciated through the relationship established among the three Do's and the question of the validity of

---

[92] *OED*, "infinite," 8. Aristotle, *Categoriae*, X.3; *De Interpretatione*, X.1. Middleton, 180.

writing itself. But this gesture pervades the entire poem. Consider, for example, the recurring attention that is paid to "the heuristic shortcomings of personifications by exploding their narrative and dramatic consistency in mid-scene" (185). An instance of this is Piers's intercession when the figure Hunger acts brutally toward the folk to keep them at their plowing. It was Piers who had asked Hunger to perform this task. The result of this request, however, is perhaps surprising.

> The immediate requirement of charity toward his "blody brethren" momentarily suspends Piers' allegorical role. He must interrupt the sequence of symbolic events which would further the narrative pilgrimage to charity, in order to act charitably.
> (185)

In doing so, linear narrative is thrown into doubt, as is, in large, the "single-mindedness of the pilgrimage ideal." Scenes such as this one compel what is perhaps an extraordinary conclusion:

> Langland's allegory considered as narrative is a study in frustration, and therein lies its value. We are made to apprehend the meaning of an idea only when all its embodiments within time and space fail us.
> (185)

The poem's own enigmatic qualities are evinced in its demonstration of its formal limits. Thus it is an allegory about the failure of allegory to express the truth. As we have seen, Chaucer alludes to this failure as well; he chooses to satirize allegory, and to opt instead for alternative literary forms that we understand to be, in contrast, "realistic." Langland is equally original. He chooses to reveal the "unreality" of the allegorical project by composing an allegory that must fail in its effort, in order that it can indicate a Christian truth incorporating the allegorical process in its enterprise of debunking that very process. In the tradition of Paul and Augustine, all that we can see will be by way of the darkened glass of the poem.

What will this "failed allegory" tell us? As perhaps can be derived from what the character Book says in the Harrowing of Hell episode, the one hope of divining the events a pilgrim witnesses is to see, as in the Augustinian sense of it, with moral eyes. In an attempt to gloss one of *Piers Plowman*'s more puzzling lines, "Badely ybedded, no book but conscience" (B.XV.534), A. V. C. Schmidt reminds us (in "Langland's 'Book of Conscience'" 482) of the myriad uses *text* and *book* could be put to by Christian theologians. He argues convincingly that the source of Langland's line is Jerome's Commentary on Daniel 7:10: "Iudicum sedit, et libri aperti sunt." Set against the unalterability of the written word is the will to be conscionable, which may deny or otherwise alter the meaning, the "bouste" of a text, a text of words. Within this tension, Langland posits the figure of the poet, who must embody and unify the dichotomy. He does so. In the last passus of *Piers Plowman* Will dreams while in a church; he is dreaming *of* a church. As

Economou writes (in "The Vision's Aftermath in *Piers Plowman*" 318), it "has given him the testament and its exegesis that allow him to articulate the yearning that charges his soul and work. It is no accident that he proposes to write this [dream] down [. . .]." For in Will's writing he is dramatizing the essential poetics of his author, who has named himself by constructing an infinite regress of reflected, mirror images. Will is the poet and theme of his own (Langland's) poem. In a poem of dreams within dreams, we find a dreamer whose fictive dream, like Chaucer's birds in the Prologue to the *Legend of Good Women*, too closely resembles an objective truth. In a church, he dreams he is in a church— God's house. From there, he goes on to carry out what he has forcefully proclaimed to be a godly activity, the writing down of his dreams.

Afterword

The Middle Ages and the Modern Persona

The formation of the modern psyche—in other words, what is usually referred to as the emergence of the individual—can be traced in Western poetry's acts of self-naming. From the twelfth through the fourteenth century, throughout Europe, these acts occurred most profoundly in the form of literary autocitation. Naming, in order to signify an authorial self, was incidental—yet it was also the mark of an all pervading presence within a literary discourse organized around it. This discourse took as its subject the dynamic of expression, especially of literary making—as the discourse participated in a symbiotic relationship with authorial self-naming. This relationship was defined by the proclamation, made through the name, of a unique narrator, and as well by an attendant, essentially philosophical speculation that embraced the very question of language per se. The relationship invested each of its members with a significance beyond what could be enjoyed alone. Thus, Chaucer's persona, a figure bearing its author's name and characterized as a poet, is also driven to fathom what the act of writing means in relation to truth generally and to personal existence specifically.

Out of this literary synergy the individual comes forth. But what is it to speak of the *individual*? Or of the *self*? These terms are fluid enough to threaten any attempt at a convincing discussion of them, unless they are employed relativistically. For example, Paul Smith (in *Discerning the Subject* xxvii) has noted that, in the field of modern psychoanalysis, theorists must simply think of *selfhood* as an "unconsciously structured illusion of plenitude"—however overly broad this definition may be. Just the same, this formulation does leave them somewhere. The poetics of authorship, which evolves in the Middle Ages, is also about plenitude. The evolving use of the authorship trope documents a gradual shifting of sites. Presence belonged to the *auctoritates* and to Christian *communitas*. They were conceived of by medieval theorists, in terms of ideology and method, as textual in nature; their ultimate authority derived from the Bible (even as certain pagan texts enjoyed wide provenance). The *text*, then, was a common denominator. The poetics of the twelfth century and even earlier—such as we observe in the songs of Guillem IX—attests the singular author, of a singular text. The singular author embraced the scriptural tradition but rewrote it as well, reenvisioned it. In doing so, the individual author became present within the individual text and, often, beyond it.

Therefore, the act revealing what was essential about autocitation was, first and foremost, of a textual nature. It resonated—in fact it perpetuated—Scripture in its praxis. The Word, an utterly textual metaphor and a basic tenet of Christian dogma, came to sanction individualized literary self-assertion that took the form of a self-commentary, of a textual self-reflection. It is within this context that later medieval writers concerned themselves with what can be called the profoundly textualized nature of poetry. What we mean when we talk about the subject, Smith continues, is "the bearer of a consciousness that will interact with whatever the world is taken to consist in" (xxvii). Slowly, the world, which had been described by Augustine in the *Confessions* as an unfurled scroll, came to be "detextualized" in inverse proportion to the "retextualization" of human authors of individual poems, of individual texts "unfurled" before their listeners and readers. These were authors who took specific names, who eschewed anonymity.

The names were fictional. They alluded to their real authors, yet they were also meant to be comprehended as separate from their authors—within their authors' texts. With the emergence of the literary persona, which in its early stages was named for its author, fiction in its modern conception appeared—as did modern notions of history and science. There could be no history as a distinct genre until there was, in contrast, fiction. This persona began as a textual voice and ended as a fully rounded, fully realized fictional being. Readings and Schaber have cleverly remarked that "[t]he history of voices forgets the voice of history, and vice versa" (16). Even so, no sure grasp of what is meant by fact, by a recounting of events apart from the mythological, could be possible prior to the invention of modern fiction.

It is this paradox that leads Leicester to reject the idea of "unimpersonated artistry" in the *Canterbury Tales*, an idea that has been put forth by many commentators, Charles Muscatine, Donald Howard, Robert Burlin, John Lawlor, Jordan and Middleton among them (3). Rather, in thinking about the *Tales* as "a collection of individually voiced texts," Leicester must first "begin with the fact of their textuality, to insist that there is nobody there, that there is only the text." Yet the absence of a somebody in the text—an absence first of all enforced by the physical writtenness of the text—is not the same as the presence of a "voice *in* the text," which Leicester refers to as the text's "subject"—for, "[i]n writing, voice is [. . .] a function not of persons but of language, of the linguistic codes and conventions that make it possible for an 'I' to appear" (9). All the same, as Benveniste has shown, unlike other pronouns the *I* is a shifter unable to refer to itself, a notion leading to the conclusion, "it is in and through language that man constitutes himself as a subject" (225).

Thus, history depends on a clear sense of fiction as a distinct discourse—to be sure, a discourse whose value has to do with itself *as* a discourse, since fiction need not, in strict terms cannot, adhere absolutely to the realm of the fact. A not so distant, but nonetheless useful, analogy for understanding the nature of fiction is Anselm's idea that statements can possess an internal, a *natural* cogency. Furthermore, the same can perhaps be said for autobiography—a genre that seems to mediate the two discourses, fiction and history, which it both emulates and produces and which, as a genre, is usually signified by either the authorial proper noun or by the unique pronoun "I." In thinking about what constitutes autobiography, we can again turn to the later Middle Ages for a powerful analogy, this time to the Dantean use of the contrastive "tu," first spoken to Virgil, by the *Commedia*'s narrator named Dante. Of course, a pivotal question that has been pursued in this book is whether it was the intention of Dante, the author, to write an autobiography of the kind the modern world recognizes as such.

The writer of modern fiction can get only so far removed from theme and character, since they have to be created out of the language of the real author. When reading fiction we may, reasons David J. Gordon (in "Character and Self in Autobiography" 105), "perceive the pressure of authorial identification with the character but are not, for the most part, disturbed by special pleading on the character's behalf," whereas autobiography asks us to make a connection between character and author. This kind of appeal to the reader, I think, did not occur to Dante. However, the *Vita Nuova* and certainly the *Commedia* are more autobiographical *and* more fictional than the *Confessions*, Dante's model. The difference between these later and earlier medieval works lies in his sense of alterity, which is part of his impulse to see himself as an individual in a manner that was quite alien to writers in the early Middle Ages. Whether or not Dante begins the modern world is a debate that is as well worn as it is finally superfluous; still, Dante's creation of his narrator looks ahead to Rimbaud's well known phrase, "Je est un autre," and surely Augustine's does not.

What perhaps begs us to view the *Confessions* as autobiography is another kind of "special pleading"—for Augustine as sinner, as convert—as, in any case, someone who realizes his responsibility vis-à-vis the divine dispensation. Hence, in Book VIII the "persona," perceiving that he is living in sin, catches sight of himself in a figurative reflection. Augustine writes that God sets him before his own eyes and forces him to see himself (VIII.7). Indeed, up to this point in Augustine's story, the eternal life of the divine had only been seen by him as "a confused reflection in a mirror," a phrase meant to echo Paul's dark glass (in I Corinthians). Now Augustine is being called upon to witness the truth. Robert Folkenflik observes (in "The Self as Other" 218) that the *Confessions* "is in the tradition of the *imitatio Christi*, but it in turn provides an exemplary life for contemplation, and the mirror is central image both within the book and for the book itself." The very idea of the book is also a mirror. Significantly, what has particularly moved Augustine toward self-realization is the story of St. Anthony, a narrative, a text (which is being related to him by his friend Ponticianus who has come to visit).

To sum up, we can say that there is an inevitability in the act of literary autocitation. The poetics of authorship evolves out of certain conditions; primary among these is sensitivity to the idea of a text, even as that idea undergoes numerous transformations. The idea is foundational to Western civilization. The writings of Plato, Paul, and most of all Augustine, have developed the concept of a text, which was, furthermore, of an ethical nature, shared within a community. In Augustine, the basic textual metaphor achieves its full effect; it can be argued that the world, for him, was a text. The medieval sense of the group, whose cement was the notion of textuality, which often manifested itself in reverence for the Bible as well as other specific texts, matured under Augustine's influence. Thus, later poets' self-naming functioned as a recognition of and a belief in a language centered in the notion of textuality; this textuality was an accurate, authentic way of describing what was real. In fact, the text was the measure, the language, of the real. To be distinct within a literary tradition, consequently, poets of the later Middle Ages could not have helped but include themselves in their attempts to point to the truth. The world that poets—especially Marcabru, Dante, and Langland—portrayed supported their self-assertions, for they were a part of that world.

These assertions employed the language of a theology and philosophy that were changing because of the spread of literacy but pivotally because of a rediscovered Aristotelian logic, one that, indirectly, mandated the poets' self-inclusions as well as their literary self-promotions. This change in literary practice became possible once text and language could be viewed as entities separate from the poet. The thing that sustained a poet's enterprise was the language used in poetry to signify the world. Once language was understood to be an entity unto itself—an understanding that was initially formulated by Anselm—the poet's meditation on his or her relationship to it could lead to a self-comprehension in which the self was posited as that which had come to exist apart from discourse. And so the poet was the user of discourse, the finder, the *trobador* who shaped the language that ultimately, by virtue of the recognition of its independence, threatened to determine the very world that had been thought to have included language as a part of it. Language was both within the world and outside it. Now, if the poet could be the definer of the poem, the *makyr*, why could he or she not define the world? Logically, such an attempt at definition was the fundamental issue that confronted poets of the later Middle Ages—an issue that ultimately came into being because of a theologian, not a maker of verse.

In one graceful turn of thought, Anselm altered the intellectual, spiritual and social makeup of the West. The effect of his emendation of Augustine's meditation on the nature of falsehoods was to liberate language and thereby to usher in a modern world. First of all, he set aside the issue of intentionality, which was, for Augustine, the primary determining factor in assessing truth or falsity. Once Anselm could recognize Augustine's distinctions, he could also realize that statements had integrity though they might fail to refer authentically to any objective truth. Anselm ascribed to any statement an intrinsic unity, a "natural" coherence. Thus he aligned language with the world while setting language at a remove from it. Language, then, did not have to conform to the strictures of the perceptible world (nor did language need to obey the poet).

In effect, Anselm had let go of the golden chain descending from Heaven. With him, a new possibility arose. Yet this new turn into the realm of semantics proper was to prove immensely problematic. Even moralistically right interpretations of expressions that of course were comprised of language, a language made opaque since the fall of Adam and Eve—as depicted by Paul's image of a dark glass—might no longer yield revelation. In the later Middle Ages, poets grapple with this central difficulty. Their texts, inherited from Augustine whose ideas concerning interpretation derived from Paul, are accessible only through a combination of hermeneutics and the presumption that any text is, in a sense, autonomous; such an equation, however, could prove hopeless in the attempt to arrive at either absolute beauty or absolute truth. Where does this leave poets like Marcabru, Dante, Chaucer and Langland, who are faced with the task of realizing the truth? They must include discussions of themselves in this attempt; otherwise, how else might they come to terms with the very separateness of language and ultimately of texts? In Langland such discussion circles back to Augustine and the question of intentionality; *Piers Plowman* investigates the role of the individual will in the achievement of salvation. Yet by the time of Langland, long after Anselm, the world has become more complicated, and in a sense modern.

Can poetry work? Can it serve? Does it lead to redemption? This set of questions forced poets to turn to a meditation on the nature of poetry and its relationship to truth, and, finally to consider their own efficacy as both poets and mortals. The stakes involved in this exercise were immense, and poets went about their task with an extraordinary vigor. Their poetic conceptions were driven by the new demands of rationalism, which generally were a function of a spreading technology of literacy. In a shift of orientation from oral to written discourse, the text came to be physically represented as separate, as existing at a distance from writer and reader. The complexity of this text necessarily deepened; since there was no hurry on the part of readers to embrace it, authors could afford to render a text that was more complicated. Literate, increasingly silent, readers could indulge themselves in it at leisure—and could reflect on the fact of its authorship.

Truth will be both atomized and narrowly defined when logic and technology come to be the dominant forces in a society. As history and fiction become separate, modern disciplines in the later Middle Ages, we see the distinction between them being modulated by the inevitably creative acts of poets. Later medieval poets discovered themselves squarely within a larger debate that formed the context of the evolution into such disciplines; these poets possessed varying degrees of objectivity regarding their role in the debate, but, intellectually curious, and acutely sensitive to the shifting and transformation of categories, they were also instrumental in this process. Marcabru is a poet who writes about the efficacy of his poetry, and of all poetry, and proclaims that the craft of song cannot be brilliantly utilized unless the poet is of good faith. Dante's journey through the three realms of experience inscribes once and for all the epistemological issues that comprise the fabric of his and possibly our own time. Langland continues this tradition. As in the *Commedia*, his persona virtually replicates its author. In *Piers Plowman* a poet is named Will. By virtue of his existence he reminds readers of the key to mortal striving, that of the individual will—not unlike Augustine's notion of intentionality. The mere embodiment of this issue, in this persona, confronts the question of writing as the way to achieve salvation. Implicitly, though, Langland is also examining the structure of this form of discourse. In *Piers Plowman's* ubiquitously illogical turns of plot, such as the tearing up of the pardon, we see the signs of a poet's attempt to unravel the *form* of his poem in order to comment on that form and ultimately to examine its larger epistemological concerns.

Langland's attempts to deconstruct a fundamentally allegorical poetic structure are perhaps more in keeping with Anselm's approach to the problem of language and meaning. Chaucer, too, contemplates the form of poetry; his attack on allegory as a viable epistemological procedure is overt, as in the Prologue to the *Legend of Good Women*. Langland's attack, however, proceeds from within, with the tacit recognition that a poetics in and of itself does not necessarily serve to render a believable description of reality. Langland's focus on the poetics asks the question, can there be unity, an internal logic or efficacy in poetry?

In effect, Langland wishes to demonstrate that there is a lack of internal cogency in allegory. Allegory might not accurately reflect actual experience; the assumption is that allegory was created to do so. More importantly, Langland implies that, structurally, allegory can be said to be "unnatural" or rather ultimately untrue. Truth, then, continues to reside beyond the pale of expression. All the same, we see this dynamic, the tension between expression and truth, most vividly portrayed in the roles that language plays in the poem. "Grammar," for Will the dreamer *and* for William Langland, like "God," is the "ground of all." Language, that is, may bridge all realms, all planes of existence be they dream, waking perceivable experience, or books—as Chaucer also recognized. For Chaucer, as well as for Langland, the *literatus* proffers the "key" of memory, and thereby a sort of truth. In other words, language strives for unity while it may, paradoxically, also intend to assert its own individuality. Accordingly, Langland's poem strives for unity by its demonstration of the ways in which poetry and ultimately language *un*do themselves. Hence, *Piers Plowman* features the search for Dowel, Dobet and Dobest; all three are grammatical anomalies. These linguistic aberrations underscore the recognition of a chasm between language, ostensibly the stuff of poetry, and allegory, which is quite possibly the very sign of all figuration and, so, necessarily, to be associated with the idea of poetry.

The sign of Langland's inquiry into the vexed relationship of language and truth is the poem's persona. In the largest terms, this persona embodies the tension between Augustine's and Anselm's ideas. Will the dreamer is also the sign of unity, for in his name the poem's theme, and authorship, come together. Comprehending this sign would be particularly welcome, since—as is evident in the great lengths Langland goes to in order to demonstrate it—there is an inherent disunity in all poetic and other expression. Langland's evocation of unity, in other words, occurs by way of oblique strategies. Self-naming and otherwise autocitation, both at the margin and at the center of his poem, remain as Langland's solution to problems of signification, problems he has inherited from past theologians and poets who comprise the *auctoritas*, that is the fabric, of Western thought and aspiration.

How might Will, then, represent the emergence of the modern persona? What affinity can this pilgrim share with, say, Tom Jones of the bildungsroman that goes by the same name? Part of the answer to this question is obvious; a persona's connection to its text may now be unavoidable—given the tradition out of which modern literature emerges—and indeed their alignment continues into the present in books like Saul Bellow's *Herzog* and Derek Walcott's *Omeros*, whose protagonists bear the names of their stories. An antagonist can do the same, as in Toni Morrison's *Beloved*. But what about Joyce's *Ulysses*, thematically organized by the Greek and then the Roman epic story recalled by its protagonist's name? More to the point, what about a work like Ashbery's *Self-Portrait in a Convex Mirror*, which does not openly posit itself within the "authorship camp," even though its title reveals Ashbery's debt to authorship poetics? Or what about any other modern work that does not, overtly, bear the sign of either author or character?

What has become of the authors' explicit self-inclusions in their texts? The answer to these questions begins by realizing that any attempt to define the modern persona must proceed from a broad base. The purview of this study does not allow for extensive probing into the nature of modern fiction and its possible relationships with fact. Still, it may be suggested here that modern authors see themselves as quite as fictional, as ephemeral, as any speaker or personage created in their texts. There is tacit agreement among writers and readers concerning these personae, an assumption that they are fictional. If we contemplate, then, our contemporary literary projects, may we not come to a fuller appreciation of what must have been the intense pleasure and gratification of authors who, for the first time, saw themselves in their own works? The mirror that contained the medieval writer's image may not be the one used today, but it surely cast a reflection.

Appendix A

Alceste as a Unifying Figure

In the daisy-Alceste figure we find, because of its idealized beauty, the paradigm of the striving for unity. Chaucer's description of Alceste is so very similar to the properties of the daisy that there can be little doubt that she does indeed personify that flower in his dream; Alceste, furthermore, exists in an enchanted garden type sequence while the daisy, of course, exists in a real—though garden-like—pastoral setting. On the exact inversion of the dream world and reality in the Prologue, see among others Malone, and Bronson; and Payne, "Making His Own Myth," 202. On the physical similarity of the daisy and Alceste, see among others Payne, *Key of Remembrance*, 106; and on Alceste as the poem's unifying force, Payne writes:

> Alceste provides the most obvious means of unifying the two different parts of the prologue. She is, first of all, the figurative transformation of the daisy; she is also the maiden of all maidens, as it had been the "flour of alle floures"; but most significantly, her relation to the poet is the same: she is to provide the "cause," the compelling attraction for the reverential poetry of the legend which Chaucer is to write in penance for his "bad" poetry. Finally, we ought to observe that these transmogrified qualities of the daisy find their physical personage in a character from an ancient legend. As a thirteenth-century rhetorician would have put it, through an invented figure of the poet's, the fact of experience and the values of tradition become identified.
> (98)

See also, in this regard, Donald Baker, "Dreamer and Critic," 11.

It should be noted that the figure, "flour of all floures," has a long and proud history from ancient times: *Flos Florum*

> is an image of perfection often used of the beloved in medieval lyrics of *amour courtois*, but it is remarkable also for the variety of its manifestations—sacred and profane, from a casual *façon de parler* to a philosophical or mystical apprehension of perfect beauty in the paradox of the many and the one [. . .]. The paradox lies in the relation between the beloved and nature, whose crown he or she is. When nature fades, the beloved can keep nature's beauty alive; when nature flowers, the beloved both surpasses nature's flowering and fulfills it.
> (Dronke *Medieval Latin* 181-82, cf. 183-92; cf the Introduction)

On the etymology of *margerite* and the connection, in English, between *pearl* and *daisy* (from the French and Latin) and the religious associations between the daisy and the Virgin Mary, see Dronke and, as well, Payne, *Key of Remembrance*.

Appendix B

Chaucer and the Allegorical Tradition

The Prologue to the *Legend of Good Women* can easily be viewed as an allegory, although many readers will pass too quickly over the poem's "analogical" elements because of Chaucer's seamless, crafted poem in which they are doing their work. An example of this subtle embedding occurs when the poem's persona returns to his house in order to rest ("to conserve" himself) for the night; but more than this, he has his house and "herber" or garden made up to be consonant with the spirit of the new summer. It is here, furthermore, that the persona will have his dream of which we will read:

> Hom to myn hous ful swiftly I me spedde,
> And in a lytel herber that I have,
> Ybenched newe with turves, fresshe ygrave,
> I bad men shulde me my couche make;
> For deynte of the newe someres sake [etc.].
> (G 96-100, F 200-206)

Robinson's gloss of these lines is particularly revealing; it is as if he has missed the lines' allegorical values: "The remark about the house with the arbor [. . . .] seems hardly applicable to Chaucer's house over the city gate, and he is known to have surrendered his lease on or before 5 October 1386 [and so on]" (842).

Perhaps a fourteenth-century reader, on the other hand, would immediately recognize the sententious and symbolical quality of the narrator's "house." In allegorical terms the house becomes, among other things, the symbol of, as well as the place for, procreation; it is the source, in other words, of the persona's poetry (the craft and the maker of the craft which is the subject of the Prologue, as Payne has observed).

Malone notices the eschewing of personified abstractions (that intend to heighten an allegorical feeling) in the G text revision of the Prologue:

> Al found they Daunger for a tyme a lord,
> Yet Pitee, thurgh his stronge gentil myght,
> Forgaf, and made Mercy passen Ryght,
> Thurgh Innocence and ruled Curtesye.
> (F 160-63)

The indication here is that Chaucer is moving away from the allegorical poetic mode in his later career (96). He will therefore effect, more and more, a seamless quality in his later poems. This is also demonstrated by the *house* image, which is not at all either a personification or an abstraction. Yet it does recall Chaucer's earlier use of this image in this way, and it does reflect contemporary rhetorical-poetic theory.

The announced purpose of Chaucer's dream in the *House of Fame*, for example, is that it will teach him something about what poetry actually is. The words that people speak, according to the eagle, have their place in the order of the universe:

> And for this cause mayst thou see,
> That every ryver to the see
> Enclyned is to go by kynde,
> And by these skilles, as I fynde,
> Hath fyssh duellynge in flood and see,
> And treës eke in erthe bee.
> Thus every thing, by thys reson,
> Hath his propre mansyon
> To which hit seketh to repaire,
> Ther-as hit shulde not apaire.
> (II.747-56)

It is important here to notice the analogy that the eagle makes between inclination ("Enclyned ys to goo by kynde") that might suggest a volition though here ordered by nature ("kynde"), and the *skill* ("skilles"—the suggestion may also include "reasoning") that is a part of this same universal ordering force. The diction in this passage, of course, is a reflection of the philosophical debate being carried on by Ockham, Holcot, Bradwardine and others. *Skill*, however, suggests also the technical virtuosity such as we might find in the poet's art, just as it resonates the deceit implicit in the bird trapper's *sophistry* in the Prologue; here it is the "artifice" of nature: so that the poet must seek, in some way, to mirror the experiential, paradigm of *kynde* in his verse. His words must possess or adhere to the force of an intuitional, pre-Gallilean gravity, the notion that all elements in the world have their proper place (Benson 983) as much as would any natural event. That is, the poet's words must have meaning, evolving in turn out of an ordering, a formalism. And, the poet's words have their proper place in the universe (they have their own gravity, as it were); every thing has its "propre mansyon."

Other instances of the use of a house or mansion as an image standing in for the idea of an originary intuition or creativity might be cited. It should be noted that this image has a grounding in medieval poetics, as Marie Hamilton has observed (in "Notes on Chaucer and the Rhetoricians" 403-09; in Payne, *Key of Remembrance* 16). "Miss Hamilton helpfully quotes, as a supporting parallel [to the *House of Fame*], five lines from *Troilus and Criseyde* which are translated from Geoffrey of Vinsauf":

> For everi wight that hath an *house to founde*
> Ne renneth naught the werk for to bygynne

With rakel hond, but he wol bide a stounde,
And sende his hertes line out fro withinne
Aldirfirst his purpos for to wynne.
(I.1065–69; my emphasis).

In light of Malone's above remarks on allegorical elements and structuring, cf. also Payne, *Key of Remembrance*, 139.

Appendix C

Ploughing as a Metaphor

In the *Etymologarium* (VI.9.2) Isidore of Seville claims that Romans wrote with a stylus made of iron or bone on tablets made of wax, and quotes "from a lost comedy by the poet Atta": ". . . Vertamus vomerem / In cera mucroneque aremus osseo"—which Curtius translates as "Turn we the ploughshare upon the wax and plow we with a point of bone" (313). See Gellrich 34 ff.

In Chaucer's "Shipman's Tale" the monk has asked the merchant for a loan, which is granted. The merchant then announces—

> "But o thyng is, ye knowe it wel ynogh
> Of chapmen, that hir moneie is hir plogh.
> We may creaunce whil we have a name,
> But goldlees for to be, it is no game.
> Paye it agayn whan it lith in youre ese [. . .].
> (VII.287-91)

—to which we may add Holloway's comments:

> The metaphors of the speech, of ploughing, of "creauncing," hold true for mercantile undertakings, yet they are blasphemy. In the *Roman de la Rose*, a Golden Calf of a poem, the plough metaphor applied to sex, "Plough, barons, plough!" to man's seed sown for the harvest of a new generation. In *Piers Plowman* the plough metaphor, as in Christ's parables, applied to preaching, to words as seeds to be sown in men's hearts. (192-93)

Elsewhere (167-68) Holloway has pointed out the "scribal" aspect of this multipurpose symbol. Her elaboration of Isidore's pronouncement is particularly germane. Isidore

> had quoted the metaphor in a lost Roman comedy [cf. above] stating that the Ancients had written furrow-wise, in Greek [. . .] *boustrophedon*, turning like oxen in ploughing, writing from left to right and from right to left alternately. A medieval adage reads: "He urged on the oxen, ploughed white fields, held a white plough, and sowed black seed" [Jeffrey 313-14]. Chaucer is familiar with the scribal metaphor though he uses it in an apparently oral tale. The knight in order to excuse his omission of a complete description of the wedding of Ypolita to Theseus explains: "I have, Good woot, a large feeld to ere, / And wayke been the oxen in my plough [etc.]" (886-887).

Reinhold Schneider, in his Introduction to an edition of *The Plowman from Bohemia* composed during this period, notes that this poem's author, Johannes von Saaz, was fully aware of the equation of writing and plowing (e.g., "I am called a plowman. My plow is the pen [. . .]"; Ch. 3). For von Saaz "took his work as seriously as the peasant does his. He delved deeply into the earth, into the hard reality of experience, to bring the truth to light" (1).

Works Cited

Primary Sources

Abelard, Peter. *Petri Abaelardi Introductio ad Theologiam, in libros tres divisa. Patrologia cursus completus, series latina.* Ed. J. P. Migne. Paris: 1844-64. 178.979-1114.

____. *Ingredientibus.* Ed. Bernhard Geyer. *Beiträge zur Geschichte der Philosophie des Mittelalters.* Vol. 21.1.1-32. Münster: Verlag der Aschendorffschen Verlagsbuchhandlung, 1919.

____. *Philosophische Schriften.* Ed. B. Geyer. Munster: 1919-33.

____. *Scritti filosofici.* Ed. M. Dal Pra. Milan: 1954.

____. *Sic et Non, prologus. Patrologia cursus completus, series latina.* Ed. J. P. Migne. Paris: 1844-64. 178.1339A-1343D.

Anselm, of Canterbury, Saint. *Dialogue on Truth.* Ed., Tr. and Intr. Richard McKeon. *Selections from Medieval Philosophers.* New York: Charles Scribner's Sons, 1929. 142-84.

____. *The Grammatico of St. Anselm: The Theory of Paronymy.* Ed. and Tr. Desmond P. Henry, Notre Dame: Notre Dame University Press, 1964.

____. *Opera Omnia.* 6 Vol. Ed. F. S. Schmitt. Edinburgh: T. Nelson and Sons, 1946-61.

Aquinas, Thomas, Saint. *An Aquinas Reader.* Ed. and Intr. Mary T. Clark. Garden City, New York: Image-Doubleday, 1972.

____. *Expositio super librum Boethii de trinitate.* Ed. Bruno Decker. Leiden: E. J. Brill, 1959.

____. *Sancti Thomae Aquinatis, doctoris Angelici, Opera omnia iussu impensaque Leonis XIII P. M. edita.* Rome: Ex Typographia Polyglotts s. C. de Propaganda Fide, 1882.

____. *Summa Theologiae.* Trans. Herbert McCabe O.P. New York and London: Black Friars / McGraw-Hill, 1963.

Aristotle. *Aristotle's Poetics.* Ed. Francis Fergusson. Tr. S. H. Butcher. New York: Hill and Wang, 1961.

____. *The Categories, On Interpretation.* Annot., Ed. and Tr. Harold P. Cooke. *Prior Analytics.* Annot., Ed. and Tr. Hugh Tredennick. Cambridge, MA: Harvard University Press / London: William Heinemann, 1983.

____. *De Anima*. Tr. W. S. Hett. Cambridge, MA: Loeb Classical Library, 1957.

____. *The Metaphysics*. Ed. and Tr. Hugh Tredennick. Cambridge, MA: Harvard University Press, 1933. Rpt. 1989.

____. *The Physics*. Tr. Philip H. Wicksteed and Francis M. Cornford. Cambridge, MA: Harvard University Press, 1963.

____. *The Poetics of Aristotle*. Tr. Stephen Halliwell. London: Duckworth, 1987.

____. *The Complete Works of Aristotle*. Ed. Jonathan Barnes. Princeton: Princeton University Press, 1984.

Augustine, Saint, Bishop of Hippo. *City of God*. Tr. Henry Bettenson. Harmondsworth, U.K.: Penguin, 1972.

____. *Confessiones*. Ed. Pius Knöll and Martinus Skutella. Leipzig: Teubner, 1934.

____. *Confessions*. Tr. and Intr. R. S. Pine-Coffin. Harmondsworth, Middlesex, U.K.: Penguin, 1961.

____. *De civitate Dei*. Corpus Christianorum Series Latina 47-48. Brepols: Turnholt, 1955.

____. *De dialectica*. Tr., Intr. and Annot. B. Darrell Jackson. Boston: Reidel, 1975.

____. *De Doctrina christiana*. Annot. and Tr. Sister Thérése Sullivan. Washington, D. C.: Catholic University of America, 1930.

____. *De mendacio*. Ed. Joseph Zycha. *Oeuvres de saint Augustin*. Paris: Desclée de Brouwer, 1948.

____. *De trinitate*. Ed. M. Mellet, O. P. and Thomas Camelot, O. P. *Oeuvres de saint Augustin*. Paris: Desclée de Brouwer, 1948.

____. *Enarrationes in psalmos*. *Patrologia cursus completus, series latina*. Ed. J. P. Migne. Paris: 1844-64. 36-37.68-1960.

____. *On Christian Doctrine*. Tr. D. W. Robertson, Jr. New York: Liberal Arts Press, 1958.

____. *On Music*. Tr. R. C. Taliaferro. Annapolis, Maryland: 1939.

____. *Opera*. *Patrologia cursus completus, series latina*. Ed. J. P. Migne. Paris: 1844-64. 32-46.

____. *The Teacher, The Free Choice of the Will, and Grace and Free Will*. Tr. Robert P. Russell. Washington: The Fathers of the Church. Vol. 59. 1968.

Aulus Gellius. *The Attic Nights of Aulus Gellius.* 3 Vol. Ed. and Tr. John C. Rolfe. Cambridge, MA: Harvard University Press, 1978.

Averroes. *Averroes' Middle Commentaries on Aristotle's* Categories *and* De interpretatione. Tr. and Intr. Charles E. Butterworth. Princeton: Princeton University Press, 1983.

____. *Great Commentary on the Metaphysics (Tafsir ma ba'd at-tabi'a).* Ed. M. Bouyges. Beyrouth: Imprimerie-Catholique, 1948.

Avicenna. *Avicennae Metaphysices compendium.* Ed. Nematallah Carame. Rome: Pont. Institutum Orientalium Studiorum, 1926.

____. *Avicenna's Commentary on the Poetics of Aristotle: A Critical Study with an Annotated Translation of the Text.* Ismail M. Dahiyat. Leiden: Brill, 1974.

____. *The Propositional Logic of Avicenna.* Tr. Nabil Shehaby. Dordrecht / Boston: Reidel, 1973.

Bacon, Roger. *Summa grammatica.* Ed. R. Steele. Oxford: Clarendon, 1940.

Bernard Silvestris. *Cosmographia.* Ed., Intr. and Annot. Peter Dronke. Leiden: E. J. Brill, 1978.

____. *The* Cosmographia *of Bernardus Silvestris.* Tr. and Intr. Winthrop Wetherbee. New York and London: Columbia University Press, 1973.

Biblia Sacra iuxta Vulgatam Clementinam. 4th Ed. Madrid: Biblioteca de Autores Cristianos, 1965.

Boccaccio, Giovanni. *Genealogia Deorum Gentilium.* Ed. Vincenzo Romano. 2 Vol. Bari: Laterza, 1951.

Boethius, Anicius Manlius Severinus. *Commentarii in Librum Aristotelis Peri ermeneias.* Ed. Carolus Meiser. Leipzig: 1887.

____. *The Consolation of Philosophy.* Tr. and Intr. Richard Green. Indianapolis: Bobbs-Merrill, 1962.

____. *In Categorias Aristotelis Libri quattuor. Patrologia cursus completus, series latina.* Ed. J. P. Migne. 64.159a-294c.

____. *In Isagogen Porphyrii Commenta. Patrologia cursus completus, series latina.* Ed. J. P. Migne. 64.71-86.

Calepino. *Dictionarii Octolinguis.* Lyon, 1663.

Cassiodorus, Senator, Flavius Magnus Aurelius. *Opera.* Turnholti: Brepols, 1958-72.

Chaucer, Geoffrey. *The Riverside Chaucer.* 3rd Ed. Ed. Larry D. Benson. Based on *The Works of Geoffrey Chaucer.* Ed. F. N. Robinson. Boston: Houghton Mifflin, 1987.

Cicero. *De inventione, De optimo genere, Oratorum and Topica.* Ed. and Tr. H. M. Hubbell. Cambridge, MA: Harvard University Press, 1953.

____. *De Natura Deorum. Academica.* Tr. H. Rackam. London / New York, 1933.

____. *De optimo genere oratorum.* H. M. Hubbell. Ed. and Tr. *De inventione, De optimo genere oratorum, Topica.* Cambridge, MA: Harvard University Press, 1942; rpt 1976.

____. *De Oratore.* 2 Vol. E. W. Sutton and H. Rackham. Eds. and Trs. Cambridge, MA: Harvard University Press, 1942; rpt 1976.

____. *Rhetorica ad Herrenium.* Latin and English. Tr. Harry Caplan, Cambridge, MA: Harvard University Press, 1954.

Damian, Peter, Saint. *Opera Omnia. Patrologia cursus completus, series latina.* Ed. J. P. Migne. 144–45.

____. *L'opera poetica di S. Pier Damiani.* Ed. M. Lokrantz. Acta Universitatis Stockholmiensis, Studia Latina Stockhomiensia, XII. Uppsala, 1964.

Dante Alighieri. *Convivio.* Ed. Maria Simonelli. Bologna: 1966.

____. *De Vulgari Eloquentia.* Ed. Aristide Marigo. Florence: Le Monnier, 1968.

____. *The Divine Comedy of Dante Alighieri.* 3 Vol. Annot., Intr. and Tr. Allen Mandelbaum.Berkeley: University of California Press, 1981.

____. *La Vita nuova.* Ed. M. Barbi. 1932.

____. *Le Opere di Dante.* 1921. Ed. Michele Barbi. Florence: R. Bemporad, 1960.

Dionysius the Areopagite. *De caelesti hierarchia* I. *Patrologia cursus completus, series graeca.* Paris: 1844–64. 3.121

____. *The Mystical Theology and the Celestial Hierarchies of Dionysius the Areopagite.* Tr. Editors of the Shrine of Wisdom. Fintry, England: Shrine of Wisdom, 1945.

Erasmus, Desiderius. *The Collected Works of Erasmus.* Ed. A. Gambaro. Annot. and Tr. B. I. Knott. Toronto: University of Toronto Press, 1986.

Geoffrey of Vinsauf. *Poetry Nova.* Tr. Margaret F. Nims. Toronto: Pontifical Institute of Medieval Studies, 1967.

Gerson, Jean. *De modis significandi.* Oeuvres complètes. Ed. P. Glorieux. Tournai: Desclée, 1973.

Hilary, Saint, Bishop of Poitiers. *Sancti Hilarii Pictaviensis episcopi* De trinitate. Ed. P. Smulders. Turnholti: Brepols, 1979-80.

Holcot, Robert. *In Librum Sapientie Salmonis.* Paris, 1511.

The Holy Bible (Douay-Rheims Version). Rockford, Ill.: Tan Books and Publishers, 1899.

Hugh of St. Victor (1096-1141). *Didascalion: de studio legendi.* Ed. C. H. Buttimer. Tr. Jerome Taylor. Catholic University of America Press, 1939. *Columbia Records of Civilization* 64 (1961). Migne, J. P. *Patrologia cursus completus, series latina.* Paris: 1844-64. 176.

Isidore of Seville. *Etymologiarum sive Originum Libri XX.* Ed. W. M. Lindsay. 2 Vol. Oxford: Clarendon Press., 1911. Migne, J. P. *Patrologia cursus completus, series latina.* Paris: 1844-64. 82.

Jerome, Saint. "*Epistola 57, Ad Pammachium.*" Ed. J. P. Migne. *Patrologia cursus completus, series latina.* Paris: 1844-64. 22.571.

____. *Sancti Eusebii Hieronymi Epistulae, Corpus Scriptorum Ecclesiasticorum Latinorum.* Vienna and Leipzig: 1910-18. 54-56.

____. *Select Letters of Jerome.* Annot. and Tr. F. A. Wright. London: W. Heinemann, Ltd., 1933.

John of Salisbury. *Metalogicon.* Ed. C. C. J. Webb. Oxford: Clarendon Press, 1929.

____. *The Metalogicon of John of Salisbury: A Twelfth-Century Defense of the Verbal and Logical Arts of the Trivium.* Annot., Intr., and Tr. Daniel D. McGarry. Berkeley and Los Angeles: University of California Press, 1955.

Langland, William. *Piers Plowman: An Edition of the C-text.* Ed. Derek Pearsall. Berkeley and Los Angeles: University of California Press, 1979.

____. *Piers Plowman: The A Version.* Ed. George Kane. London: University of London / Athlone Press, 1960.

____. *The Vision of Piers Plowman: A Critical Editon of the B-Text.* Ed. A. V. C. Schmidt. London, Melbourne and Toronto: J. M. Dent & Sons / New York: E. P. Dutton, 1978.

____. *Piers Plowman: The Z Version.* Ed. George Rigg and Charlotte Brewer. Toronto: Pontifical Institute of Medieval Studies, no. 59, 1983.

____. *Will's Visions of Piers Plowman, Do-Well, Do-Better and Do-Best.* Ed. George Kane and E. Talbot Donaldson. London: The Athlone Press, 1975.

Latini, Brunetto. *Il tesoretto.* Ed. and Tr. Julia Bolton Holloway. New York: Garland, 1981.

Macrobius. *Commentary on the Dream of Scipio*. 1952. Trans. William Harris Stahl. New York: Columbia University Press, 1966.

Martianus Capella. *De Nuptiis Philologiae et Mercurii*. Ed. Adolf Dick. Stuttgart: Teubner, 1969.

Migne, J. P. Ed. *Patrologia cursus completus, series graeca*. 166 Vol. Paris: 1844–64.

———. Ed. *Patrologia cursus completus, series latina*. 217 Vol. Paris: 1844–64.

Ovid. *Metamorphose*. Ed. William S. Anderson. Leipzig: Teubner, 1977.

Peter of Spain. *Tractatus (Summule Logicales)*. Ed. and Intr. L. M. de Rijk. Assen: van Gorcum, 1972.

Plato. *Cratylus*. Tr. Benjamin Jowett. New York: Random House, 1937.

———. *Lysis, Symposium, Gorgias*. Ed. and Tr. W. R. M. Lamb. Cambridge, MA / London: Harvard University Press, 1925. Rpt. 1991.

———. *Euthyphro, Apology, Crito, Phaedo, Phaedrus*. Ed. and Tr. Harold North Fowler. Intr. W. R. M. Lamb. Cambridge, MA: Harvard University Press / London: William Heinemann, 1960.

———. *Plato's Cosmology: The* Timaeus *of Plato*. 1937. Tr. Francis M. Cornford. New York: Bobbs-Merrill, n.d.

Priscian. *Institutiones Grammaticae. Grammatici Latini Prisciani* (incl. *Institutionum Grammaticarum, Opera Minora*, and *Grammatici Caesariensis*). 3 Vols. Eds. Martin Hertz and Heinrich Keil. Leipzig: 1858.

Quintilian. *Institutione Oratoria*. Ed. A. G. Gernhard. Liepzig: 1830.

———. *Institutio oratoria*. 4 Vol. Tr. H. E. Bulter. Cambridge, MA: Harvard University Press, 1953.

Siger of Courtrai. *Summa modorum significandi*. Ed. G. Wallerand. *Les Oeuvres de Siger de Courtrai*. Les Philosophes Belges, 8. Louvain, 1913.

Stoicorum veterum fragmenta. 4 Vol. Ed. H. F. A. von Arnim. Leipzig, 1903–24.

Thomas of Erfurt. *Grammatica speculativa*. Ed. and Tr. G. L. Bursill-Hall. London: Longman Group, 1972.

Thurot, C. "Extraits de divers manuscrits latins pour servir à l'histoire des doctrines grammaticales au moyen âge." *Notices et Extraits del Manuscrits de la Bibliothèque Nationale* Vol. 22. Paris, 1974.

Virgil (Publius Vergilius Maro). *The Aeneid of Virgil.* Tr. Allen Mandelbaum. Berkeley: University of California Press, 1971.

William of Ockham. *Ockham: Philosophical Writings.* Ed. and Tr. Philotheus Boehner. Edinburgh and London: Nelson and Sons, 1957.

____. *Opera Philosophica et Theologica ad Fidem Codicum Manuscriptorum Edita.* Cura Instituti Franciscani. Vol. 1. St. Bonaventure University. St. Bonaventure, NY, 1970, 1974.

____. *Ordinatio. Scriptum in librum primum Sententiarum (Ordinatio).* Ed. Girard I. Etzkorn and Francis E. Kelly. *Opera Theologica* Vols. 1–4. 1967, 1970, 1977, 1979.

____. *Quaestiones in librum secundum, tertium, et quartum Sententiarum (Reportatio).* Eds. Girard I. Etzkorn, Gedeon Gál, Romauld Green, Francis E. Kelly, and Rega Wood. *Opera Theologica.* Vols. 5, 6 and 7. 1981, 1982, 1984.

____. *Quaestiones variae in libros Sententiarum.* Eds. Girard I. Etzkorn, Francis E. Kelly and Joseph C. Wey. *Opera Theologica.* Vol. 8. 1984.

____. *Quodlibeta septem.* Ed. Joseph C. Wey. *Opera Theologica.* Vol. 9. 1980.

____. *Reportatio. Opera Plurima.* Vol. 4. Lugduni, 1494. Repr. London: Gregg Press, 1962.

____. *Summa logicae.* Ed. P. Boehner. St. Bonaventure, NY: Franciscan Institute, 1951–52.

Zechmeister, J. Ed. *Scolia Vindobonensia ad Horatii artem poeticam.* Vienna, 1877.

Secondary Sources

Abshear-Seals, Lisa. "Boccaccio's Criseida and Chaucer's Criseyde." *Spectrum* 27: 25–32.

Adams, Hazard. Ed. *Critical Theory since Plato.* New York: Harcourt Brace Jovanovich, 1971.

Adams, Marilyn McCord. *William Ockham.* 2 Vol. Notre Dame, Indiana: University of Notre Dame Press, 1987.

Adams, Shirley. "The Role of Sense Perception in the *Divine Comedy.*" University of California, San Diego, 1983. Dissertation Abstracts International Vol. 44/11-A: 3379.

Agamben, Giorgio. *Il linguaggio e la morte: un seminario sul lungo della negatività.* Turin: Giulio Einaudi, 1982.

Alexander, Archibald. *Theories of Will in the History of Philosophy*. New York: Charles Scribner's Sons, 1898.

Allen, Judson Boyce. *The Ethical Poetic of the Later Middle Ages: A Decorum of Convenient Distinction*. Toronto: University of Toronto Press, 1982.

____. *The Friar as Critic*. Nashville: Vanderbilt University Press, 1971.

Amassian, Margaret, and James Sadowsky. "*Mede* and *Mercede*: A Study of the Grammatical Metaphor in *Piers Plowman* C IV.335-409." *Neuphilologische Mitteilungen* 72 (1971): 457-76.

Arbery, Glenn C. "Adam's First Word and the Failure of Language in *Paradiso* XXXIII." *Sign, Sentence, Discourse: Language in Medieval Thought and Literature*. Eds. Julian N. Wasserman and Lois Roney. Syracuse: Syracuse University Press, 1989. 31-47.

Auerbach, Erich. *Dante: Poet of the Secular World*. Tr. Ralph Manheim. Chicago and London: University of Chicago Press, 1961.

____. *Literary Language and Its Public in Late Latin Antiquity and in the Middle Ages*. Tr. Ralph Manheim. New York: Pantheon-Random House, 1965.

____. *Mimesis: The Representation of Reality in Western Literature*. Tr. Willard R. Trask. Princeton: Princeton University Press, 1953.

Baker, Donald C. "Dreamer and Critic: The Poet in the *Legend of Good Women*." *University of Colorado Studies in Language and Literature* 9 (1963): 4-18.

Baldwin, Charles Sears. *Medieval Rhetoric and Poetic (to 1400): Interpreted from Representative Works*. Gloucester, Mass.: Peter Smith, 1959.

Beal, Rebecca. "Beatrice in the Sun: A Vision from Apocalypse." *Dante Studies* 103 (1985): 57-78.

Beaujour, Michel. "Speculum, Method and Self-Portrayal." John D. Lyons and Stephen G. Nichols, Jr. Eds. and Intr. *Mimesis: From Mirror to Method, Augustine to Descartes*. Hanover and London: University Press of New England, 1982. 188-96.

Beer, Jeanette. *Medieval Translators and Their Craft*. Kalamazoo, Mich.: Medieval Institute Publications, 1989.

Bennett, J.A.W. *Chaucer at Oxford and at Cambridge*. Oxford, Oxford University Press / Clarendon Press, 1974.

Benton, John. "Individualism and Conformity in Medieval Western Europe." *Individualism and Conformity in Classical Islam*. Eds. A. Banani and S. Vryonis Jr. Wiesbaden, 1977. 145-58.

Benveniste, Emile. *Problems in General Linguistics*. Tr. Mary Elizabeth Mee. Miami Linguistics Series, no. 8. Coral Gables, FL: University of Florida Press, 1971.

Bergin, Thomas. Ed. *Italian Literature: Roots and Branches*. New Haven: Yale University Press, 1976.

____. "The Provençal Gallery." *Speculum* 40 (1965): 15-30.

Bethurum, Dorothy. "Chaucer's Point of View as Narrator in the Love Poems." *Publications of the Modern Language Association* 74 (1959): 511-20

Blackburn, Paul. Tr. *Proensa: An Anthology of Troubadour Poetry*. Ed. and Intr. George Economou. New York: Paragon House, 1986.

Blamires, A. "A Chaucer Manifesto." *The Chaucer Review* 24.1 (1989): 29-44.

Blasucci, Luigi. "Discorso teologico e visione sensibile nel canto XIV del Paradiso." *Rassegna della Letteratura Italiana* 95.3 (1991): 5-19.

Bloch, R. Howard. *Etymologies and Genealogies: A Literary Anthropology of the French Middle Ages*. Chicago: University of Chicago Press, 1983.

Bloomfield, Morton W. "Fourteenth-Century England: Realism and Rationalism in Wyclif and Chaucer." *English Studies in Africa* 16 (1973): 59-70.

Bolter, Jay David. *Writing Space: The Computer, Hypertext, and the History of Writing*. Hillsdale, NJ: Lawrence Erlbaum Associates, 1991.

Booth, Wayne C. *The Rhetoric of Fiction*. Chicago: University of Chicago Press, 1961.

Borzi, Italo. "Il Canto XVII Del *Purgatorio*." *Letture degli anni 1976-79*. 363-87.

Bosco, Umberto, Giorgio Petrocchi, and Ignazio Baldelli. Eds. *Enciclopedia Dantesca*. 6 Vol. Rome, 1970-1978.

Boucher, Holly Wallace. "Nominalism: The Difference for Chaucer and Boccaccio." *Chaucer Review* 20.3 (1986): 213-20.

Bowers, John M. *The Crisis of Will in* Piers Plowman. Washington, D. C.: Catholic University Press, 1986.

____. "Piers Plowman and the Police: Note toward a History of the Wycliffite Langland." *Yearbook of Langland Studies* 6 (1992): 1-50.

Boyde, Patrick. *Perception and Passion in Dante's* Comedy. Cambridge: Cambridge University Press, 1993.

Brenkman, John. "Narcissus in the Text." *Georgia Review* 30 (1976): 293-97.

Burckhardt, Jacob. *The Civilization of the Renaissance in Italy.* 1860. Tr. S. G. O. Middlemore. London: Phaidon Books, 1965.

Burke, Kenneth. *A Grammar of Motives.* 1945. Berkeley: University of California Press, 1969.

____. *The Rhetoric of Religion: Studies in Logology.* Berkeley: University of California Press, 1970.

Burrell, David B. "Aquinas on Naming God." *Theological Studies* 24 (1963): 183-212.

Burrow, J. A. *Langland's Fictions.* Oxford: Clarendon Press, 1993.

Bynum, Caroline W. "Did the Twelfth Century Discover the Individual?" *Journal of Eccelsiastical History* 31.1 (January 1980): 1-17.

Callus, D. A. Ed. *Robert Grosseteste: Scholar and Bishop.* London: Oxford University Press, 1955.

Cassell, Anthony. "Santa Lucia as Patroness of Sight: Hagiography, Iconography, and Dante." *Dante Studies* 109 (1991): 71-88.

Chartier, Roger. "Figures of the Author." Brad Sherman and Alain Strowel. Eds. *Of Authors and Origins: Essays on Copyright Law.* Oxford: Clarendon Press, 1994. 7-22.

____. *The Order of Books.* Stanford: Stanford University Press, 1994.

Chaytor, H. J. *From Script to Print.* Cambridge: The University Press, 1945.

Chenù, Marie-Dominique. *La Théologie au douzième siècle.* Paris: J. Vrin, 1957.

____. *Toward Understanding Saint Thomas.* Tr. A. -M. Landry, O. P. and D. Hughes, O. P. Chicago: Henry Regnery Company, 1964.

____. "Theology and the New Awareness of History." *Nature, Man, and Society in the Twelfth Century.* Tr. Jerome Taylor and Lester K. Little. Chicago: University of Chicago Press, 1968.

Clanchy, M. T. *From Memory to Written Record: England, 1066 - 1307.* Cambridge, MA: Harvard University Press, 1979.

Classen, Albrecht. "The Autobiographical Voice of Thomas Hoccleve." *Archiv fur das Studium der Neueren Sprachen und Literaturen* 228.2 (1991): 299-310.

____. "Autobiography as a Late Medieval Phenomenon." *Medieval Perspectives* 3.1 (Spring 1988): 89-104.

____. "Hoccleve's Independence from Chaucer: A Study of Poetic Emancipation." *Fifteenth Century Studies* 16 (1990): 59-81.

Coleman, Janet. *Medieval Readers and Writers 1350 - 1400*. New York: Columbia University Press, 1981.

____. *Piers Plowman and the Moderni*. Rome: Edizioni di storia e letteratura, 1981.

Colish, Marcia L. *The Mirror of Language: A Study in the Medieval Theory of Knowledge*. Rev. Ed. Lincoln and London: University of Nebraska Press, 1983.

____. "The Stoic Theory of Verbal Signification and the Problem of Lies and False Statements from Antiquity to St. Anselm." *Archéologie du signe*. Eds. Lucie Brind-Amour and Eugene Vance. Toronto: Institut Pontifical d'Études Médiévales, 1982. 17-43.

Copeland, Rita. *Rhetoric, Hermeneutics, and Translation in the Middle Ages: Academic Traditions and Vernacular Texts*. Cambridge: Cambridge University Press, 1991.

Copleston, F. C. *Aquinas*. 1955. Baltimore: Penguin, 1963.

____. *A History of Medieval Philosophy*. New York: Harper and Row, 1972.

Corti, Maria. *An Introduction to Literary Semiotics*. Tr. Margherita Bogat and Allen Mandelbaum. Bloomington and London: Indiana University Press, 1978.

Culler, Jonathan. *On Deconstruction: Theory and Criticism after Structuralism*. Ithaca: Cornell University Press 1982.

Cunningham, Valentine. *In the Reading Gaol: Postmodernity, Texts and History*. Oxford, UK and Cambridge, MA: Blackwell, 1994.

Curtius, Ernst Robert. *European Literature and the Latin Middle Ages*. Tr. Willard R. Trask. 1953. Princeton: Princeton University Press, 1990.

Cropp, Glynnis M. "The *Partimen* between Folquet de Marseille and Tostemps." *The Interpretation of Medieval Lyric Poetry*. Ed. W. T. H. Jackson. New York: Columbia University Press, 1980: 91-112.

Delaney, Sheila. *The Naked Text: Chaucer's* Legend of Good Women. Berkely, Los Angeles, London: University of California Press, 1994.

de Looze, Laurence. "Signing Off in the Middle Ages: Medieval Textuality and Strategies of Authorial Self-Naming." *Vox intexta*. Eds. A. N. Doane and Carol Braun Pasternack. Madison: University of Wisconsin Press, 1991. 162-82.

De Man, Paul. *Allegories of Reading: Figural Language in Rousseau, Nietzche, Rilke, and Proust*. New Haven: Yale University Press, 1979.

____. "Autobiography as De-Facement." Paul De Man. *The Rhetoric of Romanticism*. New York: Columbia University Press, 1984, 70.

Derrida, Jacques. *The Ear of the Other: Otobiography, Transference, Translation.* Ed. C. V. McDonald. Tr. P. Kamuf. New York: 1985.

———. "From Psyche." Jacques Derrida. *Acts of Literature.* Ed. Derek Attridge. New York and London: Routledge, 1992.

———. *Of Grammatology.* Tr. G. C. Spivak. Baltimore: Johns Hopkins University Press, 1976.

Di Scipio, G. C., "Dante and St. Paul: The Blinding Light." *Dante Studies* 98 (1980): 151-57.

Donaldson, E. Talbot. *Piers Plowman: The C-Text and Its Poet.* 1949. Yale Studies in English Vol. 113 / Archon Books, 1966.

Dragonetti, Roger. *La vie de la lettre au moyen âge.* Paris: Editions du Seuil, 1980.

Dronke, Peter. *Dante and Medieval Latin Traditions.* Cambridge: Cambridge University Press, 1986.

———. *Medieval Latin and the Rise of the European Love-Lyric.* 2 Vol. London: Oxford-Clarendon, 1968.

———. *Poetic Individuality in the Middle Ages: New Departures in Poetry 1000–1150.* Oxford: Clarendon, 1970.

Eckhardt, Caroline. "The Art of Translation in *The Romaunt of the Rose.*" *Studies in the Age of Chaucer* 6 (1984): 41-63.

Economou, George. "Self-Consciousness of Poetic Activity in Dante and Langland." *Vernacular Poetics in the Middle Ages.* Ed. Lois Ebin. *Studies in Medieval Culture XVI.* Kalamazoo, MI: Medieval Institute Publications, 1984. 177-98.

———. "The Vision's Aftermath in *Piers Plowman*: The Poetics of the Middle English Dream-Vision." *Genre* 18 (1985): 313-21.

Edwards, Robert R. *Ratio and Invention: A Study of Medieval Lyric and Narrative.* Nashville: Vanderbilt University Press, 1989.

———. *The Dream of Chaucer: Representation and Reflection in the Early Narratives.* Durham and London, 1989.

Estrich, Robert. "Chaucer's Maturing Art in the Prologues to the *Legend of Good Women.*" *Journal of English and Germanic Philology* 36 (1937): 326-37.

Everett, Dorothy. "Some Reflections on Chaucer's 'Art Poetical'." *Proceedings of the British Academy* 36 (1950).

Ferrante, Joan M. "'Ab joi mou lo vers e'l comens'." *The Interpretation of Medieval Lyric Poetry*. Ed. W. T. H. Jackson. New York: Columbia University Press, 180. 113-41.

____. "Words and Images in Dante's *Paradiso*: Reflections of the Divine." *Dante, Petrarch, Boccaccio: Studies in the Italian Trecento in Honor of Charles S. Singleton*. Eds. Aldo S. Bernardo and Anthony L. Pelligrini. Binghamton, NY: Medieval and Renaissance Texts and Studies, 1983. 115-32.

Finke, Laurie. "Dowel and the Crisis of Faith and Irony in *Piers Plowman*." *Kierkegaard and Literature: Irony, Repetition, and Criticism*. Eds. Ronald Schleifer and Robert Markley. Norman: University of Oklahoma Press, 1984.

____. "Truth's Treasure: Allegory and Meaning in *Piers Plowman*." *Medieval Texts and Contemporary Readers*. Eds. Laurie Finke and Martin B. Schictman. Ithaca and London: Cornell University Press, 1987: 51-68.

Fletcher, Angus. "Allegory in Literary History." *Dictionary of the History of Ideas*. Vol. 1. Ed. Philip P. Wiener. New York: Charles Scribner's Sons, 1973. 41-48.

____. *Allegory: The Theory of a Symbolic Mode*. Ithaca: Cornell University Press, 1964.

Folkenflik, Robert. "The Self as Other." *The Culture of Autobiography: Constructions of Self-Representation*. Ed. Robert Folkenflik. Stanford: Stanford University Press, 1993. 215-36.

Foucault, Michel. "What is an Author?" *Language, Counter-Memory, Practice: Selected Essays and Interviews*. Ed. and Intr. Donald F. Bouchard. Trs. Donald F. Bouchard and Sherry Simon. Ithaca: Cornell University Press, 1977. 113-138.

Frank, Robert Worth, Jr. *Chaucer and the* Legend of Good Women. Cambridge, Mass.: Harvard University Press, 1972

____. "The *Legend of Good Women*: Some Implications." *Chaucer at Albany*. Ed. in Rossell Hope Robbins. New York: Burt Franklin, 1975. 63-76.

Freccero, John. *Dante: The Poetics of Conversion*. Ed. Rachel Jacoff. Cambridge, MA: Harvard University Press, 1986.

Fries, Maureen. "The 'Other' Voice: Woman's Song, Its Satire and Its Transcendence in Late Medieval British Literature." *Studies in Medieval Culture* 15 (1981): 155-78.

Frye, Northrop. *Anatomy of Criticism: Four Essays*. Princeton: Princeton University Press, 1957.

Fumagalli, Maria Theresa Beonio-Brocchieri. *The Logic of Abelard*. 1969. Tr. Simon Pleasance. Dordrecht, Holland: D. Reidel, 1970.

Gardner, John. *The Poetry of Chaucer*. Carbondale and Edwardsville: Southern Illinois University Press, 1977.

Gellrich, Jesse M. *The Idea of the Book in the Middles Ages: Language, Theory, Mythology, and Fiction*. Ithaca and London: Cornell University Press, 1985.

Ghisalberti, F. "Arnolfo d'Orléans: Un cultore di Ovidio del sec. XII." *Memorie dell' Instituto Lombardo*. Classe di Lettere. 24.4.

Gilby, O.P., Thomas. "Peter Abelard." *The Encyclopedia of Philosophy*. Vol. 1. Ed. Paul Edwards. New York: Macmillan / London: Collier, 1967: 3-6.

Gilson, Etienne. *Elements of Christian Philosophy*. Garden City, NY: Doubleday, 1960.

____. *History of Christian Philosophy in the Middle Ages*. New York: Random House, 1955.

Godzich, Wlad. *The Culture of Literacy*. Cambridge, MA: Harvard University Press, 1994.

____. "Foreword." Eugene Vance. *From Topic to Tale*. Minneapolis: University of Minnesota Press, 1987. x-xix.

Goldin, Frederick. Tr. and Intr. *German and Italian Lyrics of the Middle Ages*. Garden City, NY: Anchor-Doubleday, 1973.

____. Tr. and Intr. *Lyrics of the Troubadours and Trouvères*. Garden City, NY: Anchor, 1973.

____. *The Mirror of Narcissus in the Courtly Love Lyric*. Ithaca: Cornell University Press, 1967.

Gonda, J. *Ancient Indian ojas, Latin *augos and the Indo-European nouns in -es-/-os*. Utrecht: N.V. A. Oosthoek's Uitgevers Mij., 1952.

Gordon, David J. "Character and Self in Autobiography." *The Journal of Narrative Technique* 18.2 (Spring 1988): 105-19.

Gradon, Pamela. "Langland and the Ideology of Dissent." *Proceedings of the British Academy* 66 (1980): 179-205.

Greenblatt, Stephen. *Renaissance Self-Fashioning: From More to Shakespeare*. Chicago and London: University of Chicago Press, 1980.

____. "Shakespeare and the Exorcists." *After Strange Texts: The Role of Theory in the Study of Literature*. Eds. Gregory S. Jay and David I. Miller. Alabama: University of Alabama Press, 1985.

Greetham, D. C. "Self-Referential Artifacts: Hoccleve's Persona as a Literary Device." *Modern Philology* 86.3 (February 1989): 242-251.

Griffiths, Lavinia. *Personification in* Piers Plowman. Cambridge: D. S. Brewer, 1985.

Guillory, John. *Poetic Authority: Spenser, Milton, and Literary History*. New York: Columbia University Press, 1983.

Hagman, Edward. "Dante's Vision of God: The End of the Itinerarium Mentis." *Dante Studies* 106 (1988): 1-20.

Hamilton, Marie P. "Notes on Chaucer and the Rhetoricians." *Publications of the Modern Language Association* 47 (1932): 403-9.

Hanning, Robert W. "I Shal Finde It in a Maner Glose": Versions of Textual Harassment in Medieval Literature." *Medieval Texts and Contemporary Readers*. Eds. Laurie A. Finke and Martin B. Schichtman. Ithaca and London: Cornell University Press, 1987.

Hans, James S. *The Play of the World*. Amherst: University of Massachusetts Press, 1981.

Harwood, Britton J. Piers Plowman *and the Problem of Belief*. Toronto, Buffalo, London: University of Toronto Press, 1992.

Hathaway, Neil. "Compilatio: From Plagiarism to Compiling." *Viator* 20 (1989): 19-44.

Havelock, Eric. *Preface to Plato*. 1963. New York: Grosset and Dunlap, 1967.

Hawkins, Peter S. "Divide and Conquer: Augustine in the *Divine Comedy*." *Publications of the Modern Language Association* 106.3 (May 1991): 471-83.

Heidegger, Martin. "The Question Concerning Technology." Martin Heidegger. *The Question Concerning Technology and Other Essays*. Tr. William Lovitt. New York: Harper and Row, 1977. 3-35.

Herzog, Michael B. "The *Book of the Duchess*: The Vision of the Artist as a Young Dreamer." *Chaucer Review* 22.4 (1988): 269-81.

Hill, John M. *Chaucerian Belief: The Poetics of Reverence and Delight*. New Haven and London: Yale University Press, 1991.

Hoepffner, Ernest. *Les troubadours dans leur vie et dans leur oeuvres*. Paris, 1955.

Holley, Linda Tarte. "Medieval Optics and the Framed Narrative in Chaucer's *Troilus and Criseyde*." *The Chaucer Review* 21.1 (1986): 26-44.

Holloway, Julia Bolton. *The Pilgrim and the Book: A Study of Dante, Langland and Chaucer*. New York: Peter Lang, 1987.

Huizinga, Johan. *Homo Ludens: A Study of the Play Element in Culture*. Boston: Beacon, 1950.

Hult, David F. *Self-Fulfilling Prophecies: Readership and Authority in the First* Roman de la Rose. Cambridge: Cambridge University Press, 1986.

Jeffrey, David Lyle. "Chaucer and Wyclif: Biblical Hermeneutic and Literary Theory in the XIVth Century." *Chaucer and the Scriptural Tradition*. Ed. David Lyle Jeffrey. Ottowa: University of Ottawa Press, 1984. 109–42.

____. "Sacred and Secular Scripture: Authority and Interpretation in *The House of Fame*." *Chaucer and the Scriptural Tradition*. Ed. David Lyle Jeffrey. Ottawa: University of Ottawa Press, 1984. 207–28.

Jolivet, Jean. *Arts du langage et théologie chez Abélard*. Paris: Librarie Philosophique J. Vrin, 1969.

Jordan, Robert M. *Chaucer's Poetics and the Modern Reader*. Berkeley: University of California Press, 1987.

Justman, Stewart. "Literal and Symbolic in the *Canterbury Tales*." *Chaucer Review* 14 (1980): 199–214.

Kamowski, William. "Langland and Wyclif on Theology: Alternatives for Reform in *De Divii Dominio* and *Piers Plowman*." Paper presented at Thirtieth International Congress on Medieval Studies (7 May 1995). Kalamazoo, MI.

Kane, George. *The Autobiographical Fallacy in Chaucer and Langland Studies*. London: H. K. Lewis, 1965.

____. *Chaucer and Langland: Historical and Textual Approaches*. Berkeley and Los Angeles: University of California Press, 1989.

____. *Piers Plowman: The Evidence for Authorship*. London: University of London / Athlone Press, 1965.

Kay, Sarah. *Subjectivity in Troubadour Poetry*. Cambridge: Cambridge University Press, 1990.

Kendrick, Laura. *The Game of Love: Troubadour Wordplay*. Berkeley, Los Angeles, London: University of California Press, 1988.

Kermode, Frank. *The Sense of an Ending: Studies in the Theory of Fiction*. London: New York and London: Oxford University Press, 1966.

Kimmelman, Burt. "Ockham, Chaucer, and the Emergence of Modern Poetics," in *Reconstructive Polyphony: Studies in the Rhetorical Poetics of the Middle Ages. Essays in Honor of Robert O. Payne*. Eds. John M. Hill, and Deborah Sinnreich-Levi. Gainesville: University Press of Florida (forthcoming).

____. "Visionary Science in Purgatorio XVII and Paradiso XXX." *Comitatus: A Journal of Medieval and Renaissance Studies* 26 (October 1995).

Kiser, Lisa J. *Telling Classical Tales: Chaucer and the Legend of Good Women*. Ithaca and London: Cornell University Press, 1983.

Kittredge, G. L. *Chaucer and His Poetry*. Cambridge, MA: Harvard University Press, 1915.

Köhler, Erich. *Trobadorlyrik und höfischer Roman*. Berlin: Rütten and Loening, 1962.

Kooper, Erik S. "Art and Signature and the Art of the Signature." *Court and Poet: Selected Proceedings of the Third Congress of the International Courtly Literature Society*. Ed. Glyn S. Burgess. Liverpool: Cairns, 1981. 223-32.

Kretzman, Norman. "Semantics, History of." *Encyclopedia of Philosophy*. Vol. 7. Ed. Paul Edwards. New York: Macmillan / London: Collier, 1967: 358-406.

Kristeva, Julia. *Desire in Language: A Semiotic Approach to Literature and Art*. Ed. Leon S. Roudiez. Tr. Thomas Gora, Alice Jardine, and Leon S. Roudiez. New York: Columbia University Press, 1980.

Kruger, Steven F. *Dreaming in the Middle Ages*. Cambridge: Cambridge University Press, 1992.

Lawton, David. *Chaucer's Narrators*. Cambridge: D. S. Brewer, 1985.

―――. "Lollardy and the 'Piers Plowman' Tradition." *Modern Language Review* 76 (1981): 780-93.

―――. "The Subject of *Piers Plowman*." *Yearbook of Langland Studies* 1 (1987): 1-30.

Le Goff, Jacques. *The Medieval Imagination*. Tr. Arthur Goldhammer. Chicago: University of Chicago Press, 1988.

Leicester, H. Marshall. *The Disenchanted Self: Representing the Subject in the* Canterbury Tales. Berkeley: University of California Press, 1990.

Lewis, Charlton T. *A Latin Dictionary*. Oxford: Clarendon, 1879, 1980.

――― and C. Short. *A Latin Dictionary*. 1869. Oxford, 1962.

Lloyd-Jones, K. "Humanist Debate and the 'Translative Dilemma' in Renaissance France." *Medieval Translators and Their Craft*. Ed. Jeanette Beer. Kalamazoo: Medieval Institute Publications, 1989. 347-71.

Lowes, J. L. *Geoffrey Chaucer*. Oxford: Clarendon Press, 1934.

Lindberg, David C. *Theories of Vision from Al-Kindi to Kepler*. Chicago and London: University of Chicago Press, 1976.

Makin, Peter. *Provence and Pound*. Berkeley: University of California Press, 1978.

Malone, Kemp. *Chapters on Chaucer*. Baltimore: Johns Hopkins Press, 1951.

Maloney, Thomas. "Roger Bacon on the *Significatum* of Words." *Archéologie du signe*. Eds. Lucie Brind-Amour and Eugene Vance. Toronto: Institut Pontifical d'Études Médiévales, 1982.

Mandelbaum, Allen. Annot., Intr. and Tr. *The Divine Comedy of Dante Alighieri*. 3 Vol. Berkeley: University of California Press, 1981.

____. "'Taken From Brindisi': Vergil in an Other's Otherworld." *Vergil at 2000: Commemorative Essays on the Poet and His Influence*. Ed. John D. Bernard. New York: AMS Press, 1989.

____. *Visione e visibilia*. Firenze: Leo S. Olschki, 1988.

Manly, J. M. "Chaucer and the Rhetoricians." *Proceedings of the British Academy* 12 (1926).

Mann, Jill. *Langland and Allegory. The Morton W. Bloomfield Lectures on Medieval English Literature, II*. Kalamazoo: Medieval Institute Publications, 1992.

Martin, Christopher. Ed. *The Philosophy of Thomas Aquinas: Introductory Readings*. London and New York: Routledge, 1988.

Mazzeo, Joseph A. "Medieval Hermeneutics: Dante's Poetic and Historicity." *Religion and Literature* 17 (Spring 1985) 1: 1–24.

____. "Universal Analogy and the Culture of the Renaissance." *Journal of the History of Ideas* 15 (1954).

Mazzotta, Giuseppe. *Dante, Poet of the Desert: History and Allegory in the* Divine Comedy. Princeton: Princeton University Press, 1979.

____. *Dante's Vision and the Circle of Knowledge*. Princeton: Princeton University Press, 1993.

McCormick, Peter J. *Fictions, Philosophies, and the Problems of Poetics*. Ithaca and London: Cornell University Press, 1988.

McClellan, William. "Bakhtin's Theory of Dialogic Discourse, Medieval Rhetorical Theory, and the Multi-Voiced Structure of the Clerk's Tale." *Exemplaria* 1.2 (October 1989): 461–488.

Middleton, Anne. "Narration and the Invention of Experience: Episodic Form in *Piers Plowman*." *The Wisdom of Poetry: Essays in English Literature in Honor of Morton W. Bloomfield*. Kalamazoo: Medieval Institute Publications, 1982. 91–122.

____. "*Piers Plowman*." *A Manual of Writings in Middle English 1050–1500*. Ed. Albert E. Hartung. New Haven: Connecticut Academy of Arts and Sciences, 1986.

____. "Two Infinites: Grammatical Metaphor in *Piers Plowman*." *English Literary History* 39.2 (June 1972): 169–88.

____. "William Langland's 'Kynde Name'." *Literary Practice and Social Change in Britain, 1380–1530*. Ed. Lee Patterson. Berkeley, Los Angeles, Oxford: University of California Press, 1990. 15–82.

Migiel, Marilyn. "Between Art and Theology: Dante's Representation of Humility." *Stanford Italian Review* 5.2: 141–59.

Miller, Jacqueline T. *Poetic License: Authority and Authorship in Medieval and Renaissance Contexts*. New York and Oxford: Oxford University Press, 1986.

Mills, David. "The Role of the Dreamer in *Piers Plowman*." *Piers Plowman: Critical Approaches*. Ed. S. S. Hussey. London: Methuen, 1969.

Minnis, A. J. *Chaucer and Pagan Antiquity*. Cambridge, U.K.: D. S. Brewer, 1982.

____. *Medieval Theory of Authorship: Scholastic Attitudes in the later Middle Ages*. London: Scolar, 1984.

Miskimin, Alice S. *The Renaissance Chaucer*. New Haven: Yale University Press, 1975.

Moody, Ernest A. "William of Ockham." *Studies in Medieval Philosophy, Science, and Logic*. Berkeley: University of California Press, 1975. 409–40.

Morse, J. Mitchell. "The Philosophy of the Clerk of Oxenford." *Modern Language Quarterly* 19 (1958): 3–20.

Murphy, James J. *Rhetoric in the Middle Ages: A History of Rhetorical Theory from Saint Augustine to the Renaissance*. Berkeley, Los Angeles, London: University of California Press, 1974.

____. Ed. *Three Medieval Rhetorical Arts*. Berkeley, Los Angeles, London: University of California Press, 1971.

Neaman, Judith S. "Magnification as Metaphor." *England in the Thirteenth Century: Proceedings of the 1989 Harlaxton Symposium*. Ed. W. M. Ormrod. Stamford: Paul Watkins, 1991. 105–22.

Nichols, Jr., Stephen J. "A Poetics of Historicism? Recent Trends in Medieval Literary Study." *Medievalia et Humanistica* NS 8 (1977): 77–101.

____. "Toward an Aesthetic of the Provençal Lyric II: Marcabru's *Dire vos vuoill ses doptansa* (BdT 293, 18)." *Italian Literature: Roots and Branches*. Ed. Thomas Bergin. New Haven: Yale University Press, 1976. 15–38.

———. "Voice and Writing in Augustine and in the Troubadour Lyric." *Vox intexta*. Eds. A. N. Doane and Carol Braun Pasternack. Madison: University of Wisconsin Press, 1991. 137–61.

Niermeyer, J. F. *Mediae Latinatatis Lexicon Minus*. Leiden: E. J. Brill, 1976.

Noakes, Susan. "Dante's 'Vista Nova': Paradiso XXXIII.136." *Quaderni d'Italianisitica: Official Journal of the Canadian Society for Italian Studies* 5.2 (Autumn 1984): 151–70.

Oberman, Heiko. *The Harvest of Medieval Theology: Gabriel Biel and Late Medieval Nominalism*. Cambridge, MA: Harvard University Press, 1963.

Olson, David R. *The World on Paper: The Conceptual and Cognitive Implications of Writing and Reading*. Cambridge: Cambridge University Press, 1994.

Ong, Walter J. *Orality and Literacy: The Technologizing of the Word*. London and New York: Methuen, 1982.

Oppenheimer, Paul. *The Birth of the Modern Mind: Self, Consciousness, and the Invention of the Sonnet*. New York: Oxford, 1989.

Owen, Charles. "The Tales of Canterbury: Fictions within a Fiction that Purports Not To Be a Fiction." *Chaucer and the Craft of Fiction*. Ed. Leigh A. Arrathoon. Rochester, MI: Solaris Press, 1986. 179–94

Pasquini, Emilio. "La metafora della visione nella *Commedia*." *Letture Classensi*. (23 Feb. 1985). 129–51.

Paterson, Linda M. *Troubadours and Eloquence*. Oxford: Clarendon, 1975.

Patterson, Lee. *Chaucer and the Subject of History*. Madison: University of Wisconsin Press, 1991.

———. *Negotiating the Past: The Historical Understanding of Medieval Literature*. Madison: University of Wisconsin Press, 1987.

———. "On the Margin: Postmodernism, Ironic History, and Medieval Studies." *Speculum* 65.1 (January 1990): 87–108.

Payne, Robert O. *The Key of Remembrance: A Study of Chaucer's Poetics*. New Haven and London: Yale University Press, 1963.

———. "Late Medieval Images and Self-Images of the Poet: Chaucer, Gower, Lydgate, Henryson, Dunbar." *Vernacular Poetics in the Middle Ages*. Ed. Lois Ebin. Kalamazoo: Medieval Institute Publications, 1984.

———. "Making His Own Myth: The Prologue to Chaucer's *Legend of Good Women*." *Chaucer Review* 9 (1975): 197–211.

Pearsall, Derek. "Editing Medieval Texts." *Textual Criticism and Literary Interpretation*. Ed. Jerome J. McGann. Chicago and London: University of Chicago Press, 1985. 92-106.

Peck, Russell A. "Chaucer and the Nominalist Questions." *Speculum* 53 (1978): 745-60.

Pound, Ezra. *A B C of Reading*. 1934. New York: New Directions, 1960.

Preminger, Alex, Leon Golden, O. B. Hardison, Jr. and Kevin Kerrane. Eds. and Trs. *Classicism and Medieval Literary Criticism: Translations and Interpretations*. New York: Frederick Ungar, 1974.

Quinn, William. *Chaucer's Rehersynges: The Performability of the* Legend of Good Women. Washington, D. C.: The Catholic University of America Press, 1994.

Quint, David. *Origin and Originality in Renaissance Literature*. New Haven: Yale University Press, 1983.

Reade, W. H. D. *The Moral System of Dante's* Inferno. Oxford: Clarendon, 1909.

Readings, Bill, and Bennet Schaber. "Introduction." *Postmodernism across the Ages: Essays for a Postmodernity that Wasn't Born Yesterday*. Eds. Bill Readings and Bennet Schaber. Syracuse: Syracuse University Press 1993. 1-30.

Reiss, Edmund. "Chaucer's Fiction and Linguistic Self-Consciousness in the Late Middle Ages." *Chaucer and the Craft of Fiction*. Ed. Leigh A. Arrathoon. Rochester, MI: Solaris Press, 1986. 97-120.

Ricoeur, Paul. *The Rule of Metaphor: Multi-disciplinary Studies of the Creation of Meaning in Language*. Tr. Paul Czerny with Kathleen McLaughlin and John Costello, S.J. Toronto: University of Toronto Press, 1977.

Robins, Rossell Hope. *Ancient and Medieval Grammatical Theory in Europe*. 1951. Port Washington, New York / London: Kennikat Press, 1971.

Roncaglia, A. "Riflessi di posizione Cistercensi nella poesia del XII secolo." *I Cistercensi e il lazio: atti delle giornate di studio dell' Istituto di Storia dell' Arte dell' Università di Roma*. Rome, 1977. 11-22.

———. "*Trobar clus*: discuzzione aperta." *Cultura Neolatina* 29 (1969): 5-55.

Ruud, Jay. "Chaucer and Nominalism: The 'Envoy to Bukton'." *Mediaevalia* 10 (1984): 199-212.

Schaefer, Ursula. "Hearing from Books: The Rise of Fictionality in Old English Poetry." *Vox intexta*. Eds. A. N. Doane and Carol Braun Pasternack. Madison: University of Wisconsin Press, 1991. 117-36.

Schmidt, A. V. C. "Langland, Chrysostom and Bernard: A Complex Echo." *Notes and Queries* (April 1983): 108-10.

____. "Langland's 'Book of Conscience' and Alanus de Insulis." *Notes and Queries* (December 1982): 482-84.

Schneider, Reinhold. Intr. Johannes von Saaz. *The Plowman from Bohemia: In the Original Early New High German and in English.* Tr. Alexander and Elizabeth Henderson. New York: Frederick Ungar, 1966.

Schwietering, Julius. *Die Demutsformel mittelhochdeutscher Dichter.* Berlin: 1921.

Shaw, Prudence. "*Paradiso* XXX." *Cambridge Readings in Dante's* Comedy. Eds. Kenelm Foster and Patrick Boyle. Cambridge: Cambridge University Press, 1981.

Shepherd, Geoffrey. "Religion and Philosophy in Chaucer." *Geoffrey Chaucer.* Ed. Derek Brewer. London, D. S. Brewer, 1974. 262-89.

Shoaf, R. A. "Medieval Studies after Derrida after Heidegger." *Sign, Sentence, Discourse: Language in Medieval Thought and Literature.* Eds. Julian N. Wasserman and Lois Roney. Syracuse: Syracuse University Press, 1989. 9-30.

Smith, Paul. *Discerning the Subject.* Minneapolis: University of Minnesota Press, 1988.

Smith, Sarah Stanbury. "Cupid's Sight in the Prologue to the *Legend of Good Women.*" *Centerpoint: A Journal of Interdisciplinary Studies* 4.3 (Fall 1981): 95-102.

Souter, Alexander. *A Glossary of Later Latin to 600 A.D.* Oxford: Clarendon Press, 1949.

Spearing, A. C. "The Development of a Theme in *Piers Plowman.*" *Review of English Studies* 11 (1960).

____. *Medieval Dream-Poetry.* Cambridge: The University Press, 1976.

____. "Verbal Repetition in *Piers Plowman* B and C." *Journal of English and Germanic Philology* 62 (1963): 722-37.

Spence, Sarah. *Rhetorics of Reason and Desire: Virgil, Augustine, and the Troubadours.* Ithaca and London: Cornell University Press, 1988.

Spiegel, Gabrielle M. "History, Historicism, and the Social Logic of the Text in the Middle Ages." *Speculum* 65.1 (January 1990): 59-86.

Spitzer, Leo . "Note on the Poetic and Empirical 'I' in Medieval Authors." *Traditio* 4 (1946).

Steinmetz, David C. "Late Medieval Nominalism and the 'Clerk's Tale'." *Chaucer Review* 12 (1977): 38-54.

Stephens, John. "The Uses of Personae and the Art of Obliqueness in Some Chaucer Lyrics" Parts I, II and III. *Chaucer Review* 21.3 and 4, 22.1 (1987): 360-73, 459-68, 41-52.

Stepsis, Robert. "*Potentia Absoluta* and the 'Clerk's Tale'." *Chaucer Review* 10.2 (1975-76): 129-46.

Stevens, M. "The Performing Self in Twelfth-century Culture" *Viator* 9 (1978): 193-212.

Stock, Brian. "History, Literature, and Medieval Textuality." *Yale French Studies* 70 (1966): 7-17.

____. *The Implications of Literacy: Written Language and Models of Interpretation in the Eleventh and Twelfth Centuries*. Princeton: Princeton University Press, 1983.

____. "Language and Cultural History." *New Literary History* 18.3 (Spring 1987): 657-70.

____. "Medieval Literacy, Linguistic Theory, and Social Organization." *New Literary History* 16.1 (Autumn 1984): 13-23.

____. *Myth and Science in the Twelfth Century: A Study of Bernard Silvester*. Princeton: Princeton University Press, 1972.

Stock, Lorraine Kochanske. "Will, Actyf, Pacience, and *Liberum Arbitrium*: Two Recurring Quotations in Langland's Revisions of *Piers Plowman C Text*, Passus V, XV, XVI." *Texas Studies in Literature and Language* 30.4 (Winter 1988): 461-77.

Stone, Gregory B. *The Death of the Troubadour: The Late Medieval Resistance to the Renaissance*. Philadelphia: University of Pennsylvania Press, 1994.

Tabarroni, Andrea. "Mental Signs and the Theory of Representation in Ockham." *On the Medieval Theory of Signs*. Eds. Umberto Eco and Costantino Marmo. Amsterdam and Philadelphia: John Benjamins, 1989.

Tateo, Francesco. "Teologia e 'Arte' nel canto X del *Purgatorio*." *Questioni de poetica dantesca*. Bari: Adriatica, n.d.: 137-71.

Taylor, Henry Osborn. *The Classical Heritage of the Middle Ages*. New York: Frederick Ungar, 1957.

Taylor, P. B. "Chaucer's 'Cosyn to the Dede'." *Speculum* 57 (1982): 315-27.

Topsfield, Leslie T. "*Jois, Amors* and *Fin' amors* in the Poetry of Jaufre Rudel." *Neuphilologische Mitteilungen* 71 (1970): 277-305.

____. "The 'Natural Fool' in Peire d'Alvernhe, Marcabru, and Bernart de Ventadorn." In *Mélange d'histoire littéraire, de linguistique et de philologie romanes offerts à Charles Rostaing*. 1149-58. Liège, 1974.

____. *Troubadours and Love*. New York: Cambridge University Press, 1975.

____. "*Malvestatz versus Proeza* and *Leautatz* in Troubadour Poetry and the *Lancelot* of Chrétien de Troyes." *L'Esprit Créateur* 19 (1979): 37-53.

Trapp, Damasus. "Augustinian Theology of the Fourteenth Century." *Augustiana* V (1956), American Series.

Trinkaus, Charles, *The Poet as Philosopher: Petrarch and the Formation of Renaissance Consciousness*. New Haven and London: Yale University Press, 1979.

Troyan, Scott D. *Textual Decorum: A Rhetoric of Attitudes in Medieval Literature*. New York and London: Garland, 1994.

Tuve, Rosemond. *Elizabethan and Metaphysical Imagery: Renaissance Poetic and Twentieth-Century Critics*. Chicago and London: University of Chicago Press, 1947.

Vance, Eugene. "Augustine's *Confessions* and the Grammar of Selfhood." *Genre* 6.1 (March 1973): 1-28.

____. *From Topic to Tale: Logic and Narrativity in the Middle Ages*. Minneapolis: University of Minnesota Press, 1987.

____. *Mervelous Signals: Poetics and Sign Theory in the Middle Ages*. Lincoln and London: University of Nebraska Press, 1986.

Van Vleck, Amelia. *Memory and Re-Creation in Troubadour Lyric*. Berkeley, Los Angeles, Oxford: University of California Press, 1991.

Vignaux, Paul. *Philosophy in the Middle Ages*. New York, 1959.

von Nolcken, Christina. "*Piers Plowman*, the Wycliffites, and *Pierce the Plowman's Creed*." *Yearbook of Langland Studies* 2 (1988): 71-102.

White, Hayden. *The Content of the Form: Narrative Discourse and Historical Representation*. Baltimore and London: Johns Hopkins University Press, 1987.

____. *Metahistory: The Historical Imagination in Nineteenth Century Europe*. Baltimore and London: Johns Hopkins University Press, 1973.

____. *Tropics of Discourse: Essays in Cultural Criticism*. Baltimore and London: Johns Hopkins University Press, 1978.

Wilhelm, James J. "Arnaut Daniel's Legacy to Dante and Pound." *Italian Literature: Roots and Branches*. Ed. Thomas Bergin. New Haven: Yale University Press, 1976. 67-84.

____. *Dante and Pound: The Epic of Judgement*. Orono, Maine: University of Maine Press, 1974.

____. *Seven Troubadours: The Creators of Modern Verse.* University Park, PA: Pennsylvania State University Press, 1970.

Wittig, Joseph. "*Piers Plowman* B, Passus IX-XII: Elements in the Design of the Inward Journey." *Traditio* 28 (1972): 211-80.

Williams, David. "From Grammar's Pan to Logic's Fire: Intentionality and Chaucer's 'Friar's Tale'," *Literature and Ethics: Essays Presented to A. E. Malloch.* Eds. Gary Wihl and David Williams. Kingston and Montreal, McGill-Queen's University Press, 1988. 77-95.

Woolf, Rosemary. "Some Non-Medieval Qualities of *Piers Plowman.*" Rosemary Woolf. *Art and Doctrine: Essays on Medieval Literature.* Ed. Heather O'Donoghue. London, 1986. 85-97.

Zink, Michel. *La Subjectivité littéraire au moyen âge: Autour du siècle de saint Louis.* Paris: Presses Universitaires de France, 1985.

Zumthor, Paul. "Autobiography in the Middle Ages?" *Genre* 6.1 (March 1973): 29-48.

____. *Toward a Medieval Poetics.* Tr. Philip Bennett. Minneapolis and Oxford: University of Minnesota Press, 1992. Originally published as *Essai de poétique médiévale.* Paris: 1972.

INDEX

A

Abbo of Fleury (10th century), 44, 45, 60, 79
Abelard, Peter (c.1079–1142), 58 n.21; and abstract comprehension, 72; and difference between people in form and matter, 19; and grammar, 58; and interrelationships among language, user, and truth, 104; and Marcabru, 91; and nature of words, 77, 81, 85; and nominalism, 161; and nouns, 58; and the past, 86; and semantics history, 81; and universals, 58, 81–82
absence, doctrine of, and Aquinas, 131, 132; and Augustine, 132; and Dante, 33, 135–136, 156, 174; and Dionysius, 132; and Langland, 203; and Marcabru, 99, 100; and medieval philosophy, 121; and ontology, 129; and self-naming, 174
abstraction, and Langland, 170; and Ockham, 195
Activa Vita (Langland: *Piers Plowman*), 219
Actyf (Langland: *Piers Plowman*), 219
Aeneas, Dante's historical antecedent, 33
Aeneid (Virgil), 29 n.32, 33 n.67, 196
Alan of Lille (1128–1202), 57
Albert the Great (c.1200–1280), 82
Alceste (Chaucer: *Legend of Good Women*), 178, 179; and Chaucer, 30, 188, 197; and Cupid or God of Love, 179 n.36, 198–199; daisy resemblance, 193; and Dante, 198–199; and dreaming, 195; an intercessor like Dante's Beatrice, 174; more than allegorical, 192–193; and naming in the Prologue to the *Legend of Good Women*, 173; and troubadour topos, 199; as an unifying figure, 237
Alcuin of York (c.732–804), 40
allegory, and Abbo of Fleury, 60; Alceste transcends, 192–193; and Anselm, 234; and Augustine, 203; and Berengarius, 60; and the Bible, 56, 71; and Chaucer, 18, 169, 184–185, 187 n.42, 194, 199, 202, 226; and discourse, 55, 186; and dream poems, 183–184; and dream vision, 186–187; and epistemology, 161; and fiction, 164, 220; and Geffrey and Will, 14, 176; and God, 222; and God of Love, 185; and grammar, 71; and house, 238–240; and Langland, 61, 164, 171, 186, 202; and Langland's Clergy, 59; Langland's Will often taken as a figure of, 164; and *Legend of Good Women* (Chaucer), 234; and the literary persona, 12; and literate societies, 56; and logic, 55, 194–195; and medieval culture, 11, 57–58; myth and truth relationship with, 55; narrative distinct from, 164; and Ockham, 194–195; and *Pearl* (anon.), 182; and personification, 161, 238; and *Piers Plowman* (Langland), 60, 122, 159, 161, 182, 213–214, 215, 226; and Platonizing principles, 170; and Prologue to the *Legend of Good Women*, 238–239; and *Roman de la rose,* 157; and Bernard Silvestris, 56, 57; and textual communities, 74
Allen, Judson Boyce, 22, 117
alterity, concept of, 21–22; and Chaucer, 24; and *différance,* 18; and Guillem IX, 24; and individualism, 27; and Langland, 24; and Marcabru, 24
amars (false love), and Marcabru, 89, 91, 106, 139
Amassian, Margaret, 211
"Amics Marchabrun, car digam" (Marcabru), 119
amor courtois (courtly love), 106, 237; see also courtly love; *fin' amors*
amors (true love), and Marcabru, 89, 106, 139
anagram, and textuality, 2–3
analogical thinking, and language as starting point, 44, 49, 190
anatomy, concept of, 186
anima (soul or mind), 19, 216
Anima (Langland: *Piers Plowman*), 216
anonymity of authorship, and St. Bonaventure, 7
Anselm, St. (c.1033–1109), on allegory, 234; and being and understanding and linguistics, 137; comprehended by

Marcabru, 111; critique of *Categories* (Aristotle), 46 n.5; on faith, 191 n.48; followed by Langland, 211; free will superior to reflex, 110; and God, 45–46; on grammar, 42, 46 n.5; influence on Guillem IX, 103, 106; and intentionality, 6, 104, 137; on language, 109, 230, 232; on language and nature, 22, 134, 159; and *lekta*, 103, 104, 210; on lies, 111; on linguistics, 162; and logic, 42; and names and naming, 9, 45–46, 47; on *naturaliter*, 133, 159; and natural language, 115–116, 135; on nature of words, 77–78; not a nominalist, 159; and nouns, 45–46, 160; and the past, 86; a philosophical realist, 19; and rationality, 103, 211; and *rectitude*, 110, 111, 120; and Scripture, 162; and semantics, 9; and truth, 104, 133; *see also specific works*
Anthony, St. (1195–1231), 231
appetitus rationalis and *voluntas* (Aquinas), 162
Aquinas, Thomas, St. (c.1225–1274), and absence doctrine, 131, 132; and Aristotle, 150, 162; and Dante, 132, 150–151, 157, 206; figurative language distrusted, 131; and grace, 143; and the Holy Trinity, 132–133; influenced by Augustine, 150; and knowing, 141–142, 150–151; and Langland, 137, 168; and linguistics, 43–44; and Matthew, 153; on the nature of a word, 77, 142; and Ockham, 39; and ontology, 38; and the past, 86; and pride, 155; on *rectitude*, 210; on sight, 141–142, 143–144, 148–149; on signs, 150–151; on understanding, 150; *see also specific works*
Arbery, Glenn C., 121, 135
Aristotelianism, 35, 40, 43, 63
Aristotle (384–322 BC), and Aquinas, 150, 162; and Averroës, 64; on categories, 39, 40 n.5, 142; and concept of imitation, 117; and Dante, 157; and the infinite, 225; influence on Chaucer, 130; Langland's Will discusses, 218; and literate culture's birth, 116; and Marcabru, 93; and nominalism, 161; and notion of *species*, 199; and nouns, 161; and predication, 81–82; and Priscian, 30; and sight, 142; and speculative grammar, 44–45; and substance and accident in grammar, 103; *see also specific works*
Arnulf of Orléans, 91
Ars Minor (Priscian), and the infinite, 224–225
art, and nominalism, 193 n.50
Ashbery, John, 1, 235
Attic Nights (Aulus Gellius), 79
auctor and *auctores*, 21, 75, 107, 197
auctoritas, 4, 28; and Chaucer, 192, 193 n.51; and Christianity, 37, 41, 42, 56, 66, 83; and *communitas*, 229; definition of, 84; derivation of, 62–63; as an epistemological method, 187; etymology of, 74; form of proof in sermons, 73; a function of intertextuality, 85; literary development of, 34, 116, 197; and Scripture, 62; and time, 74
Auerbach, Erich, 23, 32–33, 132
Augustine, St. (354–430), and absence doctrine, 132; and act of creation, 123; Aquinas influenced by, 150; and autobiography, 9; Chaucer influenced by, 130; on concept of reading, 71–72, 73; and concept of "I", 88; concepts of love, 101–102; and confession, 24; and the *Convivio* (Dante), 7; and cosmology, 52, 113; and Dante and autobiography, 156, 157; and darkened glass image, 226; on dialects, 124; and eloquence, 89; and epistemology of memory, 43; and etymology, 52; on grace, 151; and historicity, 67; and intentionality, 6, 79, 135, 232, 233; on language, 109; and *lekta*, 81, 104, 180; levels of meaning, 129; on lies and falsehood, 103, 111, 181 n.40, 232; and link between reader and maker, 86–87; and Marcabru, 89, 91–92, 94, 101, 111, 115; medieval poets influenced by, 232–233; and *De Mendacio* (Augustine), 181 n.40; and metaphor, 6, 35, 88, 157; and *mundos*, 151; and oneself as example, 8; on Plato's *logos*, 50; and *potentia ordinata*, 181–182; and presence doctrine, 131; on reading, 107; and rhetoric, 42, 80; on Scriptural interpretation, 74, 113; on sight, 149; on signs, 150–151, 161; St. Anthony story influenced, 231; and text and textuality, 35, 51–52, 72, 231; and text as organizing community, 88; and

Index

Thomas of Erfurt, 151; on true things as unteachable, 43; on truth, 12, 42, 116, 159; and unintentionality, 127–128; and will, 12, 113; on words, 78, 123, 182 n.41; *see also specific works*
authority, and individuality in the Middle Ages, 6, 9; *see also* authorship
authorship, 6, 10, 34, 136–137, 165, 173, 200; *see also auctoritas*
authorship trope, and Chaucer, 195, 199; and Dante, 8; and the disciplines, 38; evolution of, 229; and Guillem IX, 10; and Langland, 133, 157; Marcabru, 133; poetics of, 37
autobiography, assumption of, 5 n.4; and Augustine's *Confessions*, 7, 9, 20; and Dante's *Commedia*, 29, 156, 206–207; and fiction and history, 12, 230, 231; and Hoccleve, 41; and Langland and *Piers Plowman*, 172, 205, 209, 213; and logic, 87; nature of, 230–231; and troubadours, 95; and *La Vita Nuova* (Dante), 231
autocitation, beginning of, 40–41; and Chaucer, 5 n.4; and Chrétien, 5 n.4; and Dante, 5 n.4, 135; forms of, 2,3; and *Piers Plowman* (Langland), 234; self-naming, 229; and troubadours, 95; *see also* authorship trope
Averroës (1126–1198), 43, 64, 146
Avicenna (980–1037), 82

B

Bacon, Roger (c.1214–1294), 44, 133
Baker, Donald, 237
Barthes, Roland, 26
Beatrice (Dante: *Commedia*), 207
Beaujour, Michel, 9
Beer, Jeanette, 66
Bellow, Saul, 234
Beloved (Morrison), 235
Benn, Gottfried, 208
Benton, John, 19 n.21
Benveniste, Emile, 26, 230
Berengarius (c.1050–1150), 44, 45, 60, 79
Bernard of Chartres (d. c.1130), 41 n.3, 63, 64
Bernard of Clairvaux (1090–1153), 20
Bernart de Ventadorn (fl.1150–1180), 95, 99–100
Bible, and allegory, 56; *exemplum* in, 74; and textuality, 53, 231–232; and *textus*, 52; *see also* Scripture

biography, and Langland, 207
Blackburn, Paul, 105
Blamires, A., 198
Bloch, Howard, 123
Boccaccio, Giovanni (1313–1375), 117
Boethius (c.480–c.524), and Aristotelianism, 40; and authority of tradition, 66; and Chaucer, 189, 191; and Dante and autobiography, 156; and historicism, 67; and the infinite, 225; and nouns, 161; and predication, 81–82; and Prologue to the *Legend of Good Women* (Chaucer), 174; and translations of Aristotle, 39, 40, 49; *see also specific works*
Bolter, Jay David, 65 n.31
Bonaventure, St. (c.1217–1274), 7
Book (Langland: *Piers Plowman*), 226
book, as metaphor, 50, 122; and Augustine, 157; and Chaucer, 195; Christian theologians' use of, 180 n.37, 226; and Hugh of St. Victor and hand of God, 180; idea and image of, 53, 157, 175–176; and Langland, 175–176; and nominalism, 157
book knowledge, and Prologue to the *Legend of Good Women* (Chaucer), 164
Book of Proverbs (Old Testament), 90
Book of the Duchess (Chaucer), a philosophical inquiry, 182
Booth, Wayne C., 10
Borzi, Italo, 141
Bowers, John, 5 n.4, 11, 174–175, 216, 216 n.88, 217
Boyde, Patrick, 140
Bradwardine, Thomas (1290–1349), 168–169, 182, 239
Brenkman, John, 12
Bronk, William, 1
Buckingham, Thomas, 163
Bunyan, John (1628–1688), 170
Burckhardt, Jakob Christoph (1818–1897), 7, 18, 18 n.19
Burke, Kenneth, 9, 212
Burlin, Robert, 230
Burrow, John A., 15 n.15, 16, 171 n.24, 209
Bynum, Carolyn, 19 n.20

C

canso, and "I", 88; and ideal form, 94; and the individual, 94; and naming, 95;

and obscure language, 94; and truth searched for, 94–95
Canterbury Tales (Chaucer), characters and interiors of, 14, 27; compared with *Pearl* (anon.), 182; compared with *Piers Plowman* (Langland), 182; compared with *Sir Gawain and the Green Knight* (anon.), 182; compared with *Temple of Glas* (Lydgate), 182; and Derrida, 186; dialects in, 124; moved from allegory, 169 n.22, 194; and pilgrimage literature, 83; problems of being a poet in, 10; and textuality, 26; unimpersonated artistry of, 230
Capella, Martianus (fl. late 4th and early 5th century AD), 145–146
caritas, and Augustine, 12
Cassiodorus (c.490–c.585), 119
Categories (Aristotle), 45; Anselm's critique of, 46 n.5; Boethius on, 161; on the indefinite noun, 225; and naming, 39–40
categories, 45, 101, 142
Chanson de Roland, 68, 69, 71, 88
Chartier, Roger, 4
Chartrian debate, 29 n.32
Chaucer, Geoffrey (c.1343–1400), and absence and presence doctrine, 128–129; *Aeneid* (Virgil) named and summarized, 196; his age, 201 n.63; and Alceste, 188; allegory abandoned by, 169, 184, 187 n.42, 198, 199, 202, 226; and alterity, 24; and *auctoritas*, 83, 192, 197; his audience, 203; and Augustine and Aristotle, 130; and authorship trope, 199–200; and autocitation, 5 n.4; and the Bible, 86; and the book as metaphor and image, 175–176, 180, 194, 195; as *compilator*, 197; and Cupid, 188; and daisy worship, 179 n.36; and Dame Julian of Norwich, 202; and Dante, 213; and Dante and Virgil, 198–199; and dreams and dream poems, 11, 176–177, 177–179, 180, 183–184, 194, 215; and experiential reality, 178, 191; and fiction, 10, 185, 201; and *imitatio*, 185; *Heroides* (Ovid) named and summarized, 196; Hoccleve comparison, 41; and individuality, 84; influenced by Augustine's *Confessions*, 124; influenced by Boccaccio, 189–190; influenced by Boethius, 182, 189, 191–192; influenced by William of Ockham, 166–167, 189, 191, 202; influenced by Ovid, 202; and intuitive knowledge, 160; and language theory, 128, 168, 213–214; and literary realism, 168, 178, 184, 191; Macrobius named and summarized, 196; and *makyng*, 181; and *margerite* genre, 194; *Metamorphoses* (Ovid) named and summarized, 196; and mimesis, 184; and naming, 128, 171–172; and narrative, 166; and narrator, 193, 196; and Nature (character), 96 n.14; and nominalism, 168, 182, 183, 189–190, 191, 199; and Ockham, 169 n.21, 188 n.45; and ontology, 189, 203; and the past, 83, 117, 192; and persona, 169, 173, 174, 178, 201 n.63; and philosophy, 166, 184; and poetic material, 6; and the poetics of authorship, 139; and reading, 117; and reason and imagination, 209; and rhetoric trope, 11, 193–194; and Richard Rolle, 202; and salvation and natural acts, 162; as *scriptor*, 197; and self-mocking, 201 n.63; and speech, 127; and Stoicism, 182; and texts, books, and stories, meaning of, 175–176; and textuality versus experience theme, 130, 220; and theology and epistemology, 168; and *traductio*, 192, 193 n.50; and *translatio*, 194; translation, 189, 194, 197–198; and truth, 177, 193, 203, 213–214, 223, 229; and unintentionality, 128; on will, 198; on wit, 198; and word's nature, 78; and writing, 241; *see also specific works*
Chenù, M.-D., 29 n.32, 62–63, 141–142
Chrétien de Troyes (fl.1165–1180), 5 n.4, 14, 26, 41, 64, 88
Christianity, 12, 21, 34, 35, 85
Chrysippus (c.280 BC–c.206), 79
"Ciceronius es, non es Christianus," 67
Civitate, De (Augustine), 140
Cleanness, 202
Clergy (Langland: *Piers Plowman*), 60, 224, 225
Clerk's Tale (Chaucer: *Canterbury Tales*), 124
cloth, and *texo*, 50, 55
Cloud of Unknowing (anon.), 160
Coleman, Janet, 48, 55, 61, 161–162, 205

Colish, Marcia L., 24, 44, 51, 71, 77–78, 80, 103
Commedia (Dante), 1, 4; and absence and presence doctrine, 99, 156; and Aquinas' *Summa Theologiae*, 23; and authorship trope, 8; and autobiography, 29, 156, 231; and discourse, 156–157; and fiction, 231; and formalism, 212–213; and imagination, 209; and individuality as an example, 7–8; and material existence, 142; and naming, 207; and Pauline theme, 153 n.39; and persona, 8; *Piers Plowman* (Langland), contrasted with, 157; as pilgrimage literature, 83; and poet's temporal context, 28; and self-naming, 31; and theology and epistemology, 168; and Thomistic philosophy, 163; Virgil's role in, 41, 156–157; and virtual witnessing, 140, 163; and will, 209; *see also Inferno; Paradisio; Purgatorio*
commemorative communities, 43
communitas and community, 6, 11, 12, 24, 43, 229
Complaint (Hoccleve), 14
compilation, defined, 65
confession, and the individual, 72–73
Confessions (Augustine), 13; and angels and silent syllables, 129; and autobiography, 7, 9, 20, 231; Chaucer influenced by, 124; and eloquence, 89; and faith's profession, 24; and fiction, 87, 231; and the individual, 72–73; and historicism, 87; and language and existence, 49–50; and Marcabru, 102; and martyrdom, 55; and metaphor, 3; and the reader, 86–87; and the word, 123; and world as scroll and skin, 50, 88, 230
Conscience (Langland: *Piers Plowman*), 163, 170, 172, 213, 216
Consolatio (Boethius), 174, 182, 186, 189–190, 190–191
conversion, of Paul, 151
Convivio (Dante), and Augustine, 213; and development of persona, 7; and reason, discourse, and light, 146
Copeland, Rita, 197
Copleston, F. C., 39, 45, 49, 119
Corbiac, Peire de (13th century), 119–120
Corinthians (New Testament), 156
corn (wheat), as symbol and metaphor, 193 n.51

Cosmographia (Silvestris), 1, 4, 55, 56, 57, 84
cosmology, 2, 52, 113
courtly love, and La Comtessa de Dia, 99; and God of Love, 185; and Guillem IX, 102, 104–105, 106; and Marcabru, 102, 104; and *Parliament of Fowls* (Chaucer), 177, 181; and Prologue to the *Legend of Good Women* (Chaucer), 185, 194; and Reinmar von Reuenthal, 98
Cratylus (Plato), 78
creating, act of, 123, 221
Criseyde, Henryson's version of, 186; Shakespeare's version of, 186; in *Troilus and Criseyde* (Chaucer), 220–221
Cropp, Glynnis, 119
Cunningham, Valentine, 17 n.17
Cupid, 178, and Chaucer's corpus, 197; and Chaucer's persona, 188; and imagination, 209–210; and Langland's *Piers Plowman*, 224; and Prologue to the *Legend of Good Women* (Chaucer), 221; and reading, 201; and *Roman de la rose* (de Lorris and de Meun), 195; as a symbol of love, 179; and translation, 180–181, 193 n.51; and *Troilus and Criseyde* (Chaucer), 196; *see also* God of Love (Cupid)
cupiditas, 12
Curtius, Ernst Robert, 7, 40, 41 n.3, 145, 176, 241
Cynewulf (early 9th century), 5 n.4, 131

D

D'Alvernhe, Peire (fl.1150–1180), 99
da Lentino, Giacomo (fl. first half of 13th century), 34
daisy, Alceste resembles, 193; and Prologue to the *Legend of Good Women* (Chaucer), 182, 187 n.42; as a symbol, 179, 193 n.51
Dame Julian of Norwich (1342–d. after 1416), 202
Damian, Peter, St. (1007–1072), 20, 91
Daniel, Arnaut (b. c.1155; fl. 1180–1200), 31–32
Daniel (Old Testament), Jerome's commentary on, 226
Dante Alighieri (1265–1321), 1; and absence doctrine, 33, 135–136, 174; and Adam, 22–23; his age, 207 n.72;

Alceste on, 198–199; and Aquinas, 132, 150, 157, 206; and Augustine, 60, 156, 213; and authorship poetics, 139; and autobiography, 156, 206–207; and autocitation, 5 n.4, 135; and Beatrice, 207; and the Bible, 86; and Boethius, 156; and categories, 142; and the Divine tautology, 213; and dreams, 171, 215; and epistemology, 118, 138, 140, 233; and fiction, 10, 29; and Geffrey of the *Canterbury Tales* (Chaucer), 172–173; himself as an example, 7–8; and historical time, 28, 165; and individuality, 84; and intentionality, 137; and knowing, 152–153; and Langland, 168, 171, 207 n.72; and language study, 20; and linguistic inquiry, 15; and love, 141; and memory, 156; and naming, 174; and *Natureingang*, 212; and *Nichomachean Ethics* (Aristotle), 155; and nouns and pronouns, 33, 45, 231; and ontology, 118, 132; and the past, 83, 117; and persona's development, 7–8, 157, 232; as a pilgrim, 9; and poesis, 156; poetic material of, 6; poetic strategies of, 9; and presence doctrine, 33, 135–136; and reading, 117; and salvation, 170, 206; and self-naming, 32, 131; and sight, 140, 144–145, 148, 149, 153–154; and solipsism of Joyce, 22; and *Summa Theologiae* (Aquinas), 141; and text, 137–138; and texts, books, and stories, meaning of, 175–176; and theology, 163, 168; and truth, 125, 233; Virgil as character, 20; Virgil as literary antecedent, 33, 157; and *virtù*, 140, 145, 150, 154–155; and will, 149; and Will of *Piers Plowman*, 172–173; *see also specific works and characters*
darkened glass (metaphor), 226, 231, 232
de Looze, Laurence, 2–3
de Man, Paul, 12
Decameron (Boccaccio), 189–190
deconstruction, 6
Decretum (Gratian), 65
Delaney, Sheila, 173, 196
Derrida, Jacques, 1, 7, 13, 26, 53, 186
Descartes, René (1596–1650), 22, 24
Deschamps, Eustace (14th century), 125–126, 127, 128–129, 130–131, 182, 194
Dia, La Comtessa de (fl. c.1160), 99
Dialectica, De (Augustine), 51, 78, 82

Dialectica (Garland the Computist), 82
dialectics, 118–120, 124; Corbiac's definition of, 119–120
dialogic discourse theory, 124
dictio, 133
Didascalion (Hugh of St. Victor), 134
différance, and alterity, 18
Dionysius the Pseudo-Areopagite (c.500 AD), 131–132; and absence doctrine, 132; Dante influenced by, 157; and God, 152 n.38; and inharmonious dissimilitudes, 132; and sight, 142
discourse, and allegory, 55, 186; and Dante's *Commedia,* 153, 156–157; and dialectical discourse, 66, 118–119, 124; and dialogic theory, 124; Hugh of St. Victor on, 138–139; and logic, 70; and *modistae,* 146; and presence doctrine, 146; and text and book image, 157; and truth, 51
dispositio, 93, 118–119
Dit du Vergier (Machaut), 182
Divine tautology, 9, 213
Doctrina Christiana, De (Augustine), 71–72, 78; and eloquence, 89; and exegetical tradition, 88; and *lekta,* 80; and Marcabru, 101–102, 115; and obscurity, 92; and signs, 127, 131; and words, 182 n.41
Donatus, Aelius (fl. mid–4th century), 40, 64
Dowel, Dobet and Dobest (Langland: *Piers Plowman*), 59, 213–219, 234; and Clergy, 224–225; definition of, 225; Langland coined terms, 170; and salvation, 221; and Will, 213; and writing, 225–226
dream poems, 11, 172 n.25, 163, 188, 191, 193; *see also* dream vision genre
dream vision genre, and allegory, 186–187; and Chaucer, 97, 176–179, 180, 193–194, 215; and Dante, 215; defined, 125, 182; and *Dit du Vergier* (Machaut), 182; and Langland, 171, 202; and *Lay de Franchise* (Deschamps), 182; and *Paradys d'Amours* (Froissart), 182; and the *Parliament of Fowls* (Chaucer), 184; and *Piers Plowman* (Langland), 204, 221; and Prologue to the *Legend of Good Women* (Chaucer), 187; *see also* dream poems

dreams and dreaming, and Alceste, 195; and Chaucer, 97, 176, 183–184, 215; and Dante, 215; and Langland, 204; and Langland's Will, 41, 170–171, 172, 226–227; and Marcabru, 171; and naming, 171; and the reader, 221; and reality, 195
Dronke, Peter, 31, 49, 57, 237
Duns Scotus (1265–1308), 167, 199–200
"dwarves on the shoulders of giants," 41, 41 n.3, 63, 86

E

Eckhardt, Caroline, 195
Economou, George, 141 n.19, 208, 209, 215–216
Edward I, king of England (1239–1307), 52
Edwards, Robert R., 11, 18, 164
Einbildungskraft (Kant), 22
"En cest sonet coind'e leri" (Daniel), 31–32
engenderment, 32, 79
ens, and *modistae,* 133–134, 137
Entheticus (John of Salisbury), 112
epistemology, and allegory, 161; and *auctoritee,* 187; and Chaucer, 168–169; and Dante, 118, 138, 140, 168, 233; and dream poems, 163; and Langland, 138, 168, 233; and literacy, 159; and Marcabru, 138; and nominalism, 181–182; and ontology, 121; and *Parliament of Fowls* (Chaucer), 177; and theology, 168
Erasmus, Desiderius (1466–1536), 66
Erec et Enide (Chrétien de Troyes), 14, 15, 20, 68
essence, concept of, existence distinguished from, 38; and *modistae,* 137; and Ockham, 39; and Siger of Courtrai, 133–134
esthetic realism, 203
Estrich, Robert, 194
Etymologarium sive Originum Libri XX (Isidore of Seville), 65, 113, 241
etymology, and Augustine, 52; and Isidore of Seville, 65, 113, 241; and Stoicism, 54; of reading and writing, 74–76
Eucharist controversy, 79
exempla and *exemplum,* 24, 73, 218
existence, 38–39

experience, and Chaucer, 168–169, 178, 198, 220; and Cupid (God of Love), 180; and language, 49–50; and the *Legend of Good Women* (Chaucer), 164; and literacy, 130; and textuality, 52; and truth, 200

F

fable, 12, 15
faith, and sight, 143
Ferrante, Joan, 95, 144 n.24
fiction, and allegory, 164, 220; and Augustine's *Confessions,* 231; and autobiography, 12, 230–231; book of culture different from, 117; and Chaucer, 10, 185, 201; and Dante, 10, 29, 117, 231; definition of, 63; development toward, 15–16 n.15, 22, 43, 87; and Guillem IX, 10; and history, 6, 37, 121, 230–231, 233; and Langland, 10, 164, 165–166; and Marcabru, 10; and names, 230; and narrative poetry, 125; and nominalism, 201–202; and parable, 220; and poetry, 11; and romance epics, 69–70; and signification, 85; and textuality, 122–123; and *La Vita Nuova* (Dante), 231
fin' amors, 101–102 n.18; and Marcabru, 116
Finke, Laurie, 204, 219, 221, 223
Finnegans Wake (Joyce), 22
Fletcher, Angus, 184–185, 199–200 n.58
flos florum, 31, 237; *see also* Alceste; daisy
flower, as symbol and metaphor, 31, 193 n.51, 237; *see also flos florum*
Folkenflik, Robert, 231
form, discussion of, 189–192
Form of Perfect Living (Rolle), 202–203
formalism, 14, 96–97, 212–213
Foucault, Michel, 3–4, 5–6, 173
Fourth Lateran Council (1215), 72
Frank, Robert, 185, 194
Franklin's Tale (Chaucer: *Canterbury Tales*), 183
Franciscan tradition, and minstrelsy, 208
Freccero, John, 7, 8, 212–213
Fredegisius of Tours (d. 834), 49
Friar's Tale (Chaucer: *Canterbury Tales*), 190
frog, used by Marcabru, 91; *see also Metamorphoses* (Ovid)

Froissart, Jean (c.1333–1400/01), 182, 194
Frye, Northrop, 186
Fumagalli, Maria, 58 n.21

G

Garland the Computist (fl. c.1040), 82
Geffrey (Chaucer's persona), and allegory, 14, 122, 176; in *Canterbury Tales*, 173; and Chaucer's narrator-poet, 10; and Chaucer's system of beliefs, 160; comical, 41; creation of, 14; and Dante, 172–173; and dream vision, 173; and experience, 198; in *House of Fame*, 173, 196; and Langland's Will, 172–173, 176; and Ockham, 200; as persona, 13; and psychology, 14; in *Troilus and Criseyde*, 173; and writing, 197
Gellius, Aulus (first century), 79
Gellrich, Jesse, 52, 86, 122–123, 195; on divine meanings, 132; on the *modistae*, 139; on the past, 117, 124–125; on Thomas of Erfurt, 134, 139
gender criticism, 6
Geneologia Deorum, De (Boccaccio), 117
genera, and grammar, 40, 45
Genesis (Old Testament), 217
geography, and myth and history, 56
Gerson, Jean, 2
Gilby, Thomas, 58 n.21
Gilson, Etienne, 35
gloss, etymology of, 74
Glossa ordinaria (Huguccio), 65
God, active presence of, 97; and allegory, 222; and Anselm, 45–46; Augustine's relationship with, 181–182, 231; Dionysius on manner of revelation, 152 n.38; Fredegisius on, 49; and freedom in world of necessity, 167; and grace, 160; knowledge comes with his assistance, 23–24; logical analysis to understand, 167–168; and Marcabru, 115; Ockham on, 192, 200; and *Piers Plowman* (Langland), 212; and self, 166–167
God of Love (Cupid), and Alceste, 179 n.39; and allegory, 185; and courtly love, 185; and dream vision, 193; and esthetic problem of Chaucer, 192; and language, 183; and nominalism, 193; and ontology, 189; and reading, 195; and *Romaunt of the Rose* (Chaucer), 179–180; and translation, 180, 192–193; and *Troilus and Criseyde* (Chaucer), 179–180; *see also* Cupid
Goddard, R. N. B., 112 n.31
Godzich, Wlad, 43, 62, 70, 94
Goldin, Frederick, 13, 43, 43 n.4, 76 n.38, 90, 91 n.5, 94, 98 n.16, 109 n.27, 146 n.27
Gordon, David J., 231
Gorgias (Plato), 75
Gower, John (1330–1408), 173
grace, and Aquinas, 143; and Augustine, 151; and doctrine, 168; and God, 160; Holcot on attainment of, 162; a natural act, 162; and reconciliation, 163; and will, 169
Gracián, Baltasar (1601–1658), 146
grammar, and Abelard, 58; and allegory, 71; and Abbo of Fleury, 44; and accident, 40, 45; and Anselm, 42; and author and text, 34; and class, 40; definition of, 71; and Foucault, 4; and history, 28; and John of Salisbury, 128; and Langland, 28, 71, 205–206; and Latin, 49; and logic, 2, 45, 59, 71, 121; and metaphysics, 45; and *moderni*, 161; and nouns and pronouns, 30, 40; and Ockham, 167; and *Piers Plowman* (Langland), 61, 212, 214–215, 234; and poetry, 134; and poets, 37; and scholasticism, 49; and science, 45, 82; and Thomas of Erfurt, 135; and truth, 49, 212, 225; and world view, 58
Grammatica Speculativa (Thomas of Erfurt), 134
Grammatico, De (Anselm), 9, 45–46
grammaticus, 46 n.5
Gratian (359–383), 65
great chain of being, 94
Greek (language), 48
Greenblatt, Stephen, 16 n.15, 20
Greetham, David, 14, 41
Griffiths, Lavinia, 159, 165, 170
group, distinguished from individual, 121
Guibert of Nogent (c.1053–1124), 20
Guido delle Collonne (13th century), 20
Guillem IX (1071–1127), and alterity, 24; and Anselm, 103, 106; and author, 229; and authorship trope, 10; and courtly love, 102, 104–107; and erotic love, 105–107; and fiction, 10; and finishing term, 75; and language-as-object, 10, 79; and language's possibilities, 110–

111; and Marcabru, 109; and naming, 108; and poetic material, 6; poetry reflected on, 108–109; and *rectitude*, 106; and romanticized love, 89; and textual communities, 76

H

Hamilton, Marie, 239–240
Hanning, Robert, 74
Hans, James, 21, 155
Harrowing of Hell (Langland: *Piers Plowman* episode), 226
Harvey, Ruth E., 90 n.3, 101, 111–112 n.31, 114–115
Harwood, Britton J., 159, 210, 210 n.79
Hathaway, Neil, 65
Hegel, Georg Friedrich Wilhelm (1770–1831), 18
Heidegger, Martin, 35, 281
Heinrich von Morungen (d.1222), 97, 199
Heroides (Ovid), 196
Herzog (Bellow), 234
Hilary of Poitiers, St. (315–367), 119
Hildegard, St. (1098–1179), 57
Hill, John M., 10
Hippocrates (c.460–c.377 BC), 181 n.39
Historia Destructionis Troiae (Guido delle Collone), 20
historical, consciousness, 18; criticism, 6; perspective, 25; time, 165
historicism, 16, 17 n.17; and the *Aeneid* (Virgil), 67; and Augustine, 67; and Boethius, 67; emergence of, 87
historiography, 17, 24–25, 64, 67, 70–71; emergence of, 43; and *Erec et Enide* (Chrétien de Troyes), 68
history, definition of, 63; and dialectical discourse, 66; and consciousness, 18, 125; and criticism, 6; and *exemplum*, 73; and fiction, 6, 36, 121, 230, 233; and Hegel, 18; and imaginative literature, 187 n.44; and Langland and redemption, 207; linear and empirically grounded, 69; and logic, 66; and myth, 48; nature of, 161; perspective, 25; and time, 165; *see also hystoria*
Hoccleve, Thomas (1360–c.1430), 14, 41
Holcot, Robert (d.1349), 104, 159, 182; and grace, 162; and humanity, 192; and Langland, 168, 209; and nominalist-realist debate, 168–169; Ockham influenced, 192; and poetry's nature, 239; and religious orthodoxy, 163

Holley, Linda Tarte, 140 n.17
Holloway, Julia Bolton, 83, 241
Holy Trinity, 44, 132–133, 167, 212
Homer, 132
homo interior, 19 n.20, 27 n.30
Homo Ludens (Huizinga), 117–118
Horace (65–8 BC), 96 n.14, 181 n.39, 193
House of Fame (Chaucer), 127, 173, 180, 196, 238–240
Howard, Donald, 230
Hugh of St. Victor (1096–1141), and language and word of God, 134; and Marcabru, 119; and presence and discourse, 138–139; and a world text, 180, 180 n.37, 194; and writing as reading, 181
Huguccio (12th century), 65
Huizinga, Johan, 117–118
Hult, David F., 10, 104
humanism, 15, 16
humanitas, 20
humilitas, 41
Hunger (Langland: *Piers Plowman*), 226
husk and seed (metaphor), 55
hypersign, persona as, 10
hystoria, 43

I

"I," and Augustine, 88; emergence of, 86–87; false in love, 108; and Langland, 213; and Marcabru, 116; and self, 26; use of, 230; and *voluntas* in *Piers Plowman*, (Langland), 216; as a witness, 163–164
idea, 50–51, 142
ideal form, 94, 96–97
ideality, discussion of, 189–192
imagination, and Chaucer, 210; and Dante, 148, 209; and Langland, 209, 216
Imaginative (Langland: *Piers Plowman*), 209–212
imitatio, 117, 185
individuality, 16, 25; and alterity, 27; and authority in the Middle Ages, 9; distinguished from group, 121; emergence of, 18–19, 69, 87–88, 166, 229; group distinguished from, 121; and logic, 70; and Marcabru, 118; and the past, 64; and *Piers Plowman* (Langland), 162; and salvation, 168; and self-naming, 229; and textual

communities, 74; and troubadours, 95–97
individuum, 19 n.21
Inferno (Dante: *Commedia*), 29
Ingredientibus (Abelard), 58
inharmonious dissimilitudes, 132
Instituto oratorio (Quintilian), 51
integumentum, 55, 88
intellectus universalium, 58
intelligens, 133–134, 137
intention naturalis, 12
intentionality, Anselm on, 137; Anselm's and Augustine's conception of, 104; Augustine on, 135, 232–233; and Dante, 137; Gellius' views on, 79; and Langland, 233; and Marcabru, 137
inter–/intratextual strategy, 88
interiority, 14, 27
interpres, 74
Interpretatione, De (Aristotle), 40
intertextuality, 22, 85
intuitive knowledge, 160, 163, 195
Inventione, De (Aristotle), 92 n.7, 93
involucrum, 55
"io sol uno" trope, 28–29, 32
Isidore of Seville, St. (c.560–636), 64–66, 102, 113, 128, 241
Isocrates (436–338 BC), 112

J

Jerome, St. (c.340–420), 66, 67, 115, 195, 226
Jesus Christ, 31, 56–57
Joachim of Flora (1130/35–1201/02), 57
joglar, 41, 88, 91, 97, 110
John of Salisbury (1115/20–1180), 66, 112–113, 128
Jolivet, Jean, 58 n.21
Jordan, Robert M., 230
Joyce, James (1882–1941), 22, 235
Justman, Stewart, 190–191, 190 n.47

K

Kamowski, William, 168 n.19
Kane, George, 16 n.15, 125
Kant, Immanuel (1724–1804), 22
Kay, Sarah, 5 n.4, 11, 28
Kendrick, Laura, 47, 88 n.49, 102
Kermode, Frank, 161
Kiser, Lisa, 185, 192
Knight's Tale (Chaucer: *Canterbury Tales*), 180

knowing and knowledge, and Aquinas, 141–142, 150–151; Chaucer's search for, 181, 193, 209; and Dante, 152–153; and God's assistance, 23–24; and imagination, 209; and Langland, 206; and Langland's Will, 222; and literature as a means to, 177; and *moderni,* 163; and *Parliament of Fowls* (Chaucer), 181; and *Retraction* to the *Canterbury Tales,* 200–201; and text and book, 157
Kretzman, Norman, 30, 81
Kristeva, Julia, 22

L

Lacan, Jacques, 14
Langland, William (c.1332–c.1400), and absence doctrine, 203; and abstraction, 170; and Aquinas, 211; and allegory, 61, 164, 171, 186, 234; and alterity, 24; and Anselm, 211; and Augustine, 222; and authorship trope, 133; and autobiography, 213; and Bible, 86, 217–218; and biography, 207; and Chaucer, 221, 234; on conscience, 213, 216; and Dante, 171, 207 n.72; and dream narrator, 11; and dreams, 170–171; and epistemology, 138, 204, 233; *exempla* used, 218; and faith, 149; and fiction, 10, 164; and God's minstrel, 209; and grammar, 28, 61, 205–206; and history, 207; and Holcot, 168, 206; and individuality, 84; and intentionality, 233; Jerome influenced, 226; and language, 165–166, 222–223; and linear narrative, 61; and linguistic inquiry, 15; and literary signature, 130–131; and logic, 205; and Longe Wille, 174; and miracles, 216–217; and *modistae,* 157; and *moderni,* 157; and naming, 156, 170; and narration, 165–166; and nominalism, 170, 193 n.50; and nouns and pronouns, 135–136, 170; and Ockham, 157, 158, 166–167, 168, 206; and the past, 117; past broken with, 83; and persona, 206, 219; and personification, 164, 170; and poetic material, 6; poetry making discussed, 170, 214, 218; and *potentia ordinata,* 213; and presence doctrine, 157, 203; pseudonym, 5 n.4; and realism, 170; on reason, 213; and salvation, 137, 162, 206–207, 222; and self-assertion, 232; and self-awareness, 172; and self-

cancellation poetics, 202–203; and self-naming, 131, 204; and theology, 168; and text poetics, 125, 137–138; and texts and books image, 157, 175–176; and truth, 61, 203, 211, 234; and will, 205–206, 209, 233; and Wyclif, 168; *see also specific characters*
language, 30; Anselm's conception of, 109, 115–116, 159, 232; Augustine's conception of, 109; being distinguished from, 121; and Chaucer, 166, 213; and Christian tradition, 203; and discourse, 6; discrete from its user, 9; efficacy of in *Piers Plowman* (Langland), 203, 212; and experience, 49–50; futility of, 13, 51, 222–223; and God of Love, 183; and Guillem IX, 10; and Holcot, 159; and intentionality, 79; and Langland, 165–166, 206, 216, 222–223, 234; and *lekta*, 80; and Marcabru, 113, 212; and *moderni*, 163; and nominalism, 159; and Ockham, 159; and ontology, 130; philosophy of, 166; reality structured through, 167; and salvation, 206; society tied together through, 109; and speech, 59; and text, 50; and thought separate, 66; and troubadours, 113, 232; and truth, 104, 202, 213, 234; and world separate from, 53
Latin (language), 45, 49, 59, 133
Lawlor, John, 230
Lawton, David, 11
Lay de Franchise (Deschamps), 182
Le Goff, Jacques, 24, 72–73
legend genre, 185
Legend of Good Women (Chaucer), 173, 192
lego, 65 n.31
Leicester, H. Marshall, 26, 186
lekta, and Anselm, 103–104; and Augustine, 80–81; Stoic theory of, 78–80, 103
Letter on Nothing and Darkness (Fredegisius of Tours), 49
Leys d'amor, 119
Liber Figurarum (Joachim of Flora), 57
Liberum Arbitrium (Langland: *Piers Plowman*), 216, 219
lies, 103, 111, 181 n.40
Lindberg, David C., 140 n.17
linguistics, 43–44, 75, 95, 162
links (verb), 75

literacy, and allegory, 56; and Anselm, 162; and Aquinas, 43–44; and Augustine, 95; and *Chanson de Roland*, 68; and Chaucer and individual authorship, 195; and commemorative communities, 43; and epistemology, 159; experience versus, 130; and individuality, 12; and logic, 43, 232; mobility encouraged through, 48; and orality, 35, 42–43; and political power, 68–69; and secular authorship, 76; societal change caused and reflected by, 70; and speaker, 9; and textual communities, 43; and textuality, 122; and writer, 9
literary individuality, 11–12
literary reality, 178
literary signature, 27–28, 130–131
literature culture, 73, 189, 192
littera, 95
logic, and Abelard, 81; and allegory, 55; and Anselm, 42; and autobiography, 87; and discourse, 70; and grammar, 45, 59, 71, 121; and history, 66; and Langland, 205; and *lekta*, 80; and literacy, 70, 232; and literate societies, 43; and *moderni*, 161; and Ockham, 159, 194–195, 200; and reading, 62; and self-naming, 84; and sermocinal science, 82; and Stoicism, 104; and theology, 162; and writing, 62
logica nova, 49
logico-empirical mode of thought, 48
logology, defined, 212–213
logos, and allegory, 194; and humanity, 54; and Langland's *Piers Plowman*, 220; verbal, 54
love, Augustine's concept of, 101–102; and Chaucer, 179; and Dante, 141; and erotic, 183; and false, 108; and Guillem IX, 106–107; and Marcabru, 93, 102, 115, 118, 120; self-consciousness, 13; *see also amars; amor courtois; amors; courtly love; fin' amors*
Lucifer (Langland: *Piers Plowman*), 222–223
Luke (New Testament), 204 n.68
lyrics, 11, 28, 90

M

Machaut, Guillaume de (c.1300–1377), 182, 194

Macrobius, Ambrosius Theodosius (fl. c.AD 400), 94, 182
Magistro, De (Augustine), 43
makyng, and Chaucer, 96, 181; and Dowel, Dobet and Dobest, 215; and Langland, 214; and Langland's Will, 209; and ontology, 187; and *Parliament of Fowls* (Chaucer), 96; and world text, 195
Male Regle, La (Hoccleve), 41
Malone, Kemp, 184, 237–238, 240
Maloney, Thomas, 44–45
Man of Law's Tale (Chaucer: *Canterbury Tales*), 173, 196, 200
Mandelbaum, Allen, 22, 23 n.25, 31, 32, 33, 144, 148 n.28, 156, 224–225
Mann, Jill, 164, 167, 211–212
Marcabru (1129–1150), and absence doctrine, 99–100; and alterity, 24; and *amars,* 91, 102, 139; and "Amics Marchabrun, car digam," 119; and *amors,* 102, 139; and Anselm, 111; Aristotle not favored by, 93; and Augustine, 89, 91–92, 94, 101, 102, 111, 115; on authorship, 95; and authorship trope, 133; and autobiography, 95; and autocitation, 3; and Bible, 86, 90; and categories, 101; Cicero influenced, 92–93; and courtly love, 102, 104; and dialectics, 118–119; and dreams and dreaming, 171; on eloquence, 110; and epistemology, 138; and fiction, 10; and *fin' amors,* 101–102 n.18, 116; and gloss used, 90–91; and God, 115; and Guillem IX, 109; and Hugh of St. Victor, 119; and individuality, 84, 118; and intentionality, 137; and Isidore of Seville, 102; and *joglars,* 41; and knowing, 149–150; and Langland, 137; and language, 79, 94, 110–111, 113, 212; and light image, 146; and linguistic inquiry, 15; and literate world, 116; and love, 89, 90–91, 93, 100, 115, 118, 120, 139; and lying, 103; metapoetical, 35; and naming, 156; on nature, 93–94, 114; and nouns and pronouns, 116, 135–136; and oral world, 116; and philosophical order, 111; and Plato, 93; and poetic material, 6; on poetry's efficacy, 233; and presence doctrine, 99, 139; and *razos,* 116–117; and the reader, 115; and rhetoric, 118–119; and salvation, 170, 206; and scholasticism, 93–94; and self-assertion, 232; and self-naming, 131; and text, 88, 125, 137–138; and *trobar naturau,* 112, 112 n.31, 119; and truth, 115–116, 233; and voice, 110; and will, 149–150; and work of others, 91; and the world's language, 113
margerite genre, 30–31, 179, 194, 237
Marriage of Mercury and Philology, The (Capella), 145–146
martyrdom, 55
material experience, 177
Matthew (New Testament), 153
Mazzeo, Joseph, 190 n.47
Mazzotta, Giuseppe, 29 n.32, 156
McClellan, William, 124
medieval life, and authority, 6; and community, 12; and group consciousness, 7; and historical consciousness, 18; and individuality, 18–19; and the mind and symbols, 190; and poetry, 20–21; and scholarship, 6; and *vanitas terrestris,* 7
medieval scholarship (overview), 6
memoria, 74
memory, culture of, 72–73; and Dante, 156; epistemology of, 43; and Prologue to the *Legend of Good Women* (Chaucer), 178, 187; and writing, 50–51
Mendacio, De (Augustine), 181 n.40
Metalogicon (John of Salisbury), 64, 112, 128
Metamorphoses (Ovid), frog from used by Marcabru, 91, 196
metaphors (books, reading, texts, and writing), 85, 121, 122; darkened glass, 226; husk and seed, 55; mirror, 13, 52, 94, 113, 156, 167; plough, 204, 204–205 n.66, 223–224, 241–242; scroll, 50, 230; *translatio,* 51; veil, 52; word, 12; world as text, 6, 194–195
metaphysics, 2, 45, 140
Metaphysics (Aristotle), 140
metatextuality, 122
Middleton, Anne, 27–28, 60 n.24, 130 n.5, 163–165, 170, 171, 174, 207, 209, 214–215, 224–225, 230
Migiel, Marilyn, 153, 155
Miller, Jacqueline T., 63
Mills, David, 60
mimesis, 184
Minnesänger, 97

Minnis, A. J., 7, 63, 75
minstrelsy, 208–209
miracles, 216–217
mirror, as metaphor, 12, 13, 52, 94, 113, 156, 167
moderni, 160, 161, 162, 163, 220
Modis Significandi (Gerson), 2
modism, 30
modistae, 82, 133, 137, 146, 157, 160
"Molti amadori la lor malatia" (da Lentino), 34
Monologion (Anselm), 45
Moody, Ernest, 159–160
moral exhortation, literature of, 18
Morris, Colin, 19
Morrison, Toni, 235
mundos, 151, 151 n.34
Murphy, James J., 119
Muscatine, Charles, 230
myth, 48, 55, 56, 57, 117

N

names, and Anselm, 45–46; and Dante's *La Vita Nuova*, 187; and fiction, 230; and *joglars*, 41; and Langland's *Piers Plowman*, 159; and *moderni*, 160; and *nomen*, 38; and Ockham, 200; and poetic authority, 41–42; and words, 187
naming, and absence doctrine, 99; act of, 38; and Peire D'Alvernhe, 99; and Anselm, 9; and *canso*, 95; and Chaucer, 128, 171–172, 173, 203; and La Comtessa de Dia, 99; and Dante, 9, 207; and Deschamps, 128; and dreams, 171; and Guillem IX, 108; and Langland, 136, 156, 170, 171, 203, 207; and Marcabru, 139, 156; methods of, 125; and Ockham, 9; and poet's self-evaluation, 98; and presence doctrine, 99; and Reinmar von Reuenthal, 98; and troubadours, 86, 135; and truth, 203
narrative, 3, 13, 24, 61, 69, 125, 164–166
narrator, 3, 11, 125, 164, 173, 193, 196, 231
natural act and law, 135, 162, 168
naturaliter, 133, 159
nature, 93–94, 114, 134, 159
Natureingang, 212
Neaman, Judith S., 140 n.17
Neoplatonism, 94
Newton, Sir Isaac, (1642–1727), 159–160
Nichomachaen Ethics (Aristotle), 155
nomen, 56–57

nominalism, 45, 97; and Abelard, 161; and Anselm, 159; and Aristotle, 161; and art, 193 n.50; and Boethius' *Consolatio*, 186; and book as symbol, 157; and Bradwardine, 168–169; and causality, 200; and Chaucer, 168, 182, 183, 189–190, 191, 199; and fiction, 201–202; and God of Love, 193; and historicization, 125; and Holcot, 168–169; and Langland, 170; and language, 159, 193 n.50; and *lekta*, 104; and narratology, 125; and nature, 159; nominalist-realist debate, 30; and Ockham, 79, 157, 160, 168–169, 189; and ontology, 162; and poetic material, 6; and *potentia ordinata*, 181; and reading, 195; and Strode, 168–169; *traductio*, 180; and will, 200; and wit, 200; the word's nature, 77; and Wyclif, 168–169
noun, and Abelard, 58; and Abbo of Fleury, 44; and Anselm, 45–46, 160; and Aristotle, 161; and Berengarius, 44; and Boethius, 161; concept of, 38; and and Dante, 45; and grammar, 40; and Langland's *Piers Plowman*, 161; and *moderni*, 160; and *modistae*, 160; and ontology, 9, 160–161; and Peter of Spain, 161; as a real entity, 49; Siger of Courtrai, 134; and text's author, 10; and Thomas of Erfurt, 133
novel, 13–14

O

obscurity doctrine, 93
Occitan (language), 113
Ockham, *see* William of Ockham
Odyssey (Homer), 132
Officis, De (Cicero), 112
Olson, David R., 5 n.4
Omeros (Walcott), 234
On His Temptations and Writings (Otloh of Saint Emmeram), 20
Ong, Walter, 30, 62, 65 n.30, 142
ontology, and Aquinas, 38; and Augustine, 52, 81; and Chaucer, 189, 203; and Dante, 118, 132; and epistemology, 121; and God of Love, 189; and language, 81, 130; and the literary act, 181; and love poetry, 28; and Marcabru, 102; and medieval poetry, 83, 138, 144; and nominalism, 162; and the noun, 9, 160–161; and

reality's expression, 117; and semantics, 30; and textual communities, 43; and words, 74, 78, 171, 182, 187, 189
Oppenheimer, Paul, 34
oral culture, 40, 73, 88, 233
orality, and literacy, 26, 35, 42–43, 61, 68, 197
Otloh of Saint Emmeram, 20
Ovid (43 BC–AD 17), 12, 91, 102 n.18, 194, 202
Owen, Charles, 10

P

Pacience (Langland: *Piers Plowman*), 219
pagan world, 86
palinode, 194
parable, 220
Paradiso (Dante: *Commedia*), 22, 141, 147, 148, 154–155, 157
Paradys d'Amours (Froissart), 182
parchment, and *texo*, 55
Paris arts faculty, papal condemnation of (1277), 167
Parliament of Fowls (Chaucer), 27, 177, 181, 184–185, 193
pars orationis, 133
partimen, 119–120
past, poetic use of, 41, 86, 118
Paterson, Linda, 89, 92, 93, 94, 110, 111 n.31
Patterson, Lee, 12, 17, 18, 67, 69, 71–72, 166, 179, 207
Paul, St. (10–c.62), and conversion, 151; as Dante's historical antecedent, 33, 157; and darkened glass, 226, 232; and distorted mirror, 156; poets influenced by, 232–233; as Saul, 152, 152 n.35; and semiological consciousness, 23; and sight, 154; and text, 231; and world as a text, 6
Payne, Robert O., 127, 128, 179, 187, 188–189, 237, 239–240
Pearl (anon.), 160, 182, 202
Pearsall, Derek, 136 n.12
Peck, Russell, 183, 189
"Per savi·l tenc ses doptanssa" (Marcabru), 118–119, 139
Perihermenias (Aristotle, Boethius' translation), 49
persona, Chaucer's development of, 169, 169 n.22, 173, 174, 178, 183, 186; and Dante, 7, 174; and dream poems, 191; emergence of, 13, 230; and fictionality, 235; a hypersign, 10; and Langland's Will, 157, 174, 234–235; a mirror image, 13; modern literary, 2, 228, 234–235
personification, and allegory, 159 n.1, 161, 238; and Langland, 164, 170; and *Pilgrim's Progress* (Bunyan), 170; and *Roman de la Rose* (de Lorris and de Meun), 170
Peter of Elia, 44
Peter of Limoge (13th century), 140
Peter of Spain (c.1271–1276), 161
Peter the Lombard (c.1095–1160), 65
Petrarch, Francesco (1304–1374), 14
Phaedrus (Plato), 50, 117
Philosophia prima (Avicenna), 82
philosophy, and Chaucer, 184; disciplines separate from, 1; and *moderni*, 161–162; and persona, 27; and poetry, 1–2, 3, 37; and self-naming, 83; and subjectivity, 166; and theology, 38, 40, 168
Piers Plowman (Langland), and allegory, 159, 161, 182, 212, 213–214, 215, 226; and animation, 171; and authorial signature, 165; and autobiography, 172, 209; and autocitation, 234; and book metaphor, 226; and Chaucer's Cupid, 224; and Christ, 222, 223; and conscience, 163, 172; and Dante's *Commedia*, 157; deconstructed, 122; and dreams and dreaming, 11, 172, 204, 221, 226–227; engendered language, 79; and epistemology, 233; and experience, 58; and God, 121; and grammar, 71, 84, 211, 214–215; and Harrowing of Hell episode, 226; and Hunger, 226; and the individual, 162; innovative, 202; and interiority, 14; and language, 58, 79, 104, 203, 212; and logic, 71; and *Logos,* 220; and Lucifer, 222, 223; and memory, 178; and metaphor, 211; and minstrelsy, 208; and names and naming, 136, 159, 171, 207; and narrator, 11; and natural law, 168; and nouns and pronouns, 159, 161; and Pacience, 219; and pardon destruction, 223; and personification, 170; and pilgrimage, 83, 157, 215, 219, 226; and Plato, 218; and plough metaphor, 241; and poetry's nature, 204; and *potentia absoluta,* 212; and *potentia ordinata,*

212; and readership appeal, 203; and *rectitude,* 210; and rhetoric, 218; and salvation, 157, 223, 204; and scholasticism, 214–215; and self-interpretation, 222; and self-naming, 234; and self-reflexivity, 204; and signification, 217–218; and speech, 59; and structuralism, 203; and textuality, 61; and theology, 163; and understanding, 207; and *voluntas* and will, 35, 137, 200, 204, 207, 216; and waking state, 172; *see also specific characters*
Pilgrim's Progress (Bunyan), 170
pilgrim and pilgrimage, 9, 83, 202, 207, 215, 216, 219, 226
plagiarism, 65, 65 n.30
Plato (c.427–c.348 BC), and allegory, 170; and Bernard, 57; and Dante, 157; and eloquence, 89; and ideal form, 50, 96–97; ; and illusion, 117; and imitation, 117and *logos,* 50; and Marcabru, 93; in *Piers Plowman* (Langland), 218; and sight, 142; and text, 231; and world as text, 6; *see also specific works*
plough metaphor, 204, 204–205 n.66, 241–242; and Chaucer, 241; and Langland's *Piers Plowman,* 223–224, 241; and *Roman de la rose* (de Lorris and de Meun), 241
Plowman from Bohemia, The (von Saaz), 242
poesis, 130, 156
poetic, fiction, 66; imagination, 144; license, 63, 65–67
poetics of authorship, 3, 7, 13, 139
poetics of self-cancellation, 203
poetics of the text, 125
poetry, and fiction, 11; function and consequence of, 233; and grammar, 134; and Langland's *Piers Plowman,* 170, 179, 204, 218; and language, 47; and Marcabru, 233; medieval, 20; and ontology, 138; and philosophy, 1, 3, 37; Renaissance definition of, 20
Porphyry, Malchus (c.234–305), 101
Posidonius (c.135–c.51 BC), 112
post-structuralism, 21, 23, 25
potentia absoluta and *ordinata,* and Augustine, 181–182; and Chaucer, 181–182; and 14th century world view, 167; and Langland's *Piers Plowman,* 212, 213; and Ockham, 200

Pound, Ezra, 155
predication, 82
Prelude (Wordsworth), 22
presence, doctrine of, and Aquinas, 132; and *auctoritas,* 229; and Augustine, 131; and Dante, 33, 135–136; and Dionysius, 132; and discourse, 146; and God, 224; and Homer, 132; and Hugh of St. Victor, 138–139; and Langland, 157, 203, 224; and Marcabru, 99, 139; and medieval philosophy, 121; and *modistae,* 146; and nouns and pronouns, 137, 138; and self-naming, 174; and Thomas of Erfurt, 134
Priscian (fl. c.500), 30
Prologue to the *Legend of Good Women* (Chaucer), and Alceste, 30–31, 173, 199, 237; and allegory, 169 n.22, 234, 238–239; and analogy, 191; and authorial intention, 200; and Boethius, 174; and book knowledge, 164; and communication, 202; and courtly love, 185; Cupid's role in, 185, 195, 221; and daisy, 182; and Dante, 198–199; and dreams and dreaming, 184, 187, 204; and esthetic realism, 203; and experience, 164, 177–178; G version, 196; and intuitive knowledge, 160, 163; and knowledge through literature, 177; and language, 103; and memory, 187; and misreading Chaucer, 197; and narratorial role, 188; and palinode, 194; and persona, 196; and perversion of skill, 181; and self-naming, 173–174; and *senex amans,* 201; and translation, 195–196; and verbal expression, 197; and waking state, 172; and witness figure, 163; and words, 190
pronoun, and Abbo of Fleury, 44; and Berengarius, 44; and Dante, 30, 33, 45, 133, 136; and Langland, 136; and Marcabru, 135, 136; and ontology, 160–161; and presence doctrine, 138; and Thomas of Erfurt, 134, 136, 137
proper noun, 10, 45, 47, 135, 137, 159, 170
proprietas, 39, 134, 138
Provençal songs, 5 n.4
pun, 41
Purgatorio (Dante: *Commedia*), 32–33; and Aquinas 150–151, 157; and Aristotle, 157; and Augustine, 157; and Dionysius, 157; and discourse, 153–

154; and imaginative experience, 148; and natural knowledge, 143; and Paul, 157; and Plato, 157; and poetic limitations, 155; and pride, 155; and reason, 153; and sight and light, 140–141, 147, 153, 154; sun's image, 154–155; and understanding, 150

Q

Quine, Willard, 1
Quinn, William, 197
Quintilian (c.35–d. after 96), 51, 55, 64, 116
quotation, 164

R

raggi, 148
ratio, 174–175, 211
rationality, 34, 103
razor, 200
razos, 115, 116–117
readers and reading, Augustine's concept of, 71–72, 73, 107; and Chaucer's narrator, 117, 193, 196; Christian way, 218; and Dante, 117; dreams and dreaming, 188, 221; and fictional persona, 235; and God of Love, 195; Hugh of St. Victor on, 181; individuality of, 71; and logic, 62; nature of, 48, 61, 124–125; and nominalism, 195; and the past, 118; and Prologue to the *Legend of Good Women,* version G (Chaucer), 196, 197; and signs, 48; and understanding, 221; and word of God, 50; as writing, 181
Readings, Bill, 24–25, 230
realism and reality, and Augustine, 55; and Boethius, 186; and Bradwardine, 168–169; and Chaucer, 168, 191; defined, 184; and dreaming, 195; esthetic, 203; and grammar, 74, 167; and Holcot, 159, 168–169; and Langland, 170; literary, 178; and *moderni,* 163; and Ockham, 168–169; and ontology, 117; as poetic material, 6; and Strode, 168–169; and symbols, 190; word's nature, 77, 171; and Wyclif, 168–169
Reason (Langland: *Piers Plowman*), 172, 174, 179, 210, 211, 212, 213,
reason, 145–146, 170, 213
reconciliation, 163

rectitude, 111, 120, 214; and Aquinas, 210; and Guillem IX, 106
Regement of Princes (Hoccleve), 41
Reinmar von Reuenthal (d. c.1205), 97–98
Reiss, Edmund, 2, 51
Remigius of Auxerre (9th century), 40
Republic (Plato), 117
Retraction to the *Canterbury Tales* (Chaucer), 173, 196, 200, 202
revelation, 222
rhetoric, and Augustine, 42, 80; and Chaucer, 11, 193–194; and Cicero, 112; development of, 13; Greek concept of, 75; and John of Salisbury, 112; and Langland, 218; and Marcabru, 118–119
Rhetorica ad Herrenium (Capella), 93
rhetorical trope, 11
Ricoeur, Paul, 155
Rimbaud, (Jean Nicolas) Arthur, 231
Robertson, D. W., 80 n.44
Robinson, F. N., 181 n.39, 238
Rolle, Richard (c.1300–1349), 202
Roman de la rose (Guillaume de Lorris and Jean de Meun), 157, 170, 195, 201, 241
Roman de Troie (Benoit de St. Maure), 20
romance and romanticism, 13–14, 18, 69–70, 71
Romaunt of the Rose (Chaucer), 179
Roncaglia, A., 111–112 n.31
Rudel, Jaufre (fl. mid-12th century), 102 n.18
Ruud, Jay, 169 n.21

S

Sacra Doctrina, De (Aquinas), 131
sacra pagina, 52
salvation, and Augustine, 222; and communication, 204; and Dante, 170, 206; and individual, 168; and Langland, 137, 157, 206, 209, 222, 233; and Langland's Will's pilgrimage, 157; and Marcabru, 170, 206; and *moderni,* 162; a natural act, 162; and Paul, 222; and text and book image, 157; and *voluntas,* 200; and writing, 203
Saul, *see* Paul, St.
Saussure, Ferdinand de, 26
Schaber, Bennet, 24–25
Schaefer, Ursula, 5 n.4
Schmidt, A. V. C., 136 n.12, 226
Schneider, Reinhold, 242

scholasticism, 40, 49, 93–94, 133, 214–215, 225
Schwietering, Julius, 7, 8
science, 4, 45, 140
Scipio Africanus, 182
Scripture, and Abelard, 161; and allegory, 71; and Anselm, 162; and *auctoritas*, 62; and Augustine, 113; and book metaphor, 50; and myth, 117; as text, 54, 55
scroll (metaphor), 50, 230
self and selfhood, 12, 13–14, 19, 20, 25, 28, 41, 87, 166–167, 204; *see also* naming; self-naming
self-naming, 5, 5 n.4; and absence doctrine, 174; and Chaucer, 173–174; and emergence of the individual, 229; evolution of, 87, 230; and Foucault, 5–6; and Dante, 32, 131; and Dante's *Commedia*, 31; and Langland, 60 n.24, 131, 204; and logic, 84; and Marcabru, 131; and medieval poetry, 42; and philosophy of language, 83; and presence doctrine, 174; and textuality, 232; and troubadours, 96
Self-Portrait in a Convex Mirror (Ashbery), 235
semantics, 23, 30, 81
senex amans, 201
Sentences (Peter the Lombard), 65
sermo humilis, 32–33
sermonizing, 73
Shaw, Prudence, 141
Shipman's Tale (Chaucer: Canterbury Tales), 241
Shoaf, R. A., 28
Siger of Courtrai (d. 1341), 44, 133, 137
sight, and Aquinas, 141–142, 143–144; 148–149, 150–151, 154; and Aristotle, 140, 142; and Augustine, 149; and Dante, 140, 140–141, 142, 144–145, 153–154; and Dionysius, 142; and Matthew, 154; and Paul, 154; and Plato, 142; and reason, 145–146; and Virgil, 145, 154; and *virtus*, 145
sign, and Aquinas, 150–151; and Augustine, 131, 150–151, 161, 181–182; and medieval intellectual, 47; nature of, 131; and reading, 48–49
signification, 9, 10, 217–218
Silvestris, Bernard (fl. 1136), 1, 55, 56, 57, 72, 95

Sir Gawain and the Green Knight (anon.), 182, 202
Skeat, Walter William, 175
skin, and text, 50
Smith, Paul, 229, 230
Smith, Sarah Stanbury, 180
Soliloquia (Augustine), 94, 181 n.40
Somnium Scipionis (Macrobius), 94, 196
"Song of Solomon," 7, 90 n.3
sonnet, 34–35
Sophistici Elenchi (Aristotle), 44–45, 49, 161
soul, 216
Spearing, A. C., 218–219, 220
species (grammar), 40, 45; *impressa* and *expressa*, 77, 77 n.39
speculative grammar, 44, 60, 82; and Abbo of Fleury, 79; and Aristotle, 44–45; and Berengarius, 79; characteristics of, 45; and interrelationships, 104; *modistae*, 82; and Peter of Spain, 161; as poetic material, 6
Speculum maius (Vincent of Beauvais), 65
"*speculum Scripturae*" (Augustine), 13
speech, and reason, 145–146, 217
Spence, Sarah, 113, 115, 212
Spiegel, Gabrielle M., 17 n.16
Spillenger, Paul, 141 n.19
Stevens, Wallace, 6–7
Stoicism, 56, 79; etymology of, 54; and *lekta*, 78–79, 80, 103; and logic, 104; and Macrobius, 182; and natural signification, 53; and real things, 80; and signification, 78; and words, 109–110; and voice theory, 110
Stock, Brian, 43, 52–53, 54–55, 57, 59, 70, 73, 73–74, 83–84
Stock, Lorraine Kochanske, 216, 219
Stone, Gregory B., 18, 26, 27, 28, 30 n.34
Strode, Ralph (fl. c.1360), 168–169, 173, 182
structuralism, 203
subjectivity, 16, 166
substance (grammar), 40, 45, 103
Suger of Saint-Denis (1081–1151), 20
Sulpicius Severus (c.363–c.420), 7
Summa Logicae (Ockham), 39
Summa Modorum Significandi (Siger of Courtrai), 134
Summa Theologiae (Aquinas), 23, 131, 141, 153, 161

Summoner's Tale (Chaucer: *Canterbury Tales*), 190
Summulae Logicales (Peter of Spain), 161
sun, image of, 154
symbols, 31, 91, 154, 179, 190–191, 237; *see also* Alceste; daisy; *flos florum;* flower; frog; sun; metaphors

T

Tabarroni, Andrea, 194–195
Tale of Melibee (Chaucer: *Canterbury Tales*), 18
Tateo, Francesco, 155
Taylor, P. B., 181 n.39, 189, 191
texo, 52, 54, 75
text, and allegory, 55; ancient texts, 4; and Augustine, 35, 55, 67, 231; author made by, 6, 123; Christian theologians' use of, 226; as a common denominator, 229; definition of, 71; and discourse, 6; and grammar, 34; idea of, 37, 54, 67; as metaphor, 35, 55, 88, 121; and Paul, 231; and Plato, 231; and reading, 61; as Scripture, 55; and *texo*, 52, 54, 75; of the world, 197; and written communication, 53
textual communities, 43, 73–74, 76
textuality, and Augustine, 35, 42, 72; and the Bible, 231–232; and Chaucer's *Canterbury Tales*, 26; and Christianity, 34; concept of, 121; disciplinary connections, 33; and fiction, 122–123; and Langland's *Piers Plowman*, 61; and narrator, 164; and reading, 84; and sermonizing, 73; and tradition, 40; and truth, 84; and word, 84; and writing, 84
textus, 52, 74
theology, and Aquinas, 168; and book and text uses, 226; and Chaucer, 168; and Dante, 168; disciplines separate from, 1; and epistemology, 168; and Langland, 168; and logic, 2, 162; and philosophy, 1, 38, 40, 168
Thomas of Erfurt (14th century), and Augustine, 151; and grammar, 135; and Langland, 137; and language, 133; and presence doctrine, 134, 138; and pronouns, 134, 136, 137; and *proprietas*, 134; and Scholastic logic, 133; and sight, 154; and speculative grammar, 44
Titurel (Wolfram von Eschenbach), 57
Topsfield, Leslie T., 111 n.31

Tractatus Morales de Oculo (Peter of Limoge), 140
traductio, and nominalism, 180, 192, 193 n.50, 193 n.51, 195
translatio, 51, 192
translation, and Chaucer, 189, 194, 195–196, 197, 198; and God of Love (Cupid), 180–181, 193; and Jerome, 51, 195; and nominalism, 180; as a phenomenon, 193 n.51; and poetic license, 67; practices, 66–67; and Virgil, 67
Trinitate, De (Augustine), 43
Trinitate, De (Hilary of Poitiers), 119
Trinkaus, Charles, 15
trobar naturau, 111, 112, 112 n.31, 119
Troilus and Criseyde (Chaucer), 202; and allegory, 169 n.22, 194; and Criseyde, 220–221; Cupid's view of, 179, 180, 196; and erotic love, 183; Chaucer's persona in, 173, 185; Gower in, 173; and naming, 173; and narrator, 173, 192, 196; its readers, 188; and *senex amans,* 201; Strode in, 173; and will, 198, 200; and wit, 198, 200
troubadour topos, 199
troubadours, 47 n.6; and Alceste, 199; and autobiography, 95; autocitations of, 95; and composition terms, 75; and dialectical structure, 35; and individuality, 11–12, 97; and language, 28, 110–111, 113; and lyric, 11–12; and Marcabru, 110; and naming, 86, 135; nature of their poetry, 212; and nouns and pronouns, 88; and obscure language, 94; oral to written communication, 88; and present and past, 21; and self-naming, 96; and sonnet, 34; *see also* Guillem IX; Marcabru
Troy stories, 20
truth, and Alceste to Cupid (God of Love), 198–199; and allegory, 55, 220; and Anselm, 133; and Augustine, 13, 42, 116, 159; authors' search for, 136–137; and *canso,* 94–95; and Chaucer, 177, 187, 193, 203, 212, 214; and Christianity, 42; and discourse, 51, 116; and *exemplum,* 73; and experience, 200; as fable, 12; and grammar, 49, 212, 225; and Langland, 61–62, 136, 170, 203, 205, 212, 234; and language, 203, 213, 220, 234; and logic, 233; and

Marcabru, 115–116; and myth, 55; Ockham on, 167, 199; and parable, 220
Tuve, Rosemond, 186

U

Ugo Catola (fl. first half of 12th century?), 119
Ulysses (Joyce), 235
understanding, and Aquinas, 148–149, 150; and creation, 221; and Dante, 150; and reading, 221
unimpersonated artistry, 230
unintentionality, 127–128
universals, theory of, 81
utterance, notion of, 82

V

Van Vleck, Amelia, 11, 88 n.49, 112 n.31
Vance, Eugene, 22, 23, 43, 50, 52, 68, 87
vanitas terrestris, 7
veil *(integumentum),* 52
verb, 38, 133, 161
verbal expression, 197
verbal, *logos,* 54; signification, 78; solipsism, 22
verbum mentis, 23, 35
Veritate, De (Anselm), 46, 103, 104, 210 n.79
via negativa, 131–132
Vidal, Peire (fl.1180–1205), 95–96
Vignaux, Paul, 162
Vincent of Beauvais (c.1190–1264), 65
Virgil *(also* Vergil, 70–19 BC), 29 n.32, 33, 67, 196
Virgil (Dante: *Commedia*), 9, 29–30, 41, 64, 66, 145, 156–157; and humility, 153–154
virtù (Dante), 140, 145, 150, 154–155
virtue, 140, n.16
virtus (Augustine), 140, 145
Vita Nuova, La (Dante), on names, 187, 231
Vogelweide, Walther von der (c.1170–c.1230), 97–98
voice, 14, 15; *see also* speech
voluntas, and *appetitus rationalis,* 162; and Langland's *Piers Plowman,* 35, 122, 137, 176, 200; and salvation, 200
Voluntate, De (Anselm), 210
von Saaz, Johannes (c. second half of 14th century), 242
Vulgari Eloquentia, De (Dante), 33

W

waking state, 172
Walcott, Derek, 234
wheat. *see* corn (wheat)
White, Hayden, 17
Wilhelm, James, 90, 105–106
Will (Langland: *Piers Plowman*), and allegory, 14, 164, 176; Aristotle discussed, 218; and author as text, 35; and Conscience, 213; Dante compared to, 172–173; and Dowel, Dobet and Dobest, 213; and dreaming, 11, 41, 170–171, 172, 222, 226–227; and Geffrey comparison, 172–173, 176; and grammar, 214, 234; and Imaginative, 209, 210; and Langland's belief system, 160; and *makyng,* 209; naming of, 11, 207; and natural knowing, 222; a natural man, 211; and persona, 14, 35, 157, 204, 234–235; and pilgrimage, 157; as a poet, 209, 219; and presence, 224; and quotation, 164; and Reason, 213; 204; and salvation, 157; and self-awareness, 172; Solomon discussed, 218; and text as author, 35; and truth, 136; and *voluntas,* 122, 216
will, and Anselm, 210; and Augustine, 113; and Chaucer, 197–198; and Dante, 149–150, 209; and dreams, 204; and grace, 168; and Langland, 206, 209, 211; and Marcabru, 149–150; and nominalism, 200; and Ockham, 210; in pilgrimage text, 207
William of Ockham (c.1285–c.1349), and abstract knowledge, 195; on allegory, 194–195; and Aquinas, 39; and Chaucer, 166–167, 188 n.45, 189, 191, 202; on essence and existence, 39; on faith, 191 n.48; and God, 192; grammar metaphorical for, 167; and Holcot, 192; on interrelationships, 104; on intuitive knowledge, 163, 169 n.21, 188 n.45, 195; and Langland, 137, 157, 166–167, 168, 206; on language, 159; and linguistics, 43–44; on logic, 159, 194–195, 200; and medieval symbolic mentality, 199–200 n.58; and naming, 9; and natural law, 159, 168; Newtonian science influenced by, 159–160; and nominalism, 79, 157, 160, 168–169, 189; and the past, 86; and philosophy, 182; on poetry's nature, 239; and *potentia ordinata,* 200; and *razor,* 200;

on reality, 202; and religious orthodoxy, 163; and truth, 167, 199; and will, 198, 210; and wit, 198; word's nature, 77

William of Saint Thierry (c.1085–1148), 20, 57

Williams, David, 201

wit, 174–175, 200

Wit (Langland: *Piers Plowman*), 198

Wittig, Joseph, 209

Woodham, Adam, 163

Woolf, Rosemary, 164

word, and Abelard, 85; and Aquinas, 142; and *auctor,* 71; and Augustine, 13, 123, 182 n.41; and autocitation, 2; and Chaucer, 190; Christian, 21, 50, 212–213; and idea, 50–51; and Isidore of Seville, 113; made flesh, 34; as metaphor, 12, 229–230; as name, 187; nature of, 77, 78, 81, 83–84, 171, 190; and ontology, 74, 78, 171, 182, 187, 189; and predication, 81–82; puzzles, 2; and *rectitude,* 102–103; and Stoicism, 109–110; and truth, 84

Wordsworth, William (1770–1850), 22

world text (metaphor), 6, 194–195

writing, and Dowel, Dobet and Dobest, 225–226; and God's word, 88; invention of, 50–51; and logic, 62; and memory and wisdom, 50–51 n.9; and ontology, 181; and orality, 88; and plough metaphor, 204–205 n.66, 241–242; and reading and Chaucer, 196; and reading and Hugh of St. Victor, 181; troubadour transition to, 88; and Will's dreams recorded, 227; and salvation, 203

Wyclif, John (c.1330–1384), 168–169, 168 n.19

Z

Zechmeister, J., 112 n.31

Zink, Michel, 18, 26

Zumthor, Paul, 15 n.14, 25, 26, 87

www.ingramcontent.com/pod-product-compliance
Lightning Source LLC
LaVergne TN
LVHW021801060526
838201LV00058B/3186